Max Dimont
December 1954

BOLLINGEN SERIES XXXVII

ERWIN R. GOODENOUGH

JEWISH SYMBOLS

in the

Greco-Roman Period

VOLUME FOUR

THE PROBLEM OF METHOD

SYMBOLS FROM JEWISH CULT

BOLLINGEN SERIES XXXVII

PANTHEON BOOKS

Copyright 1954 by Bollingen Foundation Inc., New York, N. Y.
Published for Bollingen Foundation Inc.
by Pantheon Books Inc., New York, N. Y.

Published in Canada by McClelland and Stewart, Ltd., Toronto

THIS BOOK IS VOLUME FOUR OF THE THIRTY-SEVENTH PUBLICATION
IN A SERIES SPONSORED BY AND PUBLISHED FOR
BOLLINGEN FOUNDATION

Library of Congress Catalog Card No. 52–10031

Manufactured in the United States of America
by Kingsport Press, Inc., Kingsport, Tenn.

TO
EVELYN
URSULA
DANIEL

PREFACE

THE FIRST THREE volumes of this study were designed primarily to present the archeological remains of the Judaism of the Greco-Roman period. A surprising collection of material appeared—surprising, that is, because later Jewish traditions little prepare one to find, in synagogues and on Jewish graves, not only motifs borrowed from paganism but, along with geometrical patterns, also human and animal figures, and even images of pagan gods, in painting, mosaic, and deep relief. A few such forms, like the lions of the Palestinian synagogues, have been found carved in the round. These figures were used by Jews of the period intimately mingled with representations of implements or symbols from Jewish cult—as, for example, Helios appears in Beth Alpha between a scene of Abraham sacrificing Isaac and the collected cult symbols, menorah, Torah shrine, lulab, and the rest. As the symbols accumulated, and were discovered on graves and funerary objects as well as in the synagogues, it became increasingly difficult to consider them as "mere decoration," or to distinguish between the Jewish devices as having symbolic value, and the pagan motifs as not having such value.

The feeling that the decorations had symbolic value was sharply intensified when we came to the charms and amulets, and read passionate incantations in which Jewish and pagan names are used interchangeably, and when we saw scores of amulets on which figures of pagan deities seem to be identified with Iao and Sabaoth. It appeared that there had been much "god-mixing" on the part of Jews as well as pagans in the period.

The task of the succeeding volumes is to devise and utilize a method of some kind for appraising such material.

First we must return to the question of the relevance of rabbinic evidence. The traditional method of classical archeology is to explain physical monuments on the basis of what we can learn from written documents of the period. Are we therefore to take the Jewish remains and interpret them perforce in terms of rabbinic proof texts, and classify as "merely decorative" whatever goes beyond the spirit or letter of rabbinic writings? The first chapter of this volume attempts to show that the Jewish archeological remains are so far from the spirit and letter of rabbinic positions that we must assume them to give evidence of the existence of Jews who, while still eagerly loyal to Judaism as they understood it, were much closer to paganism than were the rabbis. But we have no writings from the Jews who made these monuments. Can symbols, then, be used as historical data without literary evidence? We can trace the symbols in relation to the history of form, or to the places and periods in which they have most commonly appeared. But can we draw conclusions from the symbols regarding the life of the people who used them, when we have no written records to go with them?

This problem is attacked directly in the most important single chapter of the entire study, the chapter outlining a methodology for using symbols as independent evidence in history. I have rewritten that chapter too many times to have any feeling of satisfaction with it in its present form. But what I do in all that follows ultimately stands or falls with the validity, or partial validity, of the method I there describe.

In the chapters that follow in this volume I attempt to evaluate the symbols of Jewish cult, a relatively easier problem than that of evaluating the pagan symbols as used by Jews, because there is of course considerable literary tradition within Judaism in regard to the cult objects, though nothing which tells us directly why Jews at the time should have wanted to put a menorah, a lulab, or a shofar on their graves or amulets. The Jewish symbols, accordingly, must be studied by the new method as well as by the older one of using such Jewish sources as seem relevant. These symbols will lead us into a Judaism much more given to mysticism than that of the rabbis, a Judaism more easily co-ordinated with pagan religious aspirations than with those of halachic Judaism—if indeed it was not, like Philo's mysticism, a weaving of a pagan mystic woof upon the warp of Jewish legalism. Such is the final impression which the material leaves with the author, and which he is trying to convey to the reader. The way is thus cleared for an attempt, in the subsequent volumes, to evaluate the symbols clearly borrowed from paganism. I regret that I saw only after the following pages were in proof the stimulating volume of Theodor H. Gaster, *Festivals of the Jewish Year*, New York, 1953.

I want to take this opportunity to thank the Harvard University Press for permission to quote widely from translations in the Loeb Classical Library, particularly of Philo, and the Soncino Press, London, for permission to quote from their translations of Hebrew texts, throughout the various volumes of this work. Acknowledgments for illustrations reproduced in this volume will be found in the footnotes, at the pages indicated in the List of Illustrations. It is a pleasure to acknowledge also the many types of help and suggestion given me by Mrs. Claude Lopez, my research assistant. Among other things, she prepared the indexes for this volume.

I shall not here rehearse the names of those of my colleagues who have helped me with this volume, as they did with the earlier ones. My gratitude to the Bollingen Foundation I must again record, even though I cannot express it. I have now seen its staff members at work, and have experienced their tirelessness in bringing the volumes of this series as near to perfection as possible.

To the dear three to whom this volume is dedicated, I can say only that I thank them for the rich and delightful years they are giving me.

Erwin R. Goodenough

Jonathan Edwards College
Yale University
October, 1953

Contents

ABBREVIATIONS

AAL, N.   *Atti della R. Accademia dei Lincei, Notizie degli scavi di antichità della Classe di Scienze Morali, Storiche e Filologiche*, Rome.

AJA.   *American Journal of Archaeology.*

Baron, *History.*   Salo Wittmayer Baron, *A Social and Religious History of the Jews*, New York, 1937.

BASOR.   *Bulletin of the American Schools of Oriental Research.* Berliner, *Juden in Rom.*   A. Berliner, *Geschichte der Juden in Rom*, Frankfort, 1893.

Beyer and Lietzmann, *Torlonia.*   H. W. Beyer and Hans Lietzmann, *Jüdische Denkmäler*, I: *Die jüdische Katakombe der Villa Torlonia in Rom*, Berlin-Leipzig, 1930 (Studien zur spätantiken Kunstgeschichte, IV).

Bonner, *BM.*   Campbell Bonner, "Amulets Chiefly in the British Museum," *Hesperia*, XX (1951), 301–345.

BT.   Babylonian Talmud, with references to the various treatises. ET refers to the English translations made by various scholars under the general editorship of I. Epstein, London, Soncino Press, 1935 et seq. Similarly, GT refers to the German translation of Lazarus Goldschmidt, pub. with the Hebrew text, Berlin, 1897; rev. ed. (German transl. only), Berlin, 1929.

Bullet. Commiss. Archeol.   *Bullettino della Commissione Archeologica Comunale di Roma.*

Butler, *Architecture, 1904–5.*   *Syria: Publications of the Princeton University Archaeological Expeditions to Syria in 1904–5 and 1909.* Div. II, *Architecture*, by Howard C. Butler: Sec. *A*, "Southern Syria"; Sec. *B*, "Northern Syria." Leyden, 1919–1920.

By Light, Light.   See Goodenough.

CIJ.   See Frey.

CIL.   *Corpus inscriptionum Latinarum.*

CL.   *Dictionnaire d'archéologie chrétienne et de liturgie*, ed. by Fernand Cabrol and H. Leclercq, Paris, 1907 et seq.

CSEL.   *Corpus scriptorum ecclesiasticorum Latinorum*, Vienna, 1866 et seq.

Cumont, "Sarcophage judéo-païen."   Franz Cumont, "Un Fragment de sarcophage judéo-païen," *RA*, Ser. V, Vol. IV (1916), 1–16. Revised and reprinted in idem, *Symbolisme*, 484–498.

Cumont, *Symbolisme.*   Franz Cumont, *Recherches sur le symbolisme funéraire des Romains*, Paris, 1942 (Bibliothèque archéologique et historique, XXXV).

Danby, *Mishnah.*   Herbert Danby, *The Mishnah, Translated from the Hebrew with Introduction and Brief Explanatory Notes*, Oxford, 1933.

DS.   *Dictionnaire des antiquités grecques et romaines d'après les textes et les monuments*, ed. by C. Daremberg and E. Saglio, Paris, 1873 et seq.

Du Mesnil, *Peintures.*   Comte du Mesnil du Buisson, *Les Peintures de la synagogue de Doura-Europos, 245–256 après J.-C.*, Rome, 1939.

EA.   *Ephemeris archaiologike.*

EP.   *Encyclopaedia biblica*, ed. by T. K. Cheyne and J. S. Black, New York and London, 1899–1903.

EJ.   *Encyclopaedia Judaica: Das Judentum in Geschichte und Gegenwart*, Berlin, 1928 et seq.

Erman, *Relig. Ägypt.*   Adolf Erman, *Die Religion der Ägypter*, Berlin-Leipzig, 1934.

Farnell, *Cults.*   Lewis R. Farnell, *The Cults of the Greek States*, Oxford, 1896 et seq.

Fergusson, *Hist. Arch.*   James Fergusson, *A History of Architecture in All Countries*, New York, 1907.

Frey, *CIJ.*   Jean-Baptiste Frey, *Corpus inscriptionum Iudaicarum, Recueil des inscriptions juives qui vont du IIIe siècle avant Jésus-Christ au VIIe siècle de notre ère*, Rome, 1936, I: *Europe.*

Garrucci, *Arte cristiana.*   Raffaele Garrucci, *Storia della arte cristiana nei primi otto secoli della chiesa*, Prato, 1872–1880. References, unless otherwise stated, are to the Jewish material in Vol. VI, 1880.

Ginzberg, *Legends.*   Louis Ginzberg, *The Legends of the Jews*, Philadelphia, 1909 et seq.

Goodenough, *By Light, Light.*   Erwin R. Goodenough, *By Light, Light: The Mystic Gospel of Hellenistic Judaism*, New Haven, 1935.

Goodenough, *Introduction.*   Erwin R. Goodenough, *An Introduction to Philo Judaeus*, New Haven, 1940.

Hamburger, *RE.*   J. Hamburger, *Real-Encyclopädie für Bibel und Talmud, Wörterbuch zum Handgebrauch für Bibelfreunde, Theologen, Juristen, Gemeinde- und Schulvorsteher, Lehrer*, etc., 2d ed., Strelitz, 1883 et seq.

Harris, *Fragments.*   J. Rendel Harris, *Fragments of Philo Judaeus*, Cambridge, 1886.

Harrison, *Prolegomena.*   Jane E. Harrison, *Prolegomena to the Study of Greek Religion*, 3d ed., Cambridge, 1922.

HDB.   James Hastings, *A Dictionary of the Bible*, New York, 1898–1904.

HERE.   James Hastings, *Encyclopaedia of Religion and Ethics*, 1908 et seq.

HTR.   *Harvard Theological Review.*

HUCA.   *Hebrew Union College Annual.*

JBL.   *Journal of Biblical Literature.*

JDAI.   *Jahrbuch des Kaiserlich Deutschen Archäologischen Instituts.*

JE.   *Jewish Encyclopedia: A Descriptive Record of the History, Religion, Literature, and Customs of the Jewish People from the Earliest Times to the Present Day*, ed. by Isidore Singer, New York, 1901 et seq.

JHS.   *Journal of Hellenic Studies.*

JJPES. קובץ, *Journal of the Jewish Palestine Exploration Society* (in Hebrew).

Josephus, *Antt.* *Antiquitates Judaicae.*

Josephus, *BJ.* *Bellum Judaicum (Jewish War).*

JPOS. *Journal of the Palestine Oriental Society.*

JQR. *Jewish Quarterly Review.*

JT. Jerusalem Talmud, with references to the various treatises. FT refers to French translation of Moïse Schwab, Paris, 1871 et seq.

Klein, *Corp. inscr.* Samuel Klein, *Jüdisch-palästinisches Corpus inscriptionum (Ossuar-, Grab- u. Synagogeninschriften),* Vienna-Berlin, 1920.

Krauss, *Synag. Altert.* Samuel Krauss, *Synagogale Altertümer,* Berlin-Vienna, 1922.

KW. Heinrich Kohl and Carl Watzinger, *Antike Synagogen in Galilaea,* Leipzig, 1916 (Wissenschaftliche Veröffentlichung der Deutschen Orient-Gesellschaft, XXIX).

Levy, *Wörterbuch.* Jacob Levy, *Wörterbuch über die Talmudim und Midrashim,* 2d ed., Berlin-Vienna, 1924.

LS. Henry Liddell and Robert Scott, *A Greek-English Lexicon.* New ed. of H. S. Jones, Oxford, 1925 et seq.

Macalister, *Gezer.* R. A. Stewart Macalister, *The Excavation of Gezer, 1902–1905 and 1907–1909,* London, 1912.

Mém. Miss. *Mémoires publiés par les membres de la Mission Archéologique Française au Caire*

MGWJ. *Monatschrift für Geschichte und Wissenschaft des Judentums.*

Mon. Ant. *Monumenti antichi, pubblicati per cura della R. Accademia Nazionale dei Lincei.*

Moore, *Judaism.* George Foot Moore, *Judaism in the First Centuries of the Christian Era, the Age of the Tannaim,* Cambridge, 1927.

MR. Midrash Rabbah, with references to the various treatises. ET refers to the English translation made by various scholars under the general editorship of I. Epstein, London, Soncino Press, 1939 et seq.

NSA. See *AAL,N.*

Osten, *Brett.* H. H. von der Osten, *Ancient Oriental Seals in the Collection of Mrs. Agnes Baldwin Brett,* Chicago, 1936 (University of Chicago Oriental Institute Publications, XXVII).

Osten, *Newell.* H. H. von der Osten, *Ancient Oriental Seals in the Collection of Mr. Edward T. Newell,* Chicago, 1934 (University of Chicago Oriental Institute Publications, XXII).

PEF,QS. Palestine Exploration Fund, *Quarterly Statement.* After 1938 called *Palestine Exploration Quarterly* (abbr., *PEQ*).

PW. *Paulys Real-Encyclopädie der classischen Altertumswissenschaft,* ed. by G. Wissowa, Stuttgart, 1894 et seq.

QDAP. *Quarterly of the Department of Antiquities in Palestine.*

RA. *Revue archéologique.*

RAC. *Rivista di archeologia cristiana,* Pontificia Commissione di Archeologia Sacra, Rome.

RB. *Revue biblique.*

RE. See Hamburger.

Reifenberg, *Coins.* Adolf Reifenberg, *Ancient Jewish Coins,* Jerusalem, 1940. Reprinted from *JPOS,* XIX (1939–1940), 59–81, 286–318.

REJ. *Revue des études juives.*

RgVV. *Religionsgeschichtliche Versuche und Vorarbeiten.*

RHR. *Revue de l'histoire des religions.*

Roscher, *Lex. Myth.* *Ausführliches Lexikon der griechischen und römischen Mythologie,* ed. by W. H. Roscher, Leipzig, 1884 et seq.

Rostovtzeff, *Dura-Europos.* *The Excavations at Dura-Europos, Conducted by Yale University and the French Academy of Inscriptions and Letters,* ed. by M. I. Rostovtzeff et al. *Preliminary Reports,* New Haven, 1928 et seq.

Scholem, *Jewish Mysticism.* Gershom G. Scholem, *Major Trends in Jewish Mysticism,* Jerusalem, 1941 (Hilda Stroock Lectures, delivered at the Jewish Institute of Religion, New York, 1938).

Schulchan Aruch. Joseph Karo, *Shulchan Aruch,* cited in transl. by Heinrich G. F. Löwe, *Schulchan Aruch, oder die vier jüdischen Gesetzbücher,* 2d ed., Vienna, 1896.

Simon, *Verus Israel.* Marcel Simon, *Verus Israel: Étude sur les relations entre Chrétiens et Juifs dans l'empire romain,* Paris, 1948 (Bibliothèque des Écoles Françaises d'Athènes et de Rome, CLXVI).

Strack-Bill. Hermann L. Strack and Paul Billerbeck, *Kommentar zum Neuen Testament aus Talmud und Midrasch,* Munich, 1922–1928.

Strack, *Intro.* Hermann L. Strack, *Introduction to the Talmud and Midrash,* Philadelphia, 1931.

Sukenik, *Beth Alpha.* Eleazar L. Sukenik, *The Ancient Synagogue of Beth Alpha,* London, 1932.

Sukenik, *Synagogues.* E. L. Sukenik, *Ancient Synagogues in Palestine and Greece,* London, 1934 (Sweich Lectures of the British Academy, 1930).

Torlonia. See Beyer and Lietzmann.

UJE. *Universal Jewish Encyclopedia,* ed. by Isaac Landman, New York, 1939–1943.

Wilpert, *Mosaiken und Malereien.* Josef Wilpert, *Die römischen Mosaiken und Malereien der kirchlichen Bauten vom IV. bis XIII. Jahrhundert,* 2d ed., Freiburg im Breisgau, 1917.

ZaeS. *Zeitschrift für ägyptische Sprache und Alterthumskunde.*

ZDPV. *Zeitschrift des Deutschen Palästina-Vereins.*

ZNW. *Zeitschrift für die neutestamentliche Wissenschaft.*

Zohar. *The Zohar.* ET refers to Engl. transl. of Harry Sperling and Maurice Simon, London, Soncino Press, 1931 et seq.

EXTANT TREATISES ATTRIBUTED TO PHILO

The English titles are those of Colson and Whitaker in the Loeb edition of the
works of Philo. Roman numerals in italics refer to the number of the volume of that
series in which the given treatise appears.

Abr. *De Abrahamo.* On Abraham (*VI*).

Aet. *De aeternitate mundi.* On the Eternity of the World (*IX*).

Agr. *De agricultura.* On Husbandry (*III*).

Animal. *Alexander, sive de eo quod rationem habeant bruta animalia.* Alexander, or That Dumb Animals Have Reason. (Accessible only in Armenian and in Aucher's Latin transl.)

Antiq. *Liber antiquitatum biblicarum.* (Pseudo Philo, ed. by Guido Kisch, 1949, transl. by M. R. James, 1917.)

Cher. *De cherubim.* On the Cherubim, and the Flaming Sword, and Cain the First Man Created out of Man (*II*).

Conf. *De confusione linguarum.* On the Confusion of Tongues (*IV*).

Congr. *De congressu eruditionis gratia.* On Mating with the Preliminary Studies (*IV*).

Cont. *De vita contemplativa.* On the Contemplative Life (*IX*).

Decal. *De decalogo.* On the Decalogue (*VII*).

Deo. *De deo.* On God. (Accessible only in Armenian and in Aucher's Latin transl.)

Det. *Quod deterius potiori insidiari soleat.* That the Worse Is Wont to Attack the Better (*II*).

Ebr. *De ebrietate.* On Drunkenness (*III*).

Flac. *In Flaccum.* Against Flaccus (*IX*).

Fug. *De fuga et inventione.* On Flight and Finding (*V*).

Gig. *De gigantibus.* On the Giants (*II*).

Heres. *Quis rerum divinarum heres.* Who Is the Heir of Divine Things (*IV*).

Hyp. *Apologia pro Judaeis.* Hypothetica (*IX*).

Immut. *Quod deus sit immutabilis.* On the Unchangeableness of God (*III*).

Jona. *De Jona.* On Jonah. (Accessible only in Armenian and in Aucher's Latin transl.)

Jos. *De Josepho.* On Joseph (*VI*).

LA. *Legum allegoria.* Allegorical Interpretation of Genesis (*I*).

Legat. *Legatio ad Gaium.* Legation to Gaius (*X*, forthcoming).

Migr. *De migratione Abrahami.* On the Migration of Abraham (*IV*).

Mos. *De vita Mosis.* Moses (*VI*).

Mund. *De mundo.* On the World.

Mut. *De mutatione nominum.* On the Change of Names (*V*).

Opif. *De opificio mundi.* On the Account of the World's Creation Given by Moses (*I*).

Plant. *De plantatione.* Concerning Noah's Work as a Planter (*III*).

Post. *De posteritate Caini.* On the Posterity of Cain and His Exile (*II*).

Praem. *De praemiis et poenis.* On Rewards and Punishments (*VIII*).

Prob. *Quod omnis probus liber sit.* That Every Virtuous Man Is Free (*IX*).

Provid. *De providentia.* On Providence (*IX*).

QE. *Quaestiones et solutiones in Exodum.* Questions and Answers on Exodus. (Supplement II to the Loeb edition, transl. by Ralph Marcus.)

QG. *Quaestiones et solutiones in Genesim.* Questions and Answers on Genesis. (Supplement I to the Loeb edition, transl. by Ralph Marcus.)

Sacr. *De sacrificiis Abelis et Caini.* On the Birth of Abel and the Sacrifices Offered by Him and His Brother Cain (*II*).

Samp. *Sine preparatione de Sampsone* [*sermo*]. On Samson. (Accessible only in Armenian and in Aucher's Latin transl.)

Sobr. *De sobrietate.* On the Prayers and Curses Uttered by Noah When He Became Sober (*III*).

Som. *De somniis.* On Dreams, that They Are God-sent (*V*).

Spec. *De specialibus legibus.* On the Special Laws (*VII*, *VIII*).

Virt. *De virtutibus.* On Virtues Which together with Others Were Described by Moses; or on Courage and Piety and Humanity and Repentance (*VIII*).

PART V

THE PROBLEM OF METHOD

CHAPTER ONE

The Relevance of Rabbinic Evidence

THOUGH THE foregoing volumes have not given the reader a complete report on the Jewish art of the Greco-Roman world as known to the present, it is apparent that much has been discovered. This Jewish art is drenched with pagan importations: indeed, Jews used pagan symbols long before they had distinctively Jewish ones, and even after they had a symbolic vocabulary of their own, the pagan motifs remained so important that they were commonly used alongside of or, as earlier, in place of symbols that were idiomatically Jewish. It has further appeared that such art was by no means limited to the diaspora, for the greatest single source of our knowledge of it is still Palestine. Old Testament illustrations have not yet been found in Palestine to any appreciable extent, but in the use of hellenized art the synagogues and graves of Palestine go quite as far as the Jewish cemeteries in Rome.

What is especially important to remember is that the decorations are found not as isolated expressions of individuals, but in synagogues and burying places, and thus can be taken to represent the religious attitudes of Jews as communal groups. Sporadic individual syncretism has appeared in the charms and amulets clearly enough, yet even here the majority of the pieces which we have felt to be "probably Jewish" seem to use predominantly and repeatedly certain common adapted motifs. Basically more important than these for the history of Judaism in the period, however, are the symbols found in the synagogues and in cemeteries, for these were the public places where Jews, in Palestine and the diaspora alike, expressed their piety. Furthermore, while we have found some very simple and unadorned sites, it has become overwhelmingly obvious that Jews everywhere borrowed in much the same way, appropriated much the same symbols, and that, from East to West, they intermingled these pagan devices with much the same selection of symbols from their own cult.

A. MODERN INTERPRETATIONS

THE PROBLEM before us is to try to outline and apply a method for appraising these data. The material stands quite by itself, without benefit of any literature to explain it, for, as has been pointed out,[1] except for the writings from rabbinic circles, we have only

1. See above, I, chap. II.

the inscriptions as literary remains of the Jews of the period. How little these tell we have already seen. No reason has yet appeared for supposing that the close-knit rabbinic group had any appreciable authority in the diaspora, and now that the archeological evidence from Palestine has multiplied, it is at least an open question how much influence the rabbis had even in Palestine in the centuries immediately after the fall of Jerusalem.

In discussing the Judaism of the period, then, we must hereafter begin with the archeological evidence, for it is the only direct testimony in existence regarding the Judaism of Jews at that time outside the rabbinic circles. All preconceptions of what Jews "could" or "must" have thought or done must make room for the fact that at least and at last we know what they did do. We have not yet come to what Jews thought as they made these synagogues and tombs, with the pagan ornaments they had at first, or with the mixture of Jewish and pagan symbols they had later. But we have come to the fact that they used such decoration, wherever we find traces of Judaism in the Greco-Roman world.

Obvious as it appears to me that this art presents a problem, it has not seemed perplexing to most of those who have studied it. Schwabe, an excellent epigraphist, who draws his inscriptions largely from among the iconographic remains we are studying, is convinced that the "fundamental Jewish attitude and tradition" reflected in this material are quite like the views expressed in the Talmud, for all that the two give one such different impressions.[2] Klein [3] is so convinced that the Talmud must have ruled Jewish life that, contrary to all the evidence of the art itself, he declares that the Galilean synagogues must be dated in the first or second century after Christ, that is, in the period before the Mishnah was codified, since after that time the rabbinic proscription of images dominated the Jews of Palestine. Such expressions of faith in the supremacy of rabbinic tradition, in spite of the evidence, are common among both Christians and Jews. Albright [4] refers to the synagogal art as so clearly an instance of a taking over of forms, a borrowing without religious significance, that he feels justified in denying religious significance to similar borrowings a thousand years earlier; his position is likewise that of faith.[5] Avi-Yonah,[6] whose contribution in gathering the material and putting it into the history of the morphological development of art is acknowledged throughout, rarely alludes to the possible meanings of the symbols. But his general standpoint may be inferred when, in discussing the decoration in the synagogue of Isfiya, he points to the vase with vine, the birds eating grapes, and the peacocks, and says that hitherto these motifs have been thought to have meaning when found in Christian churches, but now that they have been discovered in synagogues it is clear that they could have had no symbolic meaning at the time anywhere, and that they are only conventional ornament used by the artisans of the region, to which "later interpretation" has given "their alleged symbolic meaning." Galling [7] discussed the evidence of the Roman catacombs in relation to Judaism, but in reviewing the paint-

2. *JJPES*, IV (1945), p. xxv. See above, I, 13.

3. Klein, *Corp. inscr.*, 71 f.

4. *Archaeology and the Religion of Israel*, 1942, 67.

5. See also Georg Schmid, *Das unterirdische Rom*, 1908, 335.

6. In *QDAP*, III (1933), 123 f.

7. "Die jüdischen Katakomben in Rom als ein Beitrag zur jüdischen Konfessionskunde," *Theologische Studien und Kritiken*, CIII (1931), 352–360, esp. 358 ff.

ings made no mention of the pagan motifs. Limiting himself to the representations of Jewish cult objects, he concluded that the Jews of Rome were "true to the Torah" (*thoratreu*). Of course these Jews must have been true to their Torah (in a Greek translation), or they would not have remained Jews. The point before us is what being "true to the Torah" meant to them.

We can, of course, heartily deny the existence of syncretism, or of pagan influence, if we omit all reference to such factors from our descriptions of the remains. Leon,[8] in reviewing the same material, freely admits the presence of pagan art in the catacombs, but assures us in a final sentence that the art, and the Roman and Greek names of the persons named in the inscriptions "should be regarded not so much as marks of assimilation as of adaptability to the customs of the people among whom they lived." They tell him nothing of any essential impact of paganism upon Jewish life or thought. Sukenik,[9] who, like Avi-Yonah, is an indispensable guide to the material, was so primarily interested in the development of art forms, and in identifying and describing the objects found, that their possible symbolic value did not really concern him. On the other hand Leclercq, with his greatly detailed knowledge of Jewish monuments and incredible mastery in the field of Christian monuments and literary sources, presents the Jewish remains only to wave aside any significance they might be thought to have had for Christians. He says [10] that the existence of a Jewish art in the sense of an original product would be hard to establish: while some Jews could obviously paint and carve, "not a single one of them was inspired by Jewish ideas." The artisans of the Christian catacombs, he assures us, drew their inspiration wholly from "Christian sources." He thinks it sufficient to state this as a fact without further argument.

From offhand assertions that the material has no bearing upon the history of the Jewish religion, or of Christianity, opinions diverge by steady gradations in two directions. On the one hand, some reject the material as evidence for Jewish religion but are aware that it presents a real problem, and marshal evidence to support their rejection of it. Others have felt that these decorations could not be thus discounted, and have argued that they had real symbolic meaning in Jewish use and show widespread hellenization among the Jews of the day.[11] Watzinger,[12] for example, reviewed the evidence carefully as he had it especially from the synagogues of Palestine. He saw that the art in these synagogues was conspicuously identical with the "Syrian-Roman decorative art, especially the

8. "New Material about the Jews of Ancient Rome," *JQR*, XX (1929/30), 301–312. The quotation is from p. 312. This has remained Leon's assumption consistently in later writings on the subject: e.g., in *JQR*, XXVIII (1937/8), 360, he denies any "recondite symbolic purpose" even to the specifically Jewish motifs.

9. Sukenik, *Synagogues*, 61–67. Jews must once have been liberal, then reacted, he says.

10. CL, VIII, 38.

11. No one, as I have repeatedly said, has systematically considered the material. But several scholars, in discussing given details, have recognized an invasion of hellenistic symbolism in this Jewish art. See esp. Cumont, "Sarcophage judéo-païen," and Lietzmann in *Torlonia*, 15–27. These authors will be considered in connection with the material they discuss.

12. KW, 184–203, esp. 201–203. This opinion was repeated by Karl Schwarz, *Die Juden in der Kunst*, 1928, 42 f.; cf. Hermann Vogelstein, *Rome*, 1940, 35–39. It goes back to H. H. Kitchener in *PEF,QS*, 1878, 126–129.

funerary art," but insisted that it could have no meaning in Judaism. To defend the thesis that it does have such significance, it would be necessary to show the relevance for Judaism of *all* the symbols thus found, he said, and indeed he himself would admit the relevance only of the lion—that is, a relevance for the rabbinic Judaism that he never ceased to think of as having been coextensive with Judaism itself. Actually, he had made a very inadequate study of Jewish tombs in Palestine, and Sheikh Ibreiq had not been really opened up; thus he could assert that "no Jewish grave" of the period "had so much as a trace of figured decoration," a statement now known to be untrue. Hence, he implies, the real pagan meanings of these symbols, which made them primarily appropriate for graves, had not been adopted by the Jews. The synagogues must then have been gifts to the Jews from official sources, Roman governors chiefly, who presented them ready-made, and the Jews had to take them as they were given, though they chipped off the offending figures as soon as it was safe for them to do so. This assumption has to be abandoned now, if only because of the discovery of the trans-Jordan synagogues in which Jews are honored by inscriptions for having given the most unorthodox of mosaic pavements. In my opinion the theory never did justice to the grave decorations in Rome, and it is now contradicted by the carvings of Sheikh Ibreiq.

Frey rejected Watzinger's thesis because of the inscriptions.[13] Frey's study of the problem seems to me the most important of any made in recent years, and his method of approach is well worth expounding, if only to show what we shall conclude to be its basic inadequacy. He made a very conscientious, indeed a deeply concerned, study of the significance of the Jewish images. His work begins with a careful analysis of the Old Testament laws, as careful, that is, as one can make who, as a Catholic, completely ignores the historical critics of the last century. He concludes that the Old Testament law was that no images were to be made of God himself, or of any being or thing whose image might be worshiped. Otherwise images could freely be made, since God himself told Moses to make the figures of the cherubim on the Ark. Hence ornamental or utilitarian images could be made, which explains the presence of images in Solomon's Temple. As the law developed through the ages, however, more and more Jews felt that the making of images of any kind (especially figures of animate beings), for any purpose, was forbidden. Frey tests his own scriptural interpretations by the traditions of the Church Fathers and the councils of the Church down through the Council of Trent, and ends by calling the Jewish attitude only "a tenacious and universally prevalent prejudice which sees in the Mosaic texts an absolute prohibition of every sort of image." Such a ruling out of images on the basis of Old Testament statements "is little in accord with the most authoritative [i.e., Catholic] exegesis."[14] By the time of Jesus, however, the view that would prohibit all images had, under the leadership of the Pharisees, quite won out, Frey says, with the conclusion that such complete prohibition was no part of the original law, but derived only from the rabbinic "hedge" about the law.

13. "La Question des images chez les Juifs à la lumière des récentes découvertes," *Biblica*, XV (1934), 265–300. For his discussion of Watzinger, see p. 292. Sukenik, *Synagogues*, 61–64, also rejected this theory, on the same grounds.

14. Op. cit., 273.

Frey has an excellent review of the literary testimony—primarily that of Josephus, though Philo is also adduced in regard to this "Pharisaic" attitude—which shows how at that time the Jews fanatically observed the stricter tradition. Frey does not consider the archeological remains which indicate that Jews in the period of Pharisaic domination, from the days of the Maccabees to the fall of Jerusalem, rejected hellenized art, or restricted their borrowings to the vine and its variants, or to the symbolic façade,[15] or to rosettes, but he describes very well from the literary sources the dominance of the Pharisees and their rejection of images in this period. Pharisaic or rabbinic dominance he rightly sees operating chiefly during the first century before the Christian era, and the first century after Christ. The apocryphal books still speak only of rejection of idols, he says, and he contrasts the proper Jewish point of view with that responsible for the offensive images in the Herodian palaces at the time.[16]

From the Palestinian literary tradition Frey turns to the archeological material for the first time in discussing the Jews of the diaspora. Jews outside Palestine, he says, were subject to the control of the Palestinian teachers to only a very limited degree, and so succumbed to the daily attraction of objects of art in the pagan world about them. But if they did not follow the Pharisaic refinements, they remained true to the original Mosaic attitude. Frey reviews rapidly the art found in the Jewish catacombs, in both painting and carving. He denies that Jews could have made the extremely pagan paintings in the Catacomb Vigna Randanini, and ranks as of non-Jewish origin, one by one, what he calls the pagan sarcophagi found in the tombs.[17] But he admits that much of the art, for example that in the Catacomb Torlonia and in the Galilean synagogues, and also the gold glass, was produced by Jews. He disagrees, however, with those who have seen eschatological meaning even in this fraction of the art which he will call Jewish, and thinks that here we have nothing but *simples motifs d'ornementation*—because, he says, it has never been established that *symbolisme doctrinal* had any part whatever in Jewish funerary art.[18] Again, he holds specifically that the Seasons and Victories on one of the Jewish sarcophagi found in Rome [19] simply stood on the sarcophagus ready-made in some Roman shop. A Jew had the menorah carved upon it, but considered himself still within the Law, "since none of these figures had an idolatrous purpose, but were purely ornamental." [20]

We are beginning to see the excluded middle which seems to me to make Frey's appraisal fallacious. His reasoning presents us with the alternative of assuming either idolatrous usage or else a mere urge to decoration. But the Christian attitude in using this same art is of course accounted for by neither of these motives. The Christians changed the meaning of the pagan figures so that they had real value in Christian terms: they were in no wise mere decoration, yet just as little were they objects of worship in the sense in which such worship is usually ascribed to pagans. Indeed, there is no reason to suppose that even in paganism the figures carved on sarcophagi were ever worshiped. The "idola-

15. See below, pp. 99–142.

16. Op. cit., 273–282.

17. See above, II, 30–32.

18. Op. cit., 288.

19. See above, III, fig. 789.

20. Op. cit., 289.

trous" horn of the dilemma existed for no one, certainly not for the Jews. That is, between the horns of "idolatry" and "mere decoration" is the *tertium quid* of symbolism. This Frey does not consider. He brushes aside the very point at issue when he says that the representations could not have been of eschatological importance because such symbolic purpose has never been established for Jewish art. The problem—and in the long run Frey is only begging the question—is precisely whether this new flood of material does not in itself at last establish just this, that at the time such representations did have symbolic value in Judaism, as they did in paganism and Christianity.

In the same spirit Frey surveys the synagogues in Galilee and in the Roman world in general as far as Dura. Unfortunately, at the time when he was writing his article Sheikh Ibreiq had not been excavated, and so he ignores the evidence of Palestinian tombs, lamps, and the like. He admits the presence of pagan ornament in the synagogues, and insists that it was Jews who made the ornament, or authorized it.[21] He traces in a few selected passages of the literature a tendency on the part of the rabbis to soften the prohibition of images, or at least to tolerate them. The second-century *Mekilta*, he says, still reflects the old condemnation, but later rabbis "relaxed this severity." He thinks that there was no real agreement on the subject, however.[22] After a few centuries, indeed, there began in Judaism a sharply iconoclastic movement which was reflected in Islam and which was at the bottom of what Frey calls the unfortunate Christian iconoclasm. This, he concludes, justified Tertullian in saying: *Synagogae Iudaeorum fontes persecutionum.*[23] Frey can finally close his study by saying that all the archeological discoveries of Jewish material *ont confirmé avec éclat la position prise par l'Église à l'égard du texte sacré.*[24] He points out the place of images in Church tradition; to him, this art has never violated the precepts of the Old Testament. "And now, if it is permitted to make images of God himself, it is not that the Church has changed the ideas presented in the Old Testament on the spiritual nature and transcendence of God, but because the Word has made divine Majesty accessible by uniting himself to human nature." [25]

That is, Frey has really not been talking about the Jewish images at all, but, probably without himself knowing it, has written a defense of the Catholic use of images: he ends in an obscurantism which will be acceptable only to those similarly committed to grounding their religious practices upon proof texts from the body of "revealed truth."

Ludwig Blau was one of the few experts in talmudic studies who have been impressed by the archeological discoveries.[26] Writing before the excavation of Beth Alpha, Dura, or Sheikh Ibreiq, and so without full appreciation of many of the ramifications now before us, Blau yet saw that we must conclude: "Not only did there exist a pre-Talmudic Judaism, but there was also an extra-Talmudic Judaism." [27] He carefully reviewed the talmudic evidence and concluded that the rabbis (some of them) tolerated figures not made for worship:

21. Ibid., 290–296.
22. Ibid., 296–298.
23. *Scorpiace*, x (*CSEL*, XX, 168, line 13).
24. Frey, op. cit., 299.

25. Ibid., 300.
26. "Early Christian Archaeology from the Jewish Point of View," *HUCA*, III (1926), 169–203.
27. Ibid., 169.

The Galilean Jews saw nothing idolatrous in the ornamentations which we regard as heathenish, since, as Kaufmann correctly observes, they were stripped of their mytho-logical content.[28]. . . Only the idolatrous side is to be taken into consideration, to the effect that all these figures which were employed in the synagogues and in the cemeteries were not felt to be idolatrous, just as in actuality they did not bear this character.[29]

Blau went on to say that all halachic prohibitions indicate an attempt of the rabbis (usually unsuccessful) to stop actual practices,[30] a fact completely apparent in the pro-hibition of the seven-branched menorah as contrasted with its seemingly universal use, but he did not set forth clearly the fact that the rabbinic proscriptions show that the rabbis (most of them) hated the figures. Indeed, he put Jewish use of these figures on a level with Christian use of them: in each case they could be used because they were no longer idols.[31]

Blau was on the right track. That the figures used by Jews in their decoration had become a part of a lingua franca of symbols, to be used with reference to gods of all sorts because they indicated no specific god at all, and that they were taken up by Jews and Christians alike on this basis, is a statement of the case to which Blau would apparently have agreed. The parallel, however, opens a door whose existence Blau did not suspect. The Christians used the pagan vocabulary to express in symbols their deepest religious hopes, and the real question is not whether Jews worshiped these figures in the synagogues and cemeteries, but whether they were not using them, like the Christians, for their symbolic value in expressing Jewish piety and hopes.

Before presenting what seems to me the critical issue, a discussion of the subject by one more scholar must be reviewed. For most recently Simon [32] has examined the problem with the outcome that he finds in the development of a Jewish art one of the most char-acteristic signs of rabbinic liberalism.[33] He says that before the decoration of the Dura synagogue there were no human figures in Jewish art, for the figures in the bacchic scenes of the Capernaum synagogue are only ornamental and probably mean nothing in relation to Jewish symbolism [34] (he quite missed the winged Victories and he too knew nothing of Sheikh Ibreiq, the evidence of which would refute many of his statements). With the instinct of a philologian he judges the reference in IV Maccabees to the possible erection of a mausoleum or memorial which would contain representations of the mar-tyrdoms recounted in the books to be more important than the actual images preserved. The statement in IV Maccabees is not the reflection of a movement of the day, he feels, but marks *le début d'une orientation nouvelle*, the beginning of Jewish art.[35]

Actually Simon's study is a fine example of the method of presenting all sides of an issue with the result that the issue is left quite undecided. He reviews the talmudic evidence on images with considerable care, and concludes: "It remains tacitly understood [in the *Abodah Zarah*] that if a Jew could, in certain cases, use images of living things, he would

28. Ibid., 177. Here (n. 17) Blau gives a very good bibliography covering discussions of the attitudes of Jews toward plastic ornament.

29. Ibid., 181.

30. Ibid., 183 f.

31. Ibid., 189.

32. Simon, *Verus Israel*.

33. Ibid., 34.

34. Ibid., 36.

35. Ibid.

create none himself." [36] But his conclusion,[37] in accord with his initial statement, is: "The images gained their place in Judaism not in the fine period of Philonic Hellenism, but in the period, and *under the auspices*, of the amoraim, authentic heirs of the Pharisees" (italics mine). Yet he admits that "rabbinic authorization only gave approval to a usage already established" in the diaspora by private and secular practices preceding the religious usage.[38]

Here is indeed a mixture of points of view in which I can see nothing coherent except that Simon admits that for a while Jews used images, and used them with rabbinic approval, though he believes that they have no importance for the history of Judaism: this position is essentially the same as that of Leon.

In all this discussion we miss the essential issue, I have said. That issue is: Where are we to find the moving cause in the taking over of images, and with what objective were they taken over? Simon and Blau, as we shall see, are quite right in recognizing that from the rabbis we have only a grudging toleration (on the part of a few) of a movement whose initiative obviously lay quite outside their control. That the initiative was a popular rather than a rabbinic one is perfectly clear. It seems also clear to me that the motive for borrowing pagan art, and integrating it into Judaism throughout the Roman world, can be discovered only by analyzing the art itself. The question is not so much whether Jews made their synagogues and graves and amulets with or without rabbinic approval, though this we must also consider. Still, it is secondary to the question which has really not been opened at all: What does the making of such synagogues and graves and amulets as we have described imply in itself? The fact of the making of images is not in dispute: we know now that Jews throughout the Empire, for a number of centuries, did make images, and then rejected them. What were Jews doing when they made such figures? What were they rejecting when they rejected them? For this a new method of study must be devised. It can consist only in a study of the images themselves—of what forms the Jews borrowed, and of how they were used, so that from both the pagan history and the Jewish use of the figures a sense of their significance in Judaism can be attained.

The first step, as I saw it, must be to assemble, and thus to present the full force of, the great body of evidence available—evidence which cannot be denied, and which, when viewed as a whole, demands interpretation as a whole, since it is so amazingly homogeneous for all parts of the Empire. The second step is to recognize that we must first determine what this art means in itself, before we begin to apply to it as proof texts any possibly quite unrelated statements of the Bible or the Talmud. That these artifacts are unrelated to proof texts is a statement which one can no more make at the outset than one can begin with the assumption of most of my predecessors, that if the symbols had meaning for Jews, that meaning must be found by correlating them with talmudic and biblical phrases. And yet to me, frankly, the relevance of the proof texts is ultimately quite secondary. We see lions, for example, in Jewish art, and know that these lions are now equated with the tribe of Judah, because in Genesis the lion is made the symbol of that tribe. But did the carved or painted lion come into Judaism as a figure to be represented before a

36. Ibid., 42.   37. Ibid., 46.   38. Ibid., 44.

Torah shrine with the purpose of illustrating that verse, or did the lion come in first, so that the application of the verse was a rationalization after the fact? Must we say that the lion either represents the tribe, that is, merely illustrates a proof text, or else is purely decorative? This is the implicit assumption of those seeking to explain by proof texts, and it seems to me quite without justification.

I have implied that the method of most of my predecessors in discussing this Jewish art has been to report a larger or smaller fragment of the archeological evidence, and then to look to the rabbinic testimony on images in order to determine the possible meaning of the figures for Jews, or show the impossibility of their having had any meaning in Judaism at all. The art has rarely, and then only in details, been studied for its possible meaning in itself; this is the task of these volumes. But before considering a way in which this meaning, if there was any, may be reconstructed, we must stop for a moment with the evidence of the rabbis on art. Incidental as is the importance that this will prove to have, it must nevertheless by all means be considered.

B. RABBINIC STATEMENTS

THE ATTITUDE of the rabbinical circle to images in the centuries when Jews were constructing the synagogues and graves we are studying cannot be reduced to a phrase. I shall weigh the evidence which has been suggested, without stopping to give credit in each case to the modern scholar who has dealt with it, since most of the material has been discussed many times.

Literary evidence, as Frey and others have recognized, shows that the antipathy of Jews to images was intense during the period of the dominance of the Hasidim and of the Pharisees, that is, from the founding of the Maccabean dynasty to the fall of Jerusalem, roughly from 150 B.C. to A.D. 70. The earlier writings, such as the Books of Maccabees, have little reference to images as an issue,[39] but we have noticed an amazingly uniform avoidance of images on all sorts of Jewish remains from that period. The testimony of Josephus strongly confirms the notion that at this time the Old Testament prohibitions of images were applied to all images, not just to those made for worship, as some of the rabbis later, at least for a time, tended to do.[40] In Philo we have an interesting contrast, for while in one passage he does say that Moses banished painting and sculpture from his commonwealth, he shows considerable liking for art.[41] Josephus, however, even condemned Solomon for breaking the law in putting bulls and lions into the old Temple.[42] And in discussing the golden eagle which Herod caused to be put on his Temple, Josephus says: "Those who propose to live according to the Law are forbidden by it to consider the setting

39. Idols were, of course, an issue: I Mac. I, 43.

40. The law as it appears in the Decalogue (Exod. xx, 4; Deut. v, 8) is explicit in forbidding the making of images of any kind. But Exod. xx, 23, and Levit. xxvi, 1, can be taken as glosses which say that the law applies only to images made for worship, idols proper. Centuries of Jewish controversy have not definitively clarified this point.

41. I have collected the relevant passages and discussed them briefly in By Light, Light, 256 f.

42. Antt., viii, 195 (vii, 5).

up of images, or to make a practice of consecrating representations of living beings." [43] In his story of the protest to Petronius against the setting up of Gaius' image in the Temple, Josephus describes the Jewish crowd as saying that under their Law they may not "put an image of God, or even of a man, in the Temple, or even in any profane part of their country." [44]

That is, the prohibition could not have been more comprehensive or specific, as Josephus states it, and as he assumes it to hold in other parts of his narrative. He quotes it again when, in his polemic against Apion, he justifies the Jews in not making images of the emperors: he protests that the Greeks were in great danger of falling into idolatry even in making portraits of members of their families. [45] The Jews of his day, according to his story, agreed that the law thus completely prohibited all images. He justified his coming up to Tiberias by saying to the Jews in Galilee that he was going to lead them in destroying Herod's palace, because it had been profaned by being decorated with images of animals. [46] He portrays the Jews of Jerusalem as ready to die rather than allow the images of the Emperor carried by the legions to be brought into the Holy City, and while it may be that Jewish aniconism was complicated with chauvinism at this point, the only reason alleged by Josephus was the law against images. The protest was so sincere that Pilate had to have the images removed from Jerusalem to Caesarea. [47]

The apocryphal and pseudepigraphical books dating from this general period are full of denunciation of pagan idolatry, [48] but have no allusion that I can find, except the single verse of I Maccabees already mentioned, to the use of images by Jews for any purpose whatever. The New Testament writers do not refer to the subject at all. Apparently Judaism in this period, in Palestine and the diaspora alike, was almost completely aniconic. We have seen in the tombs of that time much evidence of symbolism in terms of the vine, the shrine, the rosette, and other almost abstract representations, so abstract that one must see the mass of them in order to feel that they may be considered as symbols at all. But animals and human or divine figures, as well as signs of the zodiac, do not appear at this time. The literary and archeological records agree entirely in showing that the Jews were during this period so much under the domination of Pharisaic or rabbinic leadership that images were completely avoided. Apparently as long as the Temple stood, and hundreds of thousands of Jews went to it annually, the point of view of the rabbis of Palestine registered throughout Jewry, in matters of observance if not of interpretation. So for all of Philo's hellenization, he was a carefully observant Jew, presumably as aniconic as any Pharisee.

A great change appears to have set in with the fall of Jerusalem. A century and a half later, the cemetery of Sheikh Ibreiq and the synagogues of Dura and Galilee were being constructed. Their ornament seems to indicate that rabbinic control had collapsed. For the

43. Ibid., xvii, 151 (vi, 2); cf. *BJ*, i, 650 (xxxiii, 2).

44. *BJ*, ii, 195 (x, 4). We shall discuss this eagle at greater length in a later volume.

45. *Contra Apionem*, ii, 74 f.(6). This danger is pointed out in Wisd. xiv, 12–31.

46. *Vita*, 65 (12).

47. *BJ*, ii, 169–174 (ix, 2 f.); *Antt.*, xviii, 55–59 (iii, 1).

48. E.g., III Mac. vi, 11; Wisd. xiii–xv; Aristeas, 134–137; Sib. Or. i, iii; Jub. xii, 1–8.

rabbis went on with their total denunciation of images for some time, in spite of what Jews were actually doing. The most important single passage relating to this is the comment on Levit. xxvi, 1, in the oldest of the midrashim, the *Sifra*,[49] whose material dates mostly from the second century after Christ or earlier. Here not only "idols" are prohibited, but also "images" and "pillars" (*mazzeboth*): he who makes such a thing does something objectionable. Specifically, the passage continues, this refers to the herms set up beside the roads, and to astrological symbols, such as the images of the sun on gables: the law prohibits not just the making of images in order to worship them, but the making of them at all. The rabbis are thinking still in terms of the Judaism of the period before the fall of Jerusalem.

From approximately the same time comes the *Mekilta*, a commentary on Exodus, in which the prohibition is made just as absolute.[50] One may not make "any manner of likeness," whether incised or in the round, of wood, stone, copper, iron, tin, or lead. No animate creature whatever is to be represented in any of these ways, whether cattle or fowl (bird), fish, locust, unclean animal, or reptile; no images are to be made of the sun, the moon, the stars, or other planets, or of angels, cherubim, *ophannim*, or of anything under the earth, which includes anything reflected in water. This law is attributed to Akiba himself. According to others, the *Shabrire*, apparently some sort of fabulous water animal or snake, was specifically not to be depicted.[51] Such elaborateness of the law is finally explained: "Scripture goes to such length in pursuit of the evil inclination to idolatry in order not to leave room for any pretext of permitting it." That is, the "hedge" around the law against idolatry is itself scriptural. All image making is forbidden.[52]

This complete rejection of images has recurred throughout the history of Judaism to the present, and also went over into Islam. When it reasserted itself as the dominant attitude in Judaism, Christianity felt the impact, and in turn for a time came near to renouncing its images. But through the early centuries of the Christian era, that is, during the period when most of the symbolism we are studying appeared on Jewish monuments, there developed in Judaism a tendency on the part of some rabbis to interpret the law more generously, though others steadily emphasized complete prohibition.

The earliest modification of absolute proscription is connected with none other than R. Gamaliel, who lived at the time of Jesus. In the Mishnah [53] it is said that he "used to have a diagram of phases of the moon on a tablet [hung] on the wall of his upper chamber, and he used to show them to the unlearned and say, 'Did it look like this or this?' " The purpose of the tablet is apparent. The days of festivals were fixed according as rustics coming in to the city reported the position of the moon. The best way to determine clearly

49. *Behar*, ix (see Jakob Winter, *Sifra: Halachischer Midrasch zu Leviticus*, 1938, 642).

50. *Bahodesh*, vi, 60–85 (ed. and transl. of Jacob Z. Lauterbach, 1933, II, 241–243). Frey had noticed this passage; see above, p. 8.

51. One wonders whether this is not a prohibition of Capricorn, a figure we have seen frequently in Jewish ornament—perhaps of Capricorn as Leviathan.

52. It is on the basis of these passages that S. Klein thought that by the middle of the second century the prohibition of images was fixed and complete. See above, p. 4.

53. *BT*, *Rosh Hashanah*, 24a,b (ET, 105–107). The whole, except for the Mishnah, is reproduced almost verbatim in *BT*, *Abodah Zarah*, 43a,b (ET, 214–216).

what they had seen was, Gamaliel found, to confront them with diagrams which they could identify. It is quite clear that harmless as this would seem to us, most of the rabbis did not approve, and such devices were not generally used; otherwise the debate would have turned on the general practice, not the single case of Gamaliel's using a chart. As the discussion continues in the Gemara, excuses are found for Gamaliel, for the law "Ye shall not make with me" implies that one should not make images of any of God's attendants, including the heavenly bodies. "Rabbi Gamaliel's case was different," is the actual consensus of the discussion. Several suggestions are made, as that Gamaliel had not made the tablet, but had had a gentile make it for him. "If you like I can say that it was in sections," that is, apparently, fitted together temporarily, if at all; "or if you like I can say that he did it for purposes of study." The implied conclusion is that Gamaliel's chart sets no precedent: his making one, however he really did it, remains unique, and a Jew who keeps the Law in the rabbinic sense does not make such things.

Another instance of a laxer attitude appears in this same passage. About the middle of the third century Rab Judah wore a ring with a seal on which a figure stood out in relief.[54] Another rabbi, Samuel, called him by a scornful name and ordered him to "put out that fellow's eye," that is, to annul the image as a human form in relief by defacing it. An older law is then repeated, namely, that if a man wanted to have such a ring it was allowed, though if the image projected in relief the ring could be used as a seal, but not worn, since the figure put into circulation would be only the impression sunk into the wax. Conversely, if the figure was cut into the stone or gold of the ring it could be worn, but never used for a seal, else an object in relief would be circulated. Apparently "figures" were acceptable, but not figures in relief, and the prejudice against making these was so great that a proper Jew could not even stamp a relief in wax as a seal; here we are still a long way from approving such images as we have seen from the synagogues. This older law Rab Judah must deliberately have been disregarding.

Rab Judah disregarded this law presumably on the basis of another principle which comes out in the same passage, a principle for which Abaye, who lived a generation later, is chiefly quoted.[55] For he at least concurs in identifying the four faces of Ezekiel's vision (Ezek. 1, 10) with those attendants of God whom it is forbidden to represent, since they fall under the exclusion of "with me," and he also concurs in ruling that the prohibition applies only if they are represented all together. In that case, representation of a human being would apparently be permissible. But the argument continues to the effect that "ye shall not make with me" implies also "ye shall not make me"—meaning, I infer, that since man is made in God's image, to represent a human figure is to represent God, and so is still forbidden.[56] This new ruling would, however, allow representation of either the lion, the bull, or the eagle, and these could probably now be used individually, *pars pro toto*, to mark an object as sacred. We begin to see how a lion before a Torah shrine could have

54. We have referred to rabbinic use of amulets above, II, 214 f.

55. Abaye, a Babylonian amora, lived 279–338, according to A. Cohen in his translation of *BT*,

Berakoth, 1921, 431.

56. This is based upon the statement of R. Huna, who had it from Abaye, but the passage is cryptic: see Cohen's note ad loc.

served in Jewish terms to indicate the presence of Deity in the scrolls of the shrine. For the lion would stand for the "living creature" of Ezekiel's vision, as attendant upon God, and would imply, without direct representation of God, that the Shekinah was in the scrolls.

Abaye goes on to forbid the making of images of the heavenly bodies and ministering angels, but a gloss, probably of the fifth century, says, "That statement refers to the prohibition of [making a likeness] for serving it." This puts the whole matter on an entirely new footing. The later interpreters would apparently have balked at no image whatever unless it was designed for worship, and all images made for worship—even an image of an earthworm—were forbidden. How far this discussion lags behind actual developments in the synagogues, however, becomes clear when it is stated in the same passage that in Nehardea (i.e., Babylonia) two rabbis, Rab and Samuel, father of Samuel, who flourished probably early in or toward the middle of the third century,[57] went together for prayer into a synagogue where there was a statue,[58] "and they were not afraid of arousing suspicion." This synagogue is mentioned as one to which the Shekinah twice came,[59] hence it was especially sacred. What the Gemara tells us here is that no one took offense because these rabbis did so remarkable a thing as to go into this building at all. They are excused, apparently, on the ground that they went in not at a time of service, for "where a whole body of persons is concerned it is different." That is, the compiler of this passage would not censure the two rabbis for going in, but he obviously did not like the presence of a statue, whatever its nature, before a praying congregation, and we feel from this passage that for rabbis to go into a synagogue which had carvings or other representations was exceptional, since such a point is made of the fact that these two rabbis did so on a single occasion.

One thing comes out very sharply: even if some rabbis tolerated such an image, the implication is that they were far from taking the initiative in introducing anything of this kind. Indeed, Abaye himself tried to prohibit representation of any part or furnishing of the Temple, specifically the menorah of seven branches. Menorahs could be made with five, six, or eight branches, he said, but not with seven, and this is the rule still observed by the orthodox, who avoid having menorahs of seven branches. Yet we know that it was precisely in Abaye's day that the popular use of the seven-branched menorah as the "hallmark of Judaism" was at its height, in Palestine as well as elsewhere. Abaye's protest at length won out, but it was a protest against a very widespread custom of his own time.

We have noted above that the passage from the *Rosh Hashanah* which we have been discussing is repeated, except for the Mishnah, in another talmudic treatise, the *Abodah Zarah*. There it is part of a much larger section,[60] which we cannot analyze in detail.[61] The

---

57. Rab fl. 154–247, according to Cohen, 437.

58. It is now traditional to say that it was a statue "of a king," but I see no reason for the tradition. The word אנדרטא is usually translated "royal statue," but it is a loan word, the Greek ἀνδριάς, which means simply a carved image of a man, and the Hebrew word has this meaning in every instance listed in Jastrow's dictionary.

59. *BT, Megillah,* 29a (ET, 175). On the synagogue, see Krauss, *Synag. Altert.,* 214–219.

60. *BT, Abodah Zarah,* 40b–55a (ET, 202–282).

61. It is systematically examined by Hans Blaufuss, *Götter, Bilder und Symbole nach den Traktaten über fremden Dienst (Aboda zara) in Mischna, Tosefta, Jerusalemer und babylonischem Talmud* (Jahresbericht des K. Neuen Gymnasiums in Nürnberg für das Schuljahr 1909/10, Suppl.), 1910. I shall use this illuminating study freely.

discussion turns mainly on what should be done with heathen idols, and how one is to know which object is an idol and which is not. The Mishnah has R. Meir prohibiting all such images, since they are all worshiped once a year, but an anonymous rabbi limits the prohibition to an image holding a staff, bird, or sphere in its hand, while another says that it applies to any image having anything in its hand. This, says the Babylonian Gemara, applies particularly to images in the cities; but images in the cities may be only ornaments, hence the blanket prohibition is thought by some not to apply to these. The Jerusalem Gemara [62] says that all authorities "allow" images which have been set up only to adorn a city. The context still deals only with images set up by pagans, and Blaufuss rightly cites as an instance R. Gamaliel's indifference to an image of Aphrodite in a bathhouse—an example to be discussed shortly. Nothing suggests that R. Gamaliel's attitude could be used as a precedent permitting a Jew to make such an image himself.

Idols can be annulled or desecrated, the discussion continues, and so made innocuous for Israelites.[63] Hence the very fact that an image is broken establishes a presumption that it has been annulled and is no longer an object of worship; but to this the stricter rabbis object. In any case, an Israelite cannot annul a pagan image or idol: only a pagan can do that. But an idol once worshiped by a Jew can never be annulled.[64] It is interesting that the rabbis especially warned against any image of a separate hand or foot, however, because these were symbols of gods and were worshiped in their own right.[65] This specific proscription of the hand because of its idolatrous suggestion is most interesting in view of the fact that at the time the pronouncement was made other Jews, at least in their paintings, were evolving the tradition of representing the Jewish God himself in the form of a heavenly hand, a convention widely adopted in Christian art.[66] One feels that such a development in art hardly came from rabbinic inspiration.

62. Quoted by Blaufuss, op. cit., 3.

63. See above, p. 14.

64. *BT, Abodah Zarah,* 42a (ET, 207 f.); cf. 51b, where it is stated (in the Gemara, with ascription to Akiba) that an idol made by an Israelite is not prohibited until it is worshiped, but it is explained in the Gemara (52a [ET, 262]) that the Israelite who made it is accursed.

65. The reference to hands seems to me to point to the hand of the Phrygian Sabazius, for this was a symbol in widespread use in the Near East at the time; this was the hand "set upon a base," as the Babylonian Gemara amplifies. The reference may, however, be to Egyptian hands, for in Egypt images of both hands and feet were worn as amulets. See C. Blinkenberg, *Archaeologische Studien,* 1904, 66–128: "Darstellungen des Sabazios und Denkmäler seines Kultes." Egyptian amulets in the form of hands have been often published: for examples from early Egyptian times to the Roman period, cf. W. M. Flinders Petrie, *Amulets,* 1914, 11, and plate 1; G. A. Reisner, *Amulets,* Cairo, 1907, 118–

120, nos. 12111–12119, plate IX (Catalogue général des antiquités égyptiennes du Musée du Caire). Blaufuss, op. cit., 15–17, gives a large number of possibilities and extensive material. The reference to feet would presumably be to a symbol of Serapis. Egyptians used images of feet as amulets from early times: see Petrie, op. cit., 11. But for the foot as a symbol of Serapis see Blaufuss, op. cit., 17 f., where many examples are cited. Images of feet, dating from various periods, were found in Gezer, and one was dug up "under the ruins of a Maccabean castle." These were supposed, when discovered, to be "votive offerings," but may have been such objects of worship as the rabbis were here prohibiting. See Macalister, *Gezer,* II, 446 f. On representations of the hand (and foot) of God, see Otto Weinreich, Θεοῦ χείρ, "Antike Heilungswunder," 1909, 1–75 (*RgVV,* VIII, i). The talmudic passage seems to say that fragments of broken idols are allowed, but not such images of hands and feet as are complete symbols of divinity in themselves.

66. Cf. esp. the representations of the hand in the

The long discussion which follows in the *Abodah Zarah* is chiefly concerned with the prohibition of heathen idols, and the definition of what is idolatrous. Since the dominant classes in Palestine and Babylonia alike were largely heathen, this was an extremely important matter. Could a Jew go to the public baths, for example, when these were commonly filled with pagan ornamental images, if not with images used in active cult? The matter was fiercely debated, with decisions from rabbi after rabbi alternating in sharp contrast.[67] The test case was the one already mentioned: namely, Gamaliel himself was reputed to have gone to a bathhouse where there was a statue of Aphrodite, and had defended his conduct on the ground, first, that the place was primarily a bath, where Aphrodite was an ornament, a thing of minor importance, and secondly, that she stood by the outlet where the water flowed into the sewer, so that in using this outlet as a toilet before her, the heathen themselves very effectively annulled any sacred character the statue might have had. Opinions of the rabbis for and against Gamaliel's judgment need not be considered; no agreement was ever reached—at least none is recorded—on the validity of his arguments or his conduct.[68] Certainly Gamaliel's complacency little accords with the strictness of such a rabbi as Menahem, son of R. Simai (probably fourth or fifth century), who was called a saint because he refused so much as to look at the image on a pagan coin.[69] And it just as little accords with this passage in the Jerusalem Gemara:

> On the Sabbath one must not look at the inscription which runs under reliefs or εἰκόνες (images). Even on an ordinary day one must not look at εἰκόνες, and on what ground? "Turn ye not unto idols." You shall not turn to pray to them. R. Jehuda said: "Thou shalt not turn even to gaze upon them."[70]

Another prohibited category was that of objects which had been offered to idols. An anonymous pronouncement in the Mishnah says that if a Jew finds on top of a *mercurius* [71] a garment or coins or utensils, he may take them for his own use, but he may not take from it such things as a grape cluster, a wreath of grain, or wine, oil, or flour, since all these are specific cultic offerings. The discussion of this in the Gemara is completely unintelligible— probably, I should guess, because the rabbis did not in general agree at all with such a

---

Moses and Ezekiel scenes in Dura, which will be discussed in a later volume; on the use of hands and feet on Jewish amulets, see above, II, 219.

67. *BT, Abodah Zarah*, 44b (ET, 220–222).

68. The point comes up again in *BT, Abodah Zarah*, Mishnah, 51b (apparently, as implied in the Gemara, a judgment of Akiba), where it is said that a garden or bathhouse connected with an idol may be used if one's use of it does not contribute to or support idolatry.

69. Ibid., 50a (ET, 251). This was apparently an old debate, for Hippolytus, *Refutatio*, IX, xxi (xxvi), tells us that one party of the Essenes would

not use pagan coins, or enter a city, since there might be an image at the gate. See Kohler in *JE*, II, 142.

70. A comment on *Abodah Zarah*, Mishnah, III, 1. Quoted by Blaufuss, op. cit., 4. D. Kaufmann, "Sens et origine des symboles tumulaires de l'Ancien-Testament dans l'art chrétien primitif," *REJ*, XIV (1887), 46 f., says that the images referred to could have been made only by Christians.

71. *BT, Abodah Zarah*, 51b (ET, 258 f.). I presume that by *mercurius* the translator meant a herm, in the sense of a roadside pile of stones to which a wayfarer added a stone as he passed.

judgment, yet had to respect it since it was in the Mishnah. The Gemara seems to conclude that the *mercurius* and everything on it are forbidden.

Why did the rabbis give so much attention to what sort of pagan images might be allowed, and what kind might not? The whole discussion seems to have arisen, may I repeat, not because they themselves were eager to appropriate images for Jewish use, but because the rabbis and Jews in general were living in countries where they were surrounded with images of all sorts; hence the question really being discussed was how Jews could use objects produced by the civilization about them. They could ordinarily purchase from the heathen almost no jewelry, indeed not even pots and pans, which were not ornamented with disturbing motifs.[72]

Whether a Jew could ever wear a ring with a figure on it was a special question. Even a rabbi hated to leave a gold ring which he might find on a road just because it had a carving on it, and a story is told of one rabbi, Eleazar Hakkapper, of the second half of the second century, who found such a ring, and caught a gentile and beat him until he would mar the image in such a way that it was annulled as an idol. Then the rabbi could take it.[73] This principle is made into a formal ruling: "When [the idolater] fashions it [a graven image] into a god do not covet it, but when he has annulled it so that it is no longer a god you may take it for yourself." [74]

Rabbi Akiba is reputed to have prohibited to Jews all idols made by idolaters, but to have allowed an idol made by an Israelite if it had not yet been used for worship. Rabbi Ishmael exactly reversed this,[75] so that one suspects that the whole matter was purely theoretical,[76] and that idols of either pagans or Israelites would, at any stage, have had short shrift in orthodox Jewish hands. Indeed the Gemara goes on to say that the whole argument has nothing to do with idols, but is concerned only with utensils used in idolatrous worship. Whatever may be done with an idol, the Gemara assures us,[77] the man who makes one is accursed. Actually the discussion probably at no point bears on so-called Jewish "use" of a pagan statue that has been worshiped, however much it may have been "annulled." I feel the same unreality in the discussion as to whether idols abandoned in time of peace, as contrasted with those abandoned in time of war, may be used.[78] It is much more realistic when the ruling that Jews may "use" an empty pedestal is qualified so that it applies only to a damaged pedestal. Even so, the use amounts to no more than that a Jew may sit on such a pedestal beside the road when he is tired.[79]

Throughout this passage, as I have said, what is really under discussion is the problem

72. In the Tosefta on *Abodah Zarah*, v, Jews are flatly forbidden to buy vessels or tools bearing heathen images.

73. *BT, Abodah Zarah*, 43a (ET, 213).

74. Ibid., 52a (ET, 263).

75. For the statements of both rabbis, see ibid., 51b–52a (ET, 260–264).

76. Like the discussion immediately following (52b [ET, 265]), as to whether it was permissible to use in the Temple at Jerusalem utensils from the Temple of Onias. The rabbis engaging in the discussion lived a century after the Temple at Jerusalem had been destroyed, and the Temple of Onias closed.

77. *BT, Abodah Zarah*, 52a (ET, 262).

78. Ibid., 53b (ET, 273).

79. Ibid. In the Tosefta on *Abodah Zarah*, v, Jews are forbidden to mount on heathen altars even to destroy them, or to use stones obtained from them.

of images as it bears on things of actual use—"precious" articles being "bracelets, nose rings, and signet rings," and "common" ones being "kettles, pots, vessels for boiling water, sheets, and towels." [80] What about such objects as these, it is asked, when they have images on them? If the image is of the sun, the moon, or a dragon, says a rabbi cited in the Mishnah [81] (the Gemara just below identifies him as R. Judah [82]), or of a human face, adds a mishnaic statement immediately quoted in the Gemara, it is to be cast into the Dead Sea, that is, utterly destroyed. But Simeon, son of Gamaliel, allowed images on common articles, forbade them on precious ones. This more generous decision deriving from the tradition of Gamaliel is based upon the assumption, apparently, that no one pays much attention, let alone reverence, to a figure on a skillet or towel: the very use to which such objects are put would be defiling to a holy image, and certainly the figure would not be worshiped. Images on jewelry are a different matter, however, for they may well have talismanic value, may serve as the guarding presence of a favorite and protecting deity. Images on common utensils are made by the heathen presumably only for "ornament"; hence there is no reason for rejecting them, and such objects may be kept. This section of the *Abodah Zarah* is the only place I know in talmudic literature where such a distinction as to intent—namely, whether an image is for ornament or for worship—is recognized, and even here the distinction is based on the intent of a pagan craftsman, not of a Jewish maker. Indeed, later rabbis continued the discussion in the Gemara,[83] but they came to no agreement. All seemingly admitted that common objects bearing almost any image were allowed, but not even such an object was permissible if it had a figure of the sun, the moon, or a dragon, or bore a representation of a human face; and some of the rabbis ruled that the passage especially forbade a Jew to make any object whatever marked with a likeness of a human face.

The general feeling in the rabbinic literature is on the whole, then, clear and consistent. Jews were forbidden to make images of human faces for any purpose whatever, and the strictest rabbis would have destroyed all objects, even of pagan origin, which might be suspected to be only as much as potentially idolatrous, because of either the images on them or the uses to which they had been put. Especially were representations of the sun, the moon, snakes, and human faces regarded as dangerous—symbols which we have seen used prominently in Jewish art and on Jewish amulets in all localities. It is Kohler's conclusion [84] that the rabbis finally stood fast on prohibiting only the four figures of Ezekiel when shown together, as well as any image of an angelic being or of the human form. In view of the objects we have seen as well as of the rabbinic statements, I suspect that these few types of representations were denounced specifically because many Jews especially liked to use them—not, however, rabbinic Jews.[85]

80. Ibid., 43b (ET, 217).
81. Ibid., 42b (ET, 211 f.).
82. Ibid., 43a (ET, 213). See above, II, 282.
83. Ibid., 42b–43a (ET, 212 f.).
84. In *JE*, II, 142.
85. See the discussion of these in Blaufuss, op. cit., 35–46. F. Landsberger in *HUCA*, XXIV (1952/3), 137, has recently called attention to a passage in *BT*, *Kelim*, xxviii, 4 (ET, 134), which refers to figures appearing on Torah mantles: "Scroll-wrappers, whether figures are portrayed on them or not, are susceptible to uncleanness." On the matter of uncleanness the schools of Shammai and Hillel, as well as Gamaliel, had differing

Lieberman [86] has recently discussed the subject and come to the conclusion that in the third and fourth centuries idolatry was no longer an especial problem to the rabbis, because Jews by then were no longer proselytizing; thus the rabbis were addressing a Jewish audience with no inclination to idolatry. If idolatry is the use of animal, human, and monster forms to represent spiritual beings and to make their power more accessible, then our archeological evidence, which Lieberman never considers, would sharply contradict his assumption. "Idolatry" seems to me another word embodying a value judgment. The Catholic uses images, but is offended when Jews and Protestants call them idols, while he himself is denouncing pagan images, for which he has no use, when he calls them idols. The rabbis seem to me to have ruled out all religious images as idols, in this condemnatory sense. They talked about idols when they meant images, because they did not like images. So orthodox Judaism has understood them ever since.

Over against this general impression we have the contrast of a few anomalous occurrences which are apparently described for their very deviation from the rule, not as precedents for later observance. Rabbi Gamaliel's moon chart is one instance. Rab Judah's and R. Gamaliel's signet rings another. The story of the rabbi who beat a pagan until he would annul the image on a ring, that of the two rabbis who went once to pray in a synagogue where there was a statue, and the episode of R. Gamaliel in the bath that had a statue of Aphrodite, all these make up a tradition of exceptions: the rule against images, especially images of the human face, is steadily repeated. It is accordingly interesting that, so far as I know, the only reference in the Talmud to mural decoration is made in the Jerusalem Gemara as a sort of parenthesis in the discussion of what objects bearing pagan images a Jew may use. "At the time of R. Johanan," the text suddenly says, "they began to have paintings on the walls, and the rabbis did not forbid it." [87] The reference is to the R. Johanan who died as a very old man in A.D. 279; hence the passage tells us that mural paintings had begun to appear in the third century.[88] Paintings not only began to be made at this time, but, in spite of all the context of prohibition in the Talmud, they were not forbidden by the rabbis of the day. A recently discovered fragment of this passage expands it to say that a century later R. Abun "did not hinder" his contemporaries from making designs in mosaic.[89]

Three other talmudic passages should be mentioned. The first contains the statement already quoted,[90] that an idol made by an Israelite, but never yet worshiped, may be used, though for what purpose is not specified. The second has also been quoted: it holds that the prohibition applies only to likenesses made to be worshiped.[91] With this goes the third statement: "What was the coin of Abraham our Patriarch? An old man and an old woman

opinions. But what the "figures" on these wrappers were no one knows.

86. Saul Lieberman, *Hellenism in Jewish Palestine*, 1950, 115–127: "Rabbinic Polemic against Idolatry."

87. *JT, Abodah Zarah*, III, 3 (FT, XI, 211).

88. See S. Mendelsohn in *JE*, VII, 211–213.

Rabbi Johanan is famous for his liberalism: he even thought knowledge of the Greek language an attractive accomplishment in women.

89. Publ. by J. H. Epstein in *Tarbiz*, III (1931/2), 20, line 15.

90. See above, p. 18.

91. See above, p. 19.

on the one side, and a young man and a young woman on the other." [92] The elder couple must have been Abraham and Sarah, the younger Isaac and Rebekah.[93] No trace of such a coin has ever been found, and it probably was a figment of some rabbi's imagination. But why imagine such a coin? Perhaps to justify the images of Patriarchs which had begun to appear in synagogues and, possibly, on Torah scrolls: but this is only one of many conceivable guesses. Certainly no weight can be put upon this evidence.

Krauss seems to me entirely justified, then, in his conclusion that "there is nothing to be quoted from Talmud and Midrash to apply to the period of the Galilean synagogues." [94] I should alter this only to emphasize that there is nothing in these writings which accounts at all for the decorated synagogues and graves, or for the syncretistic amulets.

Baron also properly recognizes that the rabbinic passages we have cited are far from explaining the "widely prevalent" art, and he goes on to comment on the statement about R. Abun quoted above:

> The talmudic teachers certainly did not encourage the painting of nude women on synagogue walls, as was done in Dura (the Egyptian princess personally fetching Moses from the river). The text indicates, on the contrary, that the practice, under the impact of Graeco-Roman mores, had become so deep-rooted that the rabbis could not avoid legalizing it, even for Palestine.[95]

It does not seem to me that the passages "legalize" such art, or any art, in the synagogues: they say simply that a few rabbis "did not forbid," or "did not hinder," that is, they shrugged their shoulders. In contrast, most of the rabbis, if we know anything of their spirit at all, would have despised not only the naked woman at Dura, but likewise all the murals and carvings and amulets representing human figures, Greek gods, the sun and moon—indeed, Helios in person—and the hand of God, or even, as we shall have occasion at least to suspect, God himself, enthroned above the tree or vine at Dura. Baron seems to me unquestionably right. What tolerance the halachic teachers showed toward the art we are studying must have been wrung from them by popular pressure, and as soon as they were again in a position of dominance, they saw to it that this art was destroyed.

Such popular pressure seems suggested in a statement in the targum of the pseudo Jonathan, in a passage paraphrasing Levit. xxvi, 1, which Krauss quotes:

> Make for yourselves no idols: idolatrous images and columns before which you would prostrate yourselves you must not make, and a stone ornamented [with pictures] before which you would kneel down you must not let stay in your land. But a *stoa* (סטיו) on which figures and likenesses are carved you may put upon the floor(?) of your sanctuary, but not to throw yourselves down upon it: for I am the Lord your God.[96]

It is impossible to determine the date of this passage without begging all our questions. Krauss thinks it very early—as much in this targum is believed to be—and thus takes it to

92. *BT, Baba Kamma*, 97b (ET, 568). See above, I, 268.

93. As Kirzner suggests (ET) in a note ad loc.

94. Samuel Krauss, "Die galiläischen Synagogenruinen und die Halakha," *MGWJ*, LXV

(1921), 211–218, esp. 218.

95. Baron, *History*, III, 52 f. For some reason this statement is omitted in the revised edition of 1952. For R. Abun, see above, p. 20.

96. Op. cit., and Krauss, *Synag. Altert.*, 348, n. 2.

antedate the opposition to images he sees in the Talmud. The question is, however, whether this passage is not, in direct contrast to the talmudic writings, the product of a more popular source, or a reading adapted to popular pressures. Here is at last a concession to the point of view which produced the art of the synagogues and graves. It is not in a rabbinic work, in the strict sense of the term, but in a text designed for the populace. Jews did, of course, say their prayers kneeling or prostrate, in the presence of these decorations. For the benefit of such worshipers, interpretations of the Old Testament prohibitions of images such as this must have been made. It is interesting that this only out-and-out sanction of images that I can find, a deliberate contradiction of the Old Testament law, is in a targum made for popular teaching. I doubt very much whether many rabbis ever approved such an interpretation.

Krauss recalls in connection with this passage the story of Rab (third century), who read the Scriptures in a synagogue in Babylon. At the proper time the worshipers all prostrated themselves on their faces—all except Rab, who refused to do so (or to pronounce the blessing after reading) because "there was a stone pavement there, and it has been taught, 'Neither shall ye place any figured stone in your land to bow down upon it.' " [97] The rabbis have many explanations of this, as does Krauss. For our purpose the scene may well stand as originally described: Rab had come into a synagogue decorated with images in mosaic which he by no means approved. He would read the Scriptures for such a congregation, but showed his marked disapproval of their decorations by not joining in their prayers. It was the common people, not halachists like Rab, who were responsible for making such images. The people had no scruples about falling down upon them to worship, but when Rab's successors finally had their way, the images, whether in mosaic, painting, or relief, were carefully chipped away. It is recounted that "although there were thirteen synagogues in Tiberias, R. Ammi and R. Assi prayed only between the pillars, the place where they studied." [98] The Talmud does not explain why these rabbis of the third and fourth centuries did not like to pray in the synagogues of Tiberias, but one can make a shrewd guess. [99]

It has often been said that the rabbinic prejudice was against objects or forms in the round, rather than in two dimensions. Accordingly, I have heard it brought out in discussion that we have in our Jewish remains practically no representations in the full round, only in relief, painting, or mosaic, and hence that these representations did not go against rabbinic feeling. This seems to me thoroughly unwarranted. The discussion of the seal ring and its impressions was carried out strictly on the basis that an object in relief was forbidden, while the representations on "kettles, pots, sheets, and towels" must have been drawn quite in the flat. I do not know a passage where the rabbis distinguished between

97. *BT, Megillah,* 22b (ET, 137). See Krauss, *Synag. Altert.,* loc. cit., where parallel passages are cited.

98. *BT, Berakoth,* 30b (ET, 185).

99. The contradictory attitude of the rabbis on the use of images has continued throughout Jewish history. Marvin Lowenthal, *A World Passed By,* 1933, pp. xxvii f., presents an interesting collection of quotations on the subject from rabbis of the twelfth to the fourteenth century. Even about the most liberal of them, however, one feels that they are exercising toleration, not initiative, in regard to the use of images.

images in the flat and in the round, except possibly the discussion of the signet ring, and if I have overlooked such a passage, the fact remains that in the discussions we have been considering the distinction never appears. In general, the rabbis were protesting against representing forbidden forms, not against round forms as contrasted with two-dimensional ones. And while in many of the passages figures are forbidden which have been used as idols, in many others the discussion is concerned simply with the forbidden images as such. The danger, of course, was always that the images might be used as idols. But the prohibitions are against making the images *lest* they be used as idols. The prohibitions, I repeat, are against making or using images, round or flat, and they have always been construed to mean this in orthodox tradition.

We may close our review of the rabbinical evidence with the latest addition to our knowledge, a psalm found in the genizah scrolls newly discovered in Palestine, and recently translated and discussed by Sonne.[100] The psalm is a denunciation of certain heretics, a pronouncement of their doom, by a man who has been "given knowledge through the mysteries of thy wonders, and through thy wondrous secret thou hast manifested thy might with me." This is said toward the close of the psalm, or just short of the place at which the manuscript becomes illegible, but the last lines which can be read seem to say that what the writer has done is beyond the scope of human flesh. It is the spirit of God within man which alone leads him into knowledge of God, his might, and his tender mercies. Only God is the source of righteousness. Sonne strangely sees in this the point of view of a Jewish Gnosticism which, unlike what he calls "genuine Judaism,"[101] contrasted flesh and spirit, and got mysteries out of the Scriptures by allegory. He has interesting evidence that R. Meir himself was influenced by this trend. It seems to me that many an ancient rabbi could have written this section, since the gnostic intrusion is slight indeed. What interests us more especially is the sort of heresy which the psalm as a whole was written to denounce. I quote the words that describe the heretics:

> But they, hypocrites, schemes of Belial
>
> do they conceive, and they seek thee with a double heart,
> and are not well grounded in thy truth. Yea, a root that
> beareth gall and wormwood is implanted in their thoughts,
>
> and they go about after the inclination of their heart, and
> inquire of thee with idols. The stumbling block of their
> iniquity they put before their face, and they come
>
> to search for thee from the mouth of false prophets,
> seduced into heresy. And they speak to thy people with
> stammering lips and with a strange tongue

100. Isaiah Sonne, "A Hymn against Heretics in the Newly Discovered Scrolls," *HUCA*, XXIII, i (1950/1), 275–313. The Hebrew text was published by E. L. Sukenik, מגילות גנוחות, Jerusalem, 1948.

101. Sonne, op. cit., 284.

> to cheat them and make them act foolishly, because they
> (the false prophets) hearkened not to thy voice and gave
> no ear to thy word. For
>
> of the vision of knowledge they said: "It is not right,"
> and of the way of thy heart they asserted: "It is not
> that." Thou, O God, wilt answer them, (namely) to judge
> them
>
> in thy strength according to their idols and according to
> the multitude of their transgressions; that they may be
> taken in their own thought whereby they turned away
> from thy covenant.[102]

Here we have a bitter denunciation of people who have turned away from God's covenant, that is, wayward Jews. Their wickedness lies in having followed Belial, so that they have a double loyalty—allegiance to God and to Belial. It seems to be the second loyalty which makes them "inquire of [God] with idols." They put a stumbling block, apparently some sort of image, before their faces, and go to "false prophets" who teach them to "speak with stammering lips and with a strange tongue." Sonne connects this latter with glossolalia,[103] but it reads with total appropriateness in view of what we find in the charms and on the amulets with their inscriptions. It was all very well to use special inspiration for spiritual interpretation of Scripture, but this other was going too far for the author of the psalm.

All that I have sought to state in this chapter is that the spirit of halachic Judaism in no way accounts for the "decorations" we are studying, because nothing in the rabbinic writings gives us a moving cause for their adoption. So long as the rabbis were in control no such ornamentation was allowed, because the rabbis knew very well that these representations were more than decorative. Once the Jewish state was destroyed, and rabbinic control became more and more theoretical, the "decorations," as well as the forbidden menorah, appeared everywhere. The people who borrowed these designs, even to representing Helios in their synagogues, had some impulse to do so which the rabbis certainly did not give them. The images came in not through toleration, but on a great wave of active appropriation which reached from Rome through Palestine, and as far as Dura. No wave rises but in response to a force, and this force and this drive to image making cannot be found at all in the rabbis.

Accordingly, to insist that the images could have meant to the Jews who made them no more than they would have meant by essentially rabbinic postulates, is quite unwarranted. We shall, of course, use rabbinic evidence constantly in discussing the meaning of the images, since many details of popular Judaism found a place in rabbinic life. But we must try to recover the popular Judaism of the period primarily from the archeological remains, for the decorations found in these express a mood and a religious attitude which rabbinic Judaism has at best only grudgingly tolerated, never itself championed or advocated.

102. Ibid., 290.   103. Ibid., 303.

CHAPTER TWO

Method in Evaluating Symbols

STUDY OF THE rabbinic evidence has led to a negative conclusion.[1] It was not because the Greco-Roman world and its images had been accepted as valid for Judaism by the rabbis that such numbers of Greco-Roman figures were used in the Jewish tombs and synagogues of the time. The rabbis held to their aniconism with occasional but on the whole very insignificant modification. Accordingly, since the images were used so flagrantly, the rabbis could have had little control over the practices of the mass of Jews, and I suspect that they had even less control over the ideas, pagan, gnostic, astrological, and mystical, which the Jews who made the amulets and ornaments may have been incorporating into their Jewish faith.

If the attitudes of the rabbis do not furnish an authoritative norm reflecting popular Judaism at this time, what, then, was the character of that popular Judaism? Does the hellenized art testify to a real invasion of hellenistic thought into common Jewish thinking, or only to a penetration of art forms for decorative purposes—a phenomenon that witnesses no basic modification of what popular Judaism had been in Palestine under Pharisaic control before the collapse of the Jewish state?

Only one body of evidence speaks directly for popular Judaism in the Greco-Roman world, namely, the archeological data. Everything else deriving from the period, conspicuously the talmudic literature, is, in relation to popular Judaism, secondary to that evidence, because the literature comes, we have seen, from a group who could not have inspired such productions, and who destroyed this art as soon as they had power to do so. As to the Jews who built the synagogues and tombs, there is no reason whatever to doubt that they were what Galling called *thoratreu* Jews.[2] But before the dissemination of the Talmud, being true to the Torah could scarcely, for Jews not in the rabbinic group, have meant fidelity to the Talmud. It meant in Philo's case, for example, complete devotion to the Torah as he had it in his Greek translation, along with a tradition for its interpretation. This interpretation agreed on many points with the rulings of the Pharisees of the day. Similarly, in the period we are studying, the Jews who were "propagating" Jews, if I may call them that, were undoubtedly keeping themselves a dis-

1. This chapter, somewhat abbreviated and adapted, was published as "The Evaluation of Symbols Recurrent in Time, as Illustrated in Judaism," *Eranos-Jahrbuch*, XX (1952), 285–319.

2. See above, p. 5.

tinct group, eating kosher food as they understood the term, observing the festivals and
Sabbaths, abstaining from intermarriage with gentiles, and avoiding any taint of what
seemed to them idolatry or recognition of pagan gods. That Jews of the diaspora were
"Torah-true" in this sense both pagans and Christians of the period attest.[3] Jews wanted
their own places of worship, which meant their own way of worship, and a close association with one another even in death, which produced special Jewish burying grounds.
All of this, however, I must constantly repeat, was completely accordant in Philo's mind
with interpreting the text of the Torah in terms of Greek or hellenistic religious values
and aspirations, and such an attitude may have been just as natural to the mass of Jews
living in gentile centers.

A. THE PROBLEM

INTO THE Torah-true lives of the great mass of Jewish devotees of the period we are
studying there palpably came an amazing use of pagan art forms. Everything specifically
forbidden in the halacha of the rabbis appears in the remains of their religious culture:
apart from the fantastic images on the amulets and charms, even the synagogues have
yielded images of pagan gods—images in the round or in relief—and such motifs as snakes,
plants, hands, animals, and birds of all kinds, as well as a considerable abstract vocabulary, comprising rosettes, a great variety of wine symbols, and wreaths, fishes, bread, and
the like.

The Jewish art becomes, then, in the phrase which Cumont applied to his Mithraic
material, a "picture book without text." The philological approach has to be discarded.
Cumont himself, in a passage recently quoted by Bonner,[4] said: "Archeology, without the
help of philology, becomes a conjectural science whose conclusions achieve only that
degree of verisimilitude which the ingenuity and eloquence of their authors can give
them." But from his Mithraic "picture book" Cumont himself gave us much more than
ingenuity and eloquence about Mithraism. When relevant literary evidence does not
exist, one cannot on that account disregard the archeological remains. Obviously, in
discussing such a symbol as the cup, for example, every reference to the drinking of wine
which we can get from Jewish literature, including that of the rabbis, will have to be
closely scrutinized; but we cannot assume from the outset (and to the end) that the rabbis
tell us all that may have been in the minds of Jews who pictured the cup, or grapes,
between peacocks in their synagogues, or who carved the cup on their graves. This
would indeed be what Panofsky called "indiscriminately applying our literary knowledge
to the [artistic] motifs." [5] The symbols must be treated as primary evidence not simply of
an art, but of the life of the Jews who made the art. To use such evidence we must learn
to read the symbols as such, and here we are on ground which the historian properly
regards as extremely dangerous, the quicksand of scholarship which engulfs, often mad-
dens, those who attempt to explore it. Clearly we cannot just sit back and make guesses

3. See above, I, 33–58.   5. Erwin Panofsky, *Studies in Iconology*, 1939, 12.
4. Bonner, *BM*, 301.

at meaning. Yet merely to assert absence of meanings is not conservatism, but is equally unfounded guessing. There must be some sounder approach.

We are, then, forced to ask the question: Does this art in itself indicate a large penetration into popular Judaism of religious conceptions, if not of rituals, from the Greco-Roman world, or is it most naturally to be taken as an adopting of meaningless art forms on a purely decorative level? We must assume that so long as the Jews were Torah-true, there were limits to ideological invasion. If Helios had been accepted by Jews as a substitute or equivalent for Yahweh, who could then be worshiped in images of Helios, worshiped *as* Helios, there would have been no reason to build synagogues dedicated to Yahweh: the Jew might as well have gone to the temple of Helios with his pagan neighbors. But there is always the possibility that the Jews who used these symbolic forms maintained the same distinction as that by which Christians saved their principle of monotheism and freedom from idolatry while availing themselves largely of the same pagan-Jewish motifs—namely, the distinction between direct worship of an image and the use of it as a symbolic aid in worship. Hence I have suggested [6] that, as between the motives of pure decoration and of idolatry, there is a *tertium quid* to be considered, the possibility that these figures had real meaning for Jews as symbols—symbols whose values they had thoroughly Judaized by giving them Jewish explanations.

This is the form the question now takes. Admitting that the Jews would not have remained Jews (as they obviously did) if they had used these images in pagan ways and with pagan explanations, do the remains indicate a symbolic adaptation of pagan figures to Judaism, or merely an urge to decoration? We are forced to try to find out more from the material itself than a mere morphological-historical approach would tell us. Clearly we must study the motifs which Jews actually chose, and the ways in which they used them—in what places, associations, and circumstances.

B. WHAT IS A SYMBOL?

An objective approach to ancient symbolism is possible only for those who are ready to combine historical with psychological techniques. Use of the techniques of either one of these sciences without aid of the other has heretofore resulted in pure subjectivism. The study of religious art by the "scientific" historians of the last half century has reflected great skill and erudition in identifying the figures represented: it has "turned vases from *objets d'art* into historical documents, dated and assigned to authors." [7] What has been done in this way is of permanent importance, and has earned such scholars the right to call themselves scientific. Most of them have suddenly ceased to be scientific, however, as they have exhausted the possibilities of such study, and gone on to assert what religious values the figures did or did not have.

For example, a century ago an important school of symbolists began to use their

6. See above, pp. 7 f.

7. A. D. Nock, "The Necessity of Scholarship," *Official Register of Harvard University* (Harvard Divinity School Bulletin), XLVII (1950), no. 29, p. 42.

imaginations and produced enormous works which were essentially fanciful.[8] Much good fancy was here mixed in with bad, but there was no criterion for distinguishing the one from the other. Scientific historians, thinking they were still being scientific, reacted against such symbolists, and asserted that the art had no meaning at all beyond the ornamental. On one occasion I was approached by one of the greatest classical archeologists and historians of the century and suddenly accosted with the pronouncement, "The carvings on the Roman sarcophagi are purely decorative."

"Fine," I answered, "but how do you know?"

His only answer was to repeat the assertion in identical phraseology three times.

Similarly Avi-Yonah, as quoted above,[9] said that if the wine cup and grapes appear on Jewish monuments, it shows that such designs had so entirely lost meaning, had become so completely decorative, that they had no meaning in Christian art either. Avi-Yonah was indeed "building a fence" about his position. It was safer to deny symbolism to all grapes than just to Jewish grapes. Such dogmatism is, like all emotional dogmatism, of great comfort to the dogmatist, in relieving him of the necessity of further question. But the questions unfortunately remain.

Up to the present there has been no serious attempt to find a method by which one could distinguish between such equally absurd extremes as, in my opinion, these symbolists and nonsymbolists present. Panofsky warned of the danger, in iconography, of "trusting our intuition pure and simple," [10] and assertions of absence of meaning in such devices as we are studying are as intuitional, fanciful, and worthless as the creation of pretty stories about their meaning. Only some objective method can save us from the one or the other type of intuitionalism.

The best approach to the nature of a symbol is suggested in the simple line of Ovid: *Crede mihi; plus est, quam quod videatur, imago.*[11] That is, a symbol is an image or design with a significance, to the one who uses it, quite beyond its manifest content. Or for our purpose we may say that a symbol is an object or a pattern which, whatever the reason may be, operates upon men, and causes effect in them, beyond mere recognition of what is literally presented in the given form.[12] Two lines crossing each other at right angles may be only

8. Cf. esp. F. Creuzer, *Symbolik und Mythologie der alten Völker, besonders der Griechen*, 1836; J. J. Bachofen, *Versuch über die Gräbersymbolik der Alten*, 1859 (reprinted 1925); Goblet d'Alviella, *La Migration des symboles*, 1891. The practice goes back to Francis Bacon, *The Wisdom of the Ancients*, 1617, who prefaced his completely fanciful series of explanations of classical myths by remarking that he was not "entering upon a work of fancy, or amusement" or intending to "use a poetical liberty in explaining poetical fables." Many before him, he says, have "delivered fables of plausible meanings they never contained," and he properly traces such interpretation back to the Stoic allegories of Chrysippus.

9. See above, p. 4.

10. Panofsky, op. cit., 15.

11. *Heroides*, Epist. XIII, 155. Quoted by Bachofen, op. cit., 43.

12. In this discussion I am throughout avoiding such metaphysical problems as primarily concern Tillich: see his essay, "The Religious Symbol," *Journal of Liberal Religion*, II (1940), 13–33. He finds in the religious symbol five elements: (*1*) its figurative quality, i.e., it is revered not for itself but for what it represents; (*2*) it seems to make an imperceptible reality perceptible; (*3*) in contrast to a "sign," it has innate power—originally, in the case of pictorial symbols, magical power—so that as a symbol loses this power, it loses its genuine

that, as they seem to be in a small child's scribbling, or when an illiterate man uses them to make his mark. But they take on great symbolic meaning when they become the co-ordinates of a mathematician's graph, or when a priest merely indicates the configuration with motions of his hand toward a congregation. Similarly they take on a great variety of meanings in many savage communities. As another example, a finger ring is in itself an ornament only, but when it is given as a wedding ring it is a symbol which helps to make the marriage effective by its very presence on the hand; continued wearing of it actually helps to stabilize the couple and to make their union enduring. A flag does more to people who see it and carry it than another piece of cloth, so that "The Star-spangled Banner" is a real hymn of the group religion, and the photograph of the raising of the flag at Iwo Jima is rapidly becoming a national "holy picture" which deeply affects Americans.

Such a conception of symbol leaves out of account many other legitimate uses of the term. Any word can be called a symbol of an external object or act, or of a conception. Aside from this, a word merely as such calls to mind something quite apart from anything in its own structure, and so a symbol in this sense is often called a sign. Similarly a representational painting or carved figure, whatever its own inherent beauty of color or form, recalls some other object, and is designed, like a photograph, to call that object to mind; but since the object represented may in itself have symbolic power in the deeper sense, a painting may be more profoundly symbolic than an ordinary word can be in its literal implication. For this reason modern artists who want their designs to be regarded without such external reference have been giving up representational form for creations which, recalling nothing on sea or land, must be thought of as realities in themselves. I suspect that such artists are still speaking symbolically, however, with the difference that they have given over public symbolism for a private one. The painting still has highly symbolic, that is, operative value for the artist himself, if only because he expresses in it, as in dreams, his emotions, his sense of relatedness and fitness in form, color, and chiaroscuro. Through this his own inherent formlessness takes on form.

Indeed, in the light of latest psychological techniques it seems highly unlikely that one can make even a geometric design without producing something symbolic.[13] I have been

symbolic character; (4) it has a socially accepted rather than a private meaning; (5) it points to the "unconditioned transcendent." Tillich is primarily concerned with this fifth element, and thus seems to me to be unrealistic in his treatment of symbols as they appear in the history of religion. Such abstraction as he achieves may be the desirable and logical end of religion, but has played and plays a part in the life of only an insignificant fraction of mankind. To say that "the soul is religious," in the sense that "the relation to the unconditioned transcendent is essential or constitutive for it" (op. cit., 20), rules out from religion that which has been the concern of the great majority of men of the past, whose gods or God

have been definitely conditioned by and thoroughly immanent in human affairs and in nature. Of this no one is more aware than Tillich himself: he simply does not like to regard such a God or gods as objects of religion, and is courageously willing to call himself an atheist in reference to such conceptions of Deity. To him "religion" is a word for an ideal rarely attained. As an historian I use the word religion in its historical rather than its ideal sense. What religion ought to be, or what men ought to worship, it is not my business to demonstrate. For the way in which Tillich uses his conception of symbols in his formal thinking, see his *Systematic Theology*, Chicago, 1951, I, 238–247.

13. Vittorio Macchioro, "Il Simbolismo nelle

impressed with the revelations of character obtained when an individual tells what is suggested to him by the odd-shaped blots of the Rorschach test. People appear to project their personalities into the blots and to turn meaningless accidental forms into symbols, to such a point that one skilled in evaluating such tests can make profound observations about the psychological structure of the subject. Even more interesting to me is a still newer test, called "mosaics" by the inventor,[14] in which one is given little flat pieces, geometric shapes, in a variety of colors and told to make with them, on a sheet of paper, "anything that looks nice to you." The technique of reading these mosaics is by no means well developed, but it is at least clear that with the colored lozenges, triangles of various kinds, and squares, people tend to make designs expressive of their own natures.

This sort of symbolic projection, it seems to me, can especially be observed in the use of "merely conventional" rosettes, columns, lozenges, leaves, and the other formal devices ornamenting the ossuaries we have seen. Indeed, it appears likely that stonecutters sometimes left round spaces on ossuaries uncut so that the person who ordered the box might select the sort of rosette which especially "appealed to him," as we say; perhaps we should say the design which was most deeply moving, or symbolic, to him. But into such a private world modern psychology would be very bold to enter, especially when it relates to a remote period. If some psychologists would like to try it, that is for them. But the present work only secondarily deals with psychology, and I make no claims in the field. Let me assure the reader at once that I shall not attempt to analyze the patterns in Jewish art to discover the personal characters of the artists who designed them. It seems clear, however, that the ancient designers—perhaps as unconsciously as people who make the modern patterns—had a sense of meanings and values inhering in what they produced and in the vocabulary of shapes with which they were working.

1. *The Psychological Approach to Symbolism*

IF PSYCHOLOGISTS are right in saying that all art forms, even geometric patterns, tend to have symbolic value, it follows that in trying to establish a method for evaluating symbolism, there is no escaping the problem of psychology. Without attempting to declare my precise debt to various schools of philosophy or psychology, I may say that I have found the language of Suzanne Langer very congenial, especially in her discrimination between the realms of denotative and of connotative thinking. Indeed, this distinction is being independently used not only by psychologists and philosophers,[15] but also by literary and

figurazioni sepolcrali romane," in Reale Accademia di Archeologia, Lettere e Belle Arti di Napoli, *Memorie*, I (1911), ii, 18 f., recognizes that no art is purely decoration: "Il simbolismo esiste dunque . . . quale fatto psicologico, fuori di ogni intenzione: e appunto perchè esso è un fenomeno della psiche, un'arte decorativa figurata in sè e per sè non esiste."

14. Dr. Margaret Lowenfeld, of London. For a bibliography and discussion of this technique of testing, see F. Wertham, "The Mosaic Test," in

L. E. Abt and L. Bellak, *Projective Psychology*, 1950, 230–256.

15. Cf. C. G. Jung's chapter, "Concerning the Two Kinds of Thinking," in his *Psychology of the Unconscious*, 1916; for the logicians, cf. Susanne K. Langer, *Philosophy in a New Key*, 1942 (reprinted 1949), *passim*, esp. the chapter, "Discursive and Presentational Forms." This kind of thinking, of course, did not begin with Mrs. Langer, but it is not appropriate here to trace her intellectual

art critics in America.[16] It is a differentiation largely between verbal and averbal thought, though this must quickly be modified, since the connotative element is very important in language also. We think, that is, on two levels, one in which language is precise, scientific, specific, and attempts to convey a single definite idea from one mind to others. This I am trying to do as I write—*préciser*, the French actually call it. It is extremely difficult to do. I can describe external incidents, such as a walk to the village, because we have the language for such communication. The formulas of chemistry and mathematics are more precise forms of expression than ordinary words. But behind all such precision is a thought world where thinking is by no means precise in the same way, where we are occupied rather with impressions and associations arising from words, tones of voice, forms of objects. We are aware of some of this, but of most of it we are ordinarily not conscious at all, and much of it can be brought to awareness only by hypnotism, psychoanalysis, or the like.

Our tastes, our habits, our judgments on most matters are determined by the connotations of words and objects, their associations in all sorts of metaphor, and not their literal meaning. When asked to explain them directly in literal terms we are entirely unable to do so, just as a man could never say what his parents, wife, or children "mean" to him. Philosophy is largely an attempt to justify in literal, denotative language the conclusions to which the philosopher has long been committed by the other type of thinking. The same is true in psychology. French has recently written:

> Common-sense psychology is unformulated. The "understanding" that it gives us is an unverbalized sense of what to expect and what to do. . . . "Intuitive understanding" is an art of knowing what to expect from others without knowing why, without being able to explain how we came by the practical conclusions on which we act. . . . The facts that are most obvious are those that we do not understand at all because we never really questioned them.[16a]

It is a splendid definition of common-sense in general to say that it is unformulated, unverbalized knowledge. The person who can "express himself" is the person who has the rare power of translating his associational connotative ideas, his image thinking, or some of it, into specific, literal language. I am attracted by Mrs. Langer's statement: "To project feelings into outer objects is the first way of symbolizing, and thus of *conceiving*, those feelings." [17] That is, insofar as a word or form "symbolizes" an emotion, it takes us beyond pure "feeling" into an intellectualized "conception" of the feeling, one which can even be used to communicate the feeling, or the conception of the feeling, to others who have the same symbolic vocabulary. The symbolic form becomes a "word," a means of communication. All discourse is a matter of symbolic communication, whether in the literal or in this connotative sense.

I have no interest in adapting this contrast in most of our thought to such categorizing

---

ancestry through Cassirer, Urban, and the symbolic logicians.

16. See, e.g., Cleanth Brooks, "The Language of Paradox," in *The Language of Poetry* (ed. by Allen Tate), 1942, 44: "Poetry is a language in which the connotations play as great a part as the denotations." Cf. Wallace Stevens, ibid., 101–104.

16a. Thomas M. French, *The Integration of Behavior*, Chicago, 1952, I, 36.

17. Langer, op. cit., 100.

words as preconscious, subconscious, unconscious. But I have enormous interest in the fact that all our most important thinking is in this world of the suggestive, connotative meaning of words, objects, sounds, and forms, that our thinking is primarily unprecise, and that our world of precision is a tour de force, a veneer which we superimpose upon our ordinary world of associative thought. The present generation is amazingly developing both these types of thinking.[18] At just the time when the vocabulary of science is becoming increasingly complex, in the attempt to achieve increasing precision, and when great scientific discoveries are being made possible through such increased precision, contemporary poetry, art, and music find that they can express the modern spirit only by abandoning the specific and formal and letting the unformed speak in ways quite maddening to those who still try to be verbally precise.

It is no accident that those who practise such modern art and writing revert, with a natural sense of fitness, to the word symbolism when they are forced to *préciser* their lack of precision. By definition the symbol is a word, a poem, musical sounds, forms which mean more to us, have more power to move us, than the word, or the thing represented, in itself. For example, the word apple, when used specifically to designate a certain kind of fruit, is a word of precision. It makes little difference whether we say "apple," *Apfel*, or *pomme*. The sounds are useful, not in themselves, but only as they suggest a specific sort of fruit. Similarly the picture of an apple in a dictionary, or in a treatise on fruit trees, is only another way of making precise the concept which is being conveyed from one mind to another. But when the word apple, in any language, refers to the apple awarded by Paris, or to the apple eaten by Adam, the form of the apple, or even the question of whether this was an apple at all, is unimportant—for the word has become a symbol for greed, jealousy, discord, in one case, for disobedience to God, sin, in another. If I say, "The lady offered him her apple, and, as from the days of Adam, he took and ate," I am not talking about an apple at all, but about woman's sexual appeal for man. It would indeed be difficult to *préciser* all that the word apple means in that sentence. For some it would mean the acceptably desired; for some it would still imply the quintessence of sin; for most of us it would carry both ideas at the same time, with associations going far down into our unknown depths and conflicts.

If this statement about the apple had been made in a poem, or in some other form of "creative" writing, the poet would think that a professor who would try to make its meaning explicit and denotative was a pedantic fool. The professor would probably think that he was being intellectual, superior, in trying to do so. The cleft between the literary, poetic mind and the academic mind is largely the cleft between the mind which expresses itself, lives directly and deeply, in symbolic meanings, and the mind which supposes this sort of

---

18. The idea is of course not new. Maurice H. Farbridge, *Studies in Biblical and Semitic Symbolism*, 1923, 4, quotes Victor Hugo's *L'Homme qui rit:*

"Il est presqu'impossible d'exprimer dans leurs limites exactes les évolutions abstruses qui se font dans le cerveau. L'inconvénient des mots, c'est d'avoir plus de contour que les idées. Toutes les idées se mêlent par les bords; les mots, non. Un certain côté diffus de l'âme leur échappe toujours. L'expression a des frontières, la pensée n'en a pas."

Hugo correctly saw that this unexpressed, non-verbal content of our minds is idea, not merely emotion.

thought to be improved by annotated editions. It is the cleft between what I am calling, with reference to symbolism, "meaning," "power," or "value" on the one hand and "explanations" on the other. The symbol carries its own meaning or value, and with this its own power to move us. Indeed, even the word *préciser* is an academician's term. The poet would rightly consider the symbolic or connotative statement about the apple quite as precise as any of the lucubrations of the professor. The explanation is for some people indispensable, but it is never the reality, our poet's thought itself.

Such distinction is most helpful for understanding creative expression in painting, music, and the other arts, where the symbols of chiaroscuro, color, or form, or the symbols of successions of melodies, harmonies, and discords become the immediate vehicles of meaning, vehicles which eternally deride every attempt to make their content verbally precise. The old distinction between the emotional and the intellectual here breaks down completely, for we see that the deepest thought and meaning lie in the immediate symbolic association. Explanations are always a weak afterthought as compared to meaning itself. And significant meaning is almost always conveyed in symbols, in which I should include now drama, myth, ritual, and all connotative aspects of words, besides distinctive visual forms.

This is the real function of dreams as conceived by the depth psychologists: they are a procession of symbols—images symbolic not only in their forms but also in what happens to the forms in the action of the dream. When we become psychologically disturbed we must have help to verbalize these deeper symbols of ours, give them explanations. Jung is saying the same of his "archetypes" when he explains that the symbol itself refers neither to the literal sun, nor to the lion or king for whom the sun is a symbol, but to an "unknown third thing that finds expression in all these similes, yet—to the perpetual vexation of the intellect—remains unknown and not to be fitted into a formula." [19] Ordinarily, however, the dream is nature's own psychiatry—a sign not that we are in psychological difficulties but that we are getting dramatic purgation as the conflicts and disturbed elements within us express themselves in the medium of dream symbolism.

2. *Religious Symbols*

MY INTEREST in all this is to come closer to an understanding of religious symbols. It now appears that we have gone a long way toward recognizing what we mean, in "precise" terms, by the word symbol. In general, a symbol is a word or form which expresses more than it indicates, and so has power beyond its literal denotation. The religious symbol is not only a direct purveyor of meaning in itself, but also a thing of power, or value, operating upon us to inspire, to release tensions, to arouse guilt, or to bring a sense of forgiveness and reconciliation. We may love the symbol, we may hate it, but so long as it is a symbol we register its message, feel its power. A most moving story was told me by a friend, a famous early refugee from Hitlerian Germany, who, when the full meaning of Nazism was presented to him at a meeting, when he grasped what was in the swastika and behind it,

19. C. G. Jung and C. Kerényi, *Essays on a*   *Science of Mythology*, 1951, 105; cf. pp. 127, 136, and Kerényi's quotation from Schelling, p. 214.

stood in the street after the session shaking his fist at the great swastika on the building and shouting at the top of his voice: "It's a damnable thing, a damnable symbol!"

His friends almost violently took him home and got him out of the country. He has been convinced ever since that some symbols are in their very form good, some evil. My point in recalling this man's experience is simply to emphasize that a symbol in religion (and under my definition of religion, I would include the swastika along with the cross as being both powerful religious symbols) is something which conveys meaning indeed, but which also has inherent power to operate upon us.[19a] Another of my friends, who was murdered for his humanitarianism, had as a child been trained in Catholicism. He renounced the credo and theology of his religion but could not escape the power of its symbols, a fact which he revealed by saying that Christianity would always be a menace as long as it used "the damned cross."

There are many ways in which symbols may have come to have such power, but that is beyond the scope of my discussion here. In fact, our lives are largely guided and molded by symbols. There are the symbolic acts of polite society, the "code" of a gentleman, which no one could codify without becoming ridiculous. The urges and repressions of phallicism produce symbols so powerful that in our civilization we can rarely contemplate them directly at all. We recognize the symbolic force of green for the Irishman, of red for the Communist. We have the public symbols of the flag, the Shield of David, the cross. And there is the world of private symbolism manifested in our dreams and neurotic compulsions.

It would be relatively easy if on this basis we could contrive in words a specific formula of meaning for each symbol, at least for the public symbols, and suppose that the given meaning, or operative value, is always conveyed by the particular symbol whenever it appears. But this is to miss the point that symbols have a way of dying, of apparently losing their power, and becoming merely ornaments. And they also have the power of coming to life again, as fresh associations and religious awakenings take old symbols for their own. This happened when the Christians adopted the ancient and universal symbol of the cross, a symbol which in pre-Christian ornament had degenerated into merely a four-point rosette, one of many forms of the rosette. Rosettes were still actively symbolic when Christianity was born, continued to be so into late Christian Byzantine times; but the four-point rosette, within a circle or abbreviated as the swastika, had come in the pagan world to have no special significance, so far as I can see, in itself. Christianity seized upon this four-point rosette within a circle, however, then still later made it specifically Christian by using a longer upright shaft, and thus took it out of the circle, although the Coptic church and the Eastern church preferred to let it stay there. Similarly the sudden revival from the dead, or from near death, which recently occurred in the case of the

---

19a. Rabbi Silverman told me of the horror of his congregation at the Emmanuel Synagogue in Hartford when it was discovered, after Hitler came to power in Germany, that in 1927 the vestibule of the synagogue had been paved with a mosaic floor in which the swastika was frequently represented. The entire mosaic was at once ripped out. Here was a symbol which, when apparently dead, the Jews could borrow, but which, when alive, had a power indeed—one which could not be endured.

swastika, a variant of the cross in a circle, was even more dramatic. Now, it would be silly to argue that Christians put nothing new into the cross, or that Hitler's swastika meant the same as the swastika on a Greco-Roman mummy, or on a Jewish tombstone from the ancient world. But it is significant that when a new movement wants a powerful symbol, it usually finds satisfaction in reviving one of the primordial symbols rather than in inventing a new one, and the presumption is that this is because there is inherent symbolic power of some kind at least dormant in an old symbol even when we suppose that it has become a purely decorative device.

Whether there is such dormant symbolic power in what may ordinarily be called dead symbols used for ornament is not for the historian to debate. He must leave this for further investigation by psychologists. Whether it is more correct to say that basic symbols die, or that they merely become quiescent, I cannot say. Yet the trouble is that one cannot leave the question without begging it. For we must continue to face the problem of the "merely decorative" as contrasted with the "symbolic" use of forms in art; and when we put the contrast in these terms, or in such terms as "live" symbols versus "dead" symbols, or "active" symbols versus "quiescent" or "dormant" symbols, we assume, in each case, a theory of the nature of the contrast. Since I must have a terminology, I shall arbitrarily, tentatively, and without prejudice, use the contrast of "live" and "dead," fully prepared to have that terminology corrected by better knowledge. For in this study I cannot wait for such problems to be solved.

3. Migration of Live Symbols

As AN HISTORIAN I see that the transition of what I call a live symbol from one religion to another represents something quite different from the transition of a dead symbol. The difference can perhaps best be indicated by illustration. If in one of the modern synagogues where ornament is increasingly being used, one should find a large cross on the Torah shrine, it would be obvious that though the worshipers still wanted to call themselves Jews (the living symbols of synagogue and Torah shrine would indicate this), they had openly taken some highly important Christian values into their Judaism. A contemporary would need no literary documents to prove this, though he might have here a "picture book without text." The live Christian symbol, the cross, would speak for itself at once. If one could get a written explanation of the phenomenon from the rabbi of the synagogue, that would be only something supplementary, and perhaps a quite sophistic rationalization. The explanation would obviously be of less importance than the immediate sense that here a *value* had been borrowed, for the cross would have direct operative power to carry Christian types of experience into the lives of the Jews of that synagogue.

From such a hypothetical, probably impossible case we may turn to actual situations. All over the world, the Catholic church (rarely the Protestant) has allowed converted natives to carry much of their old symbolism into the new Christian chapels. The phenomenon is most familiar in the Latin-American countries, where native forms, symbols, and even elaborate rites are kept up along with the Christian ones. The Catholic clergy are quite aware that this gives to the local Christianity a coloration different from that of the

Catholicism of Italy or Ireland. So long as the symbols or rites thus retained are alive, actively operative, they cannot be carried over without bringing into the new religion the older values. Explanations must then be given, as when, in a story F. C. Conybeare liked to tell, a Jesuit priest got a community on one of the Pacific islands to give the name Francis of Assisi to a tribal statue which they insisted on having at least in the narthex of the chapel. The renaming did soften the paganism of the figure a bit, but did more to soothe the conscience of the priest than to put the values of the Italian saint into the savage figure. For the natives, we may be sure, the image kept its original living values in spite of the ridiculous explanation of it taught them by the priest.

The migration of symbols in the ancient world followed, I believe, the same lines. A dead symbol can be appropriated without adaptive explanation. So the egg-and-dart molding, which originally may have had symbolic value, had become a quite conventional ornament long before the beginning of the Christian era, and its appropriation by Jews and Christians probably meant nothing more than that this type of design for a molding pleased them; no explanation was necessary. The zigzag line, so much used in Romanesque architecture, is less certainly an instance of the retention of something purely formal, for it is the primordial symbol of water, and even in Romanesque ornament was used over church doorways in a manner suggesting that the flow of divine grace—which was the symbolic meaning of water in antiquity—was still felt as operative through the symbol by those who entered under it to worship in the churches. Even more clearly alive were the symbols I am studying—the eagle, the lion, the fish, the winged Victory and the wreath, the caduceus of Hermes, the figure of Orpheus with the animals. The persistence of these in Jewish and Christian art cannot be presumed to be the persistence of the merely ornamental, of dead emblems, for these were living symbols in paganism and Christianity, so that presumably, to my mind inevitably, they were living symbols to the Jews. Stripped of their old pagan explanations, as the Jesuit stripped away the name and mythology of the native idol when he called it Francis of Assisi, these motifs must have been retained by Christians, and by Jews, only because there was a value in them which they wanted to preserve for themselves. If Orpheus became for Christians a symbol of Christ taming the passions, he probably had been Moses or David, or some other Jewish figure, doing this for Jews when portrayed in a synagogue. The *value*, we see, is meaning in the connotational or associational realm. This remains constant in the migration of a symbol. The new religion will give new explanations of the symbol, precise verbalizations in the vocabulary of its own literal thinking. The historian of symbols has, then, the double task of finding the basic, unchanging values, together with the ever changing verbal explanations given by each new religion in adopting the old symbols.

Indeed, when the religious symbols borrowed by Jews in those years are put together, it becomes clear that the ensemble is not merely a "picture book without text," but reflects a lingua franca that had been taken into most of the religions of the day, for the same symbols were used in association with Dionysus, Mithra, Osiris, the Etruscan gods, Sabazius, Attis, and a host of others, as well as by Christianity later. It was a symbolic language, a direct language of values, however, not a language of denotation. Orpheus could become

Christ because he had ceased to be the Orpheus of Greek legend before the Christians borrowed him, and had come to represent mastery of the passions by the spirit—a role in which he had no specific name or mythological association. Helios driving his chariot through the zodiac could be used by Jews to represent their cosmic Deity because in the thinking of the day, especially the sort of thinking associated with Neoplatonism, this figure had come to stand not for the traditional anthropomorphic god at all, but for the Supreme Principle—a concept borrowed and used by all sorts of religions at the time. Thus its presence, to our knowledge, on the floors of three synagogues in Palestine would seem to indicate that Jews had in their Judaism not Helios, the pagan god, but the value of that figure in contemporary life.

4. *The Lingua Franca of Symbolism*

T o   u n d e r s t a n d the Judaism which used these pagan symbols, then, it is necessary to reconstruct the lingua franca of the religious symbolism of the time. To do so requires investigation of the use of each of the symbols in as many as possible of the pagan religions, even going back to the earliest occurrences of the forms in Mesopotamia and Egypt when they can be traced that far. If continuity of symbolic values can be demonstrated in all these religions, it would establish meanings for the lingua franca which, as they seem to have stability in other religions, would increasingly suggest themselves as the values of the symbols also for Jews. We seem to have familiar evidence of such continuity of meaning in the wine symbols, the cup, the vine, the grape, and the like. In Christianity, Christ is the vine; his blood, or his divine nature, is mystically given the communicant in the cup. But instantly we are reminded that for Dionysiacs and Orphics, Dionysus was the vine, and that the bacchanals received his divine nature in the cup. In both paganism and Christianity this participation meant mystic assimilation in life, and immortality after death. The symbol is really a common denominator, valid in an identical sense in both religions. For in both religions the cup and vine symbolize mystic union with the saving god, and eternal life. The bird eating the grapes of the vine is another symbol common to both religions: it is ordinarily taken in each case to stand for the devotee obtaining this divine life. So we have now the tentative suggestion that the religious experience which these particular symbols represented, the value they brought, was an experience of mystic union in which the devotee shared in the divine life of the saving god and was thereby assured of immortality, an experience which in each religion might have had a mythological explanation with or without association with the myths and cult of Dionysus himself.

In all this, however, we have constantly to bear in mind that the meaning or value of any given symbol is not a denotative, precise meaning, but a connotative one—a meaning in a language designed to speak to the mind, but having more immediate relation to the emotions than to verbal thinking. Beyond simply arousing emotions, however, these symbols carried potent ideas, even though the name or the myth linked with a given symbol changed repeatedly in the verbal formulations of the various cults. The reconstruction we are undertaking is one which will hardly please the modern philologist, who will expect me to say in precise words what Helios meant, or Orpheus, or the winged Victory, or the eagle. The religious symbolist, I repeat, is in this respect like the poet, who is usually, and naturally, disturbed at the misrepresentations attendant upon any attempt to make his language literally explicit by paraphrasing it. Wallace Stevens, himself a master of connotative expression, protests against literal "truth": "We have been a little insane about the truth. . . . To fix it is to put an end to it. Let me show it to you unfixed." [20] Literary criticism must give one ability to reread a poem with a new and direct sense of its "unfixed" meanings, the ability to feel the impact of its usually paradoxical metaphors until their resultant values register directly in mind and emotion alike.

Indeed, it has been objected with reason that it is quite misleading to contrast the denotative and the connotative, the verbal formulation and the symbolic meaning, as though the contrast were one between the precise and the imprecise. As a correspondent, A. B. Stridsberg, wrote me: "Nothing could be more definite, more existent, more real— even more precise—than symbolic meaning." With this I fully agree, though for convenience I keep the term "precise" for the verbally explicit. Thus the end of a study of symbolism is to have the symbol work upon us directly in its own right.

Accordingly, long as this study will become, there will be relatively little meaning in a literal or discursive sense got out of the symbols we examine. More and more we shall see that people used symbols which could pass thus from religion to religion precisely because the forms did not have any literal, denotative meaning; they spoke to a level of consciousness or mentality much less concerned with precision, but much richer and more important, than the level that responds to denotation. Christianity and Judaism alike rejected Dionysus and his rites and myths with horror, while they kept his symbols. They rejected the specific and kept what I may call the subspecific—linguistically subspecific, that is.

There is, however, a meaning, a very definite meaning, in the symbol, which is grasped by the devout quite as directly as verbal language, in the great majority of cases far more directly. That explanations of why the cross is important would so widely conflict, cannot obscure the fact that actually the cross itself carries a much more concrete and definite meaning or idea than all the verbal explanations of it put together. Theology is for the few: the cross is for all, the intellectual and the childish alike. It is this language which the historian of symbols must come to understand: he must let the lingua franca speak to him directly as the poet speaks in his metaphors, or as Bach with his masterful precision speaks in his fugues to those who know Bach's untranslatable language.

5. Modern Symbolism

JUNG feels deeply a danger that symbols may overwhelm us: they have a seduction, a dissolving power that can take us to destruction, to chaos. He sees in them autonomous forces which we study or release at our peril. The danger, however, seems to me to lie not in the symbols with their relative clarity and security, not even in the primordial symbols, but

---

20. "The Noble Rider and the Sound of Words,"
in *The Language of Poetry* (ed. by Allen Tate), 122, 124.

in the chaos of reality in the world and in ourselves, a chaos which first takes on meaning in the symbol. This formlessness behind the symbol which the symbol begins to make manageable is the element that, without the help of symbols, can destroy us. At our peril we look behind the symbol, for it is the symbol which finally stands between us and the meaningless.

At the same time it is in the world of symbol that we are creative. All advance in thought, as Mrs. Langer has pointed out, consists in the making explicit, that is, the expression in definite form, of that which comes to us as metaphorical, associational perception. As the immediate expression of our connotative minds, fresh creation of forms bids fair to be the future of religion. Mrs. Langer [21] says that the conflict of religion and science is the conflict between a primitive, "a young and provisional form of thought," and discursive, literal, scientific thinking, which must succeed religion if thinking is to go on. With this I completely disagree. She herself admits, as just indicated, that new formal thought usually begins in the pregnant realm of "suggestion," of symbol, and we can look forward to a time when literal thinking will have displaced figurative thinking only as we look forward to a time when man will have ceased to be human. Ours is so tremendously vital an age because, as I have said, we are now doing both types of thinking, doing so consciously, and because, as never before, in both philosophy and psychiatry, we are trying to co-ordinate the two types by understanding a little better the connotative processes of thought. We are not only trying to make our experience of nature intelligibly denotative in science; we are trying to use connotative thinking more freely in the arts, and, by coming to understand better the relation of the two types of thought, to use both more constructively. Religion will take on fresh life as it becomes less bound to the discursive and more free to create metaphorically. Indeed, it is something very like a revival of religion which modern art, music, and poetry, as well as modern psychology, are holding before our eyes. I see nothing "young and provisional" in such thinking.

A slight contribution to this attempt to understand the nonliteral, symbolical mentality is what this study aims to make. When I speak of understanding this type of mental activity, I by no means suggest surpassing it. I certainly have myself reached no full understanding. The modern mind tries to understand increasingly in order to utilize increasingly, not to create within itself illusions of understanding. This is the difference between science now and science fifty years ago, which was so confident that it had come to understand. Now we recognize that understanding is simply an infinite limit which we approach, and which orients our entire equation, our curve, at whatever point on the curve we may be, but a limit at which it would be ridiculous to consider that we have arrived.

The symbols we are studying operate in and emerge from the deepest levels of subrational thinking. They have a history which begins far earlier than history itself, and many of the earliest symbols still have potency, even in our time, when society seems to a large extent to be losing all sense of their importance. There is point in Mrs. Langer's suggestion [22] that most of the basic symbols of religion are nature symbols, that the modern

21. Op. cit., 164 f.   22. Ibid., 235.

intelligentsia live largely cut away from any association with nature, and that consequently a large part not only of the fading importance of religious symbols, but also of modern emotional instability, is to be attributed to the fact that our lives no longer incorporate the basic symbols of sin and salvation, of life and death. Doubts of the "meaning of life," she says, rarely occur in people who live as sailors do, that is, who, living with such symbols in nature, still find reality "meaningful" enough.

It is of equal importance in relation to our present sense of confusion that our educational system is directed almost entirely to rational, discursive treatment of literal fact. As long as purely intellectual training was supplemented by the chapel, this did little harm, but now man is trying to live by literal bread alone, and the intelligentsia are suffering from a sort of avitaminosis. We need more than calories to be healthy, and we need more than information to live balanced lives psychologically. The modern world has thrown out the old symbols, along with their explanations. The symbols speak to man, I have quoted Mrs. Langer as saying, on the "young and provisional" level, but it would be better to say on the subliterate level. For untold millions of years man was apparently only an animal: then for untold thousands of years he had a subliterate, subdiscursive intelligence. Upon these two stages most of us have now superimposed rationality in the full sense. All three of these levels are still represented in all of us. We trace the evolution from the animal stage in the development of the embryo; we just as truly relive the evolution to the subliterate (but intelligent) stage in infancy and childhood. The final rational adult strangely accepts his animal nature and treats it with respect, while he tries to believe that now he has "put away childish things." The great contribution of Freud has been to recall to us (many of the "rational" still childishly reject the idea) that this childish, subliterate element is as much a part of any individual's constitution as are his legs or liver, and that to neglect and abuse this part of oneself is as perilous as to neglect one's physique. Man has always stabilized this subliminal aspect of himself with symbols, and now we have none of real value. For a Cadillac car may symbolize a bank account, but our need of stability goes far deeper than material prosperity can reach. The pathetic avidity and abandon with which most of Germany accepted the swastika testified not to the merit of what the swastika brought with it, but to man's craving for basic symbols.

To the well-being of our physical side, analytical and discursive thinking has contributed enormously since it began, several centuries ago, on the study of physical anatomy. We have already made a bungling start on the "anatomy of melancholy," on the problem of man's subrational being, in depth psychology, in sociology, in anthropology. We have, to say the least, still a long way to go. It is my hope that the present work will contribute a little to the understanding of man as we trace some of our symbols in their transition through the ages. To the contemporary bearing of my work I shall only occasionally allude, though we shall repeatedly discover present value in many of the symbols examined, and the undertaking as a whole, like all historical studies, will finally have value only as it has contemporaneous value. For the most part, however, we shall be keeping our eyes on the immediate problem, which is the attempt to arrive at such relative understanding of the Jewish symbols that we shall be able to grasp their value for those who used them.

6. *The Paradox of Symbols*

AS REGARDS explanations, we must also bear in mind that in the case of a symbol of any deep importance, no single explanation of its power or scope ever suffices. One of the things that modern depth psychology has taught us is the paradoxical character of man's being. Love involves hate, death is the reverse of life, and the one seems to imply the other. Freud had to give up much of the consistency of his system when he was forced to put the "death urge" alongside the constructive "life urge" in the libido.

> The governing laws of logic have no sway in the unconscious; it might be called the Kingdom of the Illogical. Impulses with contrary aims exist side by side in the unconscious without any call being made for an adjustment between them. Either they have no effect whatever upon each other, or, if they do, no decision is made, but a compromise comes about which is senseless, since it embraces mutually exclusive elements. Similarly, contraries are not kept apart from each other but are treated as though they were identical, so that in the manifest dream any element may also stand for its contrary.[23]

Religion, it will increasingly appear, has offered man psychic therapy because it has recognized these opposites in his nature, and combined them, so that he could find life through death, save his soul by losing it, come into divine love by hating the devil and all his works. A proper religious symbol presents this paradox directly to the believer. The agony, distortion, and death of the cross bring one into divine peace, while the misbegotten religious art of the school of Hoffmann which made its way into so much of our recent stained glass, and which we still give children in the Protestant (and often in the Catholic) Sunday schools, turns out to be only emetic sentimentality, since it tries to present the sweetness, love, and kindness of God without any terror or agony. A good symbol, such as the Indian device of a cobra striking above a lingam, presents life and death together. It must always be recalled that the symbol is of value precisely as it pulls together, in nondiscursive form, propositions, desires, and attitudes which discursive formulation can only brand as impossible of combination. The language of our symbols, like the symbolic language of poetry, is what Cleanth Brooks called the "language of paradox." [24]

This is the *value* of the symbol—its power to unify a cluster of ideas or emotions or drives. The destructive chaos at the bottom of our lives, the chaos of mutually antagonistic and yet equally urgent drives, what might be called our fundamental schizophrenia,

23. Sigmund Freud, *An Outline of Psychoanalysis*, 1949, 53.

24. Op. cit., 44. Brooks (p. 58) quotes Coleridge's statement that poetry "reveals itself in the balance or reconcilement of opposite or discordant qualities: of sameness, with difference; of the general, with the concrete; the idea, with the image; the individual, with the representative; the sense of novelty and freshness, with old and familiar objects; a more than usual state of emotion, with more than usual order."

is controlled only as we get symbols in which both sides of our natures can simultaneously express themselves. I strongly suspect that what we call meaning—in the sense in which a man might say that Christianity is or is not meaningful to him, or that Communism does or does not make sense to him, or that mysticism is or is not meaningless—rests primarily on the test of whether the symbols offered by such a belief or religion, or by the symbolic acts of its practice, do or do not effect a resolution of the given individual's inner conflicts: if, when the symbol is shown, or the symbolic act is performed, it operates on the person, he is "strangely warmed," or, in Plato's term, the symbolic words light a fire within him. This fire or light brings the life of order and inner harmony, and is itself one of the primordial symbols. For the chaos behind the paradox is death and darkness: reconciliation, even in the paradox of symbols, is life and light. The experience may be one of sudden illumination as the symbol becomes "meaningful," that is, generative within the individual. Or we may be capable only of blind and often savage adherence to the symbols of our class, with chaos, darkness, and terror the apparent price of abandoning or even questioning them. Indeed, the conservative is right: he faces dissolution within himself if he must lose the old symbols without finding meaning or value in new ones, and this he is usually unable to do. The struggle between the old and the new is so rarely affected by a rational approach because rational arguments are relatively so superficial. A man "convinced in words," Plato was aware, is left of the same opinion still.

This is well illustrated by the history of the symbols we are studying, which went from paganism to Judaism and Christianity. Jews and Christians rejected the old explanations, the myths and mythological representations, while they kept their sanity by retaining the symbols themselves. One of the most notable things about the forms we are studying is that they are stripped of all their old mythological settings, because the settings implied pagan explanations. The hypothesis on which I am working, or which I am testing, is that in taking over the symbols, while discarding the myths and explanations of the pagans, Jews and Christians admitted, indeed confirmed, a continuity of religious experience which it is most important to be able to identify. For if there was such continuity of value, as the history of art may reveal it in the continuity of symbolic forms, the history of art will have much more to teach the history of religion than we have hitherto suspected. The discontinuity of myths and explanations is of profound importance in human history, and this discontinuity is what the history of religion has hitherto been chiefly concerned to indicate: but for an understanding of man, the phenomenon of a continuity of religious experience or values would have much more significance than that of discontinuous explanations.

Another most important aspect of symbolism lies in its simultaneous multiplicity of forms and sameness of values. The symbols of Christianity, for example, are indeed many. There are the cross, the crucifix, the Holy Family, the figures of Mary and Christ, the dove, the vine, the cup, the fish, the book, the lamb, the tree, the light, the cherub, the throne, the hand, the eagle, the bull, the bleeding heart, the angel, AΩ: one could go on almost indefinitely. Yet all of these will fit into a single formula, namely, the idea that the eternal God lovingly offers to share his nature with man, to lift him into eternal participation in divine life and happiness. Each symbol presents a facet of a single jewel. Devotees or artists, by virtue of their peculiar tastes and conditioning, will each find some of these symbols moving and the others rather meaningless—for them. A religion which hopes to become the religion of a civilization must make room for individual sensitivities by having a varied symbolism. We shall come to the richness of the Christian offering through an awareness of the nature and appeal of each of its symbols, but we must understand that all of them are simply roads to the same goal, each attractive in its own way. The One cannot be fully the One unless it has within it the potency of the Many. Herein lies the difference between a "great" religion and a sect. The great religion offers many roads, the sect few, or only one. In dealing with the richness of pagan and Jewish symbols we must bear this in mind: we must feel the special values of each, but always with a view to discerning the symbol's end—which presumably will be an end common to all the symbols.

C. THE JEWISH SYMBOLS

WE ARE NOW perhaps ready to discuss more directly the problem of whether the Jewish symbols were symbols at all, or only space-filling designs. Several considerations seem to me to indicate that the designs were really religious symbols to the Jews.

The first reason has already been discussed—namely, the fact that the symbols which Jews borrowed from paganism were all living symbols, in paganism earlier and contemporaneously, and in Christianity contemporaneously and later. To be sure, we can find many ancient instances in which Victories and cupids and wreaths were primarily decorative, as the cross is often used by Christians largely for decorative interest. But these very devices were also constantly used with serious symbolic meaning, on tombstones and amulets and in graffiti, by pagans as well as by Christians later, and I do not see how any Jew could then have borrowed them, especially for use in synagogues and on graves and amulets, without a feeling that they had significance.

Secondly, the vocabulary of symbols which the Jews borrowed is on the whole extremely limited. Except on amulets, not much over a score of designs are to be found in all the hundreds of instances of such borrowing that appear in remains from southern France, Italy, Sicily, Malta, North Africa, Egypt, Palestine, Asia Minor, and Mesopotamia. If, then, decoration was the motive, why this extraordinary agreement on what could and what could not be borrowed? After I had collected two-thirds of the surviving specimens of this art, it was hard to keep going to get the rest from the more scattered sources, since everything I was finding was so similar to what I already had. For their synagogues and graves, Jews obviously favored some pagan symbols, definitely avoided others—a phenomenon explicable perhaps on the assumption that only certain devices were acceptable to them, that is, that what they did take they took not for its decorative appeal but for its symbolic value to themselves. This selective vocabulary is, however, extremely interesting, because it is exactly the vocabulary of early Christian borrowings from paganism, a fact suggesting that the Christians did not take the forms from the pagans directly, but that along with Old Testament figures, the pagan emblems came into Christian art from Jewish usage.

Thirdly, the symbols used in Judaism frequently cannot be called decorative by any stretch of the imagination. Aside from the crude amulets, we have seen many instances in which the Jews who scratched the grotesque drawings on their tombstones were scarcely activated by artistic inspiration. They wanted those symbols on the graves for something other than decorative effect, and that other can have been only the symbolic values of the forms.[25]

Fourthly, on these graves and in the synagogues pagan and Jewish symbols are found so intimately intermixed, not only in a given cemetery but on a single grave or in one synagogue, that it is impossible, in my opinion, to say that when the menorah appears it has symbolic value, while there is no such value in the peacocks, wreaths, birds, Victories, and other motifs beside it. Far from feeling that the presence or absence of pagan symbols on a grave distinguishes the Judaism of the person buried in it, I venture that the choice between a menorah and a bird eating grapes was a matter of indifference in this environment, so much had the two come to symbolize the same essential religious attitude.

And lastly, I must point out that the very places where these symbols are found indicate that their symbolic value for the religion of the group as a whole was extremely important. In Rome and North Africa the ceilings of Jewish burial places are covered with them: hence the symbols must have been acceptable to the group, not just to a few aberrant individuals. In North Africa the mosaic pavement of a synagogue is elaborately ornamented with pagan devices, and most of the synagogues in Palestine, to say nothing of Dura, show such motifs in profusion, with Jewish and pagan forms so intermixed in the designs that it becomes impossible to maintain that the pagan symbols were merely decorative and the Jewish ones meaningful. But if the pagan symbols were meaningful in the synagogues, this implies irresistibly that they were meaningful for the Judaism of the group which constructed these buildings and worshiped in them.

All these considerations force me to conclude that, generally speaking, Jews throughout the Roman world borrowed these emblems with deliberate symbolic intent. We have no literature telling us of a Judaism which could do this, but the conclusion seems ineluctable that such a Judaism did exist for centuries. And it is a likely hypothesis that on the completion and dissemination of the Talmud, and with the beginning of Christian persecution of the Jews, a great reaction set in which abolished this Judaism and destroyed its writings.[26] This possibility is heightened by our knowledge of the efficacy of Jewish censorship. If we were dependent upon Jewish tradition and Jewish preservation of records, we should never have heard of Philo and the Jewish Hellenism of his day. Philo and Josephus were both preserved by Christian copyists and in Christian circles, and we should not have known even Philo's name if Christians had not adopted him. The same is true, so far as I know, of the Wisdom of Solomon and the works of Josephus. That is, Jews have not only failed to preserve accounts and the literature of hellenized

25. See, e.g., above, II, 3–50: "Symbols Used with Jewish Burials in Rome."

26. For a fuller discussion, see I, 7–17.

Judaism; their records do not even mention it. On the basis of what Jews themselves have transmitted, it would be ridiculous to suggest that Philo and hellenized Judaism ever existed. Furthermore, once Jews and Christians came to complete antipathy, Christians had no interest in preserving the writings of contemporary Jews. Hence it is highly possible that there once existed a considerable literature of the Judaism of these synagogues and graves—writings which have disappeared as completely as rabbinic Jews would have had Philo and his Judaism disappear. Thus, absence of literature reflecting the kind of Judaism which, we are beginning to suspect, went with these symbols, proves nothing. Still, the symbols exist as data clamoring for explanation, and they must be allowed to speak for themselves.

We shall often, in the case of some given symbol, leave considerable doubt as to whether it had a significance recognized explicitly by the group, was a means of communication, or had become "purely conventional" in the sense that its symbolism had ceased to be consciously recognized. In all these matters the clear either-or so dear to the scholarly mind rarely applies. Indeed, in Panofsky's phrase, we must interpret iconographic material by synthesis rather than analysis.[27] An object may be used as a symbol, used in an almost compulsory way, when all explicit understanding of its value had disappeared. A splendid instance of this is the Christian use of lamps in graves through the Byzantine period. Such use of lamps long antedated Christianity, deriving apparently from the symbolism of light as life. The practice was taken over by the Christians as a matter of course, and, in the way I have suggested, the old value was Christianized by being expressed in Christian terms. In earlier Christian usage the explanation was often written on the lamp itself, in the form of a Greek motto, "Jesus Christ, the Light of the world"; that is, still equating light with immortal life, the Christians asserted that the true Light is Christ. The custom was maintained for centuries, but once the idea had come to be an axiom to later generations of Christians, the motto was more and more carelessly written, and soon it was so put on that it is almost always completely illegible.[28] The lamp itself, however, now commonly with a cross on it, or bearing the old menorah, which had become a Tree of Life, continued to be placed in Christian graves—continued, apparently, to express and encourage hope of immortality. It persisted because, in terms of our definition of symbol, it did something to the people who used it. Thus, whether the explanation is recalled or not, lamps continue to be placed in Oriental graves, and lighted candles are still important beside a Jewish or Christian corpse.

In the next volume we shall come to judge it quite likely that the Jewish ritualistic use of wine is a similar symbolic expression which had much explicit meaning when it first came into Judaism, but, along with the kindling of the Sabbath lights, is now one of the most beloved and moving observances of Judaism, for which Jews give only the most trifling explanations, usually none at all. It still does something to Jews far beyond the physical effect of drinking the blessed wine, and beyond anything accounted for by

27. Op. cit., 8.   28. For examples, see Macalister, *Gezer*, I, 357, 366 f.

the explanations. Hence we cannot say that a symbol is dead merely because an explanation may not be at hand.

D. EVALUATING THE JEWISH SYMBOLS

THE QUESTION regarding Jewish symbolism is, then: If the designs were not put into the synagogues and tombs casually, just to look pretty, but to do something to those who made them, to those who looked at them as they worshiped, and for those who finally were buried beneath them, what was their value, what was it hoped that they would do?

Since we cannot begin by asserting what these symbols meant ideologically to the Jews who used them in the Roman world, what their basic value was, we must go a long way round. At the outset we must utilize our discovery that these are symbols which had become a religious lingua franca in the world about the Jews who borrowed them. The most important of them were originally Dionysiac, and though the vocabulary had been expanded to include a few symbols from Syria (the specifically solar eagle), from Egypt (the rows of wine jars and baskets, the waterfowl), and from Mesopotamia (the zodiac), it was still essentially Dionysiac. This group of symbols was accepted by the Nabateans, Syrians, and Egyptians, in the religions of Asia Minor, by the Etruscans, by the imperial Romans as they came under hellenistic influence, by the Jews, and later by the Christians. How did people of the ancient world use these motifs, and what did they mean? They were indignantly rejected by Jews of the Maccabean period, and most of the Romans of the Republic had little use for them. But they are rampant in Pompeii, and are found on most of the second-century Roman graves. Is it possible to reconstruct the lingua franca of these symbols in their varied uses so that the values thus discovered may be applied to a Jewish milieu from which we have no literature? It would seem that if we can decipher the lingua franca we shall have the basic value which passed with the symbol so long as it was alive.

This is indeed a long way round, but I can see no possible short cut. The phenomena of syncretism in the ancient world must be re-examined in the perspective of the symbols.

One thing becomes instantly apparent. The lingua franca as it was used in all religions was made up primarily of abstract symbols, not of mythological scenes. We have already noted this in regard to Jews and Christians, who could use the vine or the cup, for example, or birds feeding on grapes, but not bacchanalian cultic scenes, or portrayals of Dionysiac mythology. We see further that for Egypt of the Ptolemaic and later periods the same holds true, as also for Nabatean remains. In Etruscan remains this exclusion does not appear, nor at Pompeii.

In Pompeii, we suspect, people were actually celebrating specifically Dionysiac mysteries. On the other hand, in hellenized Egypt we find Osiris with grapes, but not with bacchanals so far as I know. Is this a meaningful distinction? I am beginning to think that it is. When we find cultic or mythological scenes with the Dionysiac symbols, we suspect presence of the Dionysiac cult. When we find only abstracted symbols of other cults, we suspect some sort of value identification, but not cultic assimilation. For in that case the cult or mythology of some religion other than the Dionysiac or Orphic is being interpreted by the adopted symbols in terms of Dionysiac or Orphic values. Was this always done consciously? A glance at the Christian usage shows at once that probably it was not. For the use of Dionysiac symbols in association with Osiris, say, may have been part of a definite identification of Osiris and Dionysus, an open identification very frequent in hellenistic literature and going back to Herodotus; but certainly no Christian thought that he was identifying Christ with Dionysus when he used the vine with a figure of Christ. Where the symbols are used apart from cultic and mythological associations pertaining to Dionysus, they need not imply a conscious reference to pagan cults and myths. In other words, the lingua franca had, apparently, come to speak not necessarily of cult or myth at all, but of something else, and of this in its own right.

Will this conception of symbols actually work out in evaluating the data of syncretism? The first step logically would be to examine the Dionysiac remains, archeological and literary, to see if possible what Dionysus himself meant to the Greeks in terms of religious experience. This ground has been gone over many times, but heretofore with the objective of reconstructing the myth and ritual of Dionysus rather than the psychological experience or value inhering in the myth and ritual. I cannot stop to write a new history of Dionysus in Greece, but the subject must be treated historically, for there is every reason to suppose that the character of the god changed very much. Originally a phallic god of fertility, whose tokens and rites were purely agrarian, his value seems to have been primarily magical, if I may use the term—the value of imparting fertility to the fields. (By magic, as I have explained earlier,[29] I mean simply a religious rite of automatic value.) Then Dionysus became, when introduced into a society which had Demeter, particularly the god of the vine. Another great change occurred when people began to project the idea of personal immortality into the general rites relating to resurrection of plant life, and a still further change came when the magical, or immediately operative, character of the god gave way, at least in the minds of thoughtful men, to the mystical.

These changes were probably brought about largely by the "Orphic reform," but we cannot trace the steps of the development. All we can see is that a change did at some time occur. But the new type of experience was lineally connected with the old. If the old rites were softened into sacraments for the mystical, the hope was still that something would really be effected by them: the devotee would be changed into a Bacchus, a divine being. He would be raised from spiritual death, like the seeds, and—for there is good reason to assume that the hope included this also—would be born again as a result of fertilization by the divine fluid which had earlier been represented by the leather phallus of the primitive rites, or in the orgiastic drinking of wine. The new conception did not entirely replace the old. The old survived, and still survives in rural fertility festivals in certain localities. But intelligent men were seeing deeper possibilities—men of sufficient breadth of view to see the values in the religious ideas of other peoples, and so to be inclined to syncretism. The process could be carried to the heights reached in Plato's *Symposium*, where Eros leads the soul to the Form of Beauty. All this needs careful documentation, and in this chapter is stated only as a hypothetical suggestion.

29. See II, 155–161.

As the history of each symbol is analyzed in the succeeding volumes, the phenomenon of the persisting values of symbols will, I believe, seem as much an historical fact, and thus a concern of the historian, as are literary and archeological data. The phenomenon needs as distinct a method of historical study, however, as is called for in dealing with literary or with archeological remains. Hence I have suggested above that one can study symbolism only by combining historical and psychological methods. For the ordinary criteria of historical judgment break down completely before the symbol, so that the historian trained only in philological and archeological techniques falls back into an emotional negativism. At the same time, various schools of psychology have been able to demonstrate, each to its own satisfaction, the omnipresence of phenomena which it could label with its particular formulations, like the "Oedipus complex," or the manifestations of the "collective unconscious," by means of arbitrary collections of myths, symbols, and rites—collections which, however, violate the elementary laws of all historical investigation. Clearly the two approaches must be used together, each deepening and correcting the other, if we are to make any progress in religious history. Modern anthropologists are in this respect far ahead of the historian, and are getting important results from introducing the psychological factor into their considerations. As I said, I have no contribution to make to psychology as such. But I am quite sure that an obvious place to begin applying the new psychology to history is in relation to the history of symbols. Perhaps, by using historical and psychological criteria together, we may at least eliminate some of the fancifulness in which either method of investigation is likely to end without the counterbalance of the other.

It became clear to me, then, that if I was to do more than other recent students in the field, I must not be content with publishing all the remains of Jewish art, with the parallels, or a sufficient number of them, from pagan and Christian art. Rather, I must use the best methods at hand for archeological identification of the evidence, and all available literary testimony, but couple with these some appreciation of their psychological implications. The psychologist may be scornful of the archeological niceties; the classicist may grow wroth at my mingling of psychological conceptions with archeological data. And both will have ample cause to point out that I am far from being a trained man in their respective fields. I have consoled myself with the fact that in opening any new approach, a man is *ipso facto* an amateur in it. Thus, at the risk of incurring the indignation of the departmentally righteous, I have persisted. I cannot hope, working in strange fields, to be free of mistakes, though I am exercising meticulous care as far as I can. But I still hope that the main implications of my work are sound. These implications, however, are largely in the field of the history and psychology of religion, and it is historians of religion and psychologists, not classicists or church historians or talmudists, who must ultimately pass on their value.

E. PSYCHOLOGY OF RELIGION

THE PSYCHOLOGY of religion which is emerging here is as a whole my own. Much as I have drawn upon the various schools of depth psychology, Freudians will be the first to say that I am not one of them, at least in any orthodox sense. For that all guilt feeling means fear of castration, and that the Oedipus complex is found in everyone in the sense that there is in every man a jealous desire to abolish or kill the father, seem to me not at all justified assumptions. Nor am I a Jungian, seeing our individual minds rooted in a collective unconscious, or the psyche as comprising the animus and anima, the shadow, and all the rest. I do not feel that it is my task to construct or to commit myself to a system of psychology as such, and shall make no attempt to do so. But in the perspective of the depths opened up by such approaches to psychology, the data I am trying to explain take on a meaning which they have in no other frame of reference. The systems of these schools have grown out of interpretation of the phenomena that analysts have observed in their disturbed patients. The symbols of the ancient world are a totally different body of data, and suggest somewhat different formulations. But it is not surprising that they should suggest much that is similar to what analysts have found, since the phenomena in both instances come from the depths of the human spirit. Fifteen years ago, E. S. Robinson, one of Yale's most promising psychologists of the stimulus-response school, whose work was cut short by early death, remarked that while he was not at all a Freudian, he felt obliged to say that Freud bears the same relation to modern psychology as Newton bears to modern physics. It is in this spirit that I shall make free to draw upon Freudianism, or Jungianism, for anything that seems helpful in interpreting the symbols, without committing myself to other aspects of these systems. I must sharply warn the reader not to assume that what follows is an adequate psychological account of all aspects of religious experience. To present my ideas on that subject as a whole is quite beyond our immediate need. In this section I bring out only those aspects of it relevant to the types of religious experience that seem to me indicated by the symbols we are trying to evaluate.

The psychology in terms of which I am thinking begins from man's basic drive for life.[30] This is by no means a novel idea: the "instinct of self-preservation" is as familiar in the old psychologies as is the "life urge" in the newer. Everything indicates that this was a very unreflective urge in primitive man, as it is in animals. Savage man and animals alike will fight to the death for their food, just as they will periodically fight to the death for a desired female. But the desire for the female certainly plays little part in the motivation of most animals (except when they are inflamed by her odor), while they spend the majority of their waking hours in the search for food. Yet the life urge seems most intimately to include the sex urge, increasingly so as man becomes more civilized, since the sexual drive not only plays a part in the relatively sophisticated desire for progeny, but also becomes a means of achieving personal expression and an enlarged experience of life.

30. Just what I mean by "life" I cannot say exactly. It includes "activity free from anxiety," as defined by Robert P. Casey, "Oedipus Motivation in Religious Thought and Fantasy," *Psychiatry*, V (1942), 228, but comprises much more than that restricted phrase suggests. Hope of immortality, freedom from frustrations, ability to live creatively in whatever sense the individual defines creativity, these are certainly also in life as we desire it. I should add that an excellent introduction to what follows, as regards ideas and bibliography, is Casey's "The Psychoanalytic Study of Religion," *Journal of Abnormal and Social Psychology*, XXXIII (1938), 437–452, in which he reviews with admirable clarity the contributions made on the subject to the date of his writing.

Accordingly, I must take the sex urge as but one aspect of the much more profound urge to life, to the realization, expansion, and perpetuation of life. In this, as far as I understand them, I agree with both Freud and Jung, each of whom insists that his conception of the libido includes much more than the sex urge as ordinarily conceived. The view of sex as the door to something greater must not be confused with the sublimations and perversions of the sex impulse which for one reason or another may take the place of direct expression of the instinct through the sexual act. Indeed, I am not sure that it is correct to say that artistic creation represents a sublimation of sexual activity, any more than one can say that because water flows better through one tap if a second tap on the same main is shut off, the greater flow of the first tap represents a "sublimation" of the flow of the second. The one tap is simply getting more water from the flow behind both. Sexual activity occurs only when the life urge expresses itself through the sexual mechanism (which comprises much more than the sexual organs). When the life stream is shut off from sexual expression, it may find other outlets, but this is only very doubtfully in any sense to be called sexual activity. Hence I prefer to speak of the life urge rather than of the libido, since the specifically sexual connotations of the latter word have caused so much confusion.[30a]

The most immediate satisfactions of the life urge are found in eating and sexual expression (and of course in breathing and bodily movement, which we take for granted); with these go the primitive outlets of warfare and the hunt, gratifications of the urge to kill, unfortunately familiar still. The urge to kill seeks direct expression now only episodically, but it has been necessary to create a substitute outlet in sport[31] and socio-economic competition. The great symbols of the life urge are by nature of three basic kinds: they are the symbols of hunting or fighting, the symbols of food and eating (or of the sources of food— the winds, rain, the sun, etc.), and the symbols of sex. In these three themes we have the meanings of the vast majority of religious symbols used by all but the most advanced and intellectualized peoples. And while any given symbol we may be discussing will represent primarily one of these three themes, it will usually also refer to one or both of the others.

30a. I feel that in this I am very close to Dr. T. M. French's "concept of the craving of all healthy organs for stimulation and functional activity." In view of this conception French adds: "Instead of postulating a basic erotic drive, we content ourselves with recognizing cravings for stimulation and functional activity for their own sake": op. cit., 147 f. He regards my "life urge" as too philosophical a conception. He may well get on without such an over-all notion in his clinical work, just as he seems to be rejecting Freud's libido as a single force manifest in various usages. But in trying to understand the data of religion we need an over-all conception, since here man seems to be functioning as a unit, in his desires to achieve immortality, or to come into a larger mystical life. A man

as a whole is a "healthy organ craving for stimulation and functional activity," and this cannot be understood in terms of his individual organs and their drives. The life urge seems to me to be for the organism as a whole what French, op. cit., 44, himself more philosophically calls the "basic functional pattern."

31. The cannibalistic natives of Truk are now so civilized that they stage excellent games of baseball between tribes which formerly waged war with one another and ate their captives. But during the games the women stand on the side lines mumbling charms to bring a plague of dysentery upon the opposing team. My colleague Murdock, recently returned from Truk, is my informant in regard to this.

Another source of religious symbolism is in the child's relation with the parents during infancy. The sex life of the great majority of men has through the ages rarely been limited to the experience of one mate, while his infancy has been concentrated into an experience of one mother. To be sure, the infant in a luxurious home may be confused by nurses, and even in the simplest home a grandmother may be a more frequent attendant than the mother. Yet any plurality of such persons makes much less impression at that stage than later: for the infant, there is simply the great beneficent personality, in which only a quite developed child can distinguish different persons. There is far greater similarity between the experience of a baby of fifty thousand years ago and our own experience at the same age, than between any of his subsequent experiences and ours at the corresponding stage. And it is the unchangeable nature of this earliest experience, along with the unchanged neurological structure of man, which furnishes the most important common ground of understanding between us and remote civilizations.

The baby has always had, if he survived at all, a passionate life urge, and very little else. To be sure, healthy infants express this life urge during the greater part of the time in sleep, a way to life through death. Their waking moments are taken up with a sense of great discomfort from hunger, thirst, and the needs of elimination, and with the ecstasy of the gratification of their desires. All babies awaken in that terrifying confusion which is sometimes upon us adults when we awaken. Their world is only a few feet, at first only a few inches, in circumference; their misery, helplessness, and terrors are their only conscious experience. They cry—and out of the void there suddenly appear a loving face and deft hands which cut the terrible aloneness and promise the satisfaction of all needs. Soon the infant is comfortable, and then comes the heavenly breast, where love and food and life are one. Insecurity, fear, and uncertainty are lost in perfect peace and trust. In heavenly security the infant sucks in the life of the great goddess, and perhaps gurgles in brief joy before he again takes the sleepy path of death to still greater life. No later type of experience ever equals the complete satisfaction of this one. In maturity an ideal love affair may reproduce some measure of it, but only in societies in which romantic love patterns prevail could such perfection last for more than fleeting moments. In no adult relation is the experience at all complete.

The pangs of later infancy come from the invasion of this ideal world by social realities and compulsions which spoil, one after another, the perfection of gratification earlier enjoyed. Defecation, from being a delight, becomes to the child a meaningless struggle; as bodily movements develop, the loving face of the goddess often grows stern as she imposes incomprehensible restrictions and prohibitions. And then the breast itself is lost. Indeed, even the initial monotheism becomes a confusing polytheism as the goddess, still supreme, becomes one among other great figures which appear and disappear like theophanies. A world has passed away, a world where a loving goddess from her own person gave full gratification to the life urge. Specific memories of these months mercifully fade away and do not haunt us, but the basic memory does remain as a symbol of the one time when life completely conquered death in love. The nostalgia of later years, even when articulated in terms of more mature concepts, is still a longing for those arms, everlasting arms in which we may find again the mother's warmth and life, keep it now at last forever; it is possibly even the wish for the complete nirvana of the womb.

Each aspect of this experience, and of the deprivation of it, has appeared clinically as a major cause of later psychological difficulty. But I think that in discussions of religion the experience as a whole, first of gratification, then of deprivation, has not been sufficiently stressed: it is the basis of at least one of the most important of the patterns of religion. This pattern produces little "social gospel": it is as narcissistic as the life of the infant. It arises from the craving of the individual for self-realization through absorption of and in the true Being, the craving for life after death, for atonement and reconciliation, for rebirth and the abiding presence of the Comforter. The "mystic marriage" in the form of union with the temple prostitute or with the Church, the bride of Christ, is really a union with the Great Mother, a return to her intimate care. We love the picture of the Christian version of this theme, Mary the Mother with her Child, for each of us is the child. We project ourselves into the picture, but never as Mary: we—at least we males—are each the Baby in her arms.[32] And the power which that Baby manifests is the power we want also to manifest, a fullness of life such as we feel we should have in the security of that embrace. *Ave Maria!* We pray for that loving protection, whether before a figure of the Mother, or in primitive sexual rites, or in the scarcely veiled eroticism of Protestant hymnody.

As the child enters upon the next stage of his development, the love and protection of the great beings of the adult world are still of deep importance. But the life of law and taboo is now the much more immediate concern of the child's consciousness. He still desperately needs for his self-realization the life and protection, the flow of loving approval he formerly had, but he finds that these are now to be bought at a price: they no longer come to him as a free gift. The mother goddess has by now become a male-female duality, or monad in two persons, father and mother, and the child soon learns (in the normal family as it has functioned through the millennia of our civilization) that the ultimate authority is not the mother but the father. "I'll tell your father," is the final threat in the child's life. The law he must obey is to him really a codification of the whims and fancies of his father. The sanction consists in the father-mother displeasure, or even those tortures of whipping which have inspired the notion of hell. From this sanction the child can never

---

32. The development has been sketched here from the masculine point of view, and with reference to a patriarchal society. I do not know feminine psychology nor the history of matriarchy. It is obvious that the basic experience of the tiny infant with the mother is the same for boy and girl. It is also evident that the girl in her own way is as anxious to achieve unity with the father as the boy can be. But somewhere in the development of most girls, there is a stage of transference, so that the girl's ideal is to become, by possessing the father, herself a mother, the Mother—just as the boy's aspiration is to become the Father by possessing the Mother. I do not think that this difference need bother us. The symbols of religion in the civilizations from which ours is descended seem to be largely the product of men rather than of women, though perhaps the appearance of the satyr with Dionysus, and the absence of such a figure from among Astarte's followers, are results of the greater influence of women in Bacchism than among the Semites. I suspect that before a Madonna and Child a woman identifies herself as much with the Mother as a man identifies himself with the Child. But I am certain that we can go a long way without having to stop at each step to discuss the feminine counterparts in experience. At least, I shall not attempt to do so.

feel safe except in the atmosphere of approval and love which only obedience seems to produce. The "superego" is rapidly forming at this time: God and my father are one, and *Ave Maria, ora pro me*—"Intercede for me with the Father"—expresses the inevitable attitude toward the mother. In many persons, religion is found at this level. To the original pure nostalgia for complete gratification has been added a sense that the price of gratification is obedience to laws, social and ritualistic, while the concept of the mediator has made its highly important appearance.

The fully "compulsory" stage postulated by Freud is a step beyond this, but not away from it. Law becomes more elaborate, mediation less significant: and from such conditions there can emerge a religion like talmudic Judaism, in which the mother element has become quite unrecognizably obscured in the dominant pattern of the relation between a boy and his father. Here the individual is given the rewards of this life and the next strictly on the basis of obedience. To be sure, the quality of mercy does not fail, and provision is made for repentance and reinstatement of the transgressor. But these provisions were never so important in Judaism that they produced a distinct divine personality to symbolize and execute them. Traditional Judaism is a civilization, a complete way of life, but only secondarily a personal source of ecstasy. It is intensely social in feeling, as the family is a social unit: the child as one member knows that the father is equally concerned with his brothers and sisters. Little of social importance came out of the cult of the Great Mother, or of Isis, or of the Virgin. The social aspects of religion first became important as the father became central, and the tendency reached its logical end when it produced a sense of the Father-God's universal rightness, and of universal Right.

Such a religion gets its hold upon its followers through the conditioning power of behavior. The family celebrations of festivals come to play a tremendous part in the child's life: and just as Christians cling to Christmas, a Jew, however far he may stray from orthodox Jewish belief, rarely ceases to feel the appeal of the festivals if he has been brought up under such influences. This gripping hold of Jewish observances is magnificently presented in Feuchtwanger's *Jud Süss* (*Power*). Years of participation can of course in some people instill a devotion to the festivals which involves a much more ecstatic and personal religious pattern than is usually associated with them. But a religious milieu such as that of rabbinic Judaism enforces the form, binds the believer to a compulsory pattern of life with the Father.

Religious experiences, while they take on many forms, can thus be distinguished as they show primarily the narcissistic mother pattern or the compulsory pattern of legalism. To be sure, the great religions have for the most part contained both of these elements. Certainly Christianity, with its Old Testament heritage and the ethical teachings of Jesus, has not been, at any time, engrossed simply in the problem of personal salvation. Even Judaism, commentators are now agreed, drew as heavily for its spirit upon the fertility religions of the Canaanites as upon the distinctive "religion of Moses." Most of Jewish ritual and the festivals go back to fertility rites. Still, there can be no doubt that the Jewish contribution to Christianity through the Old Testament and the Synoptic Gospels predicated a relation between a Father and his children, while the Greek contribution of Paul, of the Fourth Gospel, and of the early Greek Christians was in the direction of a personal religion of salvation which in emotional pattern resembled much more the ancient fertility cults than the teachings of the rabbis.

Regarded in the light of such a contrast of types in religion, that is, the contrast between the mystical and the legalistic type, the Jewish archeological material became increasingly anomalous as I studied its associations elsewhere. The symbols borrowed from pagan art by the Jews were precisely those symbols which stood for the type of religious experience and longing most completely at variance with the tendencies of rabbinic Judaism at the time. That is, the rabbis were developing Judaism increasingly to reinforce its legalism, its compulsory or Father pattern. The victory of Yahwism over the Canaanites was at last becoming complete. Fertility rites, the cycle of Adonis dead and risen, the birth of the sacred child at springtime and at the winter solstice, the holy trinity of Father, Mother, Son, in which the Son was identical with the Father, all these were being finally expelled from Judaism, even in its Hosean form. God was a loving Father, but intensely masculine, and the task of his children was to study and obey his Law.

Nothing in this led or could have led anyone to suspect that in the very centuries when the rabbis, in their scholastic groups in Jamnia and Babylon, were patiently working out the Talmud, with its almost exclusively legal interest, the mass of the Jews were breaking down the traditional restrictions and filling their synagogues and tombs with symbols partly Jewish and partly appropriated from those aspects of paganism which we shall see were especially hateful to the rabbis. In Christianity these same symbols were being used in turn to represent just those aspects of the new faith most repugnant to the rabbinic schools. Nothing whatever warrants either saying that the symbols had no meaning in Judaism, or insisting that if they had meaning, that meaning must somehow be found in rabbinic thinking. The symbols themselves point to meaning, and to a meaning which the rabbis deeply repudiated.

We have suggested that the lingua franca of symbolism, the medium of continuity of values in symbolism, is the key to understanding the symbols borrowed by Jews, and that this lingua franca can be read, and the values of the symbols recovered, only as we consider the figured symbolism in the light of the newer psychology. And we have suggested that with such psychological understanding we must follow each symbol relentlessly through, in all of its typical appearances in those countries and ages whose influence carried on, directly or indirectly, into the Greco-Roman world. The elements of the psychology of religion just suggested were the product of this search, not its guide.

This psychology of religion, I have said, centers upon the phenomenon of a great life urge, a drive to self-fulfillment which may express itself in a desire for mystic union with the Mother-Father, or for security through obedience to the Father. But the symbols, as I studied them, amazed me by seeming at first to reduce themselves in almost every case to a basic erotic value. As I took up each symbol I hoped that I should at last get something different. But when even the dove, the duck, and the quail were by specific ancient testimony given erotic explanations, I felt myself overcome by the evidence itself. To the investigator this experience is much more moving than it can ever be to the reader. Only by taking this book apart and looking up these symbols for oneself, could the experience of the author be duplicated. For as I analyzed symbol after symbol, I found myself driven with relentless regularity to identical explanations, and to ascribing identical values to all the symbols—driven not by my predilections but by the evidence itself.

The basic value, I have said, appeared definitely an erotic one. This was the major element all the symbols had in common. How could this have happened, when religious eroticism had been so driven out of Judaism? It was partly in view of this that I looked afresh at the place of the erotic in religion in general. Was it eroticism in the sense in which we use the term—namely, something akin to *ars amatoria*, expressing or enhancing the pleasure of intercourse? It suddenly occurred to me that in order to evaluate a leather phallus as a phenomenon in Greek society it was necessary to think of it in the context of Greek society, instead of projecting our still half-Victorian conceptions back upon it, or of thinking how inappropriate it would be in a synagogue or church. Whether you and I think the phallus a proper symbol for deity has nothing whatever to do with the patent fact that many Greeks, Syrians, Phoenicians, and Egyptians—with hosts of others— thought it the most appropriate symbol of all. Whatever you and I think about sexual intercourse and its place in society, many ancient peoples regarded it for millennia as one of the best forms of temple worship. Whether or not you and I are accustomed to be amused by sexual humor, the peoples of the ancient world loved it and used it as a feature of their religious festivals. I rigorously refused to interpret pillars, upright stones, altars, etc., as phallic, after the manner of many historians of phallicism (though I am far from denying the possibility of their ultimate phallic symbolism); yet I was driven by the associations in which the symbols that I was investigating were used by Greeks, Egyptians, and many others, to recognize in most of them a basic phallic meaning.

What, then, was that phallic meaning? In our day of repressed sex, phallic symbolism in dreams and gestures is usually taken to come from repressed desire for a sexual experience. But to carry this over to sexual symbols appearing in an age that knew little such repression, and to suppose that a phallus was used by ancient worshipers similarly to symbolize literal sexual desire not otherwise to be released, is utterly unjustified—equally so on the part of those who make such interpretation directly, and on the part of those who implicitly register the same judgment when they refuse to consider this type of material at all. In the earliest periods of our cultural development, when the symbol was most frankly used, as it was in Greece and Egypt, there was apparently not much sexual repression in society, in our sense. Even the almost universal taboo against incest seems to have been little known in Egypt. Nor is there any indication that religion was using phallic symbols as they were used in Pompeiian brothels, for sexual titillation. Quite the reverse: everything indicates that the early devotee wanted by means of his phallic rites to be gratified with food, and with the perpetuation of his life. He used the symbols of gratification nearest and most naturally at hand in order to get what he wanted. That is, he used phallic symbols to represent his desire for food and life, because he had sex but did not always have enough food. Similarly in our society, analysts tell me, food—which we have —is often in our dreams a symbol for the sexual experiences that we think society is keeping from us. We use what we have as symbols of gratification of desires for what we do not have. It is in fertility rites to assure crops and flocks that the phallic symbol or rite seems most characteristically to appear, because crops and flocks represented food. The personal application of such symbols and rites, even their use to secure personal immortality, seems secondary to and is probably historically later than their use to get crops and flocks. It was the most obvious kind of sympathetic magic to try to make a field fertile by setting up a phallus in it, or by simulating or actually performing intercourse on it or for it. The utter frankness of the symbol in its early occurrences shows that it had an origin and function completely unrelated to anything like modern "nastiness." Men wanted crops and flocks, and used the phallus as a magico-religious symbol for its power to produce them. Not that they eliminated the element of pleasure suggested in the symbol. Why should they? A bull is not less serviceable as a general symbol of food because one likes beef. That sexual humor might be sinful apparently never occurred to them.

I recognized that, as Fromm has recently said, one of the most important of the contributions of Freud and Jung has been their rediscovery of the universal language of symbolism, a language current in every age and civilization, but in our own held down almost exclusively within the unconscious mind, and in dreams. Once I came to recognize the complete naturalness of phallic symbolism as used in early times, and its freedom from the moldiness of repressions, the symbol language became clearer to me as I followed the history of the symbols. For as developing civilization began to distinguish between the spiritual and the fleshly, the good and the bad, the pure and the impure, the symbols lost their directness. The hideous silenus-satyr no longer raped maenads on the vases, nor, in ithyphallic representation, plucked and trampled the sacred grapes; rather, satyrs became graceful young men giving no hint of lechery, and with only pointed ears and the merest suggestion of a tail to show their ancestry. As competitors to them there appeared innocuous babies, the cupids or Erotes, still love symbols by their very name, and still performing the religious functions in the vine and elsewhere which the lascivious satyrs had earlier carried out. Then the cupids supplanted the satyrs altogether, and the satyrs survived in iconography only as devils, symbols now of the forbidden. The devil of Christianity is still a Pan or satyr, primarily inviting us to sexuality. He is the devil because frank invitation to sexuality speaks of sin to us, and taboo.

Suddenly it occurred to me that I had, in my hands, the historical antetype of such material as is found in a typical psychoanalysis. Where analyses had over and again revealed that modern religions, especially those of the more ardent types, had at their roots a sexual motivation, I was seeing an original body of sexual symbols in religion disappear into indirection as society demanded their repression. The satyr had become a cupid, I repeat. But in their new and almost unrecognizable form, these symbols kept their old central place in the new religions which more "civilized" cultures were developing. Or, to put it in another way, a social analysis of the symbols of modern religion seemed to push back in history to the same sort of early association as is still to be found in the individual.

How did this come about? The religion of mysticism I have described in terms chiefly of the parallel of the infant longing to find complete gratification of its life urge in the person, the life substance, of the goddess, or the Mother-Father. It is therefore very perplexing that the symbols of mystical experience are almost universally the symbols of sex. How is this possible, especially in view of the fact that I have distinguished sex as a phenomenon of maturity, and as being only one outlet of the life urge?

This seems quite the most difficult problem of all in my nascent psychology of religion, and one that is extremely dangerous to try to answer for any period but our own. Here anthropology might help, by reconstructing what puberty means for the lad or girl in a society without restrictions, or at least without our restrictions, since I doubt that any contemporary society is without very definite sexual taboos. Yet the fusion of the two motifs, sex and the mother, however it comes about, seems to me most natural. The boy's whole nature at puberty is stirred by new longings, an awakening of the old drive to complete himself in someone else, but now he has a new means of accomplishing it. That this should recall the gratification of his babyhood seems again inevitable, as well as that the experience with a woman should, if only temporarily, identify itself with his earliest experiences with the mother. In adolescent years a boy is usually most moved by a woman older than himself, and even when at a later stage his craving is for the young girl, the virgin whom he can protect, and to whom he can play the ruling father, the girl nevertheless must often play the mother to him if he is to be happy with her. The mother of his religious image, the Great Mother, of whom he still dreams, becomes the Virgin Mother, I am sure, because when he is an adult the mate he desires is a virgin, and because the Mother of religion is the immediate projection of the mother as sought afresh by the mature man in a young virgin. In the highly complex picture of maturity, the young man gets his normal self-realization as he takes his father's role with the new little mother. Union is now naturally expressed in the symbols of sexual union.[33] For to the mature person the sexual act itself usually seems most important because it gives a sense of realization of life.

Hence in this mature quest for the mother, or for life in the mother, a quest which has produced formal religions and mystical symbolism, the magico-religious symbols of the fertility cults were the ones most naturally at hand to be developed and perpetuated. Religion evolves not by invention of new symbols but by putting new meanings into old forms. There seem to have been historically three major steps in this development. At first the sex symbol was the instrument of literal fertility magic to bring crops, as when a figure of Priapus was placed in a garden. Later, the significance of man's sex experience as a door to greater personal life came increasingly to be felt, and sex symbols or acts were used as open means of achieving union with the deity, male or female. Finally, all conscious reference to the sexual act was eliminated, and the overtly sexual pictures and rites were abandoned, so that religion could achieve the "higher" gratification. Indeed, in "higher" religions, like those described in Plato's *Symposium* and the *Bacchae* of Euripides,

---

33. It is likely that the desire for the virgin goddess, who is the Virgin Mother, reflects also the repressions of incest taboo affecting the boy in the relation with his mother, who, to him, is simultaneously Virgin and Mother. But the man wants a virginal wife largely to signify that he has broken that incest taboo and fulfilled the desire of his life.

the sexual act is deplored or despised. This change has created the amazing anomaly that the greatest single tension in most "higher" religions is precisely the tension between spirit and body—sex as means to union and life as over against religion, which seems to achieve its goal in the individual in proportion to his renunciation of the sexual act. Marriage of course gets a religious sanction, but sex is tolerated only within the frame of this sanction; as a value in itself, sex is repudiated. The Catholic church is only quite logical when it curses anyone who will not admit that the state of virginity is superior to that of matrimony. To Philo sex is always sin—as it has been to millions of Christians down to the present day—except as it serves the single purpose of begetting children.

Yet within "higher" religion, many of the less crudely sexual symbols, such as the dove and the erotic metaphors of mysticism, have lived on. Even in ancient Egypt, the more thoughtful minds developed the idea that the supreme God is hermaphroditic, reproducing himself by having within him organs both male and female—being Father and Mother, while the Child is only an alter ego of the Father. The three, Father, Mother, and Child, are one. This conception was very common in the late Roman empire: it emerged openly in the Orphic hymns, and seems to lie behind not only the hermaphroditic figures of late antiquity, but also the effeminate representations of Dionysus and Apollo which fill the museums. The same three, with the great emphasis upon the miraculous begetting of the Child, are still the supreme objects of worship in Christianity.

It is with the divine Child that modern man, still the baby, can identify himself more easily than with the Father's majestic greatness, and in asserting the identity of the Son with the Father in the divine realm—the Son being man himself—he finally resolves the Oedipus situation, if I may use that useful but dubious term, by becoming himself one with the Father in cosmic completeness.

Symbolic representation of this experience, or projection, or idea, may depict only the Child with its Mother: in this the Father is mysteriously implied. Sometimes we represent the three, the "holy family." On the other hand, though in halachic Judaism the Father has the kindness and brooding wings of the Mother ascribed to him, the image of Wisdom as the distinct Mother breaks through so rarely as to suggest that the occurrence marks an invasion of foreign symbolism, the use of a conception which halachic Judaism never really naturalized for itself.[34] In such Judaism the devotee is still the son, and the Psalms are full of the language of childhood. But in rabbinic tradition the mystical element of identification has been repressed: the way to the Father, I have said, is through obedience—a pattern which, while it alleviates the sense of guilt, still accentuates the duality of Father and devotee. It is in religions centering not in obedience, but in the birth and death and resurrection of the god or his son, that mystical assimilation of the devotee with the Father,

34. The figure of Wisdom is a perennial subject of debate. See, for most recent discussion, Helmar Ringgren, *Word and Wisdom: Studies in the Hypostatization of Divine Qualities and Functions in the Near East*, Lund, 1947; Ralph Marcus, "On Biblical Hypostases of Wisdom," *HUCA*, XXIII, i (1950/1), 157–171. In mystical Judaism the Mother perforce returns to her great importance. It is necessary here only to recall Philo's allegorizations of the wives of the Patriarchs each as Virtue or Sophia, and the part played in the *Zohar* by the "supernal Mother," the Shekinah, as well as the tension between male and female in the *sephiroth* as described throughout that work.

or Father-Mother, is the objective. For in identifying ourselves with the Baby, and identifying the Baby with the Father, we make ourselves one with the Father. Thus our cycle becomes complete. The reality and life as well as the protection of Baby, Mother, and Father are at last fully our own: the "Oedipus conflict" and the vagaries of the "id," if one likes these terms, have been so wholly resolved, and the life urge has come into so full a satisfaction, that we see no terror even in death for this new-found masterly existence. The death of the Child and his resurrection, motifs so apt to appear in the symbolism of the divine family, are elaborations of this experience that enable even the death urge to take us away from our guilt and inadequacy into a more serene spiritual life.

This is, apparently, what lay behind the movement which we generally call Orphism. Of course the new pattern appealed deeply to only a minority, as religion of deep emotional content appeals to only a minority in any generation. The majority are always easily content to delegate the responsibilities to others and merely to perform the rituals, such as wearing an amulet or attending stated functions and festivals. Yet it must be repeated that it is always the devout, the fanatics, who disclose the real meaning of the symbols of all religions, meaning which is felt by others in proportion to the emotional depth of their religious experiences. The new, restrained symbols (rarely altogether new) of the refined Bacchism varied, as will appear; but most commonly in one way or another they represented the power of the life fluid still. And though the life fluid no longer overtly flowed from the divine phallus, it still caused the devotee to be born anew as the divine person, insofar as it gave immortality.

From this point of view the meaning of the symbolic lingua franca seems to become much clearer. The symbols which Jews, and secondarily Christians, borrowed from paganism, relentlessly trace back to a common body of symbolic roots. They turn out to have been used in other religions always (so far as their values can be determined at all) as emblems of a certain type of religious experience. Dionysiac symbolism had little appeal for Romans so long as they held to the old flavor of their own religion, though the symbols immediately appealed to the Etruscans. In Israel, Yahwistic leaders had for centuries fought the conceptions and practices of the fertility cults of their neighbors: much had crept into the great Temple from these cults, as well as into the lives of Jews in general, but Yahwism finally triumphed, and with it the drive to abolish everything that was still recognizably akin to Baal and Astarte. That is, the formal state religions, the religions which expressed themselves in fixed laws and observances, such as the official religions of Athens, Rome, and Jerusalem, had a basis quite other than that always implied in the symbols we are studying, and correspondingly had little use for them.[35]

The evidence appears to show that these symbols were of use only in religions that engendered deep emotion, ecstasy—religions directly and consciously centered in the

35. Casey, in the essays cited above (n. 30), seems to imply that all religions have been concerned with the Oedipus motivation and castration fear. I cannot follow him in this, for it seems to me that there is a profound difference between religions which have had use for the symbols under discussion and those which have not. I might mention here L. R. Wolberg, "Phallic Elements in Primitive, Ancient, and Modern Thinking," *Psychiatric Quarterly*, XVIII (1944), 278–297.

renewing of life and the granting of immortality, in the giving to the devotee of a portion of the divine spirit or life substance. Though they were symbols not to be seen in the forum at Rome, they were everywhere in mystical Pompeii and ecstatic Phrygia and North Africa. Largely absent from official Athens, they were common in the popular Athens of the vases. Never found in the life and teachings of the Pharisees, they became central in Christianity as tokens of its hope of divine life here and hereafter.

These are the symbols that were used in the synagogues and on the graves of Jews throughout the Roman empire. It must be recalled again that we are studying the symbols so intensively just because they have come from the Jews of Rome, North Africa, Palestine, and Dura—Jews from whom we have no literary survivals, and whose Judaism it is yet our desire if possible to begin to understand.

At the end we shall see that these symbols appear to indicate a type of Judaism in which, as in Philonic Judaism, the basic elements of "mystery" were superimposed upon Jewish legalism. The Judaism of the rabbis has always offered essentially a path through this present life, the Father's code of instructions as to how we may please him while we are alive. To this, the symbols seem to say, was now added from the mystery religions, or from Gnosticism, the burning desire to leave this life altogether, to renounce the flesh and go up into the richness of divine existence, to appropriate God's life to oneself.

The experience, as we shall see, apparently implied at times an initial destruction of the self, life achieved through death, and this was expressed in pagan hunting scenes, in the god Dionysus as the hunted hunter, in the rabbit, deer, or bull torn by other animals, in the mask of the all-devouring lion; it was the basis for all mystic interpretation (of whatever antiquity) of the sacrificial systems of pagans and Jews. In Christianity the idea persisted in the Lamb who was slain and in whose death we also die, that we may rise in his resurrection. Though it is not suggested that in Judaism the animal torn had such specific reference as the lamb had to Jesus in Christianity, the religious patterns seem basically identical in emotional values.

Or the experience could be represented in the opposite terms—in terms of victory in the mystic ἀγών or conflict, in the spiritualization of the wars and religious games of Greece, even of her cock fights. For the afflatus of victory in these corresponds amazingly with the afflatus of religious achievement. When religion has brought a man into such richness of life and love that even death is defeated, his tombstone may well show in triumphant symbols that victory and its crown belong to the entombed. This crown of victory was for Philo the final Vision. For all, it meant immortality. Hence the various symbols of victory in the Jewish synagogues and on the graves would seem to indicate that the Jews who used them also looked for this victory, this crown.

Or the experience could also be symbolized quite differently, in figures of birth, of craving for the divine fluid, and of getting it. Thus, with the original phallic meaning entirely obscured to Christians and Jews, and largely repressed even by pagans, all of them alike, pagans, Jews, and Christians, still sought the cup with its medicine of immortality, the life juice of God himself, which in early times was released by the lustful satyr, but now in all three religions was made available by the endearing little Erotes, whose symbolism of love was not obscured even when they had lost their wings. And for the devout of all three religions the vine was depicted holding within its folds a multitude of symbols of life, symbols of God's mercies to man, and of man's safety in God's love of him, and in his love of God.

Or the experience could be depicted in terms of the zodiac, the planets, the cosmos, with which man unites himself as he becomes the macrocosm, or as he is borne by the solar eagle to the top of the universe—indeed outside it altogether, to that Sun and Ideal World of which the material sun and universe are only imperfect copies.

Or the old identification of one's being with the life of the fields could survive in the Seasons, depicted in synagogue and tomb with their fruits, to represent the great cycle of death and resurrection in nature, the cycle in which men first, perhaps, saw definite promise of their own immortality.

These ideas have as little place in normative, rabbinic Judaism as do the pictures and symbols and gods that Jews borrowed to suggest them. That such ideas were borrowed by Jews was no surprise to me after years of studying Philo, for in him I had long known intimately a man who thought these conceptions to hold the deepest meaning of the Torah itself. Neither will the presence of such ideas in Judaism astound students of Cabbala. What is perplexing is the problem of how Jews fitted such conceptions into, or harmonized them with, the teachings of the Bible.

To this we shall come in the last volume of this study, where we shall consider the Old Testament illustrations in Dura. In both Philo and the Cabbala the method of assimilation is by way of allegory, though the elaborate numerical treatment of the Hebrew text by Cabbalists—the technique is called gematria—is of course different from Philo's manner of allegorizing. When that numerical method first appeared I shall not attempt to say. But it is obvious that no religion could have borrowed the group of mystical ideas which I suggest are implied in the symbols without harmonizing them in some way with its own myths or biblical stories, or conforming its own myths with the mystical ideas. Otherwise the borrowing would have meant actually abandoning the old religion and taking on a new one. Jewish explanations must have been given to the old pagan symbols and their values if the devotees remained Jews, as they patently did. We have a vivid example of the process when Plutarch interprets the myths of Isis to make them into expressions of the mystical Platonism of his day. He demonstrates also how Dionysiac myths had previously been retold to adapt them to the same mystical philosophy. Philo shows the same process of adaptation for earlier hellenistic Judaism. In the complete absence of writings from Jews who used the symbols, the great importance of the Dura synagogue is that it presents, in the setting of the symbols, a pageant of Old Testament scenes completely allegorized: the paintings are in no case simple illustrations of Old Testament episodes or passages. Through them we can catch actual glimpses of the integration of Old Testament story with the theme of mystic hope in this later and otherwise unknown stage of hellenistic Judaism.

It seems the most natural thing in the world that in the centuries after the fall of Jerusalem, when Jews were without a national center or, because of their loss of Aramaic, a single unifying language, and when there was no Talmud to control their interpretations of the Old Testament, or of the Law, many of them should thus have accepted the mystic ideas of Hellenism, and fused these with their Jewish traditions. That the Jews survived as a group at all is the great miracle; survival remained possible, even as miracle, only as they kept their sense of distinction constantly vivid by observing the injunctions of the Law, especially by marrying for the most part within the group, and by holding their Torah as utterly unique. But there was nothing in their Judaism to keep them from being in other respects hellenized or gnosticized, and attracted by the philosophy of the late Roman world. How far Jews went at that time in adopting the gentile idea that religion, and par excellence their own religion, is a mystic source of life for this and the next world, we have no way of knowing. Probably, as in Philo's day, there was no unanimity: some Jews were almost complete Gnostics and laid the foundations of later Cabbalism, while others were of what Philo called the "literalist" type. The most difficult point of all to believe is the point about which there can be no dispute whatever, namely, that these Jews were so hellenized that they could borrow for their amulets, charms, graves, and synagogues the mystic symbols of paganism, even the forms of some of the pagan gods. For no error of induction or fancy in my own thinking can obscure the fact that Jews did borrow this art, not sporadically, but systematically and for their most sacred and official associations. This is a fact I have not invented, and now no historian of the field may ignore or slight it.

PART VI

SYMBOLS FROM JEWISH CULT

CHAPTER THREE

Introductory

I F WE ARE to try to reconstruct the Judaism of the Greco-Roman period from its
symbols, we must obviously begin with the definitely Jewish symbols. Of these we
have found a considerable number: the menorah, the Torah shrine and scroll, the ethrog
and lulab, and the shofar are the most important. Occasionally we find along with these
a form that may have been meant for a circumcision knife, as well as a peculiar shovel.
Representations of the shovel appear in places reserved for Jewish cult objects in a way
that will make it seem likely that such an object, presumably designed for burning incense,
was used in ancient synagogues.

We have seen that we cannot assume a priori that the rabbis controlled the religious
life of the Jews who used the symbols we are studying. If that is true, we cannot limit
ourselves to rabbinic texts to discover the symbolic meaning of these cult objects. While
it would be absurd to say, without deeper consideration, that the people of the diaspora
must have had an attitude different from that of the rabbis, it is equally absurd to assume
that they must have had the same attitude. We must begin by leaving both possibilities
open, if we are not to beg the whole question from the start.

We are from the outset struck by the sharp contrast between modern usage as regards
cult objects and the ancient practices. The menorah, for example, is still found in most
Jewish homes in the form of a Hanukkah lamp of eight lights, and many families of
modified orthodoxy have a seven-branched menorah as well. The seven-branched menorah
is, I judge, coming into increased favor in synagogues, to stand beside the Torah shrine,
but representations of the menorah very rarely appear on modern gravestones. The shofar,
ethrog, and lulab are now only adjuncts of the appointed Jewish festivals: I have never
seen a modern instance of use of any of these as a symbol in itself, or as a decoration.

The present-day orthodox Jew likes to have a Shield of David, the six-point star
made of two equilateral triangles, in a great variety of places.[1] He may have one on his
tallith, or prayer shawl, and a synagogue will certainly show many of them. Yet here we
have an excellent example of the symbol as paradox, as discussed in the preceding chapter.
When the Nazis required Jews to wear the Shield of David as a badge, it was a brand of

1. Gershom G. Scholem, "The Curious History   of the Six-pointed Star," *Commentary*, VIII (1949),
243–251.

shame and disgrace, and the Jews who have survived in Europe show the insignia they were forced to wear as though they were (and indeed they were) symbols of horror and degradation. It was precisely in those years, however, that the Shield of David came to be more important than ever in Judaism. Jewish girls in America began proudly to wear the shield in gold on their necklaces: it became the emblem of Israel. In it the lowly is exalted, and as representing both lowliness and exaltation, it has now become a symbol for Jews in a sense in which it was never so regarded before. But Jews in general are completely unable to say why they use it or what it means. No cultic story or myth accounts for it. For them the shield is the shield is the shield. It is Judaism, as the Union Jack is England.

The same feeling seems to me as an outsider to hold in regard to most of the rites of Judaism also. Jewish rites are observed with a deep sense that the Jew would be a traitor to his forebears if he did not observe them. The rites in this sense express a profound loyalty which has survived Hitler in many parts of what was once his Europe, even as it survived the Inquisition in Spain. I intend no hint of disrespect for the beautiful ceremonies of Judaism when I say that this loyalty is not centered in a conscious or articulate sense of the symbolic importance of the acts of cultus in themselves, a sense that there is an *opus operatum* or spiritual gift which the performing of a given rite brings the individual Jew. Indeed, Jews have sharply denied to me any such deeper meaning in, say, the kiddush. They wish to point the sharpest possible contrast between their wine cup and the cup of the Eucharist. A Christian who is used to the active symbolic meaning of the Eucharist often observes the ceremony of wine drinking in the kiddush ritual with something of an initial shock. One sees that every Jew present, including the rabbi, feels that the rite must be performed, but, let me repeat, performed because it is a rite their grandfathers practised for hundreds of years, not because they, as Christians do, see any deep meaning in the drinking of a blessed cup in itself. The Seder, or ritualistic observance of Passover, similarly includes wine, the bitter herbs, and a series of beautiful blessings. But all the explanations that largely constitute the ritual tell that the Jew does what he does in memory of God's goodness to his People in the past, that the Jews at the table are keeping themselves in the tradition of their fathers. Still, the wine, the bitter herbs, the mazzoth, and the rest are given no symbolic values which relate the Jew to God individually. They are not used sacramentally as in themselves vehicles of God's grace to the participant. The same could be said of the ethrog, lulab, shofar, tallith, and other cult instruments of Judaism. Only before the Torah scroll does the sense of a divine presence immanent in a physical object fully appear in the attitude of the modern Jew of even the strictest orthodoxy.

I would not at this point be misunderstood. Jewish ritual is highly important to the orthodox Jew. He will die rather than give it up, and he finds the deepest "meaning" of life through its practice; only chaos seems to him the alternative to careful observance. In this sense his ritual and the objects used in it are indeed symbolic. But symbolism in orthodox Judaism has the symbolic value of conformity; it is much more like the symbolism of the political conservative, who finds in a routine of life, dress, form, his basic security. The eating of fish on Friday night and on the Seder eve, for example, is felt to be part of the proper procedure of the festive meal. For the Jew the fish in itself has not the active value which fish on Friday has to a Catholic—the value of specific and dedicated asceticism, of sacrifice, a way of pleasing the God who demands asceticism and sacrifice. Neither Jew nor Catholic, however, has a theory of symbolic value about eating fish as fish. It is not the fish in its own right which is the symbol, but the tradition, whose acceptance is indicated, and whose value is gained, by compliance, by eating fish at the traditional times. In saying this I am recognizing, not belittling, the symbolic value of conformity to tradition. I do not stop to discuss it further here because it is not the type of symbolic value that this work is designed to expound: but that legalism, conformity to an approved code of action, embodies perhaps the most important single symbolic value in human life is at least a very defensible statement. As we go on in the next volume to study the use of the fish—to keep to this example—we shall, however, find reason to suppose that it may still speak to Jews and Catholics with symbolic values beneath the legalistic value, on a level of which they are not remotely aware.

What we face is the question whether Jewish observance was always thus. Were objects of Jewish cult in olden days as devoid of inherent—perhaps I should say explicit— symbolism as the same objects are today? Was the fish, for example, always only a symbol of conformity to tradition?

One great difference between the period we are studying and modern times is that the vocabulary of symbols which we are considering was a novel group of devices for Jews to use in their synagogues and tombs. We have seen[2] that before the fall of Jerusalem symbols of Jewish cult never appeared on graves at all. We have no synagogues surviving from that early period, but presumably the same would have been true of such synagogues. Representations of bunches of grapes and of wreaths appear on Jewish graves in Palestine dating from the period of Pharisaic domination, and we are told of the golden grapevine in the Temple itself, but to identify Jewish remains of that period is often extremely difficult precisely because no distinctive Jewish marks were used. Jews were making copious use of rosettes, façades with columns, grapevines, and acanthus, but this meant only an adapting of motifs used by all peoples in the region. After the fall of Jerusalem, it was not long before the symbols of the Temple, and of the festivals, which till then could be celebrated properly only in the Temple, began to appear everywhere, especially on Jewish graves. In the third century, the menorah had become almost *de rigueur* for Jewish burials throughout the Roman world, but the menorah flanked by other cult objects was, apparently, still better.

That is, these Jewish objects seem to have been transformed into symbols used in devotion, to have taken on personal, direct value. In a great catacomb like Sheikh Ibreiq, a menorah was not needed on a grave to indicate that the person interred in it was a Jew, for probably only Jews were allowed to be buried there. Yet scores of menorahs are in the cemetery. The same is true of the great Jewish catacombs at Rome. In both places the Jewish symbols seem to have been chosen with a sense of their meaning, however badly the forms are executed. Indeed, I have suggested that precisely the crudity with which

2. Cf. above, I, 84 f.

many of these emblems are represented indicates that they had a meaning in connection with death and life for those buried behind them. On modern Jewish graves there is nothing comparable. The very fact that in the Greco-Roman period these cult objects had just emerged into common use would make it likely that they had some active meaning in themselves, since newly adopted symbols are much more apt to be meaningful than old ones whose use may, to the conscious mind at least, have become only traditional. The variety of the devices seems to me also to imply that they had individual symbolic meaning. If the symbols indicated simply Judaism in general, there would have been no need of so many. As in modern Judaism, a single emblem like the Shield of David would have sufficed, and indeed served much better as a "hallmark."

The pagan symbols used with the Jewish ones suggest also that the Jews of the day were extremely sensitive to symbols. It is easy here to appear to be reasoning in a circle— presenting the Jewish symbols as evidence that the pagan motifs had symbolic value for Jews, and at the same time making the pagan devices attest the symbolic character of the Jewish objects represented. The fact is, however, that in this art we have the two together, and that each does strengthen the claim of the other to symbolic value.

Furthermore, Jews devised their Jewish symbols for personal use in the very period when symbols were of the greatest importance in all religions. The cup and sheaf of wheat of Dionysus-Demeter, the sistrum of Isis, the dying bull of Mithra, and the zodiac, which was entering all the religions, are the pagan response to the *Zeitgeist* which produced the lamb, the book, the ΑΩ, the cross, the dove, and all the other motifs in Christianity, and the snake, cups, and the like in Gnosticism. People of every sort of mythological heritage wore amulets bearing a figure, or a cluster of figures. At no time in ancient history do we find that men were insensitive to such figures; but at no time do we find them more sensitive to or imaginative in producing such creations than in the period of the late Roman empire. They were apt especially to put these symbols in their places of worship, and to carry them along to their graves. The symbols appear on tombstones and on lamps found in tombs, as well as on cult objects. The very idea of putting cult symbols on graves is itself one of the most important evidences of hellenization among Jews of the time. It was because gentiles were being buried with emblems from their religions, especially from the mystery religions, that Jews wanted to be buried with similar protection. For this they borrowed many pagan symbols, as we have seen, but that their Jewish cult objects became funerary motifs is witness to the fact that, as substitutes for pagan tokens, these devices themselves had taken on new values from the Greco-Roman world. These new values presumably were felt in the synagogue rites involving the cult objects as much as in their funerary use as symbols.

It is precisely in such usages that we find Jews mingling their own new symbols with their borrowings from paganism. When we see the Jewish symbols mixed in with pagan "magical" symbols on amulets,[3] it is most natural to believe that the Jewish symbols are there with the pagan ones because both were thought to have power in themselves.

The way in which the pagan and the Jewish symbols are used interchangeably makes

3. Cf. II, 208–295.

it somewhat difficult to think that the Jewish symbols had less active force than the pagan ones. A wreath supported by Victories may contain a scallop shell—symbol, as we shall see, of new life and of immortality—or it may contain a menorah. Birds eating grapes may be alone, crudely scratched on a gravestone, or they may stand beside a menorah or an ethrog, or a Jewish symbol may appear by itself on a grave or lamp. The natural assumption would be that the pagan symbol and the Jewish symbol had met on common ground somewhere in the believer, just as Judaism and Greek philosophy became mingled in Philo at a point midway between the two, so that while the Greek philosophy took on Jewish flavor, Philo's Judaism was filled with Hellenism. He still kept the Jewish festivals, for example, but explained that he did so in order that through them he might achieve a mystic development, and come into possession of what were actually the Greek virtues. Indeed, those who want to know whether Philo was more a Greek or more a Jew miss the point that the value of the Torah for Philo lay precisely in the fact that it had become for him the true revelation in which both Judaism and Hellenism seemed to find expression. So with Jewish ritual: always, the Greek idea was read into the Jewish symbols and symbolic acts by Philo and his group, for it was in the union of the Greek and the Jewish that they found escape from chaos.

In the art we are studying we have evidence of a group of Jews who went even farther, so far that they used the pagan symbols together with the Jewish ones: they were not limiting themselves to taking pagan ideas to explain Jewish rites or symbols. Philo and Josephus, for example, thought that the stones on the high priest's breastplate represented the zodiac; later, in three synagogue floors to our knowledge, Jews put the zodiac with Helios in a panel alongside a presentation of the properly Jewish symbols. This was indeed a mingling of Judaism and pagan astralism, and we may naturally assume, as a hypothesis to be tested in our evidence, that the new and bolder combination was an advancement of the earlier and less daring fusion. That is, what little we know of this Jewish assimilation of paganism shows that, except in the pre-Maccabean apostasy, hellenized Judaism could use very few of the actual pagan symbols until late in its development: in the Philonic stage not the figured symbols but the ideas, the aspirations, of pagan mysticism were appropriated—appropriated by finding these ideas and objectives in a symbolic interpretation of the Torah itself, and of the cult objects of Judaism. When the Jews went so far as to take in the pagan figured symbols also, we have a final act which at the stage of development represented by Josephus, or even by Philo, would have been regarded as blasphemous. Such a breakdown of Jewish prejudice required a long preparation, which apparently began when Jews infused their Jewish ritual and its symbols with hellenized, mystic meaning.

If that actually was the process, it becomes intelligible why a Jewish cemetery in Rome might have adjacent graves marked with pagan or Jewish symbols indifferently, or with a combination of the two. It is indeed quite possible that a Jew who had only a menorah on his grave was a Jew who was "orthodox" in his abhorrence of pagan symbols, who perhaps had the point of view of rabbinic Judaism. It has been suggested that the absence of pagan symbols in the Catacomb Monteverde means that it was used by a more orthodox group than that represented by the burials in Vigna Randanini. But when in a single cemetery graves have now Jewish symbols and now pagan, or both together, the suggestion is strong that one Jew meant with his menorah very much what another meant with his bird eating grapes, and that while the symbols in themselves attest the aspiration to immortality as variantly as do the cross and the lamb and the grapevine in Christianity, the motifs in the Jewish cemetery, menorah or grapes, lion or ladder, were all, like the Christian symbols, expressions of a common Jewish hope of salvation. From what I have read in the writings of Judaism, and heard from Jews of our own time, it seems to me incredible that we should find the Jewish and pagan symbols thus together if Jews of that day had not felt that the symbolic values of both were very similar.

Nothing I have said should suggest that all Jews of the period were engaged in profound mystical speculation or experience. By way of analogy, may I point out once more that Catholic Christians are by no means all especially profound in their religious thinking. But if we are to understand Catholic symbols, we must begin with Catholics who recognize and appreciate the deep mystical potentialities of those symbols: this is the value we must suppose them to carry for Catholicism. If most Catholics never find those depths or heights, their religious experiences can still be understood in terms of a greater or lesser understanding and appreciation of the true meaning of the symbols. How much personal piety or spiritual achievement lies behind the use of the cross upon any given Catholic grave, the grave and its cross can never tell us. Similarly it is absurd to think that all Jews of the time under discussion had an exalted perception of mystical meaning in their rites and symbols. To try, for example, to read such meaning generally into the amulets would be obvious nonsense. What I am trying to say is that the Judaism which less profound Jews —such as those who were buried in Vigna Randanini with one or another symbol on their graves, or who worshiped at Capernaum, Beth Alpha, or Hammam Lif—may have failed to understand, was a Judaism seemingly filled with hopes and incentives quite different from the hopes and meanings which an insensitive but orthodox Jew might have been failing to perceive in halachic Judaism. Perhaps I should say "additional" rather than "different," for the menorah and all the other Jewish symbols certainly must at that time have stood as they do today for the great Jewish tradition, the unique treasure of God's revelation of his will to the Jews which every Jew must guard with his life.

That such additional meaning was in Greco-Roman Judaism and its symbols is, of course, a *thesis to be examined, not an assumption to be initially asserted or denied.* I say here only that the hypothesis most obviously suggested by the peculiar data is that the idiomatically Jewish symbols did in some way mean more in themselves to ancient Jews than they do to modern Jews with their halachic background, and that this different meaning evolved largely through the reading of pagan mysticism into the Jewish symbols. That hypothesis must now be tested.[4]

4. As this volume is in type I can only refer the reader to a study by Cecil Roth with many interesting suggestions: "Jewish Antecedents of Christian Art," *Journal of the Warburg and Courtauld Institutes,* *XVI* (1953), 24–44.

CHAPTER FOUR

The Menorah

THE SEVEN-BRANCHED candlestick [1] (properly lampstand [2]) or menorah is the Jewish emblem most frequently found in all the uses of the art we are studying. So familiar is it in this art, and in Jewish art and cult throughout all later time, that Jews themselves for the most part would be surprised to know that such representation was strictly forbidden by the rabbis. Three practically identical passages in the Talmud [3] say that one must not make a house like the Temple, or a table like the sacred table in the Temple, or a menorah like that in the Temple, of whatever material. To avoid such imitation, it is stated, one may make a menorah of five, six, or eight branches, but not of seven.

Kaufmann [4] is the only scholar I recall who was aware that this presents an anomaly in view of the fact that it was precisely the seven-branched menorah which was universally reproduced, so much so that it became the mark of Judaism in the period almost as distinctively as the cross became the token of Christianity. Kaufmann tried to find a solution of the difficulty by saying that the rabbinic prohibition was against making a menorah for daily use, not against depicting one in painting or relief. It was an actual lampstand of metal such as that in the Temple which was prohibited, not a picture of one, he argued. But this seems to me to ignore what the evidence will appear most clearly to suggest, namely, that whether Jews had such menorahs in their homes or not, they made them, and used them as among the most important appurtenances of their synagogues. And it ignores the fact that the prohibition is still observed by punctilious Jews, who prefer to have in their homes and places of worship an eight-branched menorah.

One menorah made of a single block stone, with the seven branches cut in relief and a hollow receptacle for a lamp upon each branch, was, indeed, found in the synagogue at

---

1. This chapter, somewhat abbreviated and adapted, was published as "The Menorah among Jews of the Roman World," *HUCA*, XXIII, ii (1950/1), 449–492.

2. Avi-Yonah, in *QDAP*, III (1933), 121, pointed out the popular error which associates the menorah with candles. See also du Mesnil, *Peintures*,

3. *BT, Menahoth*, 28b (GT, X, 483); *Abodah Zarah*, 43a (ET, 214); *Rosh Hashanah*, 24a,b (ET, 105 f.). See Nowack in *JE*, III, 531–533.

4. In *REJ*, XIII (1886), 53. Cecil Roth, in a letter, mentioned a monograph by J. Zwarts, *De zevenarmige Kandelaar in de Romeinse Diaspora*, Utrecht, 1935. I have been unable to find the book.

Hammath.[5] The question is only, then, whether the cast-metal menorahs, as illustrated everywhere, were used in synagogues.

A. THE MENORAH ON THE MONUMENTS

THE MENORAH has been much discussed with regard to its original meaning, but without any satisfactory demonstration. It is likely that the biblical passages saying that a menorah was in the ancient Tabernacle are insertions and inventions of a later time.[6] Ten lamps are reputed (in late interpolations) to have been in the Temple of Solomon, and we come upon the first assured appearance of the seven-branched menorah in the description of the Temple of Zerubbabel. This menorah was destroyed by Antiochus, but another was put in its place by Judas Maccabeus, and that menorah of Judas was one of the three famous cult objects in Herod's Temple. It is this same menorah which is pictured, literally or fancifully, on the Arch of Titus, fig. 1,[7] though the animal figures on the base are suspect, and Cook thought that the menorah as a whole might well have been carved on the arch very freely from descriptions given by prisoners rather than from the original. The upper level of the base shows, in the end panels, two sea lions, and in the central panel an open wreath or garland held up by a typical eagle of the East at each side. In the lower level, on the left, are two confronting figures which may be griffins; in the center is a sea monster, possibly Capricorn, and at the right are two confronting lions, couchant. An early eighteenth-century engraver may have been right in giving the long tails of sea monsters to both the griffins and the lions.[8] The fact that the pagan sculptor of the arch decorated the base of the menorah with these very hellenistic figures by no means assures us that there were such representations on the Temple menorah, though motifs of this kind have appeared in the tombs and synagogues,[9] and the possibility that they were on the original menorah cannot be categorically denied. Confronting animals or birds in association with the earlier tree form were, as we shall see, very old.

How the menorah came to be put into the Temple, and why, we cannot say with certainty. Indeed, in the vision of Zechariah (Zech. IV, 10), the lights, it is thought, most probably stand for the planets, for in the verse it is said that the seven lights of the candlestick are the seven eyes of Yahweh, wandering through the whole earth.[10] Yet we cannot

5. See above, III, fig. 562; cf. I, 216.

6. The best single account of the history of the menorah, with all references, is still that of S. A. Cook in *EB*, I, 644–647, supplemented by the same author in *PEF,QS*, 1903, 185 f.

7. From a photograph by Alinari (no. 5840 B, Rome); used by permission.

8. Adrian Reland (Reeland), *De spoliis templi Hierosolymitani in arcu Titiano*, Utrecht, 1716, plate at p. 6; reproduced in William Knight, *The Arch of Titus and the Spoils of the Temple*, London, 1867, III.

9. See Galling in *ZDPV*, XLVI (1923), 40.

Sea monsters will be discussed in the following volume. The garland is very common (see above, I–III, Indexes, s.v.), and though I have not seen a sea lion in such material, we have noted both a Capricorn (III, fig. 475) and a sea horse (III, figs. 742, 749). Griffins are quite familiar, as well as lions; see III, Index 1, s.vv. "Griffin," "Lion." The Jewish lion is not usually couchant; however, a lion in this posture is found on three gold glasses: see III, figs. 966 f., 971.

10. H. Gunkel, *Schöpfung und Chaos*, 1895, 127 f. Gunkel's idea that the passage interprets the lights of the menorah as representing the planets has been

be sure of an astral interpretation until we come, in the Greco-Roman age, to Philo and Josephus. In the vision of Zechariah there is likewise a tree motif: two olive trees, one on either side of the candlestick, supply the seven lights with oil from a spout to each lamp. The spouts strikingly suggest the Egyptian tree with Nut in it, pouring the fluid of life from a spout; but whether or not there was any connection at all, Jews of course did not include Nut in their symbolism. These trees at the side of the menorah, since the menorah itself may be taken to symbolize the planets, perhaps simply preserve the original meaning of the menorah as a tree. The form of the menorah suggested to Cook and many others that it originally represented the sacred tree, the Tree of Life, with lights or fruit hanging on it, since light and life were from early times almost interchangeable.

That the menorah was originally a tree seems to me now almost certain in view of the representation of the ancient cosmic tree of the Sumerians, fig. 2,[11] in which the tree grows on the cosmic mountain in such a way that it offers a close parallel both to the menorah as a whole and to its universally emphasized base. This similarity appears especially in the base of the menorah as depicted on the Arch of Titus. An earlier sacred tree from Susa, fig. 4,[12] and, even more important, that of Khafaje, fig. 3 [13]—motifs found on objects which go back to the fourth millennium B.C.—suggest the same relation. We now see that the buds called for on the branches of the menorah were to take the place of the leaves or fruit on a tree and indicated that the tree was living even when presented as a menorah. The device got to Palestine very early, for fig. 6,[14] reproducing a pitcher dated 1295–1262 B.C., found at Tell el-Duweir, shows the tree in this form. It is now impossible to determine whether this was the ancestor of the seven-branched menorah of the Temple, but the similarity in form is so striking that we may perhaps assume that the menorahs of our later period reflect the tradition of the Temple, which in turn reflected the older representation of the tree. Interesting in themselves, though too remote from Judaism to be used as evidence for the meaning of the menorah, are a pair of candelabra painted on the wall of the Villa of Diomedes at Pompeii. The candelabra are in the form of palm trees with seven branches and pendant fruit.[15] In the menorah, the tree, as a symbol of life, was made a bearer of lights, and my pupil W. M. Goidel has recently suggested to

often repeated, as by B. Baentsch, in his comment on Exod. xxv, 31–40, in *Handkommentar zum Alten Testament*, 1903, p. 227. W. F. Albright, *Archaeology of Palestine and the Bible*, 1932, 161 f., says that the seven-branched candlestick in Palestine goes back to the Iron Age. His evidence applies to lamps with seven wicks, but not at all to the lampstand shaped like a tree, as in the Old Testament description and in the representations of our period.

11. From Christian Zervos, *L'Art de la Mésopotamie*, 1935, 226. The design is from a stone bowl of about 2300 B.C. found at Susa, and now at the Louvre. On the history of the Tree of Life in Mesopotamia, see Geo Widengren, *The King and the Tree of Life in Ancient Near Eastern Religion*

(Uppsala Universitets Årsskrift, 1951, IV). Widengren discusses briefly the connection with the menorah (pp. 63–67).

12. From Nell Perrot, "Les Représentations de l'arbre sacré sur les monuments de Mésopotamie et d'Élam," *Babyloniaca*, XVII (1937), plate I, 2.

13. From ibid., plate I, 3.

14. From J. L. Starkey, "Excavations at Tell el-Duweir, 1933–1934," *PEF,QS*, 1934, plate IX, at p. 166. See du Mesnil, *Peintures*, 21.

15. W. Zahn, *Die schönsten Ornamente und merkwürdigsten Gemälde aus Pompeii*, etc., 1844, III, viii, 89. In the illustration only one of the trees is represented as a candelabrum, but Zahn calls them both candelabra.

me that for this the burning bush or tree was a parallel. The latter was a direct symbol of Yahweh, who "dwelt in the bush," so that it was the form in which God first revealed himself to Moses. I do not by any means feel that the planetary symbolism excluded that of the burning Tree of Life in the minds of later devotees.[16] The whole problem of this symbolism in the Greco-Roman period, however, must await discussion until we see how the menorah, a thing of unknown origin, reserved to the Temple—with the rabbis forbidding all reproduction of it in the seven-branched form outside the Temple—was actually used in our art.

First, so far as I can see, there is no reason whatever to suppose that the menorahs found on graves and synagogues [17] all stem from the representation on the Arch of Titus, and that Jews copied this,[18] or to agree that the symbol "of course refers to the Temple in Jerusalem." [19] Rather, Watzinger,[20] while he will appear to have limited too strictly the meaning of the menorah, was right in suggesting that it was not the menorah of the Temple which was represented thus universally, but that menorah which had somehow, in spite of rabbinic protest, become one of the most important articles in the synagogue.[21]

Such a conclusion seems inevitable from the great number of representations of the menorah along with other utensils of synagogue worship. At Beth Alpha,[22] for example, the design in the upper of the three panels of the synagogue floor seems to present a collection of such cult utensils. The Torah shrine or ark at the center, with the curtains drawn back at either side, marks the groups unmistakably as being from the synagogue. High in the gable of the ark is a hanging lamp—presumably even then a lamp hung always lighted before the Torah shrine [23]—while strange birds like American turkeys,

16. Nowack, in *JE*, III, 531–533, also combines the two.

17. See Frey, *CIJ*, Index, p. 663, s.v. *Chandelier*, for all occurrences of the menorah in Jewish inscriptions of Europe; Klein, *Corp. inscr.*, pp. 38, 49, 68, 82–85, 88, for menorahs accompanying inscriptions from Palestine. See also I. Loeb, "Chandeliers à sept branches," *REJ*, XIX (1889), 100–105; Kaufmann in *REJ*, XIII (1886), 52–55; KW, 191, n. 4, and fig. 291; Avi-Yonah in *QDAP*, III (1933), 121, n. 2; Beyer and Lietzmann, *Torlonia*, 16 f.; Ben-Zevil in *PEF,QS*, 1930, 211; Nowack in *JE*, III, 531–533.

18. This suggestion was first made by Kaufmann, loc. cit., and has been frequently echoed.

19. Vogelstein in *MGWJ*, LXXVII (1933), 306 f. But Vogelstein thinks that all the Jewish tokens early lost any specific symbolism, and became merely general signs of Judaism: e.g., the person on whose grave such a symbol or symbols appeared was thereby declared to be a Jew, if the devices were not "purely decorative." The use of the menorah in the synagogues, which we shall discuss immediately, seems to contradict him on all

counts.

20. In KW, 191. Grotte, in *MGWJ*, LXV (1921), 28, protests against this with no grounds at all.

21. Agreement with this view is found in Sukenik, *Synagogues*, 55 f., and Beyer and Lietzmann, *Torlonia*, 18. It may have been the priestly group who brought the menorah into the synagogue after the Temple was destroyed, in which case it would have been they whom the rabbis were rebuking.

22. See above, III, fig. 639.

23. Sukenik, *Beth Alpha*, 22, thus identifies the object, and comparison with the similar objects hanging from menorahs beside an ark at Naaran (see above, III, fig. 646) makes this the most plausible guess. Objects of the same form seem to be on either side of a menorah on the stone door of a tomb in Kefr Yasif: see III, fig. 44. A second-best guess is that these objects are not lamps but chalices for the kiddush—second-best because the objects in both cases are suspended, and such a position for the chalice is very strange.

which we are possibly to see as peacocks,[24] guard it on either side at the top, and a pair of lions are similarly stationed at the bottom. Lions are to this day part of the usual decoration on or before the Torah shrine in a synagogue. Then there are four other emblems, each presented in a pair, one on either side of the ark: they include the lulab with ethrog, the shofar, the incense shovel,[25] and the menorah. Finally, there is at the right a tree with a bird perched on it, balanced by a flowering branch on the left. Sukenik's statement [26] that these suggestions of trees are obviously only decorative space fillers is one of the few points of his description in which we cannot follow him, for in the case of a group of emblems in which everything is so clearly at once realistic and symbolic, it is extremely dangerous to make such a judgment about one given object solely because we cannot identify its symbolism. It is possible that at this time the Tree of Life, for example, was used by the Jews much more than we have known, and to this we shall return in a later volume.

Be that as it may, we find at Beth Alpha a pair of menorahs flanking the ark of the synagogue, and essentially the same motif appears upon several gold glasses from Rome,[27] on which, with freedom of individual design, but with definite identity of basic idea, the menorah and other implements of synagogue cult are represented with the Torah shrine. And there are many other parallels from synagogues and graves of Palestine and of Rome,[28] so that it seems to me highly probable that menorahs did actually flank the Torah shrines in the synagogues of the day.[29] Indeed, we recall that a synagogue inscription at Side in Pamphylia mentions the refinishing of two seven-branched lampstands (δύο ἑπταμύξους).[30] The menorah was also widely shown grouped with other cult objects, such as the lulab, ethrog, shofar, Torah scroll, circumcision knife, palm branch (lulab?), and incense shovel. These occur in every sort of combination, and I can see nothing to suggest why one of these objects rather than another, or one group of them rather than another, should accompany the menorah in any given place. Such combinations survive from the synagogues of Jerash,[31] Capernaum,[32] Pekiin,[33] Priene,[34] Gaza,[35] Hammath by Tiberias,[36]

---

24. Sukenik's conjecture (op. cit., 25) that they are ostriches is likewise feasible in view of the manner in which the birds are drawn, but it is strange that ostriches are found nowhere else in Jewish art, except possibly on amulets, and I think it most likely that they are completely misdrawn peacocks. They do not resemble the "ostriches" on amulets: see above, II, 242 f. Morgenstern suggested to me that they might be phoenixes, another possible interpretation.

25. See below, pp. 195–208.

26. Op. cit., 34.

27. See above, III, figs. 973 f.

28. Sukenik, op. cit., 26 ff. See above, III, figs. 58–61, 440, 602, 646, 706 f. See also Frey, *CIJ*, nos. 315, 327, 401, 460, and 712(?).

29. I am glad to agree on this point with Galling in *ZDPV*, XLVI (1923), 40 f., but when he says that the synagogal menorah has nothing to do with the Temple menorah (in *Theologische Studien und Kritiken*, CIII [1931], 358), he goes too far. The menorah of the synagogue seems to me to be the descendant of the menorah of the Temple.

30. Sukenik, op. cit., 26, n. 4. Cf. A. W. van Buren in *JHS*, XXVIII (1908), 195–197, no. 29; N. and M. D. Chaviara in *REJ*, LVIII (1909), 61–64; see above, II, 81.

31. See above, III, fig. 656.

32. See III, fig. 478.

33. See III, fig. 573.

34. See III, figs. 878, 882.

35. See III, fig. 583.

36. See III, figs. 564–566.

Pergamum,[37] Eshtemoa,[38] and Hammam Lif.[39] Menorahs appear very frequently scratched on tombstones, wherever Jewish graves of the period have been found, as well as on other objects.[40] There is no escaping the conclusion, it seems to me, that the menorah of our period represents primarily the synagogue (or household) menorah, and that the reference of the design to the menorah of the Temple is quite secondary.

If the menorah was thus actively important in the synagogue, it is amazing to find it represented so freely along with pagan emblems. In Frey's reproductions of grave inscriptions, we find it beside many different devices—an omphalos (no. 148 [41]), a bird (no. 152), birds, two at a tree and another eating grapes (no. 306 [42]), a bull (no. 171), and portrait busts (no. 675 [43]). The most striking single example of the menorah in pagan setting is on the famous sarcophagus fragment from the cemetery of Vigna Randanini.[44] Here the menorah is the only Jewish object: it is on a shield or in a circle held aloft by two Victories, flanked by the Seasons, and Dionysiac putti appear below. In synagogues, we find the menorah flanked by birds at Priene,[45] within a crown of Victory at En Nabraten,[46] with lulab and shofar at Ashdod,[47] Gaza,[48] Nawa,[49] and Gadara.[50] It appears with the vine, also twice with wreaths and rosettes, on stones probably from a synagogue at Nawa,[51] and between two rosettes in the synagogue at Yafa.[52] At Ascalon it is with Jewish cult objects, but in a scroll of rosettes in a vine.[53] On lamps and amulets it appears in association with various symbols.

It is not surprising, therefore, that the menorah is the only Jewish cult emblem which is used by itself on monuments, and whose presence marks the object or structure without further question as Jewish. I shall not attempt to list the hundreds of occurrences of the menorah thus alone, as it has been found in every region and upon every sort of object in the Jewish remains of the period.[54]

We recall that the menorah, which seems so closely associated with the synagogue,

37. See III, fig. 877.

38. See III, figs. 606, 609.

39. See III, figs. 890 f.

40. E.g., Frey, *CIJ*, nos. 118, 139, 151, 193, 200, 225, 234, 250, 254, 281*a*, 283, 312, 318, 346, 351, 361, 374, 382, 385, 397, 416, 418, 478–480, 484, 493*a*, 499, 523, 525, 545, 578, 595, 646, 652, 667, 671, 682*a*, 691*a*, 692, 713. See also below, n. 54.

41. See above, III, fig. 781.

42. See III, fig. 729.

43. See III, fig. 857; cf. II, 59.

44. See III, fig. 789; cf. II, 26.

45. T. Wiegand and H. Schrader, *Priene*, 1904, fig. 586; see Sukenik, *Synagogues*, 43.

46. See above, III, fig. 518.

47. See III, fig. 571.

48. See III, figs. 583 f.

49. See III, fig. 624. Dalman describes the stones here as probably from a synagogue.

50. See III, fig. 574.

51. See III, figs. 618, 622.

52. See III, fig. 570.

53. See III, figs. 575 f.

54. For the extraordinary variety of presentations of the menorah, and of the symbols accompanying it, see the Indexes of the preceding volumes, s.v. "Menorah." See also Frey, *CIJ*, Index, p. 663, s.v. *Chandelier*. The only exception that I know to the rule that a menorah marks an object as being Jewish is the phenomenon of decadent menorahs which are common on Christian lamps from Syria of the sixth to the eighth centuries. O. R. Sellers has isolated the problem and discussed it in *BASOR*, no. 122 (April, 1951), 42–45; ibid., *Supplementary Studies*, nos. 15 f., 1953, 48–53. Simon in *RA*, Ser. VI, vols. XXXI/XXXII (1949), 971–980 (*Mélanges Charles Picard*) has pointed out a few Christian usages of the menorah as evidence of people who were only half converted to the new religion.

does not appear in even one instance which can with any confidence be dated before the destruction of the Temple, and that its great popularity apparently begins in the late second or early third century. On one lamp of a style we should call hellenistic, that is, a style dating predominantly from the second century B.C. to a century after Christ, the menorah does appear,[55] but we know that this style of lamp persisted well on into the second century after Christ, and nothing compels us to date this lamp earlier. In the great mass of the decoration on ossuaries, most of which seem to antedate the fall of Jerusalem, the absence of the menorah is a most conspicuous feature, though three out of over a hundred have designs which might suggest such an object.[56] On not a single ossuary have I seen a menorah in the form that is almost universal later. Similarly, in the early rock-cut tombs in the neighborhood of Jerusalem, which by reason of their splendor are unanimously supposed to have been built when the city was thriving, the menorah does not once appear. Antigonus, a most unpopular ruler, did put the menorah upon his coins,[57] but the innovation was apparently so ill received that it was never repeated, and even in the intensely patriotic days of the Second Revolt, the menorah was not used on any coin now known. Apparently the rabbinic prohibition against taking Temple objects, in any sort of replica, outside the Temple, for any use, was in force even before the destruction of the Temple, and was disregarded only after that catastrophe had crushed not alone the Temple but with it the effective center of Jewish discipline. The appearance of the seven-branched menorah along with pagan symbols therefore represented no greater defiance of the halachic point of view than did the popular use of this sacred Temple symbol by itself.

B. MEANING OF THE MENORAH

CONFRONTED WITH such a mass of menorahs, represented in such a variety of settings, we ask at once what the symbol meant, if it had any meaning at all beyond the fact that the object it marked was the property of a Jew, or was of Jewish origin.

1. Modern Interpretations

OF THE menorah as thus used, there have been only four important interpretations from the standpoint of symbolism. The first, given by most writers, is the one just stated, namely, that the menorah was the hallmark of Judaism, that it characterized a site as a place where a Jew worshiped his God, or a grave as being that of a pious Jew, and that there is nothing more to be said about it. Such a limited interpretation appealed to Beyer and Lietzmann,[58] since the symbol occurs on so many objects in relation to which, as they say, an otherworldly interpretation would not be appropriate. This argument rests upon the fallacy of supposing that if a symbol has a given meaning or value, it must always carry that value in full consciousness wherever it is found. Otherwise it never has this value at all.

---

55. See above, III, fig. 266; cf. I, 145–147.
56. See III, figs. 197 f., 200; cf. I, 125 f.
57. See above, I, 273; III, figs. 674 f.
58. *Torlonia*, 16–18. Galling, loc. cit., on the

whole agrees with them; cf. idem in *ZDPV*, XLVI (1923), 25–29. The judgment of these scholars is final for Jack Finegan, *Light from the Ancient Past*, 1946, 359.

If it ever has other-worldly reference, it must always have such meaning. The same reasoning would lead to the conclusion that since the cross appears on a bottle of Benedictine, it has no real religious symbolism for our generation of Christians, since clearly the deeper meanings given the cross are inappropriate on a bottle of cordial.

Largely on the basis of such an argument, however, these authors reject a second interpretation, that of Cumont,[59] an interpretation suggested to him by the sarcophagus fragment (III, fig. 789) to which we have earlier alluded many times. Cumont placed the menorah in an astral setting (the Seasons), and adduced evidence (without sufficient exposition) from Philo and Josephus to show that the lights meant the seven planets, from which, since both the heavenly lights and those in the Temple were thought of as "eternal," he concluded that the souls of the departed on whose graves the symbols appeared would "shine . . . as the stars for ever," according to the phrase in Dan. XII, 3. Beyer and Lietzmann objected. They did not deny the possibility of such a meaning in the menorah: they held only that Cumont's evidence was not convincing, and they felt no need of such an extreme interpretation. I must, on the whole, agree with Beyer and Lietzmann in thinking that Cumont had not "proved his case," or even established a reasonable probability. Cumont tried to narrow the symbolism down too closely to a single astral meaning. But when Beyer and Lietzmann refuse to consider either Philo or Josephus as witness for contemporary Judaism in the diaspora or in Palestine, one wonders. That is, it would appear that Beyer and Lietzmann, as well as Cumont, have simply left the matter open for further investigation without prejudice.

A third meaning was suggested by Rengstorf.[60] He objected to the common conception of the menorah as the hallmark of Judaism, and like Kaufmann [61] took his start from the talmudic prohibition against the making of a seven-branched menorah. He says that because of that prohibition no Jew could have made one, and that this is confirmed by the fact that none has ever been found. Hence, he concludes, the menorah represented on graves could not have reflected a menorah used in synagogues. Rengstorf did not know of the stone menorah found in the synagogue of Hammath in Galilee.[62] He ignored the fact that very few metal objects that were not preserved in graves have survived from antiquity: thus, if most synagogues had menorahs of metal, as I suppose, it may well be that they were long ago melted down for other purposes. So he decided that the menorah on graves must be an ideal sign, a reflection of the heavenly menorah, and that it was so often represented with the Torah shrine simply to indicate the light of the Law by which a Jew hoped to be saved. It will come to appear to us a perfectly correct assumption that the light of the menorah was a saving light, and that this light was revealed also in the Torah; but Rengstorf's argument rests upon too many inaccurate assumptions to be of much use.

59. Cumont, "Sarcophage judéo-païen," 1–16. In reprinting this article in his *Symbolisme*, Cumont softened his insistence on astralism (pp. 495 f.). Baron, *History*, III, 53, showed that he too was impressed by the menorahs, but had no interpretation.

60. In *ZNW*, XXXI (1932), 35–37, 39–41, 52–58.

61. See above, p. 74, n. 17.

62. See above, pp. 71, 75.

A fourth interpretation, first suggested by E. Bekker,[63] but much elaborated by E. Peterson,[64] is that the menorah on graves was an apotropaic symbol. They admit the cosmological interpretations, but since they obviously can conceive of no proper place in Judaism for such notions, they think that the menorah on graves was intended to frighten away grave robbers, human or demonic; it served for warding off, as when a Catholic crosses himself before a corpse or anything "supernatural."

That the menorah was regarded as having power in itself, apotropaic if you will, but as being also something more, and that, in any case, if it was a hallmark, it was not merely this, we have found abundantly demonstrated by the menorahs on amulets.[65] For something worn on the person, with a religious symbol on it, can safely be presumed to be worn for protection at least, if not for edification. The menorah would not appear upon amulets so often if it had not carried some idea of a direct potency. We saw this reflected explicitly in an amulet bearing a menorah and the inscription, "For the salvation of the Lady Matrona," [66] where "salvation" seemed to refer not only to the lady's general protection but also to her safe passage to heaven. The menorah seems likewise to have been used for its direct power when stamped upon bread.[67] It is highly likely that many Jews used the menorah on amulets and graves with apotropaic purpose, but this significance, like that of the use of the sign of the cross just mentioned, seems to me entirely secondary to a deeper meaning and power in a symbol. Only the deeper meaning would make such secondary usage possible, and it is the profounder meaning that we are seeking.

We shall look for this deeper meaning in four distinct types of sources, namely, in certain inscriptions, in the interpretations of the menorah by Josephus and Philo, in the references to the menorah in rabbinical writings, and in the references to it in the *Zohar* of Cabbalism. A great complexity of meanings will emerge from these sources, but also one common meaning underlying interpretations of apparently the most contradictory sort.

2. In the Inscriptions

ONE OF THE relevant inscriptions was found upon a tombstone from Almyr in Thessaly.[68] The lettering on its face was restored by Frey (following Bees), as reading, [M]νῆμα Εὐσεβίου Ἀ[λ]εξανδρ[έως] καὶ Θεο[δώρα]ς γ[υναικὸς] αὐ[τοῦ], "Tomb of Eusebius the Alexandrian and of his wife Theodora." On the back of the stone is an inscription, fig. 5,[69] which Spyridiakes,[70] Bees,[71] and Frey agree should be restored to read, [E]ἰκ[ὼν] ἐνορῶ[ντος] θεοῦ, "Image of God who sees." Spyridiakes, who supposed the stone to be a Christian one, recalled the similar statement in Zech. IV, 10, mentioned above, where the seven lights of the menorah are explained. The Sepuagint renders this: "These seven are the eyes [of

---

63. *Malta sotterranea*, 1930, 130.
64. Εἰς Θεός, 1926, 278–290.
65. See above, II, 217 f., 220–222.
66. See II, 219.
67. See II, 218; cf. III, fig. 1018.

68. Frey, *CIJ*, no. 696; cf. above, II, 136 f.
69. From Frey, loc. cit.
70. In Ὄθρυος, IV (1901), 37, n. 2. This article is not accessible to me, but the author's remarks are quoted by Bees.
71. In *EA* (1911), 105, no. 40.

the Lord] which look upon all the earth." The verbs ἐπιβλέπω and ἐνοράω both mean "gaze upon," and can be used quite interchangeably. We are very likely dealing here with variant translations of the passage in Zechariah, but if so, both show the same mistranslation. For in the Hebrew text the participle מְשׁוֹטְטִים describes the eyes of Yahweh as "roving about within (or wandering through) all the earth." That is, the Hebrew suggests, as we have seen,[72] that the seven lights are the seven planets roving about, and at the same time are the eyes of Yahweh. The attributive "roving about within" of the Hebrew has become "looking down upon" in the Septuagint.[73] On the tombstone we have a comparable yet different conception, namely, that the seven lights collectively make an image of God as he "looks upon"—with no indication of the object of his gaze, which may be still the earth as in Zechariah, or something more personal and mystical. About this we can decide nothing: but this interpretation of the inscription would mean that the menorah on the tombstone was specifically called an image of God as he "regards" in some sense, and hence that at least for this Eusebius of Alexandria the menorah was much more than a hallmark of Judaism. It was a religious icon in the true sense of the word, a symbol of God himself. The possibility that Eusebius was the inventor of this conception of the menorah is very slight, and just as slight are the chances that every Jew anywhere who scratched a menorah upon his father's tombstone had the same sense that he was putting up a symbol of Deity: but the possibility is strong that we have here a clue to the meaning of the menorah for those who did understand.[74]

This interpretation, which I earlier accepted,[75] Bonner has challenged in one of his valuable letters to me. The letters ΙΚ seem to him quite insufficient to be read as εἰκών, while ενορω, if restored as ἐνορῶντος at all, would without an object at most mean "having sight, i.e., not blind." He has suggested restoring the word as μ]ενορω[θ, and so making the phrase mean "the menorahs of God," that is, the seven lights each regarded as a menorah. This last suggestion seems to me quite unsatisfactory, ingenious as it is, first because the menorah is the whole lampstand, so that "menorahs" would be quite inappropriate for a single menorah, and secondly because such a restoration implies a familiarity with Hebrew which cannot be assumed in the Jewish writers of such Greek inscriptions. Bonner felt the word *eikon* to be questionable because of the Jewish prejudice against images, but he had not seen the body of material we are considering. All I can say in conclusion is that he has unsettled the confidence I had in the interpretation of the inscrip-

72. See above, p. 72.

73. The Hebrew is difficult, for it is hard to see how the planets, or any "lights," could wander about "through" or "within" the earth. The original words may have said in one way or another that the "lights" wander through the heavens looking down upon the earth. The LXX rendering would then have preserved "looking down upon the earth," the Hebrew "roving about within." It may be, of course, that the LXX text represents the original Hebrew statement, later clumsily altered to make the reference to the planets more

specific. In any case the Hebrew cannot be quoted as contradicting Gunkel's planetary interpretation, since the Hebrew, read literally, makes no sense at all.

74. Just as in Catholic Christianity the full meaning of the cross upon a tombstone may or may not have been understood by some given individual upon whose grave it is found.

75. In my previous discussion of the inscription, II, 136 f., and in *HUCA*, XXIII, ii (1950/1), 461–463.

tion by the scholars named in the preceding paragraph, an interpretation which Leon also questioned, as he writes me. But I still feel that the phrase "of God who sees" refers in some way to the menorah itself.

With this in mind, two other inscriptions become significant for us. On a tombstone reported as at Venosa in Apulia is the device shown in fig. 7.[76] The Hebrew is difficult. Frey wanted to make of the letters a badly spelled *shalom*, but this the leaf in the middle of the word, if nothing else, seems to me to preclude. As they stand the words mean "of fire," so that, written over the menorah, they perhaps say: "The menorah is a symbol of fire." If this is what the Hebrew indicates, it would fit in well with the other suggestions regarding the meaning of the menorah that we have come upon thus far, but I would put no weight upon the idea, especially since Leon writes me that at Venosa he could find no trace of this inscription, but did discover many errors in the publication of the other Hebrew inscriptions of the catacomb.

Beyer and Lietzmann[77] follow Cumont[78] in calling attention to a possibility of interpreting similarly another inscription, this one from the Catacomb Monteverde in Rome.[79] The stone presents, along with birds eating grapes, a large menorah with the word Ἀστήρ above it. Beyer and Lietzmann read this as a name. "Of course," they remark, "the Greek form, not rarely met with, reproduces the Hebrew 'Esther,' but its position above the candlestick says clearly that this Esther is herself now a 'star,' gone to her heavenly abode." One wonders whether the person buried here was really named Esther. The deceased may have been not a woman at all, but a man of any name who had become a "star," elevated by the great God whose astral symbol the menorah is declared to be. We have seen the word also upon a gold ring of the sixth century from Bordeaux,[80] on which Ἀστήρ stands with three menorahs. Cumont seems to me quite right in reading *Aster*, but wrong in doubting that there could be anything of eschatological reference on a seal.[81] Inasmuch as the ring presumably owes its preservation to its having been buried on the finger of a corpse, possibilities of eschatological implication are by no means excluded. In Christianity likewise, devices embodying eschatological values have also all sorts of other and lesser uses, as we have repeatedly insisted. The ring would appear to have eschatological reference, as well as the tombstone inscription. The idea of salvation as a return to the stars is documented by Cumont from paganism,[82] but it seems to me to be probably an old "Orphic" notion, since it so clearly appears in Plato's *Phaedrus*,[83] where it is said that the soul before its fall shared in the great diurnal revolution of the "gods,"

76. From Frey, *CIJ*, no. 574.

77. *Torlonia*, 17.

78. Cumont, "Sarcophage judéo-païen," 12 f.; see the additions in Cumont, *Symbolisme*, 495.

79. See above, III, fig. 729; cf. II, 9.

80. See III, fig. 1009.

81. Cumont, *Symbolisme*, 511. Leclercq in CL, VIII, 211, quotes two other Jewish inscriptions to show that Aster is a common Jewish name: one

reads *Claudia aster hierosolymitana*, etc., the other *Avilia aster Iudea*, etc. In each case, *aster* may not be a name at all, but possibly a reference to the lady's having gone to heaven.

82. Op. cit., 495; cf. p. 282 for a number of pagan tombstone inscriptions in which the deceased is said to have gone to dwell "among the stars."

83. Esp. 246 E–247 C; but see 246 B, and the second speech of Socrates throughout.

obviously here the heavenly bodies, and returns to them when again properly oriented and controlled.

Another inscription of significance to us, already mentioned, was found on a fragment of a column in Henchir Fuara in Algeria.[84] Here, above a menorah, is written: *D[eus Abr]aham. Deus Isac.* Since Hebrew names are not inflected in Latin, this should probably be read, "The God of Abraham, the God of Isaac." This is another instance in which the menorah seems definitely labeled as a symbol of the God of the Jews. It recalls the suggestion that the burning bush of Moses was presumably also a symbol of Yahweh.

The menorah seems again to be identified as a symbol of God on a little stone of talismanic value,[85] on which, above the menorah, are mystical letters that have meant nothing to anyone. The legend *Iaō* within the outlines of the candlestick is quite intelligible, and the last four letters of the second line, ΥΠΕΠΙ, we took to be the remains of יהוה, so often represented by ΠΙΠΙ in Greek manuscripts. Regarding this second line we could only speculate. The *Iaō*, however, appears to mark the menorah as a symbol of God. In the light of these associations, the words εἷς θεός appearing with a menorah on another tombstone earlier mentioned[86]—the inscription is placed between the pictured faces of a man and his wife—seem perhaps still another such label.

Thus various inscriptions lead us to believe that the menorah was the symbol of God, and that it symbolized God by virtue of its lights.

3. In Josephus and Philo

THE POSSIBILITY that the menorah was in those days deeply symbolic, by reason of both its "fire" and its seven fires, is strengthened when we see what it meant to Philo and Josephus. In simplified explanation for outsiders,[87] Philo says that the menorah (in the Temple or Tabernacle, as mentioned in Exod. xxv, 31–37) symbolizes heaven,[88] by which he means specifically the planetary system. The central light of the seven is the sun; it has three planets on either side, to which it gives light.[89] Josephus' references are similar to the exposition in this passage of Philo. As part of a general and very brief statement that each of the cult objects in the Tabernacle had cosmic significance, Josephus says of the menorah only that the seven lamps represent the seven planets,[90] to which he adds elsewhere that the menorah is made up of seventy portions, which gives ten portions to each of the seven planets, thereby, he vaguely implies, representing the decans.[91] More, obviously, lies behind these brief references than is specifically said.

Fortunately Philo tells us about this in another passage, in *Quaestiones in Exodum* (II, 71–81), a section in which he says that he is drawing his material from the "allego-

---

84. See above, II, 88 f.; *CIL*, VIII, 16701; Paul Monceaux, "Inscriptions juives," *RA*, Ser. IV, Vol. III (1904), 369, no. 146.

85. See above, III, fig. 1027; cf. II, 220.

86. See III, fig. 857; cf. II, 59.

87. On the different types of writing in Philo as he speaks to different audiences, see my *Introduction*, chap. ii.

88. *Mos.* II, 105.

89. Ibid., 102 f.

90. *BJ*, V, 217.

91. *Antt.*, III, 144 f., 182. See Thackeray's notes ad loc., Loeb ed. That Josephus was not simply copying Philo in all of this appears from frequent differences in detail. See my *By Light, Light*, 99.

rists," [92] so that we may safely assume from his own pages that his interpretation is not his own creation. His exposition here elaborates in detail the significance of the menorah as a symbol of heaven with its "light-bearing stars." The menorah was to be made of pure gold, he argues, because, though the rest of the universe is made up of the four elements, heaven is made of a single substance, the "quintessence," which is shortly given its other name, "aether." [93] The menorah was to be "turned," because heaven is so made that it is a figure of the "periods of the cycles"; each star is made to revolve, and the natures of all the stars are devised with divine skill. The structure of the menorah reflects the fact that the heavens themselves are a unit, though containing so many members. [94] For its branches, Philo says, go out obliquely, rather than at right angles, to correspond to the obliquity of the zodiac, while the central light is the sun, the three above are Saturn, Jupiter, and Mars, and the three below are Mercury, Venus, and the moon. [95] Three bowls or cups like almond nuts are required, as well as a ball and a flower, on each branch. The three bowls indicate to Philo the three zodiacal signs of each of the seasons, the balls suggest the cosmic sphere, and the nuts and flowers (lilies) are vaguely and extensively allegorized, also in terms of seasons, or brightness, in the random way Philo has when dealing with a detail for which he can think of no good single symbolic explanation. [96]

On the shaft of the menorah (Exod. xxv, 34) are to be four of the cups, representing, Philo says, the four seasons. [97] The seven lights show forth the Hebdomad, itself a divine symbol, and they represent the seven planets by whose movement through the zodiacal signs all sublunary things are brought together into concord. [98] But the second half of Exod. xxv, 37, reads in the Septuagint, φανοῦσιν ἐκ τοῦ ἑνὸς προσώπου —a cryptic statement with no warrant from the Hebrew, and meaning, I should guess, that the lamps were to present a single front, that is, that they should be on a line. [99] Whether this is the meaning or not, Philo was aware that πρόσωπον has an astrological meaning which Liddell and Scott give as "decan considered as the *domain* of a planet." [100] This meaning of the word at once allowed him to make the verse say that the planets do not wander through all parts of the heavenly sphere, but are limited to the southern half: hence the shadows they cast fall always to the north, never to the south. [101] By still more ingenious play upon words the next verse is made to say that all the light of the stars comes from a single source, the

92. Cf. §71. In the passage as a whole, Philo is allegorizing the table in the Tabernacle, but two sections later he turns to the menorah, and there is no reason to suppose that he is not indebted for this also to "those who are nourished by visible food in the form of allegory."

93. *QE* ii, 73; cf. §80.

94. Ibid., 74.

95. Ibid., 75.

96. Ibid., 76.

97. Ibid., 77.

98. Ibid., 78. Marcus, in his note ad loc., Loeb ed., recalls *Heres*, 225.

99. Similar language is found in LXX, Num.

viii, 2 f., esp. verse 3, ἐκ τοῦ ἑνὸς μέρους κατὰ πρόσωπον τῆς λυχνίας ἐξῆψεν τοὺς λύχνους αὐτῆς, which means, I suppose, that the lights were arranged so that the wicks all pointed in a single direction, i.e., toward the front.

100. For references see *LS*, s.v. πρόσωπον ii, 2.

101. *QE* ii, 79. Philo's statement is correct inasmuch as the planets move within the ecliptic and so are always south of one who stands north of the tropics. But he is wrong, of course, about the shadow, since from the March to the September equinox the sun rises and sets north of an east-west line, and thus in the evening and morning does cast a shadow to the south.

aether.[102] The final ramifications of this allegory, by which Philo expounds the fact that the menorah is to weigh a talent, contribute nothing except a further testimony to the unity of the heavenly sphere, and to the fact that it surpasses all human mensuration.[103]

Philo finally interprets the "pattern on the mount"—the design shown to Moses for the menorah—in purely Platonic terms,[104] but everything he says about the heavens up to that point could have been taken from any "Chaldean" or Stoic astronomy, in which the material universe is itself the ultimate reality. Certainly in this account he gives no hint that the planets are the "eyes of God," that anything but the aether is higher than the planets, or that the planets do not themselves and of their own force control and harmonize sublunar matters.[105] That is, Philo seems, in the composition of the *Quaestiones* here, to be following some other person's exposition without critical alertness. We cannot determine whether that source was a Stoic work on the planets, or, as I think more likely, a commentary on the menorah by a Jewish "allegorist" who was more open than Philo normally was to the Stoic point of view. In any case, the Stoic interpretation of the menorah in this passage is fully contradicted by two other passages in Philo's more deeply allegorical writings.

For in these writings Philo's allegory expresses his own Platonic notion that the ultimate reality is immaterial, and that even the heavenly bodies are only reflections or images of a supernal reality. In a brief reference in *De congressu* (§8), he comments upon the story of how God showed Moses the heavenly pattern of the menorah.[106] There, he says, it is stated that the menorah "gives light from one part only, that is, the part with which it looks toward God. . . . It sends its beams upwards toward the One,[107] as though feeling that its light is too bright for human eyes to look upon it." Now, we have just seen [108] that in what seems the more Stoic interpretation, Philo makes this passage mean that the planets keep their paths in the southern celestial hemisphere. In the *De congressu* passage, however, we find a strikingly different, theistic interpretation. The planets are in attendance upon God, shine to him alone, are quite beyond our natural perceptions.

To understand what this may mean we must look at the context, where it appears that the reference to the menorah is a passing illustration in one of Philo's most abstrusely mystical discussions. The passage is a long allegory of Sarah, who here symbolizes a peculiar quality within man, "a ruling power present in me," ἀρχή μου.[109] At first this power makes itself apparent in the various virtues a man has, but in the full development these become "generic virtue" (γενικὴ ἀρετή). This is Sarah as contrasted with Sarai,

---

102. Ibid., 80.

103. Ibid., 81.

104. Ibid., 82.

105. This seems to me to be true in spite of the ambiguity noticed above, p. 83.

106. Exod. xxv, 37. Colson and Whitaker point out that Philo quite correctly contrasts this with the narrative of the making of the menorah, Exod. xxxviii, 5 f. (xxxvii, 17), where the statement which follows is not repeated.

107. I cannot follow Colson and Whitaker in changing the ms. reading of τὸ ἕν to τὸ ὄν. Philo would certainly have carried the ἕν over from the scriptural statement to his allegory, and the unity of the source of light is stressed even in the passage in *QE* just discussed.

108. See above, p. 83.

109. To understand the passage one must compare *Cher.* 4–8.

and this Sarah is at once barren (or virgin) and exceedingly prolific, for she cannot be impregnated by evil, but is fecund indeed in producing virtuous states and acts in man. Fully to appropriate this power is to come to the state in which Sarah's offspring in a man are children which he has himself begotten upon her. Now in ordinary course she is virginal to man, indeed remains virgin to God even while he opens her womb and impregnates her (*Congr.* 7). She is, Philo continues, just like the menorah, whose light, in the proper sense, and in the "ideal" form of the menorah, shines only to God. Impossible as it is for most men to beget by this divine Virtue, one who has made proper ascent and preparation can come to do so. That is, the menorah has temporarily ceased to stand for the planets, and is a symbol of the saving "female principle" which Philo has so deeply taken to himself from pagan mysticism. The menorah is the outflowing manifestation of God's power, the Light-Stream shining forth from God to man, but most properly shining back to God, beyond man's power to comprehend.

Philo's most important single passage on the menorah (*Heres* 216–229) goes even farther toward immaterialism. Here he starts from a still different point of view, with the peculiar conception that the Logos is a great Knife, or Cutter, and at the same time is Glue. I have analyzed the notion elsewhere,[110] and here need say only that it appears to be a primitive Pythagorean formulation whose history cannot be traced, but which seems to have suggested a number of ideas in Greek philosophy. The conception is at once a theory of numbers and a myth of creation. As a theory of numbers it explains that the entire numerical system arose from what Plato in the *Philebus* calls the limit ($\pi\acute{\epsilon}\rho\alpha s$) and the undefined ($\ddot{\alpha}\pi\epsilon\iota\rho\sigma\nu$), which are identified respectively with the monad and the indefinite dyad. That is, we begin with two principles, identity or individuality, and mere quantity. Identity imposes itself upon quantity by bisecting it and gluing it together again. Identity, in making its first bisection, produces the number two; when it inserts itself between the two parts as the Glue, it makes the number three. Thus, by further cutting and combining, the whole of the system of numbers is produced as a series of specific differentiations within indefinite quantity. The even numbers arise from bisection alone, the odd numbers from bisection plus the presence of identity between the two parts. In physical creation the process is the same, inevitably so, according to Pythagorean ways of thinking. The first two bisections produce the four elements: then the world is made by further cuttings and joinings as the Logos is now Knife and now Glue. The most famous single illustration of such a process appears in Plato's *Symposium*, with its theory of creation by bisection, a conception over which classicists have always felt obliged to be amused, since it is put into the mouth of Aristophanes.[111]

This theory of creation by bisection is the background of Philo's most important passage on the menorah. The lampstand is discussed first from the point of view of number

110. "A Neo-Pythagorean Source in Philo Judaeus," *Yale Classical Studies*, III (1932), 117–164.

111. Anyone who understands humor does not refuse to consider an idea because it is quizzically suggested. The cartoons in *Punch* and the *New Yorker* frequently have serious intent and deepest social importance. The same theory of creation is taught at one point in the Talmud, where humor is conspicuously lacking. See my study just cited, p. 162, where further references are given.

theory and its religious implications, secondly from that of cosmic theory. The seven lamps, the most noteworthy part of the symbolism, represent the number seven: in this case the Logos is between the two groups of three, both separating and joining them. The Seven or Hebdomad is a pure existence which the One begot without using any female, or any type of matter, as mother (*Heres* 216). This prime product of the One is sometimes called Sophia by Philo; it is here the Logos, which is only another name for the many-named single streaming outflow of God's nature. The function of this Stream from God is that it permeates all things, as the creative and cohesive force in the universe, and this is likewise represented by the malleability of the gold of which God ordered the menorah to be made (§217). And the specification of nuts and flowers as ornaments on the branches further brings the nature of the Seven, or of the Logos, into every part of the menorah, although the seventh lamp, the central one, seems especially to symbolize the Logos (§§218–220). From the cosmic point of view the seven lights are again the seven planets, whose function—especially that of the central planet, the sun—is likewise to send light to the earth, by which Philo implies the stream of the Logos, which is Light.[112] The centrality of the sun among the planets is stressed, and thereby the implication is still that the central light is of especial symbolic importance (§§221–224). Thus, in the menorah God has given us a model of the celestial sphere and at the same time a representation of the human soul: herein the theory that the soul is a microcosm is assumed though not elaborated (§225).

In the Tabernacle or Temple, the altar for incense symbolizes the four elements, or matter. The table symbolizes the animate world, and the menorah represents the celestial world, represents that world in the act of giving thanks (§226). This last Philo does not explain, but I think we do him no injury in recalling that the light which rises to God from the menorah is turned back to God, its source, as Philo speaks of it in the passage of *De congressu* that we have examined. He closes the allegory of the menorah by repeating his notion that only the weight of the menorah is specified, not its dimensions, because heaven is of infinite magnitude, bounded only by God, who is also its charioteer and pilot (§§227–229).

These passages together throw much light, I am convinced, upon why, of all the instruments in the Temple, it was the menorah that especially assumed a place in the synagogue, and so survived in Judaism. Philo and Josephus alike give these allegories of the menorah, along with similar allegories about the rest of the furniture of the Tabernacle, in order to integrate into Judaism the current idealistic astralism as contrasted with the materialistic. In this astralism the universe was conceived to be always the product of God's streaming power, and to be in the act of worshiping the Creator, so that its worship

---

112. This is stressed by Clement of Alexandria (*Stromata*, v, vi; ed. Stählin, II, 349, lines 9–12), who may have been working from Philo here, but who makes Philo's Logos into Christ. Thus he says: "The golden lamp presents another figure of the symbol of Christ, not merely by virtue of its shape, but in that it casts light (φωτεμβολεῖν) 'at sundry times and in divers manners' upon those who believe upon him, those who get both their hope and sight by the ministry of the first things created (τὰ πρωτόκτιστα)." That is, the light of the universe symbolizes the true Light, the Logos or Christ, who gives hope to all believers.

is the great and true priestly worship taking the soul of man to God. But most of the other objects in the Tabernacle which seemed to Philo to symbolize this cosmic priesthood were quite unadaptable to the synagogue. For example, there were the veil of the Temple, on which, says Josephus, the starry panorama was revealed (except for the signs of the zodiac),[113] the incense altar, the table, the robes of Aaron. While the symbolism of all of these pointed likewise to the cosmic worship,[114] none of them, except possibly the veil, could easily, if at all, be transplanted to the synagogue, or become a symbol in the abstract, such as the menorah became. With its seven lights vividly representing the seven planets, and with light itself as its function, the menorah—whether in the Temple, or in the synagogue, or on a grave—told men that there is a great Light from God coming into the universe, chiefly manifest in the planets, but none the less powerful in all other things. So the menorah is an "image of God." For its light is the Light from God; it is Sophia or the Logos, the presence of God in the world at once as its ruler and as the priest leading the world back to God. That true High Priest is the Savior of men, and it does not matter for the conception that the human priest is no longer in the Temple reflecting the cosmic worship. Aaron and his robes perished finally with the Temple of Jerusalem, but the High Priest of the universe, the Logos, could still live on with hellenized Jews to be the message and meaning of their Judaism.

The menorah as representing this Light of the world, or Logos, is God's mercy revealed to the Jew in at once a cosmic and a Jewish sense. It was really not important whether one took a Stoic or a Platonic view of ultimate reality. What modern readers find hard to grasp is that all this allegory was developing with no ecclesiastical whip to keep the thought in a single "orthodoxy." Philo himself deplored Stoic materialism, but often quotes with approval allegories based upon Stoic assumptions. The main thing is that the menorah is a symbol of God and his rule: you explain it your way, I in mine, is the attitude. The two schools were united in reverence for the biblical descriptions of the menorah, and, I am sure, for the object itself. That is, the value was as specific as the explanations were varied and ambiguous.

This would be the meaning of the menorah if we can suppose that the interpretations of Philo and Josephus, and of the other Jews they reflect, were the interpretations which prompted the taking of the menorah from the Temple to be the general symbol of Jewish faith. Beyer and Lietzmann, we saw, protested that Josephus and Philo could not be assumed to represent the current Judaism. Without great support from other evidence, no isolated writer or writing can be taken as doing so, not even, in the first Christian centuries, the Talmud. But three things suggest that the interpretation of the menorah given by Philo and Josephus was the general one in their day and, presumably, for some time afterwards. The first is Philo's frequent reference to others whose opinions he is expressing, his saying even that "everyone knows" about the planetary symbolism of the seven lights. Secondly, Josephus agrees with Philo about the menorah and in interpreting the Tabernacle worship in cosmic terms, but disagrees with him on so many details that he seems to have another source and not to be drawing upon Philo for the interpretation.

113. *BJ*, v, 214.   114. See my *By Light, Light*, chap. iv.

That is, he is one of the "many" to whom, Philo implies, the reference of the menorah to the planets is known. Thirdly, Philo and Josephus set forth a notion which appears again, isolated but recognizable, in the midrashim, and clearly in the Cabbala.

4. In Rabbinic Writings

THE RABBIS seem to me as a whole to have opposed the sort of attitude toward the menorah that we have been discussing. That is probably the reason why, as we saw,[115] they so specifically forbade the use of a menorah with seven branches. In the Talmud I have been unable to find a single passage which attempts to explain the menorah symbolically. One passage [116] says that in the Temple or the Tabernacle the three lights on each side faced the central light, and the central light faced the Shekinah, which seems a definite acceptance, or modification, of the symbolism of the seven lights as the planets, but a tanna, Nathan, says that this means only that the central light is the most honored.[117] He may well have said this to contradict the mystical or astrological interpretation. We have seen evidence in our material that such an arrangement of the lights was popular.[118] Most representations of the menorah show only the branches, or indicate only flames on them. In a relatively small number the little lamps are depicted, and in a few of these the side lamps are oriented toward the center.[119] The rabbis were almost certainly speaking of an arrangement of lamps used at least sometimes in the synagogues.[120]

In most of the midrashim the rabbis continue to ignore the menorah, though since the midrashim are scriptural commentaries, these writers are forced to mention it more frequently than the authors of the Talmud. When they do so, however, their explanations usually betray the halachic and rabbinic point of view in contrast to that of hellenized Judaism. For example, a passage in the *Sifre* on Numbers (Num. VIII, 1–3),[121] again alludes to the fact that lights of the side lamps turn toward the central one. In the *Mekilta* [122] the passage in which the menorah is mentioned is considered along with four other passages of the Torah simply because they all have ambiguous syntactical construction. In both that treatise and in the *Midrash Rabbah* on Exodus, the extended passages on the menorah in Exod. XXV and XXXVII receive no direct comment at all. In this midrash, the astral interpretation of the Tabernacle is perhaps dimly echoed in the statement that the gold clasps in the Tabernacle looked like the glittering stars in heaven.[123] More information

---

115. See above, p. 71.

116. *BT, Megillah*, 21b (ET, 131).

117. *BT, Menahoth*, 98b (GT, 708).

118. See above, II, 103, 110 f.

119. See III, figs. 769, 929, 967. An interesting survival of the idea appears in the representation of the menorah in the manuscripts of Cosmas Indicopleustes: see E. K. Riedin, *Christian Typography* (in Russian), Moscow, 1916, I, 260, fig. 268. The three lights on either side have each one little wick facing outwards, wicks which clearly stand for lamps. The central light on this menorah is a trefoil.

120. There was much discussion among the rabbis of how the lights of the Temple menorah were oriented. Paul Romanoff, *Jewish Symbols on Ancient Jewish Coins*, 1944, 33–37, has collected these passages, with the conclusion (p. 34) that the rabbis had lost all memory or tradition of how the lights were arranged.

121. See German transl. of K. G. Kuhn, 1933/6, 160. He refers to W. Bacher, *Die Agada der Tannaiten*, 1902, II, 439, n. 6.

122. Lauterbach ed., II, 143 (*Amalek*, i).

123. *MR, Exodus*, XXXV, 6 (ET, 435).

comes in the comment on the command (Exod. xxvii, 20) to bring pure olive oil for the lamp, where, through a combination of verses, Israel becomes itself the ideal olive tree which supplies the fruit, and at the same time is light for all men.[124] The lamp is also God who gives the light, and it is likewise the Torah; but all of these statements are left unconnected with the menorah itself.

The menorah does, however, appear again, with a very important explanation, at the end of this work. I quote the passage in the translation of Lehrman:

> [Because] you have made curtains of goats' hair [therefore] will I protect you with a cloud in the Messianic Age. . . . [And because] you have made an ark-cover will I forgive all your sins; [and because] you have made a table will I save you from [Gehinnom] that stands ordered, and will set [order] for you a table in the World to Come. [Because] you have made a candlestick for me, I will cause it to shine for you sevenfold in the Messianic Age. . . . [And because] you have made an Ark unto me in which the Torah is kept, [for this reason] will I give you endless reward.[125]

Lehrman's footnotes show that the passage perplexes him, since its presence at the place where it appears is, even in this midrash, an anomaly. What we do have recorded, however, is a tradition which made these objects, among them especially the candlestick and the Torah shrine—"the Ark . . . in which the Torah is kept"—into symbols and promises of salvation or endless reward in the Messianic Age. Here is an interpretation which would throw much more direct light on the use of the menorah, with or without the Torah shrine, upon graves. And in view of the objects represented in Beth Alpha and on the gold glasses, it is equally significant that in this passage the curtains are named along with the candlestick and Torah shrine as carrying power or promise of forgiveness of sins. The passage, however, is so unusual that it cannot be taken as generally valid among the rabbis, and used to explain the occurrence of the menorah upon graves. But we must bear in mind that in spite of their hostility to the use of the menorah and to its mystical interpretation, the rabbis have recorded this account of the symbols. I doubt very much that the explanation was as unusual in the Jewish world of the day as it appears to be in the rabbinic literary remains.

Not identical in its interpretation, but similar, is another passing mention in the Midrash,[126] where the menorah, which is said to represent the Torah as light, is called the crown of good deeds; for actual good deeds (that is, deeds in accordance with the commandments) make atonement, as repentance does, for one's sins, and are "a shield against punishment." That the light of the menorah corresponds to the Torah is implied in another midrash,[127] according to which God said to Moses, after the princes of the twelve tribes had brought their offerings to the Tabernacle:

> Say to thy brother Aaron: Greater than the gifts of the princes is thy gift; for thou art called upon to kindle the light [Num. viii, 1–3], and, while the sacrifices shall last only as long as the Temple lasts, thy light of the Law shall last forever.

124. Ibid., xxxvi, 13 (ET, 436–440).

125. Ibid., l, 5 (ET, 560 f.).

126. *MR, Numbers*, xiv, 10 (ET, 612 f.).

127. *Tanhuma* (ed. Buber), בהעלתך, 6, as translated in *JE*, I, 4.

That is, in the rare instances in which the rabbis do discuss the menorah, they make it into a symbol of the light of halachic Judaism, the Torah which gives commands, inspires obedience, and promises a Messiah and a Messianic Age.

When, however, the *Midrash Rabbah* comments on Num. VIII, 1–2, we find surprisingly hellenistic explanations. Here it is first told that Moses was quite unable to make the menorah, until God indicated the pattern directly with his finger, or told him to put a talent of gold in the furnace, which would come out fully formed. A third version seems to be that Moses hit the gold with a hammer, and the menorah took shape of its own accord. All of this means that God made the menorah, and accordingly said to Moses that if Israel

> "will take care to kindle lights before me I shall preserve your souls from all evil things."
> For souls are likened to a lamp; as it says, "The spirit of man is the lamp of the Lord" (Prov. xx, 27).[128]

God is the Light of the universe, the passage continues, yet he commands that a lamp be lighted to give light back to God, as a blind man was asked to kindle a lamp in a house for a man who had guided him to it. So God has led Israel by his light, and in gratitude Israel is to give light in return, thereby enhancing its dignity before the other nations, for as Israel elevates the lighted menorah, Israel is itself elevated.[129] The light of the menorah does not perish as must even the Temple, but in its continued burning symbolizes the fact that God's blessings endure forever for his children.[130] This explanation seems a clear reference to the menorah of the synagogue, which actually did still burn after the Temple had been destroyed.[131]

In the next section of this midrash the interpretations given are again cosmic. The seven lights of the menorah of Zerubbabel, that is, the menorah of the vision of Zechariah (Zech. IV, 10), are, it is said, the seven planets, "which run to and fro through the whole earth." From this the exposition goes on to show that the light of God is greater than that of the heavenly luminaries. Light shines out from the Temple windows, for example, not into them; "lightning owes its origin to the celestial fire," and while man must light one fire from another, God kindled the primordial light of creation out of darkness.[132] A man-made menorah, or a light which a man can kindle, is of course inferior to the light of God: it is as when a man has invited a king to eat with him, and puts out all his best, only to find that the light and the other furnishings which the king has brought with him put all he has to shame, so that the man wants to hide his poor utensils. But the king will not allow him to do so, and uses the man's equipment rather than his own. So God came in the Shekinah when Moses made the lamp. This too I feel must be taken to indicate that the lighting of the menorah in the synagogue still brought the Shekinah to the faithful.[133] And again we have it made plain that the lamp is an image or symbol of God himself.

---

128. *MR, Numbers*, xv, 4 (ET, 645).
129. Ibid., §5.
130. Ibid., §6.
131. It is possible, but not so natural, to see in this passage a reference to the light burning before the Torah shrine.
132. Ibid., §7.
133. Ibid., §8.

The interpretations continue, and again become cosmic: from the celestial light (that is, God) comes the light of the sun and the moon, and only a hundredth part of the celestial light ever reaches mankind. Thus "the Holy One, blessed be he, was constrained to dwell with mortals in the light of a lamp." [134] And so a "pure menorah" came down from heaven. It is recounted again how Moses found difficulty in copying the divine model, with the solution that this time Bezaleel, whose name is here interpreted to mean "In the shadow of God," helped Moses out of the difficulty and made the metal menorah. Bezaleel's ability to do this is explained by the suggestion that he had a special relation or access to the divine light. [135] The Temple in which his menorah was kept was destroyed, but the menorah was one of five things which were taken away and hidden by God (the others were the Ark, the fire on the altar, the Holy Spirit, and the cherubim). And, it is said, "when the Holy One, blessed be he, in his mercy will again build his Temple and his Holy Place, he will restore them to their position in order to gladden Jerusalem." [136] That is, the menorah is here too, at the end of this remarkable series of explanations, one of the chief symbols and hopes of the Messianic Age, in which, of course, the Temple is to be restored.

This extraordinary passage impresses me as one of the unusual incursions into rabbinic literature of that mystical Judaism which we know chiefly from Philo, but which will seem, as we continue, steadily to emerge as the popular Judaism of the age, the Judaism behind the art symbols we are studying. For in this case the number of parallels between the precepts of the rabbis and Philo's exposition is astonishing. Both identify the seven lights with the planets, though the Midrash has no explanation, and it is only in Philo that we see reason for such an identification. Both derive the light of the menorah or the planets from a single supernal fire or light which is God, a conception clearly identified with the pagan notion of heavenly aether by Philo, but left unexplained again by the Midrash. The Platonism of Philo seems echoed in the great stress which the Midrash lays upon the disparity between the divine model of the menorah and the human copy. The rabbis too knew that the central light was the important one, but it is only in Philo that we have some explanation of that importance. Just as Philonic, though less vividly so, are the passages which insist that God's light comes to man, and that it is for man to give light to God in return: in both the rabbinic view and Philo's, the menorah is the soul of man sending light back to God, but chiefly it is the light of God.

What is especially notable about the Midrash passage, however, is that it expresses a type of Judaism which has always been distasteful to most of the rabbis, a Judaism which finds its meaning not so much in study of the Torah, in order to learn and do the will of God, as in a mystic union between man and God. The stream of mercy, light, goodness, the Shekinah, the Logos, spirit, Sophia—call it what you will—was the central interest of this essentially nonhalachic type of Judaism. I see in the parallels cited not a single instance indicating that, in the language of the old philologians, the authors of the Midrash had "read" Philo. But I do see coming into rabbinic thinking (and this is by no means the only instance of such invasion in the Midrash) a mysticism whose chief exponents are

---

134. Ibid., §9.
135. This mystical meaning would be unrecognizable in *BT, Berakoth*, 55a (ET, 357).
136. *MR, Numbers*, xv, 10 (ET, 651).

Philo at one end, and, as we shall see, the Cabbala at the other—a mysticism which was accepted by many rabbis, but which obviously was flowing into their circle from the outside, and was not an idiomatic product of their own group. These midrashic passages find a proper context in Philo and the Cabbala as fully as they are anomalies in official rabbinic literature. I should guess that the passages of Exodus which mention the menorah are skipped in the *Mekilta* and *Exodus Rabbah* precisely because the menorah (as *Numbers Rabbah* shows) was at the time so widely thought to be a mystic symbol. We are perplexed only as to how the passage in *Numbers Rabbah* could have survived. All that can be said is that we owe to such anomalous survivals in the Bible and rabbinic literature much that is most important for our knowledge of the development and richness of Jewish history. The general attitude of the rabbis seems to be expressed in the repeated command not to use a seven-branched menorah, and in their general ignoring of the symbolism of the menorah except in this one passage.

It is still sound to hold that Philo and Josephus, especially Philo, cannot be taken unsupported as guides to the popular Judaism of their day, but in regard to the menorah Philo's attitude seems less isolated. It begins to appear quite likely that the menorah, a symbol of God himself, held out a mystical and eschatological hope to Jews in the Greco-Roman world. They presumably insisted upon using the menorah with seven branches in spite of rabbinic prohibition because the astral symbolism was so meaningful to them, and I suspect that the rabbis as a whole tried to prevent the use of the seven-branched menorah because they did not like this astral mysticism. The archeological evidence shows, however, that the rabbis did not for several centuries make their point.

5. In the Zohar

THE ZOHAR, the chief single text of Cabbala,[137] has also much less notice of the menorah than we should expect. It is in its turn a sort of midrash of the Pentateuch, and, for all of its extensive mystical imagery of light, it disappoints us by skipping entirely the two important passages on the menorah in Exodus, as do the *Midrash Rabbah* and the *Mekilta*. But, again like the earlier midrashim, it does consider the passage in Numbers (VIII, 1–3) in which Aaron is commanded to light the seven lights. The allegorical method of the *Zohar* is much more difficult than that of the earlier rabbis or even that of Philo; however, it will not be necessary for us to examine the section in too great detail.[138] It begins with an abrupt correlation of the lighting of the menorah with the phrase in Ps. XIX, 5, "Which is as a bridegroom coming out of his chamber," and "R. Judah" says:

> Happy is the portion of Israel in whom the Holy One, blessed be he, delights and
> to whom he gave the Torah of truth, the Tree of Life. Whoever takes hold of this achieves

137. The *Zohar* is a product of Spanish-Jewish mysticism of the last quarter of the thirteenth century. Built upon a great tradition of Cabbalism, it was the supreme expression of mystic Judaism, and "became a canonical text, which for a period of several centuries actually ranked with the Bible and the Talmud." The best introduction to the *Zohar* is in Scholem, *Jewish Mysticism*, chaps. v and vi, from which (p. 153) the foregoing statement is quoted.

138. *Zohar*, *Beha Alothekha* (Num.), 148b–151b (ET, V, 203–210).

life in this world and in the world to come. Now the Tree of Life extends from above downward, and it is the Sun which illumines all.[139]

Here the menorah is made at once a "Sun," the "Torah of truth," and the "Tree of Life" (a name of God).[140] The text goes on to say that the sun races from east to west to shed illumination on his bride, the moon: thus the lighting of the lamps "contains an allusion to the celestial lamps, all of which are lit up together from the radiance of the sun." When, without further explanation, another speaker at this point abruptly begins a new exposition, the editors suspect that there is a lacuna in the text. But already we have met with three of our main explanations of the menorah from earlier sources: the menorah symbolizes the stars (the planets) illumined by the sun; and it is simultaneously the Light-Stream, the Tree of Life, the Torah, and the bridegroom illuminating his bride. The last detail recalls the menorah whose light is Sarah in mystic communion with God, according to Philo's exposition. To grasp this point, the *Zohar* now tells us, is to achieve life in this world and in the world to come, which brings in the eschatological motif suggested both in the rabbinical writings and by the usage on graves.

The speaker whose disquisition breaks abruptly into the preceding discussion tells how God gave men acts to do, conspicuously at the time of the slaying of the first-born in Egypt, which would "bring about the working of Mercy and Rigour at one and the same time." All this leads to the statement that the lighting of the menorah is another such act, by which the lighting of the heavenly lamps is simulated on earth, and so all the worlds are pervaded with gladness.

Another digression follows, this time about the ark as it rested on Ararat. The relation of this to the menorah is again not apparent, but we suddenly come to a story [141] about some companions who entered a cave lit by a lamp, and a voice was heard saying:

> "When thou lightest the lamps the seven lamps shall give light in front of the candle-stick." Here (said the voice) the Community of Israel receives the light whilst the supernal Mother is crowned, and all the lamps are illumined from her. In her are two small flames, companions of the King, as it were, which kindle all the lights on high and below. R. Jose, on hearing this, rejoiced, and reported it to R. Eleazar, who said to him: "Let us enter therein, for the Holy One, blessed be he, seems to have appointed for us this day as one on which a miracle should happen to us." When they entered, their eyes met there two men engaged in the study of the Torah. R. Eleazar proclaimed: "How precious is thy lovingkindness, O God! and the children of men take refuge in the shadow of thy wings" (Ps. xxxvi, 8). The two men stood up, then they all sat down in joyful mood. Said R. Eleazar: "The Holy One, blessed be he, has shown us loving-kindness in letting us find you in this spot. Now, light the lamps!"

Here two more of our earlier motifs reappear. The menorah is illumined by the "supernal Mother," who again sharply recalls Philo's Sarah, or heavenly Virtue, Sophia or the Logos, the cosmic feminine principle; and the description of the men studying the Torah

139. Ibid. (ET, V, 203).

140. See Simon's appendix, *Zohar*, ET, V, 394.
141. *Zohar*, *Beha Alothekha* (ET, V, 207).

by the light recalls the repeatedly expressed notion that the Torah is man's light. The cave itself has symbolism also, but I am not sufficiently a student of the *Zohar* to discuss its meaning.[142]

When the men have settled down together in the cave, four rabbis discourse on how the oil of the menorah and incense together make a unity, a unity found by means of an Aramaic pun.[143] The conclusion is that in the two is represented "the exaltation of the supernal beings after having drunk their fill of the waters of the River, so that blessings and joy are diffused throughout." Not content with this figure, another of the speakers likens the union of menorah and incense to the issuance of "causes from the supernal side of the Most Profound, which is called Thought." And again it is through Aaron that the supernal menorah with its seven lamps is lighted, and the menorah, together with the altar of incense, ministers to the joy of all existence. All three of these explanations are clearly allegories of the menorah as an offering which rises to God: the basis in each case is the light which, in Philo and the Talmud, rises from the seven lamps of the menorah to God.

So mystical is this material in the *Zohar* that we should have no right to conclude that anything lies behind it but fantastic allegory on Scripture, were it not that the earlier writers give us, in so many instances, the same interpretations, and at the same time so many intimations that they are speaking not merely of the ideal menorah described in the holy writings, but of the menorah as it was used in synagogues and on graves.[144]

C. CONCLUSIONS

As we look back over the evidence we have been considering, it becomes clear that a highly suggestive parallel has been set up. On the one hand we have the Jews putting the mysterious menorah into the Temple of Zerubbabel, writing it back into the law of Sinai,

---

142. One familiar with Plato sees in the symbolism of the cave throughout the *Zohar* a figure of life on earth, just as it is in the *Republic*, VII. Thus the lighting of the lights in the cave of the *Zohar* would refer to the ritualistic lighting of the lights on earth, to which the passage gives a metaphysical explanation and reference.

143. See *Zohar*, ET, V, 208: *beha 'alothka* ("when thou lightest") means literally "when thou makest ascend," the first applicable to the menorah, the second to incense. The whole discussion recalls the use of spices in place of incense, and the union of light and wine in the Habdalah. See below, p. 202.

144. I do not at this point consider the Christian use of the menorah, because, as a symbol in art, it was not used at all in the early church. The early Fathers allegorized it as the figure of Christ the Light of the world, or of the Church, but the design itself had no appeal to Christians as a symbol, since

it was too completely the property of Judaism, though it was often used, especially in Eastern Catholicism, on the altar. One lamp from Carthage, which has been a subject of much dispute, shows Christ with the menorah in reverse at his feet; see above, III, fig. 957. This has usually been taken to signify Christ trampling upon Judaism, but it seems a conclusive argument to me that if Christ were crushing the menorah, it would be lying horizontally under his feet: I feel rather that the design shows not the humiliation of Judaism, but the fact that historically Judaism was the foundation of Christianity. Christ is frequently identified with the menorah by the Church Fathers, and an inscription from Africa shows the menorah adapted as the cross: see above, II, 102. On the whole subject see Martigny, *Dictionnaire des antiquités chrétiennes*, 1877, 115 f.; Leclercq in CL, III, 215–220; also Loeb in *REJ*, XIX (1889), 102.

and then taking it out from the Temple again for use in synagogues, on graves and amulets, and, presumably, in the home. It was thus taken out in spite of the fact that the rabbis forbade its use in the seven-branched form. In parallel with this usage, we have literary allegories of the menorah which show that at least from the time of Philo on, if not from the time of Zerubbabel and Zechariah, the menorah was significant for Jewish piety in a great variety of senses, but essentially as a mystic symbol of Light and Life—God present and manifest in the world—through which the Jew hoped for immortality. To the more mystical it was also the illumination from the supernal Mother. No direct evidence has appeared which would take all that meaning over from Philo, Josephus, the Midrash, and the *Zohar*, and make it the meaning which consciously was in the minds of all those who put the menorah on tombstones and into synagogues through those centuries. Since we do not have a specific statement from an authoritative Jew of the time, it will always require a leap to go from these literary interpretations to the menorahs actually used in the synagogues and depicted on monuments.

With all this literary evidence in mind, it will be illuminating to return for a moment to a few of the monuments. We have seen the menorah repeatedly identified as the image of God. The literary sources have suggested that the side lights are to be so oriented that they set off the central light, and this we have seen to be true in regard to a number of representations of the menorah in antiquity. Even more directly inspired by the symbolism of the important central light is the menorah as depicted in the synagogue at Nawa in Palestine, whose central light is elevated, and marked by a "round object," here used as the mystic sign of divine Light [145] so beloved by the Jews—marked as the supreme light of the seven. This design makes no attempt at realism: it is the allegorical meaning of the writers in direct representation. Indeed, we have three instances in which all seven of the lights are represented by such disks,[146] while on a great number of little clay lamps the central light of a menorah is made into the actual light of the lamp.[147] It is even more striking to recall the shrine at Sheikh Ibreiq [148] enclosing a menorah and balanced by another aedicula whose central object is a Torah shrine, or a pair of closed doors, approached by seven steps. This arrangement reminded us of the two temples balancing each other in Dura, one of which is likewise a closed shrine whose stripes of color suggest seven steps, while the other has a large menorah at its center. These two shrines at Dura long ago associated themselves in my mind with the two formulations of mystic ascent found in Philo, one of which has the menorah as its chief symbol.[149]

From Sheikh Ibreiq also we recall the man in armor, carved in deep relief, who wears a menorah on his head.[150] In discussing this figure,[151] it seemed to us that the menorah was a symbol of the warrior's sanctity, and notably a symbol of sanctity in terms of light. We have come upon a similar notion in the midrashic statement that the menorah,

145. See above, III, fig. 621; cf. I, 237. We shall discuss the "round object" in later volumes.
146. See III, figs. 334 f., 341.
147. See III, figs. 262, 338; cf. I, 158.
148. See III, figs. 53, 55, 62; cf. I, 93–95.

149. I refer to the formulation of the "Mystery of Aaron" as contrasted with that of the "Higher Mystery" in my *By Light, Light*.
150. See above, III, fig. 56.
151. See I, 92.

representing the Torah as light, is the crown of good deeds, though I doubt that there is any connection between this statement and the carving in the tomb.

If, then, it is a leap from the allegories of the menorah to the representations of the menorah on the graves and in the synagogues, it is by no means a desperate leap. From what evidence there is, we must suppose that little, probably, as the elaborations of Philo and the Midrash were grasped by most of the Jews who put the menorah on their graves, or on the little oil lamps they took with them in burial, those who knew and understood, in this era, saw in the lampstand a true symbol of God, the source of their Light, their Law, the Tree of Life, the astral path to God, the mediating female principle, the Mother, who brought men to the Light and who brought the Light to men. For the human soul as a microcosm ascends by this path to immortality in terms of metaphysical-mystical conceptions, or to immortality in terms of the Messianic Age. The menorah concentrates all Jewish hopes as it manifests God's mercy and forgiveness and his incomparable provision for salvation. It was a popular symbol precisely because, like all good symbols, it could be given so many interpretations.

Most of my readers will have anticipated the thought with which I must close this chapter—namely, that the symbolism of the lights has by no means entirely disappeared from Jewish life. Now still the lighting of lights is the beautiful opening of every Jewish Sabbath and festival, and the lighting of the lights is one of the few ritualistic acts performed by the mothers of Israel. Were I a Jew who from infancy had watched his mother, on Sabbath after Sabbath, light the lights, touch her eyes, and bless God, and then had watched my wife doing this before my own children, and finally had seen my daughters do it also, I could think of no symbol of hope more appropriate to put upon my grave than a menorah.[152] The conception thus symbolized is explicitly illustrated in a Christian version. Figure 10 [153] reproduces a design from a medieval manuscript whose illuminations have long been recognized as implying a Jewish original. It shows the menorah in cabbalistic elaboration, with the supernal Mother, crowned and enthroned, at the top. She has of course in this Christianized version become the Virgin Mary, but she is in a place —above the menorah—where no Christian would have thought of putting her without some Jewish suggestion. "Here the Community of Israel receives the light whilst the supernal Mother is crowned, and all the lamps are illumined from her," we have heard the *Zohar* say. I suspect that most of the Jews of the Roman period who put the menorah with its lights into their synagogues and upon their graves knew very well what they were doing.

This is the conception that seems still to be symbolized as the mothers in Israel give light to the candles, and then touch their own lights, their eyes. In this rite all the hope which men for ages have found in God, in light, and in the Great Mother, still carries on

152. The basic irrelevance of many of the explanations of ritualistic acts propounded in orthodox tradition is well illustrated in the reasons given for this ceremony by Samuel M. Segal, *The Sabbath Book*, 1942, 21. He says that women must kindle the lights because Eve, in committing the first sin, extinguished the spiritual light of the world, hence woman's kindling of the lights is a penance; also that woman is the housekeeper, hence she must see to the lights.

153. From an illustration in Cosmas Indicopleustes; Riedin, op. cit., 260, fig. 269.

as a value in Judaism, little as Jews trained in the rabbinic tradition have been taught consciously to recognize it. Bella Chagall has described the impression which the ceremony made on her as a little girl:

[Mother] quickly washes her face and hands, puts on a clean lace collar that she always wears on this night, and approaches the candlesticks like a new mother. With a match in her hand she lights one candle after another. All the seven candles begin to quiver. The flames blaze into mother's face. As though an enchantment were falling upon her, she lowers her eyes. Slowly, three times in succession, she encircles the candles with both her arms; she seems to be taking them into her heart. And with the candles her weekday worries melt away.

She blesses the candles. She whispers quiet benedictions through her fingers and they add heat to the flames. Mother's hands over the candles shine like the tablets of the decalogue over the holy ark.

I push closer to her. I want to get behind her blessing hands myself. I seek her face. I want to look into her eyes. They are concealed behind her spread-out fingers.

I light my little candle by mother's candle. Like her, I raise my hands and through them, as through a gate, I murmur into my little candle flame the words of benediction that I catch from my mother.

My candle, just lighted, is already dripping. My hands circle it to stop its tears.

I hear mother in her benedictions mention now one name, now another. She names father, the children, her own father and mother. Now my name too has fallen into the flame of the candles. My throat becomes hot.

"May the Highest One give them his blessing!" concludes mother, dropping her hands at last.

"Amen," I say in a choking voice, behind my fingers.

"Good Shabbes!" mother calls out loudly. Her face, all opened, looks purified, I think that it has absorbed the illumination of the Sabbath candles.[154]

The writer's husband, Marc Chagall, has caught the mood in his drawing.[155]

154. Bella Chagall, *Burning Lights*, New York, 1946, 48 f. Quoted by permission of the publishers, Schocken Books, Inc.

155. From ibid., frontispiece; reproduced by permission of Schocken Books, Inc. For a woman's hands blessing the lights in a representation on her own tombstone, see Rahel Wischnitzer-Bernstein, *Symbole und Gestalten der jüdischen Kunst*, 1935, 88; cf. pp. 87–89. The effect is by implication to make the dead woman into a universal principle, eternally giving blessing. It seems to me no coincidence that the ancient ritualistic use of sex still survives in the old requirement that on the evening of a Sabbath or festival (that is, after the wife has lighted the lights), the husband must have intercourse with her. I should guess that it is with his wife as the Light of God that he has relations.

CHAPTER FIVE

The Torah Shrine

I N S P I T E O F the central position of the Torah shrine in modern Jewish worship, those who know modern and even medieval Judaism are little prepared to see how the shrine was used in designs on ancient Jewish tombstones and synagogues. Judaism of the rabbinic tradition feels the sanctity of the shrine almost entirely in terms of the sacred scrolls within it. In the ancient period, by contrast, the shrine seems to have had sanctity in its own right, wherein it was much like the Ark of the Covenant, whose function, to be sure, had been to hold the sacred tokens of God's dealing with the Israelites in the desert; but the Ark was itself a sacred object sanctifying the objects within it as much as they sanctified the Ark.

The Torah shrines of the first centuries of our era are in structure and symbolism closely similar to the other shrine forms of antiquity, and we must approach the Jewish shrine from the more general point of view. In describing the synagogues, their general plan, their façades and screens, the designs of the windows, as well as the shrines depicted not only in synagogues but also on graves, lamps, glasses, and ossuaries, we have had to make some reference to the significance of the shrine form, but a review of the relevant material as a whole, and of its implications, is definitely needed.

A. THE SHRINE IN ANTIQUITY

T HE STRUCTURE of the Jewish shrine, we have said, is that of ancient shrines in general. The shrine presents itself in two forms, a simple one with a single opening, and a more complicated one with triple or multiple openings. Both forms go so far back in history that it is impossible to say either that the one is originally an elaboration of the other, or that the first is a simplification of the second. Without prejudice as to which of the two is the earlier, it will be best to begin discussion with the simpler one.

A shrine in the ancient world was a little temple, designed to be the house of a god. In modern times one may put a holy image, say of the Virgin, simply upon a pedestal in one's house or garden, or beside a road, but the image appears as though more reverently treated when it is set in a shrine. The shrine is sanctified by the image, and at the same time itself sanctifies the image. The same feeling appears to have been strong from the earliest periods of antiquity. The gods of ancient Mesopotamia, for example, are presented often enough simply as figures complete in themselves, or as receiving the homage of human beings, but very commonly indeed they are put within a shrine and one has the impression that their sanctity is thereby enhanced. Figures 8,[1] 9,[2] 11,[3] 12,[4] and 13 [5] show a group of such early shrines (Jamdat Nasr period): here we feel at once that the shrines in themselves indicate a divine presence, even more strongly than do the animal or human figures beside them, though only the shrine in fig. 12 is possibly designed to mark its contents.

Even in these shrines, however, we see certain details to which it would seem strained to give importance if we did not find them so persistent in later centuries. A little gable is over the door, or, in several cases, appears as a zigzag in a sort of entablature. On two of the shrines there are rows of little round bosses, the counterpart of which will appear in "round objects" on Jewish Torah shrines. The seal in fig. 14 [6] has at the upper right, beside the shrine, a peculiar upright object ending in a volute at the top; a streamer, like a veil, hangs down part way along the standard. This device, which also appears on what are called altars, fig. 16,[7] would, if drawn in a horizontal position, recall the volute of an Ionic capital. Andrae called it a "gatepost with streamer." [8] Frankfort noted that it was "the prototype of the written name-sign of Inanna, the Mother Goddess," as she is mentioned in later religious texts.[9] In view of the interpretation of the shrine to which we shall come, it is interesting to see the door thus early marked as associated with the Mother Goddess. The volute with streamers long persisted, and we shall see its crude descendants as acroteria on Jewish shrines; apparently, then, the form had great religious value. That the same feature should be associated with both shrines and altars seems to me quite natural. Actually it is often extremely difficult to distinguish between altars and shrines; in the case of the seal just described I am not at all sure that the form on the bull's back is an altar, as von der Osten calls it, and not a shrine, possibly two shrines, each with three openings.[10] Anyway, we have the voluted object itself beside a shrine in at least one case; probably other cases exist.

The shrine in fig. 13 has a door with three panels: thus it seems likely that the paneled

1. From Edith Porada, *The Collection of the Pierpont Morgan Library*, 1948, plate v, fig. 22 (*Corpus of Ancient Near Eastern Seals in North American Collections*, I. Bollingen Series XIV).

2. From ibid., fig. 23.

3. From ibid., fig. 24.

4. From ibid., fig. 25.

5. From ibid., plate I, fig. 3e.

6. From L. Delaporte, *Catalogue des cylindres orientaux . . . du Musée du Louvre*, II, 1923, plate 63, fig. 5 (A 27).

7. From Osten, *Newell*, plate III, 22 (courtesy Oriental Inst., Univ. of Chicago); cf. p. 139, where this form is discussed as a "standard." The

device is very common: see, for other uses of it, Henri Frankfort, *Cylinder Seals*, 1939, plates IIIa, e, and VI.

8. W. Andrae, *Das Gotteshaus und die Urformen des Bauens im alten Orient*, 1930, 49; see plate II.

9. Frankfort, 15; cf. Porada, Text, 3.

10. Osten, *Newell*, 117, has a page of "altars"; in many instances among these, the identification of the form as an altar seems to me quite arbitrary. Cf. Ernest Mackay, *Report on Excavations at Jemdet Nasr, Iraq*, II, 1931, plate LXXX, 2 (Field Museum of Natural History, *Anthropology, Memoirs*, I, ii), illustrating a device that Miss B. L. Goff has noted as another ancestor of the acroterium.

door was also early important. Figures 15 [11] and 17 [12] show two seals on which the shrine is primarily the paneled door; on one of them is a four-petaled rosette that Miss Porada calls a "star spade." Such a shrine or door sometimes also has wings (fig. 18 [13]), which Frankfort followed Ward in plausibly connecting with the gate of the rising sun, with Ishtar, and with the Jewish "wings of the morning." [14] We shall see that the mizrach of Judaism, the tablet hung on the east wall of a room to show the direction in which one should pray, still has primarily a design of doorways. The wings may also have influenced the form of the later acroteria.

Closely related to such shrines is the right-angled or rounded frame within which a divine figure stands, figs. 19 [15] and 20.[16] This, especially the round-topped frame, is said to be of Syrian origin, but an Assyrian divinity would be framed in the water of a "spouting vase." To this vase we shall return in the next volume, but it is interesting to note figs. 21 [17] and 23.[18] Figure 22 [19] shows a pair of what Miss Porada calls "manikins" each under such a rounded canopy. Ward [20] thought that when a king is under such a canopy it indicates deification, and recalled that Assyrian kings liked to place sculptured portraits of themselves in niches near the scenes of their conquests. He might have added that we have been putting statues of saints and heroes in niches ever since, so generally that the expression, "A niche is waiting for him," is a colloquial reference to immortality. I should guess therefore that the "manikins" of fig. 22 are deified human beings shown beside the gods on the seal.

The round-topped shrine and the gabled shrine were at times combined. This was done by putting an arcuated lintel above the opening, beneath the gable. I do not recall a Mesopotamian example of the round-topped shrine under a gable, but fig. 24 [21] shows a round-topped shrine within a rectangular one, and we shall see such combinations again shortly.

These forms were used in the neighborhood of Palestine, if not in Palestine itself, from early times. Figure 25 [22] shows such a shrine from early Phoenicia. The device has often been published as a "Phoenician house," but with its little image it seems clearly a shrine.

11. From Porada, op. cit., plate xxiv, fig. 217. See, for a fine collection of such paneled doors, L. Legrain, *Ur Excavations*, III: *Archaic Seal Impressions*, 1936, plate 40.

12. From Porada, op. cit., fig. 218.

13. From ibid., plate xxxv, fig. 225. Cf. ibid., figs. 222*e*–233*e*.

14. Ps. cxxxix, 9. Frankfort, op. cit., 128; W. H. Ward, *The Seal Cylinders of Western Asia*, 1910, 125.

15. From Porada, op. cit., plate cxlv, fig. 960*e*.

16. From Osten, *Brett*, plate ix, fig. 90 (courtesy Oriental Inst., Univ. of Chicago); cf. p. 14. See also Frankfort, plate xliv *d*.

17. From E. D. Van Buren, *The Flowing Vase and the God with Streams*, Berlin, 1933, plate iii,

fig. 10; cf. p. 38. The seal is at the British Museum (no. 89771).

18. From a photograph kindly sent me by the Semitic Museum of Harvard University. A drawing was published by Ward, op. cit., 217, fig. 656. Cf. Van Buren, op. cit., 39.

19. From Porada, op. cit., plate cxliii, 946*e*. See also ibid., fig. 978 E, and Frankfort, op. cit., plate xxi *a*.

20. Op. cit., 225, in commenting on his fig. 682.

21. From L. Delaporte, *Catalogue du Musée Guimet: Cylindres orientaux*, 1909, fig. 117 (Annales du Musée Guimet, XXXIII; used with permission of Presses Universitaires de France).

22. From Marcel Dieulafoy, *L'Art antique de la Perse*, 1884/9, II, plate xviii, 1.

Another small shrine from Syria or Palestine (Second Iron Age), fig. 26,[23] was apparently sacred to Astarte, to judge by the dove with spread wings at the top; probably her image originally stood within it. A new feature emerges in both of these: the doorway is framed by a pair of columns with "Ionic volutes." One wonders whether these columns are not a development of the older voluted "staff with streamers." But it is a question whether the shrine hallows the image, or the image the shrine, so definitely do we feel the sanctity of both objects.

The importance of such forms in Egypt in early times likewise needs little more than mention. Figure 27 [24] shows a shrine on a boat in a design from a prehistoric tomb in Egypt. Presumably it is the boat by which, throughout Egyptian history, the soul goes into the next world. Probably the soul itself is conceived as being in this round-topped shrine, but again, as in Babylonia, the sanctity of the shrine seems primary and self-sufficient. Indeed, in fig. 28 [25] the paneled doors reappear. How this feeling regarding the sanctity of an enclosure evolved to create the great temples of Egypt, and the elaborate tombs, it is quite beyond my power, or our purpose here, to trace out.

The force of the "sacred enclosure" is definitely increased by size and magnificence: to understand this, one has only to recall how the most irreverent feel awed when they walk into one of the great cathedrals of Europe. The importance of portals in all of this architecture cannot be overstated. One is reminded of the great pylons before the Egyptian temples,[26] and the way in which the sanctity of a god is indicated by depicting his pylon behind him,[27] and, in tombs, the emphasis upon doors, leading even to the peculiar convention of the false door. The pyramids themselves are orientated to this symbolism, as witnessed by fig. 29,[28] picturing a shrine of Ptahmose, a high priest of Memphis.

The power of the symbol in itself, however, is reflected much better in the simpler representations. For when there is no concomitant of size or display, the enclosure speaks its language much more directly. Figure 31 [29] presents a single example from among a number of such designs; it is on a wooden stele dating from the XXIId Dynasty. Unrelated to an actual building, with no structural function—being just a doorway or shrine as such, used to frame a sacred object—this form appears everywhere in Egyptian remains. I give only a few random examples. Figure 33 [30] shows a sarcophagus from late dynastic Egypt, with a rounded top; the gods stand each under a little round arch, and the corner posts of the shrine are built up to serve as acroteria at the bases of the larger arch. The importance of the little arches is made unmistakable by the fact that each of them has the same type of acroteria. In the later Saitic period the dead Apis is shown within a shrine

23. From Iliffe in *QDAP*, XI (1944/5), plate XXI.

24. From J. E. Quibell and F. W. Green, *Hierakonpolis*, 1902, II, plate LXXVII (Egyptian Research Account, V).

25. From Erman, *Relig. Ägypt.*, 180, fig. 76. Erman says that the shrine is from the temple of Abydos, but gives no further information: cf. ibid., p. 329, fig. 140.

26. See ibid., 168 f., figs. 67 f.; cf. p. 352, fig. 149; plate 9, at p. 368.

27. E.g., ibid., plate 5, at p. 142.

28. From ibid., 280, fig. 108.

29. From J. E. Quibell, *The Ramesseum*, 1896, plate XXI, 12; cf. p. 11 (Egyptian Research Account [II]). See plate XX, and the tombstone of a Syrian queen in Erman, op. cit., 347, fig. 147.

30. From Erman, *Relig. Ägypt.*, 287, fig. 113.

on a boat, fig. 30,[31] and here the shrine has an outer and an inner doorway [32]—four columns in an arrangement often revived later, though the Greeks developed a better way of presenting the notion, i.e., the arcuated lintel within a gable. But it is clear that an idea, a symbolic motive, is producing the form, and expressing itself in it, rather than that an architectural form is by association becoming symbolic. From the Greco-Roman period, but still basically Egyptian, is the shrine of Harpocrates shown in fig. 32,[33] while the shrine form is used to consecrate and give immortality to a mummy when put on the covering of the feet, as in fig. 34.[34]

From what source the form came into Jewish usage in the Greco-Roman period seems to me now impossible to determine. It is presumably a Greco-Egyptian version of the motif that appears in the shrines in Marisa,[35] but we cannot guess how much the paintings in Marisa influenced the Jews. It is quite clear that the first important occurrence of the shrine form in the Jewish art we are studying was a part of, or derived from, the general Syrian adaptation of the hellenized version of the symbol.

That the Greeks used the form for temples and shrines and many other purposes has recently been set forth in a careful study.[36] But as we examine the form our point comes out rather clearly—namely, that the shrine as such, or the façade isolated from the shrine, was used to consecrate and immortalize human beings as well as to house gods or mark their sanctity. The ultimate lineal descendant of this device is a convention already mentioned, the niche in which a statue is placed to enhance its dignity—a convention which went from classical to Gothic architecture without the least change in value.

B. THE FAÇADE

ONE FORM which emerges in the hellenistic period, with early ancestry and precedents, to be sure, but with strictly fresh emphasis, is the threefold entrance, or façade with three

31. From ibid., 323, fig. 133.

32. It is only on second glance that we see that this is the idea behind the Egyptian shrine shown ibid., 173, fig. 71.

33. From ibid., 393, fig. 166.

34. From ibid., 411, fig. 175c. Cf. the child's sarcophagus, ibid., 410, fig. 174.

35. See above, III, figs. 8, 12, 16.

36. Elizabeth Hazelton Haight, *The Symbolism of the House Door in Classical Poetry*, 1950. I have not attempted to work the contents of this book into the substance of my argument. Miss Haight makes little reference to structural design, except in regard to the door of entrance to the stage in Greek drama, though at the end she shows herself quite aware of the importance of the pictorial material, and promises to bring out a further study based upon it. But from literary allusions she has found (pp. 147 f.) that the door was in the first instance a "door of

reality," "the symbol of sex-love, for the door of maidenhood, which must be forced, for the door of the home, which must be built and protected. So the door may stand for all the integrity of family life, for the hospitality of the house, or for the violation of hospitality from without or from within: the door opened, the door closed."

Also, there are "doors of fancy's flight," "of escape through education or religion and doors of closure on secluded wife or imprisoned father, or across the pathway between earth and heaven. The mystic door of heaven . . . the indubitable door of hell."

In drama the door became a person, addressed in serenades, curses, and the like, and then even had a speaking part. Anyone interested in the symbolism of the door will find rich material and interpretation in this book which, like the present study, is essentially only a single chapter in, or starting point for, a history of the symbol.

openings of one kind or another. We must stop for a moment to consider some of the important manifestations of the form, though its history cannot be attempted.

The façade with three entrances made its earliest appearance, so far as I know, in Egypt, where it was devised, interestingly enough, not for temples but for tombs. Figure 35 shows a tomb of the Vth Dynasty—perhaps 2500 B.C.—as I photographed it beside the pyramids of Gizeh. Another example, more frequently reproduced, the tomb at Beni Hasan, fig. 36,[37] is of much later date. It has columns amazingly like the later Doric columns of Greece; but this sort of façade was not frequently used in Egypt, where the form by no means became standard for the entrance to a temple, as it did elsewhere.[38] It did persist, however, in Egypt and North Africa generally into hellenistic times. Figure 37 shows a hypogeum of the third century B.C. in Alexandria, the rock-cut subterranean tomb of Moustapha Pasha. Figure 38 shows a rock-cut tomb in Cyrene, probably of pre-Christian date, and we have seen a similar hellenistic tomb in Barca, Cyrenaica.[39]

In Greece this façade is by no means unknown; it occurs in the famous temple of Nike on the Acropolis at Athens.[40] But the peristyle commonly built round Greek temples obscures the fact that the temples proper were ordinarily entered by three doors, as in the case of the temple of Theseus in Athens, fig. 39.[41] This was by no means structurally or artistically necessary, as the Parthenon itself reveals,[42] and seems to have become so common a feature rather because earlier Greek shrines in all probability had usually had three entrances, and the temple is merely the shrine elaborated by putting the peristyle about it.

That Roman temples should have imitated this Greek custom is quite to be expected,[43] but there is considerable evidence of an earlier use of the façade with three openings on Etruscan temples, as in fig. 40.[44] We have often remarked a curious similarity between Etruscan and Syrian remains; this similarity is notable here also. For in the Nabatean temples built before Roman times the threefold entrance was of the greatest importance, and it is apparently from these that Jews got their immediate inspiration, as did the Romans when they built in Syria.[45] That the Roman usage was not merely conventional

37. From Percy E. Newberry, *Beni Hasan*, I, 1893, frontis. (*Archaeological Survey of Egypt*, I). The tomb has been published often: cf. F. M. Simpson, *A History of Architectural Development*, 1905, I, fig. 6, at p. 8. Newberry dates the tomb in the XIIth Dynasty, the middle of the third millennium; R. Pfeiffer, in *An Encyclopedia of World History* (ed. by William L. Langer), 1940, 23, dates this dynasty between 2000 and 1788 B.C.

38. We recall as exceptional instances the little temples of Elephantine and Philae: P. Planat, *Encyclopédie de l'architecture*, I, ii, 393, fig. 21, and plate LXXIX, at p. 394.

39. See above, III, fig. 98.

40. Cf. the temple at Rhamnus: Fergusson, *Hist. Arch.*, I, 269, fig. 148.

41. From Planat, op. cit., I, ii, 414, fig. 4. See also the plan of the temple of Diana at Ephesus (ibid., 413, fig. 3), and that of the temple of Poseidon (ibid., 412, fig. 1). One recalls also the two porches of the Erechtheum (ibid., 416, fig. 8), and the temple at Selinus: Fergusson, *Hist. Arch.*, I, 270, fig. 151; François Benoit, *L'Architecture: Antiquité*, I, 1911, 280, fig. 184.

42. Planat, op. cit., 415, fig. 6.

43. E.g., ibid., 420, fig. 2; 421, fig. 3.

44. From ibid., 420, fig. 1. Cf. the reconstruction in Fergusson, *Hist., Arch.*, I, 292, fig. 167.

45. This feature, as well as its effect upon early Christian churches in Syria, is very clearly expounded by H. C. Butler, "Nabatean Temple Plans and the Plans of Syrian Churches," *Studien*

could be demonstrated at length, but a single example, fig. 41,[46] suffices. Here, in an elaborate composite of symbols, to which we shall often return, the hopes of future life of a family are clearly presented with repetitive emphasis in the four columns and three openings, and the paneled door, opened or closed.

In Syria and elsewhere in the Near East the same façade was used constantly upon tombs. How far back the practice goes we do not know, but this façade, or at least the tetrastyle porch, was put on the tomb of Darius, fig. 42.[47] It appears also on a tomb in Lycia, fig. 43,[48] and on one at Yapouldak in Phrygia, fig. 44,[49] dating not long after his time. In the Greco-Roman period such a façade became very popular throughout Syria. There its applications range from a simple entrance, fig. 45,[50] to the elaborate rock carvings especially associated with Petra, figs. 46,[51] 47.[52] The tomb shown in fig. 48 [53] interests me, for in this instance the façade was never completed. I doubt that the builder ever intended to finish it, for the carving was begun at the top, and as a result was much more difficult to execute than if it had been started at the bottom. It seems to me that the owner wanted the symbolism of the façade on the tomb for its own sake, though he knew from the beginning that he could not afford to carve the whole front.

The façade form appears to me also to emerge in its own right upon tombs built in several stories. Usually these consisted of a basement which was the sepulcher proper, and a shrine form built above it, while above this in turn there was often a second shrine or a pyramid or cone.[54] Figure 50 [55] illustrates the form in its fullest development. More sharply presented is the façade on a tomb at Mylasa in Caria, fig. 51.[56] The convention

zur Kunst des Ostens (Joseph Strzygowski *Festschrift*), 1925, 9–16. See also A. Kammerer, *Pétra et la Nabatène*, Atlas, 1930, plate 115.

46. A fragment from the tomb of the Haterii, at the Lateran Museum, Rome (Alinari photograph, P.L. no. 6387). It has often been published.

47. From Dieulafoy, op. cit., I, plate x; cf. III, plates I, IV. See also Planat, op. cit., I, ii, 330, 332, and Fergusson, *Hist. Arch.*, I, 204, fig. 92. Fergusson suggests (p. 203) that this is a reproduction of the façade of the palace of Darius, transferred thence to his tomb as his eternal palace. For the palace of Cyrus, see Dieulafoy, op. cit., I, plate XII; for the palace of Darius, ibid., II, plate XIII. Palaces and tombs indeed have at least this feature in common, and I should suspect that the façade on the palace attributed divinity to the king within.

48. From Dieulafoy, op. cit., I, plate xv. Cf. Charles Texier, *Asie Mineure*, 1862, plate 25 (top); Fergusson, *Hist. Arch.*, I, 237, fig. 121.

49. From Benoit, op. cit., I, 217, fig. 143, vi; cf. iv and v.

50. From Léon de Laborde, *Journey through Arabia Petraea*, etc., 1836, 185. Cf. C. de Vogüé,

Syrie centrale: Architecture, 1865/77, II, plates 82, 84, 88, 91 f.

51. Published by courtesy of the Palestine Archeological Museum (no. 12.482).

52. From de Laborde, op. cit., plate facing p. 168; cf. plates facing pp. 185, 191. Tombs with three openings at Petra can be quickly reviewed in Kammerer, op. cit., plates 40, 44, 46 f., 69, 71, 107, 126.

53. A tomb at Petra; from de Laborde, op. cit., 156.

54. The form seems to be a combination of the façade with such simpler use of the round shrine as appears in the monument of Lysikrates at Athens: Benoit, op. cit., 288, fig. 190.

55. From ibid., 470, fig. 313: a so-called tomb (perhaps it is a monument in the form of a tomb) at Saint-Rémy in France. Our façade appears on the second story. In the monument of Igel, near Treves (Fergusson, *Hist. Arch.*, I, 362, fig. 232) the arch has become a circular ornament. See also the tomb of Dugga, in Fergusson, *Hist. Arch.*, I, 372, fig. 243, and the tomb of Theron, near Agrigentum, in Pirro Marconi, *Agrigento*, 1929, 125 f., figs. 79 f.

56. From Texier, op. cit., plate 27.

went even to India, where, notwithstanding other modifications, the three openings between four columns persisted.[57] Such Jewish structures as the "Tomb of Absalom" [58] are clearly adaptations of this form in which the basement has disappeared, while the four columns still stand on each side in the lower story.

Incidentally, while the material here discussed is primarily from the Near East and from Greco-Roman civilizations, the form appears also in China, with no indication, to my knowledge, of Western influence. Figure 52 [59] shows what Sirén calls the "P'ai-lou or memorial gateway built of wood, at the lake of the Summer Palace, Peking. These characteristic structures, usually of wood, mark the entrance to a sacred or beautiful spot or commemorate some event or person." The basic form and its value are clearly identical with what we are seeing in the West.

The façade had another interesting function among the Romans, one which has been actively perpetuated to present times—namely, when it was built without relation to any other structure and used as a form in itself in the triumphal arch. Discussion of the triumphal procession and of the arches has been very extensive.[60] It has been pointed out that the custom of making an army pass between the parts of the divided body of a sacrificial victim, or between sticks, was a rite of purification after bloodshed or defeat even among the Hittites,[61] and that in Roman usage the army was similarly purified and given a rebirth, certainly with religious implications, by the preparatory sacrifices, by the crowns of Victory, and supremely by passing through an arch.[62] Though the practices may be very old in their details, and the ancestor of the arch of the Romans may have been simply a pair of posts joined by a crossbeam, like that of the Hittites, it is important for our purpose that at the height of Rome's splendor the purificatory structure identified itself with the old shrine façade. While the arch forms kept the Roman character, the Greek tetrastyle superimposed upon them makes them also a presentation of openings between columns.[63]

Quite apart from association with triumphal processions, the arch seems to have become a sanctifying instrument in itself. The Arch of Titus, for example, was built after Titus' death, was dedicated to him as deified, and its sculptures portray his apotheosis. It had nothing to do with triumphal processions of Titus, and a great many of the later

57. Planat, op. cit., 351.

58. See above, III, fig. 28.

59. From Oswald Sirén, "Architecture," in R. L. Hobson et al., *The Romance of Chinese Art*, Garden City, N. Y. [n.d.], plate facing p. 46, 1. (Used with permission of *Encyclopaedia Britannica*.)

60. A complete review of the arches of antiquity, with discussion of the origin of the form and its meaning, is given by H. Kähler in PW, Ser. II, Halbband XIII, 1939, 373–493. His review of earlier studies seems to me complete and very judicious. W. Ehlers has made a similar review of the *triumphus*, ibid., 493–511.

61. O. Masson, "A propos d'un ritual hittite," *RHR*, CXXXVII (1950), 5–25. It has been re-

called that similar rites were used in adoption ceremonies which Diodorus Siculus calls "imitation of true birth": see T. Zachariae, "Scheingeburt," *Zeitschrift des Vereins für Volkskunde*, XX (1910), 141–181.

62. F. Noack, "Triumph und Triumphbogen," *Vorträge der Bibliothek Warburg*, *1925–1926*, 1928, 195.

63. Kähler, op. cit., 480, says that the majority of arches have only one opening: the ratio is almost 6 to 1 in the Latin West, 4 to 3 in the Greek East. Very rarely they have two openings. But a large proportion of the arches with one opening present the value of what Noack calls *Dreitorigkeit* by means of columns or side windows.

arches were likewise posthumously erected. Lehmann has suggested that the ashes of Titus were put into his arch, so that the structure was his immortalizing tomb.[64] Kähler thinks that Titus was not buried in the arch, yet agrees that it "is to be regarded as a memorial glorifying the apotheosized emperor." [65] On the Arch of Trajan in Benevento the Emperor is represented in the reliefs directly as a deity.[66] Noack seems to me right in saying that even when the arches appear to have been intended as ornamental structures in provincial cities, they did not lose their religious character.[67] Kähler [68] has questioned the probability of any essential connection between the arches and the ceremonies and processions of triumph, and has apparently made an excellent case. In his view the arches were primarily designed as memorials so closely associated with deification that in imperial times they came to be reserved for honoring emperors alone. His excellent summary of the material, and of the interpretations of his predecessors, concludes with a sound discussion of the arch as a symbol, and thus as a device of apotheosis. This agrees exactly with our explanation of the façade in general. At the end, however, he seems to me to have lost sight of the basic fact that the arch is a portal in the form of a shrine, or of a shrine entrance, and that it is a thing to pass under. This primary element in the form cannot be overlooked, I believe, in the final appraisal of its meaning.

Kähler gives on a single page a highly valuable collection of drawings showing the variety of forms in which the arch was built.[69] Here at a glance one can see that a few of the earlier arches consisted simply of an opening to be passed through, but that soon the columns of the shrine appeared on them; eventually four columns, whether with one or with three actual openings between them, became an invariable feature. For example, in the Arch of Titus, fig. 53,[70] the four columns are so completely subordinate to the great central arch, and to the structure as a whole, that one does not sense their symbolic importance until it is recalled that they reflect this significant tradition. In this arch the side entrances are only false windows, but with these the impression of three openings is still preserved. In the arches of Septimius Aurius and of Constantine, and in the arch at Orange in France, the side openings are presented as smaller arches, but the tetrastyle façade remains. The peculiar Arch of Janus Quadrifrons in Rome had six niches for statues on each side, but no columns, while the Arch of Augustus at Rimini, fig. 54,[71] brings in the alternative arrangement of an arch under a gable supported by two columns, a form to which we shall come in a moment. That the arch had symbolic force for the Romans we saw in fig. 41, especially in the arch with three openings pictured at the upper right, and this becomes clear again in fig. 55,[72] showing another piece from the same tomb.

64. "L'Arco di Tito," *Bullet. Commiss. Archeol.*, LXII (1934), 89–122.

65. Op. cit., 387.

66. Noack, op. cit., 198.

67. Op. cit., 169.

68. Op. cit., 488–493.

69. Op. cit., 485.

70. From William Knight, *The Arch of Titus and the Spoils of the Temple*, London, 1867, frontis.

71. From Planat, op. cit., 269, fig. 6. In the same work, all the arches mentioned in our discussion here, except the Marble Arch of London, are depicted in an article by Pierre Benouville (pp. 263–274). Cf. the Arch of Hadrian in Athens, illustrated in A. Baumeister, *Denkmäler des klassischen Altertums*, 1885, 286.

72. From Alinari photograph no. 29906, Rome. The stone is at the Lateran Museum in Rome.

The panel is traditionally supposed to depict "monuments on the Via Sacra," but if these were monuments on that street, which I doubt, they are certainly represented on the tomb for their symbolic value. In the "Arch of Isis" at the left we even feel the influence of what we shall see was the old tradition of the three openings for Father, Mother, Son, the holy trinity of paganism. On this one stone the motif of four columns with three openings is presented five times, certainly with reference to immortality.

The tradition persists in modern arches. The Arc du Carrousel in Paris and the Marble Arch in London have each the three openings and the tetrastyle façade, while the Arc de l'Etoile in Paris lacks the façade entirely. How close the symbolism of the triumphal arch was felt to be to that of the tomb is shown again in a tomb at Laodicea (Latakia) in western Syria, fig. 56,[73] where the whole pattern of the triumphal arch is clearly carried back to the grave, not functionally, but superficially, to symbolize the immortality of the occupant. The tetrastyle façade can no longer be considered simply as a representation of a temple: it is a symbol with value in itself, the value of giving immortality.

How profoundly the façades of Christian churches have been affected by this convention hardly needs to be elaborated. The columns of antiquity did not survive into medieval architecture, of course, but the basic conception that a sacred façade should present a gable having below it, preferably, three doors—in turn represented as arches—is obvious. In the church at Poitiers, fig. 57,[74] the façade is still recognizable, with the horned acroteria surviving as small turrets. The builders of the church needed actually only one entrance, but the form of the façade with three entrances was still obligatory. In the church of St. Stephen at Caen, fig. 59,[75] the value of the four columns is presented by the four buttresses at the front, and the acroteria have become towers. That church towers have such an ancestry is obscured in later Gothic structure when the two towers are pulled together by an open arcade, as in Notre Dame at Paris—an arcade which hides the gable behind it.[76] Of course churches often were given more than three doors, especially the churches of Italy; one thinks at once of the five entrances (seven arches) of St. Mark's in Venice, for example, and the seven arches on the cathedral at Pisa, though only three of them open as doors.[77] Indeed, given these basic elements of the façade, every imaginable variation has been used not only in façades,[78] but also in rood screens and windows, just as we

73. From de Vogüé, op. cit., I, plate 29. For Syrian triumphal arches, see Kammerer, op. cit., plates 99, 116.

74. From a photograph published by courtesy of the Archives Photographiques d'Art et d'Histoire (no. 2194). See also, for the cathedrals at Siena and Orvieto, Fergusson, *Hist. Arch.*, I, plates facing pp. 610, 616. On the façade of the cathedral at Piacenza there is even reminiscence of two of the columns of the earlier façade: A. Rosengarten, *Handbook of Architectural Styles*, 1878, 261.

75. From Fergusson, *Hist. Arch.*, II, 113.

76. In Notre Dame this quite conceals the gable;

in the cathedral at Chartres the gable is still visible from the front.

77. For St. Mark's, see Fergusson, *Hist. Arch.*, I, 533; for the cathedral of Pisa, ibid., I, 587. See also the five doors of San Miniato, ibid., I, 585.

78. We recall the three arches in a second story above the single arched doorway in the church at Loupiac (Fergusson, *Hist. Arch.*, II, 78) and the lateral entrance to the cathedral at Palermo (ibid., 28). The funerary value of the device seems freshly to recur in a tomb near the church of St. Pierre, Toulouse (ibid., 80).

saw in the case of synagogue windows.[79] I illustrate with a single window, fig. 58,[80] from the interior of San Vitale in Ravenna.

A conspicuous instance of the use of the façade simply for its symbolic value appears in two façades of the Orthodox Baptistery in Ravenna.[81] But the most obvious example is the iconostas of the Eastern churches. Of this we spoke in the first volume, when we suggested that the screen with three openings may have direct ancestry in the Jewish screens.[82] The Eastern ritual consists largely of bringing consecrated objects, or the blessing of the Presence, from behind this screen to the congregation, and something corresponding to this in Jewish worship has seemed the only reason for the special adyton in Jewish synagogues. Perhaps research into early phases of Eastern ritual would make the parallel more apparent, but meanwhile, from the standpoint of the vital continuity in use of the façade as a sacred form without structural purpose, the iconostas obviously is highly important. I show one further example here, fig. 60.[83] It is the iconostas in Sancta Sophia in Istanbul, built in the sixth century. The pseudo ciborium over the altar in a fifth-century church near Spoleto, fig. 61,[84] shows the form again used for consecration. In fig. 62 [85] we have the façade sanctifying a pulpit of sixth-century Ravenna; in fig. 63 [86] it sanctifies an eighth-century chancel in Nola.

This symbolism is still alive in our own usage, completely as it has faded from our awareness. Even today, with no remotest recollection of parallels from the past, we feel that a cemetery should be approached through an impressive gateway, arched or gabled. Whatever our conscious motivation, we usually build the entrance in this form. There is one such gateway, fig. 64,[87] presenting still a façade of three openings, quite near my study, and I pass it every day. It is the entrance to the Grove Street cemetery in New Haven, designed by Henry Austin and built in the late 1840's. Upon it is inscribed, "The dead shall be raised." That promise comes most appropriately from the old façade, which here as in the ancient tombs and triumphal arches has no structural function. The declaration primarily concerns the dead who lie buried behind the façade; it speaks the eternal hope of man to those who bring their dead through it, or who arrange to be borne through it themselves at the end. One could easily collect hundreds of parallels in which the façade, or the arch, sanctifies ground behind it and those buried in that ground. For example, burying the Unknown Soldier of France under the Arc de Triomphe in Paris seemed to everyone the surest way to guarantee him immortality.

The persistence of the form can be explained, as is often done, on the ground that it is "just" an effective presentation of an entrance, an expression of the human "urge" to

79. See above, III, figs. 462 f., 521.

80. From Fergusson, *Hist. Arch.*, I, plate facing p. 548. The Moslems took the device and used it in their own way: see, e.g., for the great mosque at Delhi, Planat, op. cit., 498, fig. 12. This type of window is very old. See the Mesopotamian example in Benoit, op. cit., 123, fig. 77, no. v, also the Syrian example in Kammerer, op. cit., plate 103.

81. Wilpert, *Mosaiken und Malereien*, III, plates 81 f.

82. See I, pp. 190, 203, 215, 230.

83. From Rohault de Fleury, *La Messe*, 1883, III, plate CCXLI; cf. plate CCXLIII.

84. From ibid., II, plate LXXXXI.

85. From ibid., III, plate CLXXVI.

86. From ibid., plate CCXXXI; see p. 22.

87. From a photograph of mine. See R. G. Osterweis, *Three Centuries of New Haven*, 1953, 272.

symmetry, or, as Jungians would probably put it, that it reflects the recurrent emergence of a basic form from the collective unconscious. My own position is between these. That three entrances make a more effective façade than two, four, five, or seven, can be felt, but not, I believe, rationally explained. It does seem to be better art: it appeals to us because it harmonizes better with a sense of propriety too deep within us for analysis. Indeed, the three openings seem to me to appear in façades so recurrently precisely as a projection from within us, rather than as an objectively "better" form. On the other hand, the idea that the form is a reality in itself, or in a collective mind apart from ourselves as individuals, goes too far into Platonism for me to feel content with it. The Jungian hypothesis that individuals derive such a form from participation in a larger common mentality seems to me to posit ultimately the same world of forms which is objective to us at least insofar as we are individuals. The Jungian collective unconscious appears to me to be another recurrence of the Platonic world of Forms, another way of stating its existence and relation to us: it seems to me suggestive and stimulating, as a revival of Platonism always is, and, essentially, as fanciful.

I do not see, however, that we need arbitrarily choose between these "explanations." The mystery of human life is not solved by clever but arbitrary simplification. Jung, we have recalled,[88] has pointed out with great force that the depths out of which these forms come into our lives, and from which they direct our conduct and expression, are dangerous depths, themselves formless, threatening our hold upon clarity, balance, even sanity, as we come directly to contemplate them. The very function of symbols is to obscure their formless origin, and to go to levels below the symbols is perilous. I incline to feel that Jung's own escape from this danger has lain in formulating the idea of the collective unconscious as a name and hence "explanation" for these depths: for when a phenomenon gets a name it becomes less formidable, on the same principle that a god with a name is less of a threat than a nameless god. The theological mind is only a special development of the mind of man throughout history in its feeling that the threat of this basic depth of our nature, the no man's land between the domains of physiology, neurology, and psychology, is mitigated if we call it by names, anthropomorphize it, and fancy we can explain its workings.

On the other hand, we are only resorting to another protective mechanism when we deny the obvious existence of these depths and of the forms they thrust upon us. Out of our depths these forms emerge with profound compulsion, just as the form of a specific kind of nest comes out of the depths of the gay little oriole. We do not look for a collective oriole psyche to explain the phenomenon: at the same time, we little understand the oriole without taking this peculiar impulse to form into account as one of its elemental constituents. I am not ready to give a name to this basic urge to form, this source of forms. If we cannot explain such things, however, we have perhaps now come far enough at last, and at least, to stop trying to explain them away, and to be able to face their existence, even though we may have to leave to our successors the long task of discovering their nature and origin. What may ultimately be determined, I shall not try to guess. I must confess,

88. See above, p. 38.

however, that a Freudian explanation of the façade as an image of return to the womb appeals to me most. It is in Freudian terms that the figure recurs in religious literature. Luther said: "Thereupon I felt myself to be reborn, and to have gone through open doors to paradise." [89] To go through a door is to be born, and death, as faith keeps telling man, is birth into a new life. "Gates ajar" still means heaven.

But why the three openings as a womb? I should mention one obvious explanation. We have seen the façade used in pagan art to frame various objects, as in figs. 295 and 297 of Volume III. In the former of these, indeed, where the three openings frame the pagan trinity of Father, Mother, and Son,[90] we have felt that we may have discovered why the façade of three openings was so especially favored—namely, to make a setting for, to represent, Deity in these three persons. But it is impossible to say whether a deep numerological compulsion did not produce the group of three as such. In that case the three openings would essentially be a derivative of the symbolism of three in itself rather than of the idea of the three gods. And there is no reason for connecting the three openings of ancient Egypt, as in fig. 35, with any such trinity of gods.

Perhaps we can summarize what we have seen by saying that the façade and the shrine have emerged as forms referable to no structural necessity, often with no structural function whatever, in a variety of objects and in a great variety of times and places. Wherever they "come from," whatever urge within us they "satisfy," their association with the holy and with the hope of immortality has been steadily persistent.

C. JEWISH SHRINES AND FAÇADES

It is in the light of this general phenomenon that I suggest approaching the Jewish shrines and façades,[91] since these so clearly present the same forms as those used by pagans. Here we may well test our theory that there was persistence of values where we find continuity of form. We have seen that the façade had a persisting value in paganism, and that this value was carried over into Christian usage. Is there evidence of a similar persistence of that value in Judaism?

1. In the Greco-Roman Period

THE COLONNADE or arcade has appeared on ossuaries [92] and lamps,[93] usually with devices under it—rosettes, "round objects," lozenges, little rectangular shapes which

89. Quoted in Roland H. Bainton, *Here I Stand: A Life of Martin Luther*, 1950, 65.

90. See above, I, 154. There are of course many examples of this usage from Syria. See S. Ronzevalle, "Notes et études d'archéologie orientale: Venus lugens et Adonis Byblius," *Mélanges de l'Université Saint Joseph*, XV (1930), 139–204, with plates XXVI–XXXVI.

91. This chapter was written before the publication of Carl Wendel, *Der Thoraschrein im Altertum*, 1950 (Hallische Monographien, XV), but the

study has been helpful in my final revision.

92. See above, III, figs. 173, 211–213a, 216–219, 244. In fig. 213 a rosette is within each opening; cf. I, 127.

93. See III, figs. 259, 261, 273–275, 284–289, 292 f., 299 f., 303–305, 313 f. Cf. I, 150, 153–155, and III, fig. 291, for a Nabatean parallel. An analogous Greek use of the colonnade with mythological figures appears on a Roman sarcophagus of possibly Jewish provenance, III, fig. 819; cf. II, 41.

might be cabinets, betyls or forms similar to betyls, and, in two cases, fishes. The colonnade has seemed to be in no sense a representation of a temple, or of any building, but rather to stand as a symbol in its own right, a form marking the sanctity of the emblems it frames. The importance of the symbol seems to have been consciously felt when on ossuaries three arched openings could be presented even without columns,[94] or when, as in a tomb in Sheikh Ibreiq, the three arches are carved with columns but with empty openings.[95] The symbolic importance of columns in themselves has often been debated, but not enough data appear in the Jewish material we are discussing to throw any special light on the question, although a glance at some of the representations, especially those in which the nonfunctional column is surmounted by a disk containing a rosette, makes it hard to believe that the column was not itself inherently significant.[96] Indeed, on one ossuary the column seems to be identified with a plant in a way suggesting that the famous companions, the "tree and pillar," may have some association here also.[97]

In general, however, it appears to be not the column that is especially important, but rather the opening between columns. This seems clear when an object is framed in the opening: it seems just as clear when the opening is presented as such. A very interesting instance occurs on an ossuary from Jerusalem,[98] one of the few carved in relief. In addition to the usual threefold division of ossuary decoration, ordinarily showing a rosette in the two outer sections and another motif in the center, the central panel itself is made into a façade of three openings: two columns frame a space in which is another pair of columns joined by an arch. The elements of our façade are here very successfully rearranged to suit the nature of the object it ornaments, and the very fact that they could be thus rearranged strongly suggests that each of the elements had an independent value. Yet all the spaces within the façade are empty. There is nothing even under the central arch.

The façade, unattached, empty or enclosing a figure, has appeared on many other Jewish objects. Figure 293 of Volume III shows a lamp with various Jewish symbols, one of which is a four-columned façade. The façade is surmounted by a gable with a semicircular piece, clearly an implied shell, joining the two central columns. The shell often appears in an arcuated lintel, or in a gable, and will be discussed as a symbol in its own right in a later volume. Nothing whatever is between the columns here, and we feel again that this façade is itself a symbol: presumably, by inference from the usage on tombs, it is still a symbol of immortality.

Two very similar lamps [99] have each a design of four columns, the outer two carrying a gable, and the inner two an arcuated lintel.[100] The arch in one case has become a line of

---

94. See III, figs. 212 f.

95. See III, fig. 54; cf. I, 93.

96. See esp. III, figs. 160–162, 165–171; cf. I, 121–123.

97. See III, fig. 167.

98. See III, fig. 213a.

99. See III, figs. 286 f.

100. Avi-Yonah, in *QDAP*, X (1942), 139, follows recent usage in calling this form the "Syrian gable," with reference to Nabatean structures in Si: Butler, *Architecture, 1904–5*, Sec. A, figs. 332, 335, at pp. 384, 386. See also ibid., plate v, at p. 56; plate xxii, at p. 348; fig. 342, at p. 396; plate xxix, at p. 409; fig. 352, at p. 410; fig. 354, at p. 413; fig. 378, at p. 435. The convention is a very important one, and examples of it ranging from Assyrian art to medieval Christian representations are given by Donald F. Brown, "The Arcuated Lintel

eight "round objects," in the other it is a semblance of a spirally carved arc of stone. In both instances the columns have spiral flutings, and the acroteria are "round objects"— small on one lamp, but including a larger "round object" in each acroterium on the other. Similar large "round objects" are inside the shrine on the first lamp, flanking the form of central interest in both designs, the chalice. From one of the chalices a vine grows to either side. It is clear that we are dealing with a definite symbolic convention whose three elements are the shrine with an arcuated lintel under a gable, the "round objects," and the cup. Our present interest is in seeing this architectural form, quite divorced from any reference to structure, used to indicate the sanctity of the cup and the "round objects" (here presumably symbolizing wine and bread). The total symbolic form would seem to sanctify the lamp, which, I strongly suspect, gave sanctity to the corpse with which it was buried. When we recall that a similar chalice with grapes within a primitive round-topped shrine is on an amulet found between the thighs of a Jewess in an undisturbed grave of the period in Palestine,[101] we may indeed suppose that this symbol was felt to have potency, and that its phallic associations had perhaps not become entirely unconscious. We shall see other chalices in shrines shortly.

Indisputably Jewish are the windows framed by this same form in synagogues of Palestine, that is, so constructed that the light comes into the synagogue through the central opening of such a façade.[102] Indeed, in our discussion of the front elevation in synagogues in general, it seemed highly probable that it was an adaptation of this façade, used upon the wall facing Jerusalem because that was the sacred side, while the entrance used by the congregation was presumably on one of the other sides.[103] That is, we felt that the façade form was put upon the synagogue to mark it as holy, rather than that the façade was a form taken from the synagogue for other, more abstract representation.

Such a free-standing façade, sanctifying in itself, has seemed also to be implied in the little aedicula painted on the entablature above the niche which was presumably the place

---

and Its Symbolic Interpretation," *AJA*, XLVI (1942), 389–399 (where earlier bibliography will be found). See also the pagan examples above, III, figs. 295, 297. I have an impression, which I cannot at all justify, that the arcuated lintel really presents the central opening as a final descendant of the round-topped object which, as we have seen (I, 150–152), was often put under the shrine; the round-topped space under a gable or flat lintel, then, is in itself a significant form. In Freudian and Jungian terms it is inevitable to guess that the round-topped object, which is often unmistakably a phallus, may continue to be this when it has become the round-topped opening under a gable, and so to suppose that representation of the phallus within what seems to have the value of the womb symbolizes intercourse, the most vivid gratification of the desire to return to the womb. The two to-

gether would accordingly have much the same value as the lingam carries in Indian symbolism. If this interpretation, or any part of it, is true, one wonders further at what point awareness of such symbolism was rejected by the conscious mind, while the value was left to survive without conscious appreciation of why the symbol has brought hope of immortality through the ages.

101. See above, III, fig. 381; cf. I, 166; II, 235.

102. E.g., III, figs. 462 f.

103. See esp. I, 181–186. For illustrations of the three-door façade on synagogues, see III, figs. 452 (Capernaum), 484 (Chorazin), 503 (Umm el-Amed), 506 (Meron), 505 (Kefr Birim), 520 (Ed-Dikkeh), 529 (Khirbet Semmaka), 561 (Hammath by Tiberias), 594 (Dura), 605 (Eshtemoa), 631 (Beth Alpha), 645 (Naaran), 656 (Jerash). For a façade on an ossuary which may stand for a tomb or a synagogue, cf. III, fig. 218.

of the Torah shrine in the Dura synagogue.[104] Here we have the façade flanked on one side by the menorah with lulab and ethrog, and on the other by the scene of the Akedah, the sacrifice of Isaac. It seems to suggest that the center of interest is that holy world which lies beyond the façade as used on tomb or temple, a world to which the symbolism of the menorah and the Akedah also points. The same symbolism will appear in the Dura painting of the Exodus.[105] There Egypt is represented by a great wall with an open door. Above the doorway is an arch, and at one side are two columns. The representation of the wall does not show the other side of the doorway, but the other two columns balancing the pair shown are to be assumed.[106] The great significance of the Exodus procession as here presented, then, is that the Israelites have come through that door, which is topped by Victories and an Ares figure [107]—that is, the Israelites seem in the Exodus to have got "beyond the façade," to have come through this "triumphal arch" into a new life. Precisely such a coming out of the material life into the world of immaterial reality was to Philo the meaning of the Exodus story.[108]

The same façade was put upon coins struck during the Second Revolt. It had earlier been used on coins of Herod Philip II,[109] but on these it is a quite abstract symbol, with the date of the coin inscribed in the spaces between the columns. Since the Emperor's head is on the obverse, there seems no reason whatever to assume, as is usually done, that the façade here represents the Temple in Jerusalem. During the Second Revolt the façade reappeared on many coins, and these invariably frame a peculiar object,[110] usually taken to be the Ark of the Covenant, while the façade is as before interpreted as the Temple.

Here likewise I see no reason to regard the façade as standing for the Temple in Jerusalem.[111] The tetrastyle was very commonly used on coins of the region as a device for enshrining a sacred object. Hill shows such coins from Sepphoris-Diocaesarea,[112] Tiberias,[113] Antipatris,[114] Caesarea,[115] Diospolis,[116] Neapolis,[117] Aelia Capitolina,[118] Eleutheropolis,[119] and Gaza,[120] and I do not doubt that many more instances could be found.[121] On these a god or goddess stands in the place occupied by what has been called the Ark on the Jewish coins. The Jews under Bar Kokba seem simply to have taken the sanctifying frame and put a sacred object of their own within it. Similarly, I do not think that the

104. See III, fig. 602; cf. I, 230.

105. To be illustrated and discussed in the last volume of this series. See the beautiful color reproduction in Rostovtzeff, *Dura-Europos*, VI, plate LII.

106. The two columns shown are one black and one red, hence they are usually identified with the pillars of cloud and of fire. This may indeed be the allusion of the colors, so that the columns are thereby made to do double symbolic service, a common thing in all symbolism.

107. We must consider Ares and the Victories in a later volume.

108. See my *By Light, Light*, 204–210.

109. See above, III, fig. 676; cf. I, 274.

110. See III, fig. 692; cf. I, 276.

111. Wendel, op. cit., 14, calls this representation, as well as the façade painted over the niche at Dura, the Temple of Solomon.

112. G. F. Hill, *Catalogue of the Greek Coins of Palestine*, 1914, plate I, 6 f. (Catalogue of the Greek Coins in the British Museum, XXVII).

113. Ibid., plate II, 1.

114. Ibid., plate II, 7.

115. Ibid., plate III, 1 f.

116. Ibid., plate V, 5 f.

117. Ibid., plate VI, 10, 14.

118. Ibid., plate X, 4 f., 7, 10.

119. Ibid., plate XIV, 17 f.

120. Ibid., plate XV, 10 f.

121. See H. Rosenau in *PEF, QS*, 1936, 157–162.

object under the façade was primarily the Ark of the Covenant. It seems rather an early form of the Torah shrine, a portable object smaller than the shrines later built into walls. For in the earlier synagogues, we have seen, worship seems to have been directed toward a sanctuary blocked off from the congregation by a screen which appears to be the ancestor of the iconostas of the Eastern church—a screen usually having three doors, behind which the most sacred objects, including the Torah shrine, were kept, and barring off the place where probably the most sacred rites were conducted.[122] Out of this adyton, we have suspected, the holy objects were probably brought, as the holy scrolls are still carried through the congregation at various points in the synagogue service. The Torah shrine which went with such a structure was, then, probably a portable or wheeled affair.[123]

The little round-topped box under the façade on the coins seems to me to be such a Torah shrine. It was probably carried on poles, as the Bible says was done with the Ark of the Covenant in the wilderness, and such is exactly the form of the Ark of the Covenant, carried on poles, which is several times represented at Dura. I reproduce three such arks as drawn by du Mesnil, fig. 65.[124] The rosettes, garlands, "round objects," and magical "characters" with which they are decorated show them to be products of the Greco-Roman period. But there can be no doubt, as I see it, that what we have here is the ancient Ark of the wilderness drawn in the form of the ark of the synagogues, not the reverse.[125] In fig. 597 of Volume III can be seen a graffito found in the Dura synagogue in which this same form is presented as a thing in itself, an amuletic device such as might appear on a grave: it is in all probability a Torah shrine, but, more deeply, it indicates the presence of God. The same object, quite small enough to be portable, stands beside a figure reading from the Law in the center of the Dura paintings.[126] That the round-topped Torah shrine could be put upon wheels we fortunately have directly attested in the splendid representation in a frieze of the synagogue of Capernaum.[127] Thus the coins of the Second Revolt seem to be sanctified by having upon them a Torah shrine under a façade.

The relation of the Torah shrine to the Ark of the Covenant has also been suggested by the fact that each was called the *'aron*, meaning ark. There is, however, good reason to suppose that this connection was originally suggested by hellenized Jews. In the Mishnah the Torah shrine is called not *'aron* but *tebah*, the biblical word for the ark of Noah, and for the ark in which the baby Moses was placed in the Nile. In the Septuagint, however, both the Ark of the Covenant and the ark of Noah are called κιβωτός, and it is this word

122. See above, I, 190; II, 74, 77, 81, 90, 92.

123. Wendel, op. cit., 19–21.

124. From du Mesnil, *Peintures*, plate XXVI. See above, III, fig. 215, where the same form appears upon an ossuary; cf. III, fig. 214.

125. This is the conclusion, reached, in a quite different approach, by Wendel, op. cit., 16.

126. The figure has been called by various names: du Mesnil, *Peintures*, plate XXXVII, published it as "Esdras." In a later volume I shall show good reason to suppose it to represent Moses. The

painting is beautifully published in color as a frontispiece in H.-F. Pearson, *Guide de la synagogue de Doura-Europos*, Beirut, 1940 (Haut-Commissariat de la République Française: Service des Antiquités), where it is called "Prophet Reading a Scroll." Wendel, op. cit., 9 f., argues that the object beside the figure is not a Torah shrine, but a *capsa*, a carrying case for a few rolls.

127. See above, III, fig. 472; with Reifenberg, I still take the object here to be an ark of the Law, though Wendel, op. cit., 8 f., says it is the Ark of the Covenant.

which was used by Chrysostom, in the early part of the fourth century, for the Torah shrine in the synagogue.[128] There can be little doubt that the term in Greek implied an association in meaning between the ark of the synagogue and the Ark of the Covenant, and that this was the common word for ark in both senses among Greek-speaking Jews, that is, among the Jews who were using these symbols, if not creating their symbolic values. Casanowicz [129] says that there is no trace of evidence that the ark of the synagogues was called an *'aron* in rabbinic circles until the time of Maimonides, so that the acceptance of this association in rabbinical Judaism would seem to have been indeed late. Both the history of the names of the two arks and the art forms for them would, then, suggest that those who devised the symbolism were thinking in Greek, and that artists represented the two originally in the same shape because for Greek-speaking Jews they had the same name and the same symbolic association. The rabbis, in finally allowing the Torah shrine to be called an ark, were, apparently at least, only accepting an association of meaning which in no wise derived from themselves. We shall consider that meaning more closely later.

It would, accordingly, seem likely that the earlier Torah shrine was a small portable box for the scrolls, for some reason made with a rounded top, and that it was originally kept behind a screen in a sacred chamber. The best-preserved of such screens, the one at Capernaum, is, we are not surprised to see, an adaptation of the façade we are tracing. This screen had four arched openings, two of them showing the arcuated lintel with shell, but the whole had no structural function except that of a screen.[130] There is reason to suppose that the arrangement here was not the usual one, and that ordinarily there were three openings. I suspect that in Capernaum the Torah shrine stood under one of the arches, the menorah under the other. By analogy with the shrine at Sheikh Ibreiq, it is natural to suppose that other sacred objects like the lulab, or statues, stood in the square openings at either side of these two arches, but for this there is no direct evidence whatever.

The shrines in the catacomb of Sheikh Ibreiq are in this connection extremely important. A number of the little shrines painted on the walls of the catacomb will be considered in a moment. The shrine carved in relief [131] is, however, of great significance. Here are actually two façades, one at either side of an opening with a little shelf at the back, on which something sacred must have stood. Graves are above the rear and side walls of the opening. The whole is clearly a unit. Each of the two façades has four columns, with an arcuated lintel over the central opening. In the façade at the left, double doors, each having two panels, occupy the central opening under an arch with shell; a lulab is in the space at one side, and the other side is empty. The lion beside the arch recalls the lions on the lintel of the shrine in Capernaum, as well as the lions commonly accompanying Torah shrines to the present day. The menorah under the arch of the similar façade at the right is what suggested to me that the second arch at Capernaum might have had a menorah beneath it, while the human figure carved in the opening at the left of the menorah

128. *Oratio adversus Judaeos*, VI, 7.

129. In *JE*, II, 109. This point is missed by Wendel, op. cit., 8.

130. See above, III, fig. 479.

131. See III, figs. 53, 55, 62–64, 66; cf. I, 94–96.

suggested by a not farfetched analogy that a similar statue might have stood in the side opening of the Capernaum screen.

In our discussion of this pair of façades at Sheikh Ibreiq,[132] it was recalled that—although the form of presentation is quite different—a corresponding pair of shrines appears among the Dura paintings. One of these is a closed temple, with its masonry painted to present seven bands of different colors, corresponding to the seven steps carved beneath the Torah shrine.[133] The other is a more open and accessible temple whose central feature is the menorah before an ark—here, since Aaron ministers before it, the Ark of the wilderness.[134] Publication of these scenes at Dura, and discussion of them, must wait for the closing volume of this study, but it seems to me by no means an implausible conjecture that the Torah shrine and menorah may have been the chief symbols behind the screen at Capernaum, perhaps on occasion to be seen under one of its arches.

Such a double presentation—a closed shrine and also an open one containing a menorah—is apparently intended also on the door of a Palestinian tomb,[135] which shows a number of panels, mostly with rosettes, separated by a central panel with "round objects." Of the two panels at the left, however, one displays a menorah with an object on each side: these may be cups, but I should take them to be hanging lamps as in the Naaran synagogue.[136] At the bottom is a little shrine with two columns; a large shell is in the arch that joins these, and a lozenge below, between the columns. To this lozenge we shall return, but here the final effect is that of a closed shrine contrasted with one whose openness suggests the availability of the menorah.

How early the elaborate screen and portable shrine gave way to a structure in which the shrine was built into the synagogue wall, there is no means of saying. Indeed, the great screen of Capernaum may be only a deliberate elaboration of a form which was ordinarily, in less opulent circumstances, much more simple. The new Torah shrine, if I may call it so, bore its own gable, acroteria, arch, and shell, or included most of these elements. These details of the shrine reflect the features of shrines in general in antiquity, as the structure of the Jewish façade reflects pagan designs. Wendel seems entirely right in concluding that the new form "marked the shrine as a *temple*, that is, as the lodging place of the Laws whose divine Author was personally present in them." [137]

The simpler version of the shrine we have already encountered. It had long been used in pagan art as an alternative for the tetrastyle façade, as in fig. 67.[138] It could appear as a door in a gabled structure, fig. 66,[139] which I take to be an earlier form, or as a gabled doorway, fig. 68,[140] which seems to me derived from the other, though both of the examples

---

132. See I, 94 f.

133. Du Mesnil, *Peintures*, plate xxxv; Rostovtzeff, *Dura-Europos*, VI, plate xlviii. See above, III, fig. 53.

134. Du Mesnil, *Peintures*, plate xxv; Rostovtzeff, *Dura-Europos*, VI, plate xlvii.

135. See above, III, fig. 44.

136. See III, fig. 646.

137. Op. cit., 23.

138. From Benoit, *L'Architecture: Antiquité*, I, 217, fig. 143, v. It is the prehellenic tomb at Ayazin in Asia Minor.

139. From de Vogüé, *Syrie centrale: Architecture*, II, plate 85; cf. ibid., I, 111.

140. From ibid., plate 95; cf. ibid., I, 118. See also plate 80, and, for the form without gable, plate 82, and Kammerer, *Pétra et la Nabatène*, Atlas, plate 45, figs. 1 f.

illustrated are probably of the fifth century, and Christian. This derivative, the doorway with its own gable, was often applied to each of the three entrances, especially in Gothic façades. Figure 69 [141] offers an early Syrian instance of the use of this most familiar convention. But it is again in Etruscan art that we see the best pagan parallel to the Jewish shrine. Figure 70,[142] reproducing a scene from an Etruscan vase, seems to show the Dioscuri in the act of kidnaping the daughters of Leucippus. They are carrying little images, apparently household gods; it is natural to suppose that these had been in the shrine behind them. This shrine astonishingly resembles our Jewish shrines in many obvious details, including, indeed, even the steps before it.

Just as the façade, even when empty, seems to have had symbolic sanctifying power, so the shrine could be represented without contents, apparently for the values inherent in its very form. We have seen [143] that the façade with central arch, quite empty, had meaning in Jewish funerary art. A sarcophagus from Palestine [144] shows an empty arch composed of two peculiar stories; its tall acroteria are a feature which will constantly recur. A little carving in the frieze in the synagogue at Chorazin first fully presents the single shrine in Jewish remains,[145] for here are two columns joined by an arch surmounted by a gable, and elaborate acroteria in the form of acanthus plants. Yet nothing is inside the shrine, nor, apparently, ever was. On the small Jewish glasses,[146] a pair of columns is often joined by an arch. A still simpler form of the shrine, likewise empty, appears on an ossuary.[147]

Within the little shrine various things could be represented. One shrine (III, fig. 44, lower left corner) shows, beneath the shell of the arch, a round-centered lozenge. The lozenge also appears twice in an actual niche for a Torah shrine at Dura.[148] The same idea is crudely presented upon a lamp from Jerusalem.[149] In several instances we have under such an arch something that looks like a betyl,[150] representations which once more recall objects in Syrian niches.[151] On other lamps the arch consecrates a chalice.[152] There is

---

141. From de Vogüé, op. cit., plate 141; cf. ibid., I, 141–152.

142. From G. Körte [and H. von Brunn], I Rilievi delle urne etrusche, 1890, II, plate XXXVIII, 4; cf. pp. 97–100. The editor (p. vi) dates the vases in this collection in the third or second century B.C.

143. Above, p. 112. See III, fig. 213a.

144. See III, fig. 247.

145. See III, fig. 497.

146. See III, figs. 393, 406 f., 415, 422, 427, 443.

147. See III, fig. 209.

148. Cf. I, 229.

149. See I, 152.

150. Cf. I, 150.

151. See A. J. Jaussen and R. Savignac, Mission archéologique en Arabie, 1909, I, 417 f. The authors illustrate and discuss a large number of similar shrines (pp. 405–441). The arcuated lintel, or arch, under a gable, and over such a round-topped

betyl, suggests that the two may be identical, i.e., that the round-topped entrance or doorway is itself a betyl form within which a sacred object is placed. So long as the second form is also a betyl, this is mere duplication, though if the arched opening is itself a betyl, its sanctifying power in relation to the object under it is clear. On the other hand, if the betyl is, as is usually supposed, a phallus, putting one into the doorway would suggest intercourse, with all the possible range of symbolism this implies. For the doorway is essentially a feminine symbol, and when the arcuated lintel is used it almost invariably is beneath the gable and within the outer columns. Explanations become conflicting: indeed, I strongly suspect that any single explanation will leave out more than it can include of the actual value of such a representation. See above, pp. 112 f., n. 100.

152. See, e.g., above, III, figs. 286–289.

a chalice under an arch also on a Jewish glass in the Metropolitan Museum.[153] We have already spoken of other such chalices within shrines.[154] The shrine consecrates various other symbols on glasses.[155] We have encountered a single shrine with a human figure under its arch on the door of a Jewish tomb.[156]

In Sheikh Ibreiq we saw a form that all agree must be taken as a Torah shrine under the full façade. The component parts, the façade or shrine, and the box or cabinet for the scrolls, are not distinguished in such representations as those of the Sheikh Ibreiq reliefs, but they appear clearly in *dipinti* in the same cemetery. In one,[157] the cabinet with its scrolls stands within the gabled shrine, but has no structural connection with it: this exactly accords with the conclusion we came to about the earlier, movable Torah shrines. The flanking menorahs and the light hanging from the gable are notable here. The same structural independence is presented in another *dipinto* in the same catacomb,[158] where the acroteria take on the horned form which will frequently appear, and the shell is put in as an essential element—which, however, the man who made the sketch was unable to draw properly. Again there are the eternal light in the gable and the flanking menorahs. Two graffiti, still more crudely executed, present the same features,[159] and show that the elements in this design were more important than their arrangement. In one,[160] the round top of the cabinet discussed above takes the place of the shell; this suggests that the round top, like the shell, goes with the tradition of the round-topped objects in early shrines, such as betyls and omphali. It begins to appear that the box with its end showing under the gable of a shrine came naturally to be given a rounded top—naturally because the idea of the round top within the shrine joined itself to the sacred object just as it imposed itself upon the lintel to produce the arcuated lintel.

On one lamp,[161] the arch has degenerated into a rounded fillet, the light of the lamp itself takes the place of a representation of the eternal light, and the Torah shrine proper is a separable box or cabinet. Under the round arch the box can, of course, have a flat top. But such a convention, if there was one, was often disregarded.

The niche in the synagogue at Dura probably shows roughly the size of such cabinets, for here there was room for a box approximately 0.75 m. square at the bottom and 1.25 m. high at the center. If it had a rounded top, the height of the rectangular box proper would probably not have exceeded one meter. This box could not have been wheeled up the steps, but was of such a size that it could have been carried about on poles or by handles.

In the great majority of representations, however, the gable or arch of the enclosing shrine or niche seems to have become a structural part of the cabinet itself, and would suggest that a change in ritual had occurred—a change from the practice of carrying the portable shrine through the congregation, to the arrangement that still prevails, in which the shrine itself is stationary and the scrolls are taken out for the ceremony.[162] On one

---

153. See III, fig. 401.
154. See above, p. 113.
155. See III, fig. 415.
156. See III, fig. 48.
157. See III, fig. 60.

158. See III, fig. 59.
159. See III, figs. 58, 61.
160. See III, fig. 58.
161. See III, fig. 292.
162. This was recognized by Wendel, op. cit.

ossuary there appears a form that may be a Torah shrine; here a paneled door closes the opening made by columns and a flattened arch.[163] Similar representations are on two other ossuaries.[164] In the first volume these were discussed as examples of the tomb portico or façade, or of the tomb door, rather than as Torah shrines. Actually, it is just as appropriate to include them as possible Torah shrines. Where they actually belong one cannot say, but it seems extremely probable that to the Jew who put this device on his ossuary, it made no difference whether one called it a Torah shrine or the gateway to the house eternal. The form itself sanctified, and gave hope, with a direct talismanic power which made explanations quite secondary.

The gabled shrine in simplest form can be seen engraved upon a bronze plate from a tomb in Palestine,[165] where it resembles the ordinary scroll case of the period. A scroll case depicted on a Roman sarcophagus, fig. 71,[166] simple as it is, gives the essential details— two doors opening out from the center, and piles of scrolls on the shelves within. The pagan example does not have the gabled top, and the omission is, I believe, significant. For the gabled top of the Jewish representations makes the otherwise simple scroll case into a shrine, so that the holy scrolls are presented in a setting which in itself indicates their sanctity.

Figure 72 [167] reproduces an illumination from a Christian Bible of the end of the seventh century [168] and shows Esdras transcribing the Law beside a gabled cabinet: some of the volumes in it obviously represent the Gospels, since their covers are marked with crosses. Leclercq [169] recognized the kinship between this cabinet and the Jewish Torah shrines, and he is right in feeling that the Christian form is not that of a pagan bookcase. It is the Jewish shrine taken over to house the Christian Scriptures, the Old and New Testaments. The same may be said in regard to a little shrine containing the Gospels, represented in mosaic in the fifth-century mausoleum of Galla Placidia in Ravenna, fig. 74.[170] It is a chest containing holy books, the shrine form adopted for the purpose.

Such a shrine could in Palestine ordinarily be shown as closed, because its contents could be understood to be something too holy for general presentation. Indeed, I know only a single Palestinian instance [171] in which the scroll itself is shown within the shrine. Actually we may well sometimes wonder whether the shrine of the representations is always and only the synagogue shrine. There is the peculiar shrine occurring on two lamps,[172] where in each case it is a gabled structure with "round objects" crudely serving

163. See III, fig. 216.

164. See III, figs. 219, 244.

165. Cf. above, I, 173.

166. From Leclercq in CL, II, 889, fig. 1554: see Saglio in DS, I, 708, fig. 852. A still simpler roll case without doors, and showing only four compartments, is possibly what is pictured in the upper right corner of a strange relief published by B. Ashmole, *Catalogue of the Ancient Marbles at Ince Blundell Hall*, 1929, plate 46, n. 298. At least, this is Rostovtzeff's guess, with which Ashmole (p. 109, n. 2) agrees.

167. From Leclercq in CL, II, 894, fig. 1556; cf. DS, I, 708, fig. 853. The drawing is from the Codex Amiatinus.

168. See H. J. White, "The Codex Amiatinus and Its Birthplace," *Studia biblica et ecclesiastica*, II (1890), 273–308, esp. 285.

169. In CL, II, 893, n. 1.

170. From Wilpert, *Mosaiken und Malereien*, III, plate 49; cf. Leclercq in CL, II, 895, fig. 1557.

171. See above, III, fig. 60.

172. See III, fig. 294.

as acroteria, and chevrons taking the place of doors. Yet it is flanked by a bird on each side, then a tree, then another bird. The shrine is in all probability a Torah shrine, but we may wonder whether the form is not again a holy element in itself.

The same problem recurs frequently. A simple gabled shrine, closed, with flanking rosette and lulab, is carved on the lintel of a doorway of the Capernaum synagogue.[173] The "round objects" seem important, as we shall often see them on these shrines. We recall the steps of the closed shrines we have just been discussing, and wonder whether the door of the synagogue could have been considered a door to the Mystery which this closed shrine represented. It is still a tradition that Torah shrines in synagogues must be approached by steps, not more than seven or less than three. The tradition is now an unexplained survival, something which, like much Jewish tradition, is important, so far as the pious Jew is aware, simply from the standpoint of conformity. That the steps were originally a mere convention in Judaism, especially in hellenized Judaism, we are coming increasingly to doubt.

The shrine may be topped by a shell-filled arch, as in a carving from the synagogue at Fahma.[174] Or the shell-filled arch may be under the gable of a Torah shrine, as in the synagogue at Pekiin.[175] Presented in the mosaic floors of several synagogues is a new cluster of symbols, for in these the shrine is between a pair of menorahs. In the synagogue of Naaran this combination appears in its simplest form.[176] Here the gabled shrine has no ornament whatever, but the "round objects" above the shrine and on the menorahs, together with the hanging lamps, give a definite impression of symbolic intent. In the synagogue at Beth Alpha [177] this cluster is much elaborated. Curtains are drawn back at either side to reveal the "mystic sights" ordinarily screened. These include a gabled shrine with shell arch and acroteria from which some sort of amulet or jewel is suspended; the eternal light is in the gable, and a vase, presumably a wine cup, is at the top of each of the three vertical posts of the shrine. Huge birds of uncertain character are upon the slopes of the gable, and menorahs and lions flank the shrine. Various other cult objects are scattered in the field.

It appears to me highly doubtful that this group, the culminating presentation of the inner symbolism of the synagogue, is without meaning. It has been suggested earlier [178] that since the worshiper approached this panel by first walking over the scene of the Akedah, or sacrifice of Isaac, then over the monotheistic symbolism of Helios in the zodiac, his coming at last to this group of unveiled emblems would, in any pagan setting, be taken to represent a higher mystic achievement reached through, first, purification, then cosmic mysticism, and, finally, access to the veiled mystery itself. It seemed no coincidence that in the synagogue at Naaran the Torah shrine with its lights should likewise have been approached over panels which included a symbol of miraculous salvation from death (Daniel with the lions) and again a representation of Helios in the zodiac.[179] Simpler, but essentially the same in purport, is the mosaic floor in the synagogue at Jericho,[180] which as a whole is

173. See III, fig. 471.
174. See III, fig. 560.
175. See III, fig. 573.
176. See III, fig. 646.

177. See III, fig. 639.
178. See I, 246–253.
179. See I, 255 f.
180. See III, fig. 666.

covered with what are probably tapestry designs, but in the middle presents a menorah in one panel, a closed Torah shrine with shell top in another.

Finally, we note the occurrence of the form on four peculiar funerary plaques.[181] Here the shrine is flanked in three cases by menorahs, in one of these also by birds, and in one by lions and birds. In each shrine there is an opening into which a little disk of glass could be set. The function of the glass was apparently to reflect light, and thereby to mark the shrine as the source of light, symbol of the Shekinah.[182]

2. In Later Judaism

THE SHRINE form we have been discussing persisted in Judaism through the Middle Ages, though we can trace the earlier presentations of the period only in manuscripts.[183] Figure 73 [184] shows a gabled Torah shrine at the center of a table of the Decalogue, as pictured in a tenth-century manuscript preserved at Leningrad. The gables, the panels on the doors, the lozenges, and the acanthus where we should expect acroteria, are all remnants of tradition. In fig. 77,[185] reproduced from a manuscript of the late thirteenth century, the shrine is so drawn that its simple arch is framed in a larger arch. A fourteenth-century drawing, fig. 75,[186] presents a gabled cupboard with paneled doors and ornaments on the gable ridges like those of antiquity. Figure 76 [187] gives us, in a fifteenth-century miniature, a medieval version of the gable, with birds perched on the tall acroteria. Figure 78 [188] shows the Torah shrine at Miltenberg, which has a Shield of David as an acroterium on the peak of the gable, and paneled doors and steps, with three windows as openings in the wall above the shrine.[189]

181. See III, figs. 440–442, 446; cf. I, 174–177. The plaques may have been made as mizrachs. See below, p. 124.

182. See below, p. 125.

183. It would be valuable to collect such material more systematically from medieval Jewish manuscripts. See, e.g., Wischnitzer-Bernstein, *Symbole und Gestalten der jüdischen Kunst*, plates I (at p. 16), II (at p. 48), IV (at p. 88). See also a mahzor title-page in F. Landsberger, "Old-Time Torah-Curtains," *HUCA*, XIX (1946), 376. It is dated 1708–1709, and again presents a single shrine; at the bottom are the scorpion and fishes of the zodiac. Its twisting columns might have suggested to Landsberger that the Torah curtains with similar columns for borders present an abbreviation of this same shrine, not, primarily at least, the columns of Jachin and Boaz as he suggests: see idem, figs. 6–9, and p. 373.

184. From Wischnitzer-Bernstein, op. cit., 25, fig. 18; cf. p. 24.

185. A miniature in a late thirteenth-century manuscript of northern Spain. See also Richard Krautheimer, *Mittelalterliche Synagogen*, 1927, 9,

fig. 20. From David H. Müller and Julian von Schlosser, *Die Haggadah von Serajewo*, Vienna, 1898, fol. 34. Another interesting representation of a shrine, appearing in a tenth-century Jewish manuscript, is shown by F. Landsberger, *A History of Jewish Art*, 1946, 203.

186. From Krautheimer, op. cit., 120, fig. 27, who says only that it is a miniature in an Italian manuscript of the fourteenth century, of which he had a print from the Gesellschaft zur Erforschung jüdischer Kunstdenkmäler, Frankfort.

187. From Krautheimer, op. cit., 121, fig. 28, who had the photograph from the same source as the preceding one; he calls it only "Miniature from the Late Fifteenth Century." It is in a German mahzor written in 1459; see Landsberger in *HUCA*, XIX (1946), plate facing p. 362, fig. 3, and p. 364.

188. From Krautheimer, op. cit., 190, fig. 65. The Shield of David appears in a photograph of a gable published by Krautheimer, op. cit., 191, fig. 66; see also p. 93, fig. 17; p. 251, fig. 98.

189. Krautheimer gives no dating for this shrine. The synagogue was, he says, owned by the congregation until 1429, then was confiscated in the great

In modern times, thanks to classical influence, the shrine became even more like the ancient ones. In fig. 79 [190] we have a sketch of the synagogue at Frankfort, built in 1711, as it appeared in 1835. In the synagogue at Prague we see, from an engraving of 1726, fig. 80,[191] a renewed emphasis upon the acroteria; a window is at either side of the shrine, and an eight-point rosette is painted above it on the wall. It is notable that in the synagogue at Miltenberg, fig. 78, the round window occupying the central position over the shrine is divided by eight radii corresponding to the eight petals of the rosette at Prague.[192] Triple openings in the wall are used to store the scrolls in some modern synagogues, as at Amsterdam, fig. 81.[193] An interesting shrine in a synagogue at Pogrebishche, Russia,[194] has four columns, birds, vines, urns, and animals.

The form still appears in modern Torah shrines. Figure 82 [195] illustrates the shrine built about fifty years ago in the synagogue of the Sephardic congregation Shearith Israel in New York. Here the narrowing of the two side openings produces the compressed version of the full façade that has often appeared; the whole is approached by seven steps, and three windows are above it. In keeping with the Sephardic tradition, there are no curtains before it.[196] The men who designed this shrine had no knowledge of the seven steps in Dura and Sheikh Ibreiq. Brunner, the architect, had, of course, studied what was available at the time about synagogal architecture in Palestine,[197] and some features of the synagogue he designed in New Haven,[198] like the windows beside the central arch, indeed the whole feeling of the building, reflect clearly an attempt to revive the Palestinian forms, though he did not "abandon" Moorish traditions as fully as he thought. The idea of the steps he

---

persecution, and restored to Jewish use only in 1754. "Now it belongs to a brewery," he concludes. The Shield of David is so unusual that I suspect it, and perhaps much that is with it, to be of late date, but I know nothing further.

190. From Krautheimer, op. cit., 231, fig. 89.

191. From ibid., 236, fig. 93. P. C. Kirchner, *Jüdisches Ceremoniel oder Beschreibung dererjenigen Gebräuche*, Nuremberg, 1726.

192. See also Krautheimer, op. cit., 156, fig. 44.

193. From Bernard Picard, *Histoire générale des cérémonies, moeurs et coutumes religieuses*, 1741, I, plate facing p. 168. Cf. Brunner in *JE*, II, 108.

194. See *JE*, II, 110. Landsberger, op. cit., 361, 382, interprets the birds as cherubim, on the basis of Philo, *Mos.* II, 98, where the cherubim are called πτηνά, and of the Christian Hebraist Johannes Buxtorf, *De synagoga Judaica*, 1643, 309 (reprinted in Blasio Ugolino, *Thesaurus antiquitatum sacrarum*, Venice, 1745, IV, 909): "They like to have birds embroidered upon them [Torah curtains], because birds hovered over the Ark of the Covenant in the Old Testament." It is true that πτηνά means birds, but it also means winged creatures in general, and

that is apparently the sense in which Philo used the word. Where Buxtorf got his explanation I do not know. For other interesting Torah shrines, see Landsberger, *A History of Jewish Art*, 235, 247; cf. the three doors of the modern synagogue at Hamburg, ibid., 328. The essential features of the façade as used in the fourteenth century appear in an eighteenth-century painting as background of the Seder, op. cit., 261. See also *Milgroim*, I (1922), 1; cf. p. 4.

195. From A. W. Brunner in *The Brickbuilder*, XVI (1907), 39. See the plans there of a number of Brunner's synagogues that have the same features.

196. Brunner in *JE*, II, 111. A very interesting example of this appears in the synagogue at Newport, R.I., the oldest synagogue in the United States, built in 1763 for Sephardic Jews. Here there are three steps, a Torah shrine without curtains, and a window at either side, to make the three openings. But Landsberger, in *HUCA*, XIX (1946), 365, considers this shrine form not general in Sephardic tradition.

197. See Brunner in *JE*, II, 109–111, and in *The Brickbuilder*, ibid., 20–25, 37–44.

198. Ibid., 38.

got not from archeology, but from the still living tradition. Yet it seems to me striking that he has, in various combinations, used the distinguishing features of ancient shrines. It is interesting to leaf through the photographs published by Loukomski [199] and see how the symbolic tradition stemming from the Greco-Roman period has been consciously observed in designing synagogues, and especially their Torah shrines. Indeed, Loukomski himself mentions the feature of the three openings as characteristic.[200]

The shrine often appears as a motif on Torah mantles, the cloths in which the scrolls are wrapped. Figure 83 [201] shows a very interesting example from the seventeenth century, now at the Jewish Museum in New York, and published with permission of the Museum. Here, beneath the emblems of divine royalty—the double eagle of political royalty, and the crown—is a complex of Torah shrines designed as a unit. In the lower part of the design two heavy columns topped by birds and flags, and joined by a lintel, constitute one façade, in itself suggesting a shrine. Within this is a second façade with double columns and an arch, enclosing an elaborated shrine with three steps before it, and with a drawn curtain on which is a Shield of David. Above this double shrine is a third, in the form of two columns joined by an arch, with acroteria on which birds are perched. This shrine is also covered, by a veil on which is no ornament. The whole is apparently a unique presentation of the symbolism of three. Torah mantles so often bear designs of the shrine obviously because of the symbolic value of the form and its elements.

Another interesting survival of the form is in the mizrach tablet. This is a drawing or diagram put upon the east wall of a room (the name means "east") "to indicate the direction of prayer for services in the home." [202] It seems to be usual to have such tablets show "the name of God, representations of the Temple at Jerusalem, of the temple mount Moriah or of the city of Jerusalem, and also, in most cases, a Menorah," [203] with various mottoes and scriptural verses. What is customarily called the Temple at Jerusalem, however, turns out to be our shrine form. This appears in the oldest mizrach I know, fig. 49,[204] a plaster plaque which, as I should guess from the spiral columns, might have been made in the eighth century. It has only the three arches under a gable, but into the three spaces were put little circular insets of glass, remnants of which are still visible in the openings. These could not have served as mirrors, since they were too small to have been of use for such a purpose. Rather, as I have suspected in the case of funerary plaques with

199. G. K. Loukomski, *Jewish Art in European Synagogues*, 1947; see pp. 32, 35, 39 f., 67, 90, 94 f., 98, 106, 108 f., 128–134, 152, 154–160, 163–168.

200. Since it is the only reference I know to what we are here discussing, Loukomski's statement (op. cit., 29) is worth quoting: "*Aron-Hakodesh* is the richest part of the Synagogue, which corresponds to a similar richness of the Altars of ancient Christian Churches. Going further back it appears that this feature was derived from the ancient theatre (three doors, 'the Tsar's Gate' in Russian Orthodox Churches, the Iconostas, etc.). It would seem that

it all links up with a culture of great antiquity." For other Torah shrines, see *UJE*, I, 475–477; *EJ*, III, 390–394; *Jüdisches Lexikon*, 1930, V, 990–993; *Evreiskaia entsiklopediia*, St. Petersburg, c. 1909, III, plates facing pp. 188 f.

201. Not numbered in the Museum's collection. For a rabbinic allusion to Torah mantles, see above, p. 19, n. 85.

202. A. Grotte in *UJE*, VII, 601.

203. Ibid.

204. Courtesy of Mr. Rudolf Jonas of Haifa; the piece is in his collection.

similar bits of glass set into their Torah shrines,[205] they may have been put there to reflect light, symbolizing the association of shrine and Shekinah.

The mizrach in fig. 84 [206] shows an especially interesting new presentation of the old symbols. Here the three arches overlap in a novel way, but are still the three arches. The menorah as a vine is in the central opening, with a couchant lion placed vertically beside it on either side. Vine motifs grow up in the age-old way from vases in the two openings at the sides. Peacocks and other birds are in these vines, and at the top of each is what seems to me to be a pelican piercing her breast. Snakes coil about the four central columns, and the necks and heads of two storks appear with them. Mrs. Wischnitzer-Bernstein says that the snakes are attacking the menorah, but are being held off by the storks. This is quite fanciful. The storks are not attacking the snakes,[207] and the snakes thrust their heads inwards toward the lights at the center and outwards toward the pelicans, in a way which by no means indicates attack. The snake, we shall see, and indeed have seen, is by no means always to be construed as a poisoning menace. Above the arches are devices that seem to me again symbols of the Shekinah: the hands of the Cohenic blessing are quite abstracted and become in value the blessing hands of God.[208] These are flanked by lions and griffins, which here, either of them or both, recall the cherubim once more, and the whole culminates in the crown with the double eagle, that is, with the crown as symbol of divine royalty, the ultimate Deity in cabbalistic terms. It is flanked by the letters of the word mizrach.

Prayers said by a worshiper facing such a tablet would be oriented toward the Shekinah, and this idea is vividly presented by all the symbols in a way which, novel though the composition may be as a whole, is basically traditional. Even the values of the acroteria, whatever those values are, seem preserved by the lighter vines in the two upper corners. The legend over the central arch reads, "Toward the face of the menorah, shall illuminate the seven lights. Know before whom you stand: before the King of Kings, the Holy One, blessed be he." Thus it is made quite explicit that the tablet presents to the worshiper, or recalls to him, the Shekinah. The motto "Know before whom you stand" is frequently put upon mizrachs and upon the curtains of Torah shrines. It is a quotation from the Talmud: "When you pray, know before whom you are standing." [209]

Another mizrach [210] shows the three arches on four columns, with flower-filled vases above the two side arches taking the place of acroteria. In lieu of a central gable, slanting roof lines are suggested by two cupids holding up between them a shield upon which is written, "The spirit of man is the candle of the Lord." [211] Before this shield burns the lamp

---

205. See above, p. 122. It is possible that all these objects are early mizrachs.

206. From Wischnitzer-Bernstein, op. cit., 62, fig. 37. The author does not date the mizrach, and I have no way of doing so.

207. As, e.g., in motifs on amulets: see above, III, fig. 1071.

208. The talismanic value of the Cohenic hands

is shown by the fact that such hands were often used in the seventeenth and eighteenth centuries as amulets to be worn on the person. The Jewish Museum of New York has a number of such amulets.

209. *BT, Berakoth*, 28b (ET, 173); Landsberger, op. cit., 377.

210. Publ. in *JE*, VIII, 629.

211. Prov. xx, 27.

of the eternal light, and beneath it is inscribed, "I will dwell among the children of Israel"; the word for "dwell" has the same root as "Shekinah," so that the saying could be translated, "I will be the Shekinah among the sons of Israel." Under the two vases with flowers one reads across, "Tear Satan," and under that, "On this side [the east] is the living Spirit." In large letters on the two sides is an acrostic which no one whom I consulted could identify. Four biblical scenes are below this, two in each side opening. The sacrifice of Isaac and the blessing of Jacob are on the left, and Moses smiting the rock and the judgment of Solomon are on the right. The central opening is most interesting. It is represented with opened curtains, and at the bottom is the legend, "The sun, until its setting, praises the name of Yahweh." Above this is "East," and, beneath the Ark of the Covenant with the Decalogue, the usual motto, "Know before whom you stand." The most mysterious scene is that within the central arch, that is, above the cherubim of the Ark and below the motto, "I will be the Shekinah among the sons of Israel." Here sits a bearded figure, hand to forehead in a gesture of bewilderment (perhaps of cursing), the other hand holding a scroll. About him is a scene of ruin and despair. It is the only scene without a label; it represents perhaps Moses or Jeremiah, but its position, and the fact that it is not labeled, like the others, suggest that while the figure has the form of Jeremiah or of Moses, it may possibly have here the value of nineteenth-century Christian representations of God himself. Whether this last is quite unjustified fancy or not, the plaque as a whole is, like the one just described, carefully composed to suggest, by its traditional symbols and mottoes, the presence of God, the Shekinah.

One other mizrach, fig. 89,[212] is really the back of a candlestand designed for the desk of the man leading the prayers in the synagogue.[213] This is a common use of the mizrach. Here we have only a single shrine, but again with snakes on the columns, the menorah flanked this time by a pair of stags, and above it the now familiar formula, "Know before whom you stand." Above this in turn are the tablets of the Decalogue flanked by lions, and over them is a crown jutting up into the low arch of the lintel. Above the arch is a plaque presenting the mystic ה, abbreviation for the "Name." The same symbol is substituted for "Yahweh" in the verse which is beside it, "I have set Yahweh always before me"[214]—a verse often used on curtains of Torah shrines similarly to indicate the presence of the Shekinah.[215] Indeed, this verse in which the ה is put in place of "Yahweh" is taken from the account of Solomon's prayer dedicating the Temple and Yahweh's answer, in which the Shekinah is promised in the words, "My name shall be there."[216] All these things would impress upon a devotee the implication that he was standing before the Shekinah. The traditional symbolism was probably by this time completely relegated to the unconscious mind for explanation, but clearly retained intact its original values. The tablet inspired a feeling of reverence.[217]

212. From Wischnitzer-Bernstein, op. cit., 73, fig. 41.

213. This plaque functioned as a mizrach, but when put thus on a cantor's desk it was properly called a "Shiviti-table": Landsberger, loc. cit.

214. Ps. XVI, 8.

215. Landsberger, loc. cit.

216. I Kings VIII, 29, 44, 48; IX, 3. See above, II, 241.

217. For other mizrachs see Jüdisches Lexikon, IV, 229 f.

Another way in which the shrine serves as a sanctifying device is in its use on the so-called breastplate of a scroll of the Law. This is a plaque suspended on a chain from the top of the scroll, so that it hangs at about the middle of the scroll like a breastplate on a man's chest. It is usually designed to represent a little Torah shrine or mizrach. Figures 85 [218] and 86 [219] show typical examples. On the first, clusters of grapes hang beside the inner shrine. On the second, besides the usual lions and the imperial eagle on the crown, a pair of cocks are at the top, and birds, in the ancient manner, guard or sanctify the inner shrine. In fig. 87 [220] two grapevines grow from pots, while in fig. 88 [221] the vines, shells, fillets, crowns, and the lions holding a basin and ewer for ceremonial washing, are beautifully presented within the basic form of the four columns, with the motto "Oaths," i.e., "Covenants," to represent the Torah.

Still another use of the shrine as a form important in itself is to be found in medieval and modern Jewish seals. Blau published the seal of David bar Samuel Zebi, who lived in the fourteenth century,[222] and the communal seal of Ofen.[223] On the first, a design of two columns joined by an arch, as we saw it especially on ancient Jewish glass, is quite enough in itself. On the second there is a wealth of interesting detail, much of which I cannot identify. The illustration shows a Torah shrine topped with a dome, whose ribs recall, probably not by chance, the lines of the old shell. Under this is a shrine with double columns on each side. The curtains are looped back to expose three objects, probably scrolls. Above these, and apparently in front of them, are devices which I cannot make out. The shrine proper is flanked by a pair of square piers, each with something that may be a crown at the top. These latter forms seem remote descendants of our ancient acroteria, especially since there hangs from each, as from the acroteria on the shrine at Beth Alpha,[224] a little chain ending in what looks like an amulet or bauble. It is clear that for the Jews who created these designs not just the scrolls were important, but also the shrine in which they were kept.

Seals of course suggest magical or talismanic value, hence it is not surprising that the shrine should often have been used on amulets to be worn for various types of protection. We have seen what seemed to be Torah shrines on amulets of the Greco-Roman period.[225] This tradition of the talismanic value of the shrine persisted. With the permission of the Jewish Museum in New York, I show from its considerable collection two amulets on which the shrine appears as the potent symbol. In the arch above the lintel in the first of

218. Made in Poland in 1824. From the Danzig Collection, Jewish Museum, New York; published by courtesy of the Museum. On the origin of the breastplate, see F. Landsberger in *HUCA*, XXIV (1952/3), 144–146.

219. Made in Galicia, probably at Lemberg, c. 1800. Mintz Collection, Jewish Museum, New York; published by courtesy of the Museum. Cf. *JE*, XI, 129, for the way in which the breastplates hang upon the scrolls.

220. Made in Nuremberg, c. 1850. No. F1897,

Jewish Museum, New York; published by courtesy of the Museum.

221. Made in Augsburg, c. 1725. Mintz Collection, Jewish Museum, New York; published by courtesy of the Museum.

222. *JE*, XI, plate facing p. 136, fig. 30.

223. Ibid., fig. 9; cf. p. 138. Both of these seals were fifty years ago in the possession of Albert Wolf of Dresden, but where they are now I do not know.

224. See above, III, fig. 639.

225. See III, figs. 1198 f.; cf. II, 287 f.

these, fig. 91,[226] is a peculiar device which suggests a shell or the rising sun; Dr. Kayser of the Museum associated its five points with the five books of the Law. Within the shrine are inscribed the first words of the priestly blessing: "The Lord bless you and keep you." The second amulet, fig. 92,[227] presents an elaboration of the façade of three doors, with the central door especially emphasized. The dome at the top still suggests the shell. It is hard to believe that these little amulets, designed to give personal protection, could have been made without an active feeling that the shrine and façade had potency in themselves.

D. SYMBOLISM OF THE SHRINE

Now that we have traced the persistence of values in the symbols of the shrine and the façade as they recur throughout the ages, and as reflected in the Torah shrine and sacred façade of Judaism, we may turn back to the earlier Jewish shrines to examine more closely how they were used. At the same time we must search out what we can find in ancient literature to suggest how Jews would have explained them. We can then go on to see what function the shrine and the façade had in Christianity and in Mohammedanism. It will appear that in both these later religions the shrine was derived from Jewish rather than from pagan usage.

1. In Judaism

As we return to the Jewish representations of shrines in the Greco-Roman period, a striking difference, in convention at least, appears when we compare those of western countries with forms found in Palestine. For while in the eastern countries the Jewish shrine was pictured invariably with the doors closed (except in the case of a single graffito in Sheikh Ibreiq),[228] in the designs of the West the doors are always open to show the scrolls inside.

We may begin with the painting in the Catacomb Torlonia [229] in which a gabled shrine, very much like those we have been seeing, is at the center of a group of symbols under parted curtains, exactly the sort of group which impressed us at Beth Alpha. The shrine itself has the familiar "round object" at the top of the gable, the roof line is crenelated or supplied with "round objects," another "round object" is in the center of the pediment, others are on the posts of the shrine, and its base is decorated with round-centered lozenges. This design, found at the back of an arcosolium, can hardly, it seems to me, be a picture of the front of a synagogue. It is the traditional abstraction of the shrine set before the worshiper in a synagogue. It presents the saving symbols of Judaism, mystic tokens which, when "revealed to sight," opened to the faithful a new world.

226. An amulet of the seventeenth or eighteenth century; unnumbered at the Museum.

227. Of about the same period, also unnumbered at the Museum. What is under the large central gable I cannot make out. Obermann, with misgivings, guessed that the legend might mean: "To Sarah, complete recovery." Beneath this is plainly *Shaddai* ("The Almighty"). For varied examples

of such later Jewish amulets, some with the form of a Torah shrine, see R. Kaufman, "Amulets," *UJE*, I, 288–291; see also Ludwig Blau, "Amulet," *JE*, I, 546–550; B. Heller, "Amulett," *EJ*, II, 735–746.

228. See above, III, fig. 60.

229. See III, fig. 817.

Less elaborately, this is what appears on several tombstones of Rome. Two of these [230] have each a very simple gabled shrine, open, between menorahs; another [231] shows an open Torah shrine and accompanying objects, though here there are no menorahs. But the most elaborate representations of the Torah shrine set in such a group are on the gold glasses of Rome. On two of them [232] the open shrine is shown between lions in an upper register, and a pair of menorahs with other cult objects is in the lower register; in one of these, curtains appear in the upper register. The double presentation occurs also on another gold glass,[233] where the upper register contains a gabled shrine with doves standing on globes, while a menorah with cult objects, and this time also lions, are in the lower register. A fragment of a similar upper register [234] shows a scroll beside the shrine, and doves. I should guess that the lost lower register of this design bore a collection of objects like those on the other glasses just described. It is interesting that in this case the top of the shrine is rounded, and that in it are drawn a menorah, an ethrog, and a shofar; this recalls the menorah in one of the round-topped shrines at Dura, fig. 65.

This division seems to me not altogether an artistic convention. It suggests again the differentiation we have so frequently met—a lower stage symbolized by the menorah, a higher stage by the Torah shrine. We have frequently found the two symbols presented together when menorahs are used to flank the shrine, but we have so often encountered them separated that their occurrence thus set apart seems now definitely to indicate an ideological convention, by which Judaism was divided into a lower and a higher stage. Such a division, as I may remind the reader again, goes very well with Philo's distinction between a lower and a higher Jewish Mystery. The gold glasses, however, do not always carry this twofold symbolism. In two of them [235] the menorahs appear in the upper register with the Torah shrine, as we have so often seen them—here because it was desired to present a quite different symbol, the fish meal, in the lower register.

I must say that I see no symbolic contrast between the closed shrines of the East and the open shrines of the West. The setting of the shrine, especially when associated with the menorah, is so similar in East and West—both when the two are represented as companion symbols, and when they seem to be somehow contrasted as higher and lower—that one gets the impression of an identity in meaning obtaining from Rome to Dura.

The representation of a shrine with closed doors is apparently a reference to some such secret as would be familiar in Cabbala or in pagan mysteries. The representation of the shrine as open—whether by means of curtains drawn apart or of opened doors—still suggests a secret matter, the revelation of which would be deeply important. Perhaps in the funerary symbolism of the West the doors are open in order to show that the deceased has gone into the world symbolized by the objects behind them. We have suspected at Beth Alpha and Naaran that the scheme of an inner room reserved for these symbols indicates that coming to this stage was the culmination of mystical ascent.

From the way symbols are usually treated, one would suspect that the Jewish devices

230. See III, figs. 706 f.

231. See III, fig. 710.

232. See III, figs. 964 (965), 966.

233. See III, fig. 967.

234. See III, fig. 968.

235. See III, figs. 973 f.

probably served to abbreviate all this, so that the shrine may have become a symbol detached and adequate in itself; it is as such an abbreviation that I must regard the Torah shrine presented as an independent form. The question is: What should we infer was the reality into which one would come, the world which lay behind the doors and curtains, and which was brought to a grave by putting the simple shrine, open or closed, upon it?

Several lines of approach bring us to a single conclusion. We have seen that the ark of the Law was in name and form identical with the Ark of the Covenant.[236] The symbolism of the two has always been closely alike. The Ark used in the wilderness, and afterwards supposedly placed in Solomon's Temple,[237] traditionally contained the tables of the Law, among other objects. Now, in later times, the shrine in which the scrolls of the Law were kept, a holy object in itself, had taken over the value of the lost earlier Ark, the value of being itself the Shekinah, or the seat of the Shekinah, the presence of God among men.[238] Hence the perpetual light burned before the Torah shrine as it had burned before the Ark. Similarly, the curtains before the ark of the Law brought into the synagogue the mysterious feeling conveyed by the curtains before the Holy of Holies in the Tabernacle, that the Real Presence, or Shekinah, though hidden from all common gaze, was there.[239]

We have here all the makings of a mystic rite, and since the form of the shrine and the fact that it was called an ark[240] suggest that the rite was devised among hellenized Jews, we look naturally to see what the parting of the curtains, the revealing of the shrine and its contents, meant in the tradition of Greek-speaking Jews. Philo throws us into an evaluation of Old Testament passages in terms completely derived from Greek mystical thought. He takes the descriptions of the form of the Ark in Exodus and allegorizes them word by word until the Ark is made to represent Deity in its sevenfold manifestation, Being and the six descending Powers.[241] We recognize an elaborate conception of God which one can call gnostic or Neoplatonic or mystic at one's pleasure. Philo describes two approaches to God, that through cosmic worship and that of transcending all material media and going to God himself. Philo found the first approach represented in the outer rooms of the Jewish Tabernacle and Temple: the symbols here, he felt, especially the menorah,

236. See above, pp. 115 f.

237. Critical study of the Bible has shown that the ancient Ark was not a single box: it is thought that, since it was a box containing the sacred lots that were cast to obtain a divine oracle, there was probably such a box at every shrine of Yahweh in early times. See William R. Arnold, *Ephod and Ark*, Cambridge, 1917, esp. the summary, pp. 131–141 (Harvard Theological Studies, III). Arnold shows how the editors of the P document, and of the Pentateuch as a whole, substituted for these boxes the imaginary Ark of the wilderness, which all readers of the Old Testament, Philo included, have taken to be the single Ark of the Israelites.

238. See Casanowicz in *JE*, II, 108.

239. I do not follow Landsberger's argument (op. cit., 359–364) that there is a distinction between representing the curtain as directly on the shrine, or, as at Beth Alpha, as a frame for a space containing other objects along with the shrine. He feels that in the first case the object represented is the Torah shrine, in the second the Ark of the Covenant. He does not consider the parallels to Beth Alpha at Torlonia (see above, III, fig. 817), and on gold glasses (III, fig. 966), where the open doors disclose Torah scrolls, and the curtains are pulled back to show all the objects. Whether the curtains are directly connected with the shrine or not seems to me a matter of local convention, which would not affect the symbolism of either the doors or the curtains, nor of the shrine itself.

240. See above, p. 116.

241. See my *By Light, Light*, 23–28.

were all to be interpreted in a cosmic sense. Contrasted with this was the inner room behind the curtain, which symbolized the world to be approached only by the intellect, the
Platonic immaterial world.[242] To go into this sacred place was possible only for one who
could wear the white robe of Yom Kippur, the high priest, and to go into this room was to
go into the Real Presence indeed.[243]

The one object in the inner sanctuary was the Ark of the Covenant, and this, accordingly, symbolized to Philo in its various parts the gradations of power descending from
the One. As I read these passages in Philo, I feel that those who consider such mystical
allegories to be only poetic flights of imagination are entirely wrong. Philo, I am sure, was
understating rather than overstating the mystic development of Judaism in his day. For
example, he says that the allusion in Exod. xxv, 20, to the cherubim turned toward each
other is

> an extremely beautiful and divine similitude. For it is necessary that the Powers, the
> Creative and the Royal, should look toward each other contemplating each other's
> beauties, and at the same time that they should coalesce for the benefit of the things that
> have come into being. In the second place, since God, who is One, is both the Creator and
> King, naturally the divided Powers should again achieve unity. For it is so advantageous
> that they be divided in order that one of them may function as creator, the other as
> ruler. For each of these is different. And they were also brought together in another way,
> that is by the eternal juxtaposition of their names, that the Creative Power may have a
> share in the Royal Power, and the Royal in the Creative. And both come together
> naturally at the Mercy Seat; for if God were not merciful to the things which now exist,
> nothing would come into existence through the Creative Power, nor would there be any
> government by the Royal Power.[244]

The significance of this passage I did not grasp when I first published it.[245] Philo, of
course, had no more than the biblical text to tell him about the Ark; its form and meaning
were in his day as much a matter of tradition as they were for the medieval Cabbalists,
and are for us today. The point is that the Ark was to him the supreme revelation of the
nature of God. It was the basis of his gnostic-mystical conception that God exists and
functions in a series of pairs, pairs which come together as a unity only at the very top.
So Philo lays great stress upon the fact that the two cherubim were represented as facing
each other, that is, he adds, they were "contemplating each other's beauties," "co-
alescing," "brought together" in "eternal juxtaposition." What he openly hints is made
explicit in the Talmud itself, where R. Kattina, who lived in the third century after Christ,
is quoted as saying:

> Whenever Israel came up to the Festival, the curtain would be removed for them
> and the Cherubim were shown to them, whose bodies were intertwisted with one another,

242. This contrast in Philo is developed ibid.,
passim; see esp. p. 113.

243. See ibid., 98, 108, 255.

244. *QE,* ii, 66; Harris, *Fragments,* 65. I have
translated the Greek fragment. For the slight
variations of the Armenian text, see Marcus'
translation.

245. *By Light, Light,* 25 f.

and they would be thus addressed: Look! You are beloved before God as the love between man and woman.[246]

The Talmud goes on shortly to discuss the meaning of an obscure Hebrew word, *loyoth*, in the description of the carvings in Solomon's Temple. It is said that Solomon had cherubim and palm trees and open flowers (rosettes?) carved on the walls of the building inside and out,[247] that upon each of the ten bases he put sculptured lions, bulls, and cherubim, and that beneath the lions and bulls were objects whose meaning as explained in the text has been entirely obscure at least since the days of the translators of the Septuagint, because the Hebrew *loyoth* has been unintelligible.[248] According to Rabbah, son of R. Shilah (first half of the fourth century), the verse means that the pairs of cherubim in all these cases "were intertwined like husband and wife," and indeed Resh Lakish, who flourished about fifty years earlier, said:

> When the heathens entered the Temple and saw the Cherubim whose bodies were intertwisted with one another, they carried them out and said: These Israelites, whose blessing is a blessing, and whose curse is a curse, occupy themselves with such things! And immediately they despised them, as it is said: All that honoured her, despised her, because they have seen her nakedness.[249]

It seems utterly useless to speculate as to whether the rabbis have not here preserved the original textual tradition, and hence whether Solomon might not actually have covered the walls of his Temple, and the bronze bases in the sanctuary, with figures of cherubim twined together in intercourse. It is possible that the original statement was to this effect, and that the text was deliberately obscured in expurgation. An alternative hypothesis is more plausible. For the following points are to be recognized. First, the conception here attributed to the rabbis is completely foreign to the traditions of Judaism as the rabbis ordinarily presented them. Secondly, it is quite in harmony with later cabbalistic speculation, by which the divine power in its descent is at once divided between the right and the left, which are the male and the female, indeed are aspects of divinity obviously deriving from the Ruling Power and Creative Power so prominent in Philo's writings, the two Powers whose ultimate reunion constitutes the secret of the unity of God. Thirdly, the idea of this union reflects the sort of thinking which lies at the very heart of gnostic speculation as contrasted with the stricter Neoplatonism. And fourthly, the conception is directly to be traced back to Philo's interpretation of the cherubim, primarily the cherubim of the Ark, secondarily those set to guard Eden.[250] What the rabbis have given us, then, is a more

246. *BT, Yoma,* 54a (ET, 255).

247. I Kings vi, 29.

248. I Kings vii, 29, 36. The attempt to make the word mean wreaths or garlands seems to me entirely without foundation: see the notes ad loc. in R. Kittel, *Die Bücher der Könige (Handkommentar zum Alten Testament),* 1900, 65; I. Benzinger, *Die Bücher der Könige (Kurzer Hand-Commentar zum Alten Testament),* 1899, 50; C. F. Burney, *Notes on the Hebrew Text of the Books of Kings,* 1903, 95.

249. *BT, Yoma,* 54b (ET, 257).

250. Another passage of Philo, *Cher.* 27 f., likewise tells of the unity of God divided between these two Powers, but reunited in the Logos, whose symbol is the "fiery sword," since here Philo is allegorizing the two cherubim of Eden. Philo's figures are becoming patently phallic, for the "fiery sword" now symbolizes to him not a threat to trespassers, but the Logos as the means of union between the two cherubim.

popular and outspoken version of a gnostic-cabbalistic idea which appears in Philo at least two centuries earlier than in rabbinic tradition. In Philo, the context is completely fitting; in the Talmud, the notion is utterly anomalous. The hypothesis most in accord with all these facts is that the tradition arose in a hellenized Jewish environment that was enriching the Old Testament statements with mystical allegory, an allegory which freely used the pagan erotic forms for expressing the nature of God and of man's relation to God.

The charms and amulets suggest that the ancient Ark and its symbolism were much in the popular mind: "I call upon thee, Chadraoun, who sittest between the two cherubim and seraphim," says one charm,[251] and two others hail "Helios on the two cherubim." [252] Indeed, we have seen one Jewish amulet which seems to present a familiar pagan altar form adapted to represent the Ark of the Covenant, with the two cherubim as two Erotes, and with the box labeled "Tetragrammaton." [253] The two Erotes as cherubim are quite in line with the erotic tradition of the cherubim in Jewish literature. Indeed, we may wonder whether the confronting Erotes on lamps were not accepted by Jews as the cherubim "with their faces one to another" who mark the place of the Shekinah.[254]

It seems to me to have been this same group which, as we saw,[255] began to call the ark of the Law the κιβωτός; they gave it this name in order to indicate that the box containing the Law was also the seat of the Shekinah. So popular did the term become, apparently, that the rabbis themselves were forced to begin much later to call the box of the Law by the name 'aron, the same word as was used for the Ark of the Covenant. All of this harmonizes very well with the fact that the ark of the Law as it is earliest depicted was a shrine resembling the Greek temple which was the abode of deity, and that the form of the shrine, as found in synagogue façades and in smaller representations, was really a symbol of the Shekinah which was logically and historically antecedent to the use of the shrine as a container for the Torah. That even before the shrine form was adopted, the box of the Law was identified with the ancient Ark, is indicated by the fact that the earlier round-topped form was quite interchangeably used for either of the two boxes. Behind both of these earlier designs we seem to discover a desire to offer a symbol of the Shekinah.

This seems to me again brought out in the various features associated with the shrine. For example, I am confident that acroteria, while not always indicated,[256] are included so often with exaggerated emphasis (as we saw them in Egypt and Mesopotamia) because they have some significance beyond being formally artistic. In the earlier instances, as on the gabled shrines represented on tombs, the acroteria are more or less elaborated acanthus forms. The acanthus acroterium persisted throughout antiquity and is still frequently used. I cannot say what deeper meaning the acanthus may have had, but I am reluctant to close the door finally on the possibility of its having had significance of some kind.[257]

251. See above, II, 198.

252. See II, 200.

253. See III, figs. 1068 f.; cf. II, 241.

254. See III, figs. 253, 255 (19a), 260.

255. See above, pp. 115 f.

256. They are lacking, e.g., in the Torlonia shrine (III, fig. 817), though here a "round ob-

ject" is at the apex of the gable, and the "round objects" as crenelations on the roof line may be there in place of the acroteria at the lower ends of the roof.

257. The acanthus raises very difficult problems. There are two basic varieties, one with thorns (*A. spinosus*), the other thornless (*A. mollis*). The

Some of the acroteria take the form of horns, like those on horned altars.[258] This kind of shrine goes back many centuries. Figure 90 [259] reproduces the much-published little gold plaque showing a Cretan shrine, and here the horns have a most conspicuous role. Not only do they appear as acroteria, but in the three lower panels, as often in other representations, they hold between them the sacred pillar; that is, they function to enclose and so to sanctify an object. Horns used in this way are characteristic in all Minoan-Mycenaean remains, and the Cretan shrines may well belong to the same type of symbolism. Such horns are famous for having come early into Israelitish use, and indeed they are known from Babylonia.[260] It is notable that birds are here, as we have often seen them on Jewish shrines.

Acroteria likewise appear to impart sacredness when, as often on Roman coins,[261] and in the Dura synagogue,[262] they take the form of winged Victories. I suspect that acroteria in their own right bring us back to our basic symbolism, with its emphasis on the sanctity of the thing enclosed. We have thought earlier that the two bell towers which came into medieval architecture in the place of acroteria may have been evolved as a perpetuation of this principle of the sanctifying enclosure. All this would be regarded by most historians of art as a development of mere forms. While I cannot say how much more is implied in these enclosing devices, or indeed what it is exactly that is implied, I still feel that we are confronted with developing forms, to be sure, but not with "mere" forms.

The birds which appear with the Cretan shrines and several of the Jewish ones [263] seem to have persisted through the centuries, though their significance must often have been explained in varying terms. One suspects that the birds, originally doves, were at first references to Astarte or Aphrodite or an equivalent, whatever the name,[264] while the Victories must have carried some of the same feeling, in that, like the birds, they had wings. One wonders, however, whether these in Jewish circles might not have become associated with the Jewish winged figures, and so have been, in value at least, our cherubim again. In such a matter one can only suggest a possibility.

Parenthetically, the acroteria, especially those at the lower corners of a shrine, which seem to constitute a variant of the sacred enclosure, recall the overwhelming frequency of

---

acanthus crown went with the purple robe (Mark xv, 17), and, like the purple, supposedly was a symbol of royalty, not only in its form, but in the type of leaf used (in this instance, of course, *A. mollis*). That the crown of acanthus was a crown of torture when put upon Jesus I am not at all convinced. The report that Jesus bled from wearing the crown came into Christian tradition some centuries later. See James Yates, "On the Use of the Terms Acanthus, Acanthion, etc., in the Ancient Classics," *Classical Museum*, III (1846), 1–21; E. Guillaume in DS, I, 12–14; Wagler in PW, I, 1148–1150. See also the note by C. B. Welles and myself in *HTR*, XLVI (1953), 241 f.

258. See esp. the shrine at Beth Alpha, above, III, fig. 639, and the shrines on gold glasses, III,

figs. 973 f.

259. From Lagrange, "La Crète ancienne," *RB*, N.S., IV (1907), 335, fig. 28; cf. also figs. 27, 29, 33.

260. Miss B. L. Goff is preparing a study of the phenomenon in prehistoric Babylonia.

261. See, e.g., the numerous references to such acroteria in Harold Mattingly, *Coins of the Roman Empire in the British Museum*, IV: *Antoninus Pius to Commodus*, 1940, 893, s.v. "Temple showing six columns."

262. See, e.g., du Mesnil, *Peintures*, plates xxv, xxxv. I hope to publish clearer reproductions in the last volume of this study.

263. See above, III, fig. 639.

264. Doves will be discussed in a later volume.

pairs of flanking objects in all ancient and in much modern symbolism. We may mention, simply for example, the pair of lions flanking the column on the famous gate of Mycenae; the animals which flank the Cretan goddess; the two "communicants" drinking through straws from a bowl between them on Babylonian seals; the powerful urge, in much of Jewish symbolism, to flank a central sacred object, such as the menorah, with other forms (we recall that in the vision of Zechariah the menorah is flanked by a pair of trees); the balancing of objects at Beth Alpha and elsewhere; and the continuance of this symbolic balancing in relation to Christian altars. The two candles burning one at either end of the altar during the service, with the cross in the middle between them, come especially to mind.

I put this forward only as a possible suggestion; but we are repeatedly finding the meaning of our symbolism in the "language of paradox," and that may well be the case here. The balancing reflects essentially, perhaps, the tension between the opposites so recurrent in our personal lives, the tension which modern critics feel as underlying all poetry,[265] so that the cross, the menorah, the Torah shrine, the goddess, or the cup, standing between balanced alternate motifs, is by its very position the symbol of the resolution of that tension, the *tertium quid* of the basic paradox of life and death. The sacred three would, by this, be a representation of the tension of life, and of the saving reconciliation of the opposites. Indeed it is in accepting and yet transcending this tension that religion offers its greatest healing. The dichotomies of love-hate, life-death, flesh-spirit, individual-society, man-God—all of these manifestations of the same fundamental tension are, in Christian terms, reconciled in the cross. This, perhaps, is what the central cross above the candles flanking it on the altar tells us in the direct language of symbolism. Indeed, as regards our whole problem of the three doors, or of three persons as a trinity (Christian or pagan in form), it is highly possible that what is symbolized is the primal triad which a century ago was popularly presented in the Hegelian formulation as thesis, antithesis, and synthesis, and which at that time seemed to epitomize the basic meaning of all life, history, and metaphysics.

Another clear reference to the ancient Holy of Holies is found in the curtain or curtains, earlier mentioned, that hung before the Torah shrine. They vividly recall the curtains of the Tabernacle behind which was the Ark, and I have no doubt that this association was definitely intended. Figure 93 [266] shows an early Christian representation of the shrine at Santa Maria Maggiore. In the full mosaic Joseph stands before this shrine on one side; at the other side is Mary, standing before another shrine.[267] Mary's shrine seems to be the Torah shrine of Judaism; but it is impossible to say whether Joseph's shrine with its eternal light and curtains is a Torah shrine or the old Holy of Holies. From the point of view of values, it really does not matter which was intended.

The shell which we have seen often on the Jewish shrines, and which was so important that it was sometimes put in as an afterthought,[268] intensifies the feeling of holiness.[269] In

265. See above, p. 41.

266. From Wilpert, *Mosaiken und Malereien*, III, plate 56; cf. ibid., I, 479.

267. See ibid., III, plate 53; ibid., I, 476.

268. See above, III, figs. 59, 440, 639, 666; cf. figs. 53, 566, 573, 602, 617.

269. The shell will also be discussed in a later volume.

one painting at Rome the sanctity of the shrine has been heightened by putting a sun and moon at the left and right of the roof line, which gives the shrine a cosmic setting.[270] The photographs only faintly show this, but in the original one can clearly see not only the sun and moon beside the shrine, but also a star above it. The editors think that the shrine represents the Temple of the heavenly Jerusalem, but it is clearly a Torah shrine with open doors, and I suspect rather that it presents the cosmic and heavenly place of the Law as a divine symbol.

The shrine flanked by the heavenly luminaries suggests also that the Law is the Light, itself a manifestation of the Shekinah. How traditional this is in Judaism is shown not only by the menorahs which flank the shrine in most representations, even to this day, but also by the eternal light which, in analogy with the eternal light in the Tabernacle,[271] burns before the Torah shrine.[272] This association with light is still marked in the synagogue also by a detail of the celebration of Simhath Torah, when all the scrolls are taken out of the shrine and carried round the synagogue in procession. Into the empty shrine there is then put a lighted candle: it is clear that quite apart from the scrolls which give it sanctity, the shrine itself has sanctity, and even in the absence of the scrolls, does not cease to give out light. In view of this it becomes clear why the "round object" is used so constantly on the ancient shrines, for we shall see in a later volume that the "round object" is itself, among other things, a symbol of light. And it was from this point of view that the peculiar little plaques bearing shrines with openings for glass [273] took on meaning as we considered them. They show that the shrine is a source of light. The devices on them obviously represent Torah shrines, as we judge from the menorahs beside them, and the plaques are clearly sepulchral fetishes. In a peculiarly vivid form they seem to have brought to the deceased the Shekinah as Light-Law. As used among the living, I suspect that they may have served as mizrachs, since this appears to be also the religious value of the mizrach.[274]

Figure 94 [275] shows a remarkable survival of the shrine—here presented as a sacred object in itself—on an illuminated page from a prayer book for festivals dated 1272. The design is that of the ancient shrine with arch and elaborate acroteria, though medievalized in many ways: its connection with the past is most strikingly shown by the sun and moon on the arch, especially in the detail that the sun is the familiar six-point rosette of Jewish ossuaries. Beneath the shrine stands a judge holding a balance very heavily weighted on one side, which I take to be a reflection of the sense that the New Year and the Day of Atonement are days of reckoning for one's sins. That the judge is God I do not say, but that the shrine hallows the judgment as divine seems unmistakable.

2. In Christianity

WE HAVE already noted how the sanctifying façade went into Christianity as an architectural device, and indeed this development could be discussed at length with reference

270. See III, fig. 811.
271. Exod. xxvii, 20.
272. See above, III, figs. 59 f., 639.
273. See III, figs. 440–442.
274. See above, p. 122.
275. From F. Landsberger, "On Mediaeval and Modern Art," *Milgroim*, no. 2, 1922, p. 4. The letters on the little flag in the arch I have not been able to decipher. *Baruch*, the first word, is clear, but whether intended as "blessing" or a proper name I cannot say.

to the recess, the niche, or the shrine form used with other sacred objects, such as statues of saints. Only a few striking instances can be mentioned.

Sloane recognized that the design of the frontispiece of the Ashburnham Pentateuch, fig. 95,[276] is a remote descendant of the Jewish Torah shrine, and especially commented on the shell under the arch. He was quite right, and I do not doubt that behind this presentation lay a Jewish frontispiece with the same design.[277] He did not, unfortunately, notice the birds in the corners, and his reproduction only suggests at the right that horns had been a part of the original design. We see the motive: the holy text was consecrated by being put within the shrine façade, which here again is a consecrating form in its own right.

No one has noticed, however, that the shrine also survived in Christian usage upon Coptic tombstones. In fig. 96 [278] we have a typical example, important because shell, horns, and birds together make it clear that this is still the same shrine. Not every one of the more than thirty instances in Gayet's collection, or of the still larger number in that of Crum,[279] has all of these details together, but the three rarely appear together even in Jewish designs. Our feeling that acroteria are important symbols, whether they are horns, birds, or acanthus, or a combination of these, is strengthened by the fact that for acroteria the Copts used a variety of devices—birds,[280] leaves,[281] palm leaves,[282] fishes,[283] hares,[284] or the ΑΩ.[285] The crenelated roof has disappeared altogether, but the "round object" occurs several times, as in fig. 97.[286] The "round object" is clearly more than a formal survival when it is assimilated into the upper part of the old Egyptian ankh to make a new Christian symbol within the shrine, fig. 98.[287] The symbolic value of the round-centered lozenge and of the "round object" seems vividly to survive in the crudities of fig. 99.[288]

The shrine in these Coptic Christian representations is usually a frame for a sacred object, but sometimes it seems to be also the doorway to the next world. Two specimens show this in an elaborate presentation of the vine with a bust of Christ, as in fig. 100.[289] Gayet suggested that the large rosettes are the bread which goes with the wine symbolized by the vine, and that the two together stand for the hope of future life. I strongly suspect that they were felt to do more than this, that they were supposed to help the soul to get to

276. From J. C. Sloane, "The Torah Shrine in the Ashburnham Pentateuch," *JQR*, XXV (1934/5), 1–12, fig. 5. Cf. the shrine in the *Liber floridus*, from St. Omer, published by Helen Rosenau in *PEF, QS*, 1936: see plate IX, at p. 163. The "temple mosaic" on Mount Nebo which she publishes in plate VIII is also interesting.

277. Probably a large number of such manuscript survivals of representations of the shrine could be collected. See also the striking manuscript drawing at Pisa, published by Rohault de Fleury, *La Messe*, 1883, III, plate CLXXXXV.

278. From A. Gayet, *Les Monuments coptes du Musée de Boulaq*, 1889, plate XXIV (*Mém. Miss.*, III, iii); for birds, see also plate LXXXVI.

279. W.-E. Crum, *Coptic Monuments* (Catalogue général des antiquités égyptiennes du Musée du

Caire, nos. 8001–8741, 1902). Almost all the shrines in this collection seem to be variants of the shrine of our fig. 96; but cf. esp. nos. 8586–8603, 8608, 8615–8621, 8662, 8665, 8674 f., 8707. See also A. Tulli in *RAC*, VI (1929), 129–140.

280. Gayet, op. cit., plates XXIV, LXXXVI.

281. Ibid., plates XLV, LXXV.

282. Ibid., plates XXVI, XXXVIII f., XLIV.

283. Ibid., plate LIII.

284. Ibid., plates LIV f.

285. Ibid., plate LXVIII.

286. From ibid., plate XLI; cf. plates LXIV, LXVI, LXVIII, LXXII.

287. From ibid., plate XLIV; cf. plates XXXI f., etc.

288. From ibid., plate LXXXIX; cf. plates XXVI, LVI.

289. From ibid., plate XI; cf. plate X.

heaven, as when the sign of the cross is made over a corpse and the coffin is sprinkled with holy water. Designs in which the shrine is made into a door are common on Coptic tombstones.[290] Indeed, when a little crowned figure appears under the arch on such a stone, fig. 101,[291] we begin to suspect that portraying a saint under an arch or in a niche is a convention for representing him as being in heaven because he has gone through what we still call "the Gates." A seventeenth-century carpet in the synagogue in Padua, fig. 103,[292] shows an arched portal, with the motto, "This is the gate of the Lord; the righteous shall enter into it," whereby the shrine is specifically designated as a gate to immortality.

As this volume was going through the press, I noticed an interesting Coptic adaptation of the Egyptian ankh as a doorway.[292a] Here, embroidered on some sort of sacred cloth, is a design which is basically the ankh. But beneath the crossbar the one upright has become two, so that the whole is a gate with a round top such as is still common in Moslem architecture. A cross is in the upper circle and a second cross is between the two uprights, while a circle of birds round the whole emphasizes the symbolic intent of the design. Here the door has become in a new form the door to life. One is haunted by the possibility, which I know no way to do more than suggest, that the round-topped doors of the mosques had this same original meaning.

Further to attest the sanctifying power of the shrine we have, incidentally, two late Egyptian mummy portraits, one of which, fig. 102,[293] besides immortalizing the deceased by clothing her in the elaborate robe of Isis, sets a little arched shrine over her head, a wholly artificial addition. To point up how all this symbolism had its roots in paganism, I reproduce in fig. 104 [294] a Punic tombstone on which the figure under the arch is being given the crown of immortality. The arch is itself within a gabled shrine, in whose tympanum the deceased appears again, apotheosized, and flanked by doves. An acanthus cup is at the top of the gable, and above it are a great number of heavenly figures and symbols, especially birds and grapes (the grapes at the right are on a vine growing from a vase), while into every possible space a "round object" has been bored with a bit. The "explanations" of these symbols in Punic terms would indeed have been different from those given

290. See Crum, op. cit., nos. 8684–8702.

291. From Brooklyn Institute of Arts and Sciences, Brooklyn Museum, *Pagan and Christian Egypt*, 1941, plate 36. Published by permission. The figure is called Coptic, of the fifth century, an *orans* (p. 23).

292. From *Mittheilungen der Gesellschaft zur Erforschung jüdischer Kunstdenkmäler*, Frankfurt a. M., I (1900), 24, fig. 15, a study presumably by Frauberger. He says that the carpet is of embroidered silk, and of the sixteenth century. Landsberger, in *HUCA*, XIX (1946), 368, says it is of the fifteenth century, and in A. G. Grimwade et al., *Treasures of a London Temple*, 1951, 53, n. 66, Kendrick and Barnett say that it is not an embroidery but a "Transylvanian type of Anatolian carpet, probably of Jewish make, of the late seventeenth century."

As to the design, however, Landsberger is probably right when he says that the object within the gateway is a fountain, and that it "is probably to be understood symbolically as the fountain of life, the fountain of the Law."

292a. P. du Bourguet, "Une Forme particulière de croix ansée sur un trésor copte du legs Raymond Weill," *Revue d'égyptologie*, VIII (1951), 21–23, with plate 1.

293. From Gayet, op. cit., plate A; cf. plate B. Gayet describes this (p. 5) as a Christian object, but not a single one of the symbols on the robe is distinctive of Christianity. See also the shrine on the feet of a mummy from Roman Egypt, fig. 34.

294. In the British Museum. Published by permission of the Museum.

by Jews or Christians, but the tomb itself might easily have been Jewish or Christian so far as the values of the symbols are concerned. We have been studying a "convention" which is much more than a convention.

3. In Mohammedanism

THE TORAH shrine seems to me to have survived in the mosque as well as in the church. The sacred façade did not become a regular form for the entrance to a mosque. In Tunis there is, indeed, an example of the use of this façade, but it is so unusual that the building is called the Mosque of the Three Doors.[295] For the last thousand years, however, it has been the custom in every mosque to indicate the direction for prayer (kiblah) by building into one of the walls what is called a mihrab.[296] The kiblah originally oriented prayer toward Jerusalem, but Mohammed himself seems to have changed the orientation to Mecca, in about the sixteenth month after the hegira. That is, the whole idea of kiblah was taken over directly from the Jews. The original ways of indicating this orientation were varied, but soon only the mihrab was used. The earliest mihrab now extant, according to Creswell, is an arch in low relief, fig. 105,[297] decorated with "round objects," lozenges, and other motifs of the sort that Jewish shrines have made familiar. Almost contemporary with this are mihrabs in the form which from the eighth century on has been quite standard, that of a niche. A mihrab from Bagdad, fig. 115,[298] is of a type favored during the early years in the East; it has the shell in its little semidome, and at the back is a degenerate presentation of the vine and vase motifs also common in Jewish art. This mihrab looks indeed like a Jewish Torah shrine.

The usual mihrab from that time to the present has been a niche, with a mimbar beside it, fig. 106.[299] The mimbar[300] was in early times a throne for the caliph or political ruler of the community, and then became the high seat for the director of the services. That is, at the beginning it had a function much like that of the Seat of Moses. In the earliest mosques it was apparently a wooden throne with several steps ascending to it; but it soon became a fixed part of the structure of the building, like the throne in the synagogues, notably that of Dura. Traditionally, its origin was in a throne from which the Prophet himself preached. But the combination of mimbar and mihrab in the mosque exactly parallels that of throne and Torah niche in the synagogue: in each case the combination is used to indicate the direction of prayer, and originally even the directions were

295. K. A. C. Creswell, *Early Muslim Architecture*, II, 1940, 325.

296. See references ibid., Index, s.vv. "Kibla," "Mihrab," "Minbar"; A. J. Wensinck in *Encyclopedia of Islam*, II, 1927, 985–987; J. Pedersen, ibid., III, 1936, 337–341; E. Diez, ibid., III, 485–490.

297. From Creswell, op. cit., II, plate 120 a; cf. ibid., I, 70. This is a mihrab in a cave beneath the holy rock under the Dome of the Rock in Jerusalem. (Used with permission; also fig. 115.)

298. From Creswell, op. cit., II, 37, fig. 26; cf. pp. 35–38 and plate 120 d. It is in the Bagdad

Museum, says Creswell, and probably was taken from the mosque of al-Mansur.

299. From a photograph by Bonfils of the mihrab and mimbar in the mosque of el-Aksa in Jerusalem. For other examples, see *Encyclopedia of Islam*, III, plates at pp. 488, 500.

300. On the mimbar see E. Diez, ibid., III, 499 f. The study of the mimbar on which all others are based is that of C. H. Becker, "Die Kanzel im Kultus des alten Islam," *Orientalische Studien Theodor Nöldeke*, 1906, I, 331–351. Both Creswell (op. cit., I, 9) and Diez give further bibliography.

identical, since in early Islam the orientation was, as it always has been in Judaism, toward Jerusalem. The orientation is also indicated by the shrine on the prayer rug.

Accordingly, there appears to be no reason to deny that the mihrab and mimbar mark a direct line of transition from the synagogue to the mosque. The mihrab has by some been derived from India,[301] but of late years it has seemed assured that it came into Islam from the Coptic Christians.[302] Creswell shows two Coptic niches, and one pulpit (not connected with a niche) with steps, which are decidedly similar to Moslem mimbars, and there is a little literary tradition—to me quite indecisive—which Creswell quotes as final. We have found extensive use of the niche among the Copts, to be sure, but no stated convention of niche and pulpit together, and nothing to indicate that the Coptic niches were devices for orientation. At the same time it has seemed obvious that a great deal went from the Jewish synagogal art of Alexandria and Egypt (all lost) to Coptic Christians. I should therefore see the Coptic niche with its pulpit as a cousin, rather than an ancestor, of the Moslem usage. When to all this is added the frequent custom of putting a copy of the Koran into the mihrab,[303] Jewish rather than Christian antecedents seem by far the more probable. In both religions, the worshiper, watched from the pulpit, prays toward the holy place through a niche in which is the Holy Writ.

4. Conclusions

IN CLOSE kinship with the Torah shrine in form and use, we find representations in the Greco-Roman Jewish art of an actual little temple, or, more properly, a shrine in three dimensions, instead of just the front of a shrine. One of these [304] is in the arcosolium of the Catacomb Torlonia that has also the Torah shrine with sun and moon.[305] Unfortunately, there remains of the little temple only the front gable and one side of the roof in perspective behind the gable. The rest of the shrine has gone with the plaster on which it was painted. But the roof here too is flanked by sun and moon. A similar shrine appears on a gold glass.[306] Like the preceding one, it much resembles the Torah shrines, though it is presented not as a façade but as an actual building, and stands in a walled courtyard with gates and palm trees, while the usual menorah, vases, lulab, and the rest appear on the wall in front. This gold-glass representation, which has been much discussed, is amazingly similar, in its essential form, to that of fig. 107.[307] In the latter, the classical shrine has turned into a synagogue of the eighteenth century, but the classical doorway persists in the portal of the city at the front. The whole is made into the heavenly Jerusalem, an eschatological symbol, by

301. As in Thomas P. Hughes, *A Dictionary of Islam*, 1885, 348.

302. Diez, op. cit., 485, says that the mihrab "no doubt" was introduced under Christian influence, but after some sentences more he says that the ascription to Hindu antecedents "has as much or as little in its favor" as that to a Christian source. Creswell, op. cit., I, 99, says "we can no longer hesitate to accept its Christian origin."

303. I have often seen this mentioned but could find no published reference to the practice. Obermann told me that it is a custom dating from approximately the ninth century.

304. See above, III, figs. 809, 811.

305. See III, fig. 817.

306. See III, fig. 978.

307. From Wischnitzer-Bernstein, *Symbole und Gestalten der jüdischen Kunst*, 125, fig. 73. The author recognizes the similarity. The design is from a Passover Haggada printed in Venice in 1740.

the same convention here as at Torlonia, in that the scene is flanked by the sun and moon. Mrs. Wischnitzer-Bernstein recognized that this design looks to the eschatological,[308] and noted its similarity to the design on the gold glass, but missed the feature of the sun and moon.

There is no consecutive tradition in Jewish life for the use of this type of enclosure to represent the messianic hope, or for the persistence of the arched doorway with gable, or of this symbolism of sun and moon. The engraver of the woodcut certainly knew nothing of either Torlonia or the gold glass. I do not like to explain these amazing reappearances of symbols by reference to Jung's theory of the collective unconscious, though I have no alternative explanation for such a phenomenon. Yet we cannot slight the phenomenon because we cannot explain it. One thing that the woodcut adds to the symbolism is the throng assembling from all the corners of the earth at the summons of two men whom Mrs. Wischnitzer-Bernstein plausibly calls Elijah and the Messiah. These people, who are surely the People, come to a spot whose sanctity is effectively indicated by its emptiness. No one is in the streets of the city at all. This emptiness, abstractness, is of the essence, for thus the Shekinah comes again to be felt. If the enclosure were filled with people, it would quite lose this symbolic force, and now that the later design has brought the point to light, the bare abstractness of all the old representations appears to be in the same way an integral part of their symbolic power.

In the preceding volumes [309] the shrine was discussed as symbolizing the heavenly Jerusalem in the form of the "house of Peace," the "house eternal." In John XIV, 2, this same "house" is "my Father's house," where, it is said, there are many "dwelling places." Such dwelling places seem to be represented in the woodcut by the tents, a form which recalls one of the strangest of the Dura paintings.[310] We seem to have in these tents a reemergence of the tents of Dura, and of the "dwelling places" of John, though that phrase is first met with in the Gospel. These tents, we shall see in the next volume, would, for the especially pious, have been made of the skin of Leviathan. Eschatology and mysticism are, as usual, coming very close together. I have suggested in the earlier volumes that all this was implied when the tomb itself was by its façade made into a shrine.

The problem of what is involved in the symbol of the Torah shrine, or of the façade which the Torah shrine primarily was, has become very complicated, but that is the way of symbols as one comes to study them. Simple or facile explanations, explanations "in a word," or in terms of "merely," or "just," are essentially ways in which we escape psychological entanglement in the essential involutions of the symbol itself, or escape its still more dangerous roots. We are, let me recall, in the world of connotation rather than of denotation, a world where "truth" never can be made verbally specific. Since I am not a student of psychology, I feel myself under no obligation to do more than call attention to the observable phenomena. The phenomena themselves are not debatable. I close this

308. She points out the many eschatological allusions in the Seder ritual.

309. See I, 75 f.; II, 113, 141. I am not suggesting, of course, that the Jew who made the woodcut was drawing on the Fourth Gospel, but rather that the phrase in the Gospel had roots deep in Judaism.

310. Du Mesnil, *Peintures*, plate xxx.

discussion of the perennial hope offered in the shrine by presenting fig. 109,[311] which shows the tomb of a Jew in Italy dated 1555. The inscription puts the man himself into the shrine, and so gives him hope of immortality.

E. SYMBOLISM OF THE SCROLL

SOMETIMES THE Jews of the Greco-Roman period contented themselves with abbreviating the shrine symbol simply as a Torah scroll. Many such scrolls can be seen, it is reported, in the catacomb of Sheikh Ibreiq.[312] In the synagogue of Priene a pair of scroll ends are under the branches of the menorah.[313] But scrolls are more common on Jewish monuments in Rome, where they appear on perhaps three graves in the Catacomb Monteverde,[314] on two graves in the Catacomb Vigna Randanini,[315] on a ceiling vault in the Catacomb Torlonia,[316] and beside Torah shrines on two gold glasses.[317] In Jewish catacombs in Rome there were found also two fragments of sarcophagi bearing portrait busts: in both cases the figure is represented holding a conventional scroll.[318] The male figure on a Jewish tombstone from Pannonia [319] holds something that is probably also a scroll. Used as symbols in Jewish burials, the scrolls were probably interpreted as Torah scrolls. There is superficially nothing special to be said regarding the symbolic value of the scroll apart from that of the Torah shrine as a whole, just as we cannot say that there is a distinction in symbolic value between the cross and the crucifix in Christian usage. Both the scroll and the shrine (with or without scrolls) seem to have brought to Jews the living and saving presence of their God. The scroll sanctifies the shrine at least as much as the shrine sanctifies the scroll, and the two are thought of together as one symbol. Certainly they are presented together at least in the open Torah shrines of the West.

A word should be said about the scroll or holy book as such, however, for the book by itself, at least to Protestant and Jewish consciousness today, is more acceptable as a symbol of the divine presence than is the shrine as such. To be buried with a sacred text was important in Egypt from very early times. The Pyramid Texts of the third millennium were probably preceded by other means of giving to the dead the consolations of revealed truth. A wall painting in one of the tombs of Beni Hasan (XIIth Dynasty) shows slaves who provide for the needs of Prince Chnemhotep in the afterlife.[320] One group of these slaves bring him scrolls. This is the same tomb whose entrance with three openings seemed to us so strangely prophetic of much later Greek shrines.[321] The custom of giving a scroll or a sacred text to a corpse continued in Egypt into Christian times, in one form or

311. From H. Frauberger, "Über alte Kultusgegenstände in Synagoge und Haus," *Mittheilungen der Gesellschaft zur Erforschung jüdischer Kunstdenkmäler*, Frankfurt a. M., III/IV (1903), 100, fig. 146. We note also the use of the device to sanctify marriage contracts, e.g., ibid., I (1900), 28.

312. See above, I, 96.

313. See III, fig. 878.

314. See III, figs. 710, 712, and 718(?).

315. See III, figs. 772, 779.

316. See III, fig. 810.

317. See III, figs. 968, 973.

318. See III, fig. 821 (the second fragment was reported but not published); see I, 27.

319. See III, fig. 857.

320. Newberry, *Beni Hasan*, I, plate xxxv (*Archaeological Survey of Egypt*, I).

321. See below, fig. 36.

another, and there is probably a similar meaning in the little scrolls in the hands of the dead on Roman sarcophagi. One recalls also the Orphic leaves used in Greek burial.[322]

The importance of this material can best be seen in the classic work of Birt,[323] from which I take a few instances. Figure 108,[324] reproducing the front of a sarcophagus, shows a woman in each of the three openings of a columned façade. In the scenes of the side openings, she is apparently being instructed by a teacher, along with another person (her husband?). In the central opening, she stands ready to go through the curtain of death hanging behind her, helped by a deeply concerned putto; she is now veiled, but clutches a scroll. She is on her way to the next life. Birt projects his classical interest and makes her a devotee of literature: he thinks she is represented as taking with her in death the books she studied in life. Perhaps I am only projecting my own interest in the same way when I say that it appears much more likely that she and her husband were students of mystic philosophy, or of some mystic *hieros logos,* and that in the scroll she carries this with her as a divine guide. The panel seems a most explicit statement in pagan terms of the values inherent in the Jewish façade, shrine, and scroll.

It is interesting that very few of the figures holding scrolls come from classical Greece,[325] but that the motif is common in Etruscan remains,[326] and really becomes of great importance in such decorations as those at Pompeii.[327] In the Greek examples the scroll appears so often along with musical instruments that one must assume that here the association is indeed with poetry, though music and immortality are too often connected in Greek art and literature to permit of certainty about this. In later representations, however, the roll is almost certainly the mystic roll which corresponds in value to the Egyptian *Book of the Dead.* The value of the scroll seems illustrated in fig. 110,[328] which, as I understand it, shows a mathematician marked by the shrine as sanctified. His mathematics, I should guess, was mystical numerology rather than mere calculation.

From Naples comes the lamp shown in fig. 112,[329] an extremely interesting object, for its stem bears the motif of branches which has appeared so often on Palestinian lamps.

322. The texts on these were edited and translated by Gilbert Murray in an appendix to Harrison, *Prolegomena.*

323. Theodor Birt, *Die Buchrolle in der Kunst,* 1907.

324. From ibid., 64; cf. pp. 63–66. See also W. Amelung, *Die Sculpturen des Vaeticanischen Museums,* 1908, II (text), 166–169; II (Plates), plate 18. Amelung dates the sarcophagus in the third century after Christ.

325. Birt, op. cit., 157, shows a beautiful single example; cf. pp. 46 f., 49, 125 f., 138, 147 f.

326. Ibid., 80; see also p. 343, s.v. *Etruskisches.*

327. Ibid., 113–123, 132 f., 135, 145, 162–165, 223.

328. From Otto von Heinemann, *Die Handschriften der herzoglichen Bibliothek zu Wolfenbüttel,* 1878, II, iii, plate at p. 124. Birt, op. cit., 191,

describes the man as a mathematician who has stopped reading to verify for himself the calculations in the scroll. The illustration is from the sixth-century Codex Arcerianus, but Birt properly suggests that a much earlier prototype lies behind it. He says that the man is raising his fingers in thought. F. Marx, "Digitis computans," *Jahrbücher für classische Philologie,* Suppl. Vol. XXVII (1902), 195–201, assumes that here are the computing fingers of the mathematician. This is justified by the fact that the illustration comes in that part of the manuscript which reproduces a brief treatise on surveying. But the man is not by any means an ordinary mathematician. He sits upon a stool whose base is a pair of human-headed griffins, and we notice the shell used as roof.

329. From Birt, op. cit., fig. 94; see his discussion, pp. 161 f.

In regard to these we were perplexed to determine when such a motif could or could not be taken to represent a menorah, and were especially impressed by the way in which the central stem of the "menorah" encircles the actual light of the lamp, and thus gives the impression of a "round object" at the top. In the Naples lamp we have the same treatment of the light at the top of the branched design. If we may judge from the illustration, the little man holds a palm branch over his left breast. But the lamp here is unquestionably an ithyphallus. The little man is reading a scroll, which according to Birt probably contains such matter as might have induced the erection. Birt finds it perplexing that on the scroll are inscribed clearly the first six letters of the Greek alphabet, but nothing more. His difficulty is that when there is something he does not understand, as here, he tries to reduce it to the comical. This little lamp was probably not a grotesque, but was made to be put into a grave, where it would bring immortality by virtue of its cluster of symbols— light, which is life, since it issues from the phallus as the symbol of life, and hope as offered by the mystic scroll, upon which, of course, only meaningless letters would be exposed to the public. A less explicit expression of the same kind, fig. 111,[330] again suggests only the comical to Birt. To represent a naked child with a scroll seemed to him something which could have been prompted only by a desire to be funny. But the child is a putto, a love symbol, so that what is implied is the hope of salvation through proper knowledge, as symbolized in the scroll, and through love. It is the same combination we saw in fig. 108, where a woman holds a scroll in death, with a putto at her feet to guide her.

It was in such an environment that Philo made a *hieros logos* of the Pentateuch, and this has been the value of the scroll in Judaism ever since. While gentiles, as is reported, were buried with their sacred scrolls, Jews naturally had the Torah scrolls carved on their tombstones. That this practice too went over into Christianity is familiar. But the famous relief presented in fig. 116 [331] shows how the motif went over via Judaism. In the center is Christ with the sacred scroll, surrounded by six disciples. But he is in a Jewish Torah shrine with curtains and arcuated lintel (which the artist quite misconstrues but retains). True, the shrine is also a city wall, that is, its symbolism is elaborated. But that this is a Christian expansion of the Jewish symbol seems to me very clear.[332]

The Jew is ordinarily no longer buried with symbols of his Torah. An eighteenth-century Jewish tombstone in Pappenheim, Bavaria, fig. 113,[333] would appear to present a strange atavism. Here the classical wreath has been revived, with its old sanctifying value, but the scroll has become the printed book. *Plus ça change, plus c'est la même chose.*

330. From ibid., 53, fig. 32.

331. From Garrucci, *Arte cristiana*, VI, plate 441; cf. Birt, op. cit., 168 f. The figure shows the lower part of the Lipsanoteca at Brescia. For a photograph of the whole, see Antonio Ugoletti, *Brescia*, Bergamo, 1909, 41 (C. Ricci [ed.], Collezione di monografie illustrate, Serie Italia artistica, L). I have not been able to consult Richard Delbrueck, *Probleme der Lipsanothek*, Bonn, 1952; see W. Deonna in *Latonus*, XI (1952), 533 f.

332. A quite novel Christian presentation in mosaic appears in the chapel of Santa Matrona in the church of San Prisco in Capua: see Garrucci, *Arte cristiana*, IV, plate 257, 2; cf. Wilpert, *Mosaiken und Malereien*, III, plate 77. In this design Mark and John as bull and eagle flank a throne surmounted by a dove representing the Spirit. Over the throne is a veil which undoubtedly is supposed to cover the objects upon it, but, as in Dura, must be represented as behind them. The objects upon this heavenly throne (set in the clouds) are a banqueting bolster as symbol of the Eucharist, and, resting upon this, a scroll.

333. From Frauberger, op. cit., 102, fig. 151.

CHAPTER SIX

The Lulab and Ethrog

THE GREAT frequency with which the lulab and ethrog appear in the representations on Jewish remains, especially in connection with funerary symbolism, surprises even those who know Jewish tradition best. For while these are objects still used by orthodox Jews in celebrating the Feast of Tabernacles, they are not symbols which it would occur to any Jew now to carve upon his tombstone.

The lulab and ethrog were carried in ceremonial processions during the eight—later nine—days of the Feast of Tabernacles. The word lulab specifically means a palm branch, but refers usually to a bundle of twigs, consisting primarily of a palm branch whose leaves are still unfolded, with three shoots of myrtle and two of willow bound to the base of the palm stalk in a specified way.[1] These, which with the ethrog make up four elements, were of course given many symbolic interpretations by the rabbis, but nothing appears in their ingenious assemblings of proof texts to reveal the real meaning or value of the lulab. In Greco-Roman times, the name ethrog had come to apply properly to a particular citrus fruit, which was tied to the lulab,[2] or carried in the left hand (with the lulab in the right hand) during the processions. In the art we are studying, the ethrog appears as a companion to the lulab, but also often alone.

A. THE LULAB AND ETHROG ON THE MONUMENTS

THE LULAB and ethrog occur first on coins. The earliest instances found to date are the representations on two disputed coins [3] which are probably to be regarded as dating from the First Revolt (A.D. 69–70). One of these shows on the obverse what is commonly taken to be a lulab flanked by ethrogs, on the reverse a wine cup. The other has two lulabs with an ethrog on the obverse, and a fruit-bearing palm tree, with baskets, on the reverse. The lulab and ethrog appear similarly on coins of the Second Revolt (A.D. 132–135),[4] and we found reason to believe in discussing coins of this type that these symbols

---

1. Construction of the lulab seems from our pictures to have varied considerably in the Greco-Roman period. For the talmudic regulations, see Casanowicz in *JE*, VIII, 205–207, and Strack-Bill., II, 780–789.

2. The long, unopened palm branch with an ethrog tied to the base will suggest a symbolism of penis and testicles to some. I can only say they make no such suggestion to me.

3. See above, III, figs. 689 f.

4. See III, fig. 692, and I, 276.

were used on them as tokens of triumph, the triumph of legalistic Judaism and of the new Jewish state.

The lulab and ethrog are especially common on Jewish tombstones, and many of them occur on the graves discussed in Volumes I and II, and are shown in the relevant illustrations.[5] They are also found in catacomb decorations, in graffiti and carvings in Sheikh Ibreiq, on lamps, on Jewish blown glasses, and on gold glasses; in all of these instances they should probably be considered as belonging to funerary usage. They appear as well in paintings, reliefs, and mosaics in the synagogues of Palestine and at Dura, and on seals.[6]

Lietzmann listed a considerable number of occurrences of the ethrog and lulab[7] in the art we are studying, but he felt that the ethrog is presented in two forms—first, as a citrus fruit of the type still recognizable as the ethrog, and, second, as a sort of root vegetable which tapers to a point below and has long leaves at the top, an object which might, he felt, be identified with almost any of the root vegetables. He called it a *Rübe,* a generic term for root vegetables, for which there is no corresponding word in English. The contrast can most clearly be seen on a Roman sarcophagus[8] on which a fine menorah is flanked on the left by an ethrog shaped like a lemon or a lime; its leaves, on a stiff branch, are the small, compact leaves of citrus fruit. At the right is the *Rübe;* it is wide at the top and tapers down into a narrow root, like a parsnip or a sugar beet, and has long, lanceolate leaves growing directly from it. As one studies these forms, however, it is increasingly to be noted that in many of them the distinction is not maintained, but details from both types are used, so that the existence of a specific *Rübe* in contrast to the ethrog becomes doubtful. One tombstone (III, fig. 773), seems to make the problem explicit by putting the *Rübe* and the ethrog side by side, and here the two forms appear as contrasted above. We have the two together also in fig. 846 of Volume III, where the ethrog is a fruit on a stem, and the other form is apparently a root, the *Rübe,* though in this case it has not long leaves but a stem with little leaves. This variation is still more strikingly apparent in fig. 814 of Volume III, where a *Rübe* is drawn in contrast to the definite ethrog balancing it; but here, while the citron with its little leaves is clear on the right, the *Rübe* has a tall clump of foliage above it, quite unlike that found elsewhere with the pointed root shape.

It should be noted that in not a single case in my collection do we have the three devices, lulab, ethrog, and *Rübe,* presented together.[9] Indeed we do not have a single object of the sort we have described as the *Rübe* appearing with the lulab at all. On the

5. See III, Indexes, s.vv. "Lulab" and "Ethrog." Cf. also Frey, *CIJ:* for occurrences of the lulab alone (including the single palm branch), nos. 30 f., 53, 61, 135, 356, 421, 425; of the lulab with a menorah, nos. 51 (cf. *Torlonia,* 30, no. 12), 89, 153, 450, 713; of the lulab with various other Jewish emblems, nos. 79, 95, 500, 523, 578, 652, 671.

6. For all these types of occurrence, see III, Index I.

7. Beyer and Lietzmann, *Torlonia,* 19–21.

8. See above, III, fig. 818.

9. One possible exception appears in a crude drawing, III, fig. 805, in which at one side a palm branch is attached in a unique way to the base of a menorah; on the other side are two objects, both of which could be ethrogs, but neither of which has the form which suggested the use of the term *Rübe.*

contrary, the last instance cited recalls that the lulab itself often is drawn with its lower part going down to a point. Thus, the design in fig. 716 of Volume III, crude as it is, shows an ethrog balancing something that, because of its base, looks like a *Rübe*, but here has a palm branch above it, and in this case is certainly a lulab. On the gold glasses too this form appears distinctly. In fig. 978 of Volume III, we find at the left of a menorah an ethrog and a lulab, the latter a long branch with a bundle at the bottom. In fig. 964 of Volume III, the lulab is drawn in careful detail, with the pointed base of a *Rübe;* an ethrog is at the left. The same lulab with a base shaped like a *Rübe* is on the gold glasses in figs. 967, 969, 974, and 976 of Volume III. A lulab on a stone in Pergamum (III, fig. 877) has a differently shaped base, while still different bases are on lulabs on coins of Palestine (III, figs. 689 f., 692). But a sufficient number of the bases of lulabs are shaped like the *Rübe*, especially in the West, where alone the *Rübe* has been thought to appear, to force me to conclude that the so-called *Rüben* are all lulabs, and that a *Rübe* as a distinct object is really not attested at all.[10]

When one reviews the representations of the lulab and ethrog, the impression arises that they were used primarily as funerary emblems, and that their appearance in synagogues and on seals is secondary to the funerary usage, just as it has often been observed that the synagogal ornament in general was taken from funerary art. It is of course possible that the lulab and ethrog, like the menorah, were often put on graves to say only "Here lies a good Jew," but we have found reason to believe that the menorah itself said basically much more than this, was indeed a seal of immortality, so that, however mechanically a given Jew may have availed himself of the lulab and ethrog, they may, in view of the uses of them that appear in the archeological remains, be presumed to have had a similar value. To recover their meaning more accurately, however, we must examine the literary tradition.

B. THE FEAST OF TABERNACLES

As long as the Temple stood, the Feast of Tabernacles was properly celebrated in Jerusalem.[11] It seems highly probable, however, that for many years, perhaps for three or

10. For a suggestion, made by several scholars, that the *Rüben* are really mandrakes, see Frey, *CIJ*, at no. 545; cf. above, III, fig. 846.

11. The literature on Tabernacles is enormous. The most important rabbinic treatment is of course that comprised in the Mishnah, Gemara, and Tosefta of the tractate *Sukkah* (*BT* and *JT*), though important allusions occur in many other places in the Talmud. The Mishnah and Tosefta of this tractate have been translated with good notes by A. W. Greenup, *Sukkah, Mishna and Tosefta*, 1925. *MR, Leviticus*, 30, and the *Pesiqta* also have excellent comments. This rabbinic material, with much more, is collected in the special essay on Tabernacles in Strack-Bill., II, 774–812. The most valuable general discussion to date is found in Harald Riesenfeld, *Jésus transfiguré*, Copenhagen, 1947, 146–205, while Benzinger in *EB*, IV, 4875–4881, Friedmann in *JE*, XI, 656–662, and Eisenstein in *JE*, XII, 476 f., are still very useful. Special studies will be mentioned as we continue, but particular note should be made of J. Pedersen, *Israel, Its Life and Culture*, III/IV, 1940, 418–425, 737–745; Moore, *Judaism*, II, 43–49; William A. Heidel, *The Day of Yahweh*, 1929, 197–249; R. Patai, "The 'Control of Rain' in Ancient Palestine," *HUCA*, XIV (1939), 251–286; T. H. Gaster, "What the Feast of Booths Celebrates," *Commentary*, XIV (1952), 308–314.

four centuries, Jews who could go to Jerusalem for the celebration did so, while the great mass of Jews who could not go to the Holy City more than once or twice in their lives, if ever, observed the festival each year at home and in their local assemblies. One bit of evidence is in the Mishnah, twice repeated:

> Originally the lulab was taken (shaken) in the sanctuary during seven days and in the country only one day. When the Temple was destroyed Rabban Jochanan b. Zaccai ordained that the lulab should be shaken in the country seven days, in remembrance of the sanctuary.[12]

This can refer only to a ritual "in the country" simpler than that in the Temple, but in practice while the Temple was still standing. We should expect the great mass of Jews who could not go to the Temple each year for the festival to have celebrated it less elaborately at home. Philo's remarks about the feast, to which we shall return,[13] as well as his explanations of the whole cycle of Jewish festivals, predicate that these festivals could be celebrated by Jews in Alexandria, and do not once suggest that the rites could be observed only in Jerusalem. It is hard to see how the Jews of the diaspora could have kept their loyalty as intensely as we know them to have done, if these festivals had for all practical purposes been taken away from them. The celebration of the feast at home and in the synagogue which has been universal since the destruction of the Temple seems, then, only the continuation of a practice that was long established before that catastrophe.

1. *Origin and Temple Celebration*

THE FEAST of Tabernacles (Sukkoth) is a harvest festival which Jews seem to have acquired, as a part of their agricultural rites, from the Canaanites. In Judges (IX, 27) we have a reference to a group at Shechem who had revolted from Yahweh and gone over to worship Baal-berith as their god (VIII, 33 f.). These men "went out into the fields, and gathered their vineyards, and trod [the grapes], and held festival, and went into the house of their god, and did eat and drink." It would appear to be in some manner a reference to this festival also when in a passage shortly preceding (IX, 13), new wine is described as that "which cheers God and man," that is, a drink which God shares with man. That dancing was also part of the festival is inferred from the story of how the Benjamites kidnaped wives for themselves from among the girls who danced at a festival in Shiloh, here become a festival of Yahweh (XXI, 19–23).[14] Originally, Sukkoth was simply a "festival of ingathering," celebrated without fixed date at the end of the fruit harvest, but it was also early called the Feast of Tabernacles from the custom, which Friedmann says still prevails in Palestine,[15] of living in little booths or huts while the harvest is going on. This

12. Mishnah, *Sukkah*, III, 12; *BT, Sukkah*, 41a (ET, 184; cf. Greenup, op. cit., 46 f.); *BT, Rosh Hashanah*, 30a (ET, 141).

13. See below, pp. 158–161.

14. Cf. I Sam. I, 3. Scholars in general consider these passages explicit witness to the Canaanitic origin of the festival. H. Gressmann, "The Mysteries of Adonis and the Feast of Tabernacles,"

Expositor, Ser. IX, Vol. III (1925), 416–432, makes a very good case for the theory that the festival was originally a feast of Adonis. He has an excellent bibliography: see esp. R. Kittel in *Orientalische Literaturzeitung*, XXVII (1924), 385–391; idem in *Deutsche Literaturzeitung*, XLVI, i (1925), 431–435.

15. *JE*, XI, 657a.

practice would seem to have been part of the Canaanite usage, but in Levit. xxiii, 42–43, the booths are adapted to be a feature of the festival for Jews, here with an obviously new interpretation, i.e., they are to commemorate the fact that the Israelites lived in tents in the wilderness. This is a fine example of an old symbolic value being retained in a new religion, with a new explanation in harmony with the religion that is freshly adapting it. Gaster [16] calls such a process "historicizing," that is, it connects a primordial ritual with an historical event. In this case the explanation is an "historicization," but explanations of symbols are not always that.

What the booths or huts represented originally we do not know, but they would seem to have been connected with the symbolism of trees. In Levit. xxiii, 39–44, which gives the most elaborate command regarding the festival, it is definitely stated that the Israelites should, after the harvest, hold a festival of seven days, in preparation for which they should "take . . . on the first day the fruit of goodly trees, branches of palm trees and boughs of thick trees, and willows of the brook; and ye shall rejoice before Yahweh your God seven days." The passage does not describe how these boughs are to be used, but shortly goes on to say that the people are to build booths to live in during the festival, while in Neh. viii, 14–18, it is specifically said that the boughs are to be used to build the booths. The Sadducees and Karaites accordingly said that this was the proper use of the boughs, while others, whom the rabbis followed, said that the boughs were to be carried in a procession. Friedmann makes the additional suggestion that they were possibly carried by the early dancers, which appears to me highly probable.

I see no reason for choosing between these interpretations. There is every likelihood, it seems to me, that some of the branches were made into huts, while others were carried: this would afford two ways of identifying the worshiper with the trees, or getting for him the numen inhering in trees. That this sort of magic, religion, or symbolism had active force in Jewish life is a matter to which we shall come in greater detail in a later volume, when we discuss the symbolism of trees more generally. I should guess that the use of branches was a part of the Canaanite heritage, since there seems no reason for it as a Jewish innovation. The booths themselves do not play a part in our symbolism, but their meaning is clearly not to be separated from the symbolic value of Tabernacles as a whole, a value which seems, *pars pro toto*, to be represented for us in the lulab and ethrog.

We may mention a unique tradition of Tabernacles as preserved in Jubilees xvi, 21–31, wherein it is said that the festival was founded and first celebrated by Abraham himself "according to the testimony of the heavenly tablets." It was observed for seven days with booths, "leafy boughs, and willows from the brook, and branches of palm trees, and the fruit of goodly trees," and the celebrants wore "*wreaths upon their heads.*"

The recent study of Riesenfeld [17] has with rich detail brought out the great antiquity of the cultic booths, and their widespread use. He sees in them associations with the place of enthronement of a king, and with the *huppah* of the marriage ceremony—in this case the divine marriage so commonly associated with fertility and the new year. These booths were the site of much of the licentiousness associated with fertility cults and marriage

---

16. T. H. Gaster, *Thespis*, 1950, 22–24. 17. Op. cit., 130–205. See also Gaster, op. cit.

rites, so that the tradition of drinking, and the sexual excesses which we shall find consistently mentioned as a danger in connection with the festival, are probably very ancient indeed. The booth also prefigured the habitation of the Just in Paradise, and Riesenfeld [18] quotes the *Pesiqta* as stating that in the future world the sun will abandon its course and consume all men for whom God has not constructed booths. This idea is probably behind the "mansions" of John XIV, 2, and the heavenly tabernacle for the saints in Rev. VII, 15.

The feast was further enriched in the postexilic era by two new ideas. The first is clearly a late Jewish amplification: the feast was thought to anticipate the Messianic Age, when, according to the prophecy of Zechariah, Tabernacles was to become a universal festival which would draw all the nations of the earth to Jerusalem in its honor.[19] In the same passage is the second suggestion, namely, that the festival guaranteed rain, and that the peoples who did not come to Jerusalem to celebrate it would be cursed with drought. I suspect that the connection of the feast with rain is actually very old. The need of fall and winter rains for the growing grain presented an annual crisis in the life of Palestine, as it still does.[20] This would seem to account for the "bowls before the altar" of Zech. XIV, 20.[21] These bowls are explained in the talmudic descriptions of how the feast was ideally celebrated in the Temple.[22] Here are mentioned the lulab, the willow branch, and the Hallel,[23] as separate items, as well as the rejoicing, the booths, the flute playing and festivity of the second evening, and the libations of wine and water. In this account the lulab is spoken of as a branch, usually of palm, but more properly it was a bundle which included, besides the palm, also myrtle and willow branches.[24] It was carried and waved, while willow branches were used to adorn the altar.[25] A procession of people carrying their lulabs marched about the altar each day; they did so seven times on the seventh day, in order to commemorate, as is likewise allegorically explained, the march about Jericho.[26] A tanna of the second century, R. Johanan b. Baroka, is reported as saying that they brought dried branches of palm trees, apparently into the Temple, "and beat them to pieces on the floor by the sides of the altar, whence that day was called 'the day of the

18. Op. cit., 189.

19. Zech. XIV, 16–21.

20. In the year in which I visited Palestine the rainfall was unusually light, with the result that the workers of a collective farm where I was entertained were obliged, notwithstanding the irrigation system, to cut their wheat for hay. In ancient times this would have meant, if not starvation, at least extreme suffering.

21. Cf. *MR, Song of Songs*, VII, ii, 2 (ET, 278 f.): "You close your work before me at Tabernacles, and I open the heavens and cause winds to blow and bring up clouds and make rain fall and cause the sun to shine and make plants grow and ripen produce, and provide each one of you with a table set out with his needs, and each body according to its requirements." See also *MR, Leviticus*, XXX, 13 (ET, 394). In *BT, Rosh Hashanah*, 16a (ET, 58), the Mishnah reads: "On Tabernacles judgment is passed in respect of rain," to which the Gemara adds: "Why did the Torah enjoin us to pour out water on Tabernacles? The Holy One, blessed be he, said, Pour out water before me on Tabernacles, so that your rains this year may be blessed" (ET, 60).

22. The passages are collected by Friedmann in *JE*, XI, 66o*b;* cf. Hamburger, *RE*, II, 666 f.

23. Pss. CXIII–CXVIII.

24. *BT, Sukkah* (ET, 164, n. 7).

25. *BT, Sukkah*, 45a; Mishnah, *Sukkah*, IV, 5. In Tosefta, *Sukkah*, III, 1 (Greenup, op. cit., 73), each person is told to take two branches of willow, one for the altar and one for the lulab.

26. *JT, Sukkah*, 54c, quoted by Greenup, op. cit., 51, n. 1.

threshing of the dried branches.' " Greenup, referring to Is. XLIV, 2–4, suggests that this may have been symbolic of the resurrection.[27]

The libations of wine and of water, which we found first alluded to in the "bowls before the altar" of Zechariah, were apparently late additions.[28] The mishnaic tradition recounts [29] that beside the altar were two basins with ducts leading down to a subterranean cistern.[30] Into one of these, water from the pool of Shiloh was poured, with great circumstance and sounding of the shofar; into the other the celebrants poured wine, though it was not strictly required that this differentiation of the two basins be observed. The ceremony goes at least as far back as the time of Alexander Jannaeus, but seems at that period to have been in dispute, for Alexander, expressing the contempt of the Sadducees for the innovation, poured the libation over his feet and was pelted by the crowd with their ethrogs for what seemed to them his impiety.[31] Whether the libation of wine came in later than that of water cannot be said: it may have been an extension of the ancient libation that accompanied sacrifices at the altar. But I suspect that like so many of the uses of wine in Jewry, the libation of wine at Tabernacles was introduced during the period of hellenistic influence.[32] The wine of the ceremony is not discussed by the rabbis, and wine has never been a ritual part of later celebration of the feast, though as a concomitant of "rejoicing" it has always been freely used.

The drawing and pouring of water was of much more lasting importance: indeed, survivals of it have been observed until very recent times, and can possibly still be found.[33] The Tosefta [34] goes into a considerable discussion of the water of the festival, which seems to me to echo some very mystical source. It offers an elaborate commentary upon the "water gate" [35] through which the water for the libation was carried up to the Temple.

27. *BT*, *Sukkah*, 45a; Mishnah, *Sukkah*, IV, 6 (as transl. by Greenup, op. cit., 51 f.). Gaster, op. cit., connects the lulab, and the ceremony of beating off its leaves on the seventh day, with fertility rites.

28. Moore, *Judaism*, II, 44, suggests that both the great illumination and the libation of water were introduced in the hellenistic period.

29. *BT*, *Sukkah*, 48a,b (ET, 226; Greenup, op. cit., 53).

30. In Tosefta, *Sukkah*, III, 15, this is called the *shith*: Greenup, op. cit., 78. Tradition is confused as to whether these basins were of silver or stucco (earthenware?).

31. Greenup, op. cit., 54, n. 2. J. Hochman, *Jerusalem Temple Festivities*, Diss., Heidelberg [1909?], 88, has suggested that actually Alexander was pouring the water on the ground as a libation in the Greek manner, and that it was against this that the people protested. Therefore the priest was to "raise his hand high" in the pouring, so that

everyone could see the water falling properly into the basin. This is an interesting conjecture. Louis Finkelstein, *The Pharisees*, 1938, I, 102–106, uses this incident as part of the evidence from which he concludes that it was the Pharisees who introduced the water pouring. His argument is on this point not fully convincing to me. R. Patai, op. cit., 276, says that the people got excited over the impiety, fearing that it meant a year of drought for them.

32. Pedersen, op. cit., 425, says: "Of the old peasant festival by which the grape-harvest was sanctified there is hardly a trace left"; cf. ibid., 422. This is so obviously true that it remains a possibility that the libation of wine at the festival, of which no early mention exists, was a hellenistic invasion. I see no way of settling the question.

33. Greenup, op. cit., 17, 25; G. F. Moore in *EB*, III, 3354; *JE*, XII, 476 f.; Patai, op. cit., 274, 276.

34. *Sukkah*, III, 3–13; Greenup, op. cit., 73–77.

35. *BT*, *Sukkah*, 48a; Mishnah, *Sukkah*, IV, 9 (ET, 226; Greenup, op. cit., 53).

The flask in which the water was brought from the pool of Shiloh becomes a miraculous font: "Water oozing and rising, as if from this flask, will in future days come forth from under the threshold of the Temple." [36] The stream is the mystical and eschatological stream of Ezek. XLVII, 1–12; the conception here is enriched with details from other passages of Scripture. The point about this great stream, which will flow to the Mediterranean, the Sea of Tiberias, and the Dead Sea, is that it is a stream of life, teeming with fish and giving life to the fruit trees (whose leaves "are for healing"), so that " 'all the waters of creation' come out of this flask." A late rabbi, Ena, is quoted in the Gemara [37] as applying to this miraculous water the promise of Is. XII, 3: "Therefore with joy shall ye draw water from the wells of salvation." The same idea was in the minds of the compilers of the Tosefta, for they associated the waters of Ezekiel's vision with the legend of the rock which followed the Israelites in the wilderness to serve as a source of water for them, and to become the well at Beer "which the princes digged." The waters from this rock also "became a great river, pouring themselves into the Mediterranean, and bringing thence all the precious things of the world." [38] This tradition of the rock which followed the Israelites is an old one, for Paul identifies the rock with Christ,[39] and the tradition probably underlies Philo's allegory that "the rock is the Sophia of God, which he cut off as the peak and first of his own Powers, and from which he quenches the thirst of the souls that love God." [40] This is not very far from the more literal statement of the Tosefta that it was the "waters of creation" which flowed from the rock of the wilderness, or from the flask of the water drawing at Tabernacles.

The mystical association with the water drawing of Tabernacles, while it appears late in the talmudic sources, is therefore perhaps of very early origin. We recall now that the cistern or pit into which the water and wine flowed is made a mystical concept in the Gemara: it was a part of God's original creation in the six days, so that the "school of Ishmael," a group that flourished in the second third of the second century, taught that the proper reading of *Bereshith*, "In the beginning," is *Bara shith*, "He created the pit." The pit itself is *hammuqey yerekayik*, the "roundings of thy thighs" of Cant. VII, 1, a phrase which the rabbis seem to me to have understood to refer to the vulva.[41] (In the next verse the image becomes that of a "round goblet" which will never lack "mingled wine.") This idea is elaborated as the Gemara goes on to associate the pit also with the "vineyard on a very fruitful hill" where a vine was planted, a town built, and a vat hewn out (Is. V, 1 f.), for this vat too, it is made clear, was the pit used for the libation of Tabernacles.[42] Patai says that the image of the water flowing down the duct symbolizes the copulation

36. See Patai, op. cit., 263 f.

37. *BT, Sukkah*, 48b (ET, 227). Ena is one of the latest rabbis to be quoted in the Talmud. He taught at Susa after A.D. 515: see Bacher in *JE*, V, 675, s.v. "Giza."

38. Tosefta, *Sukkah*, III, 11–13 (Greenup, op. cit., 76 f.).

39. I Cor. X, 4.

40. *LA* II, 86, where Philo is commenting on the

tradition of the word as found in Deut. VIII, 15. See my *By Light, Light*, 210 f.

41. *BT, Sukkah*, 49a (ET, 229), in a statement ascribed to Rabbah bar bar Hana, a first-generation amora of Babylon: see *JE*, X, 290 f.

42. *BT, Sukkah*, 49a (ET, 230). This saying is ascribed to R. Jose, presumably Jose b. Halafta, a tanna of the second century: *JE*, VII, 241.

of the upper (male) and the lower (female) waters.[43] Indeed, he has shown that in Hebrew tradition all rain was regarded as the sexual union of the upper waters with the lower, and that the earth is said to "open" to the rain "as the female opens to the male." [44]

To me it seems that behind all these sayings lies not only rain magic, but a very mystical approach to Tabernacles. The mystical figures of speech antedate the destruction of the Temple, since they bring in ideas to be found in Paul and Philo, and their application to Tabernacles, while not attested until the second century after Christ, likewise possibly reflects the ideas in the minds of many of those who celebrated Tabernacles in Herod's Temple. The libations of wine and water were a symbol and a means of fecundation of both the land and the soul of man by God. The wine and water were poured into the vulva, the life-giving streams were full of fish and gave life to the fruit trees: this carried always its probable original meaning, that of rain magic, with, for many, a sense of spiritual participation in God's gifts to men. The details recall the ceremonies of mystery religions, indeed of cult practices in Greece, all of the Near East, and Egypt, in which fluid is poured out for the dead, especially poured through tubes into pits—so much so that we must suspect an eschatological reference when R. Jose says that the cavity of the cistern reached down into the "abyss." The pit may well have had such associations for the Jews, as for all the people about them, that the libation was understood to give *refrigerium*,[45] some sort of life or survival, even to those in Sheol, the abyss.

It is, then, not surprising that together with the libation which had such mystical and eschatological implications, with the tree carrying, the living in booths made of trees, and, indeed, the tree threshing, there should have been preserved the ancient rejoicing and dancing. For the high point of the feast, according to the Mishnah,[46] was the evening of the first day, when a number of lamps were set up and lighted, and a torch dance was executed in the Temple before all the people, executed by "the pious men and saints." Jews still love to quote the statement in the Mishnah about this night of celebration: "He who has not seen the rejoicing at the place of the water-drawing has never seen rejoicing in his life." Later sources fondly exaggerate both the illumination and the rejoicing. The Mishnah says, "There was not a court in Jerusalem which was not made bright by the light of the water-drawing"; and an anonymous tanna is reported to have said, "A woman could sift wheat by the illumination of the place of the water-drawing." [47] In this connection it seems to me not without significance that it is stipulated that the wicks of the lamps used for this illumination should be "made out of the worn-out drawers and girdles of the priests." [48] This amazing detail in the Mishnah is passed over by the

43. Op. cit., 262. Patai sees the "real significance" of all this as pertaining only to "rain magic," in which I would dispute merely his exclusive emphasis upon this aspect of the festival.

44. Ibid., 261 f. The author presents a large collection of rabbinic passages.

45. André Parrot, Le *"Refrigerium" dans l'au-delà*, 1937. See my review in *JBL*, LVII (1938), 104–106.

46. *Sukkah*, v, 1–4 (Greenup, op. cit., 55–58; the notes here are valuable). *BT, Sukkah*, 50b–51b (ET, 236–244).

47. *BT, Sukkah*, 53a (ET, 252).

48. *BT, Sukkah*, 51a (ET, 242); Greenup, op. cit., 56 (cf. n. 5). The Hebrew word for drawers is clear enough. The "girdle," המין, is discussed by Josephus, *Antt.* III, 154–156—where he uses the same word (originally Persian) in Greek (ἐμίαν)

Gemara and the Tosefta, and indeed it would have taxed the ingenuity of the rabbis to explain from their own point of view this clearly phallic association with the lights,[49] which recalls the association of phallic flow and light-stream common in Egyptian and Dionysiac thought.

In this sort of light, to a great din of music from instruments of "all kinds without number," highly acrobatic dances were carried out, with contortionism, tumbling, and juggling skill greatly emphasized. Rabbi Simeon b. Gamaliel could keep eight lighted torches in the air without dropping one, if we are to believe the accounts,[50] and R. Levi permanently lamed himself with his contortions, but he juggled eight knives; Samuel balanced eight glasses of wine (without spilling a drop), and Abaye manipulated "eight eggs, or, as some say, four eggs." Even the rabbis grow skeptical, it appears, as they tell these stories. The spectators were in a highly festive mood, so much so that the normal separation of men and women proved inadequate, and the rabbinic court (*Bet Din*) had to order galleries especially constructed for the women.[51] The clear implication is that while the rabbis and priests tried to keep the sexual symbolism from setting off an overt sexual rout, they failed repeatedly as they tried by one device after another to segregate the women from the excited men.[52]

As the rabbis danced there was a procession led by two trumpeting priests, and the dancing rabbis themselves are reported to have spoken cryptic sentences indicating repentance and reconciliation with God, or such mystic phrases as that of the elder Hillel: "To the place which my heart loveth, there my feet lead me; if thou comest to my house (saith God) I will go to thine."[53] It was apparently while he was dancing that Hillel "saw a skull floating upon the face of the water," and said to it, "Because thou didst drown others, they have drowned thee, and they that drowned thee shall be drowned also."[54] Astonishing as these details are, there is obviously much more which does not become explicit. Increasingly we are forced to the conclusion that upon the original Feast of Tabernacles a large number of fresh ceremonials, or new interpretations of the old ceremonials, have thrust themselves, but with the original fertility values only re-emphasized. In the account in Judges the dancers were sometimes men, the harvesters; sometimes they were women, young marriageable women with no men to protect them from kidnaping. In the talmudic description they seem to be especially the priests and rabbis.

The details of this celebration fit in completely with the scheme in which Gaster [55] outlines the "seasonal pattern of ritual." The pattern universally manifests itself in use of

—as a most luxurious "sash," tied so that it covers the body from the waist to the armpits, and having long ends hanging down to the ankles.

49. Patai, op. cit., 264, has no references to support his statement that the drawers of the priests symbolize rain clouds.

50. *BT*, *Sukkah*, 53a (ET, 254); Tosefta, *Sukkah*, IV, 4 (Greenup, op. cit., 81); *BT*, *Taanith*, 25a (ET, 131).

51. *BT*, *Sukkah*, 51b (ET, 245 f.); Tosefta,

Sukkah, IV, 1 (Greenup, op. cit., 80).

52. Cf. Patai, op. cit., 261. He sees in the fire dances only more rain magic. I see this, but also more.

53. Tosefta, *Sukkah*, IV, 3 (Greenup, op. cit., 80 f.). Cf. *BT*, *Sukkah*, 53a (ET, 253).

54. *BT*, *Sukkah*, loc. cit. Slotki refers to Mishnah, *Aboth*, II, 6, and says that this drowning means "divine retribution."

55. Gaster, *Thespis*, 2–33.

lights or fire, sexual promiscuity (against which the rabbis always had to watch), shouting, libations, feasting (including drinking), and physical combat or demonstrations of physical prowess, which the dances of the rabbis and priests seem to represent.

There is good reason to suppose that behind and beneath these observances, specifically the Jewish ones, there often lay profound mystical feeling and eschatological hope. Thackeray [56] seems to me to put the matter correctly when he says that to get what he calls the *key-notes* (italics his) of the festival we must look not to the sacrificial ordinances of the Priestly Code but to the ritual, the popular ceremonies; and these present centrally the two ideas of water and light. True, the water pouring was a ceremony for getting rain: "Pour out water before me on Tabernacles, so that your rains this year may be blessed." [57] And the night of illumination, ending with a blast of the shofar at cockcrow—a festival of the equinox—presented such aspects that the implication of sun worship had to be denied: "Our fathers who were in this place turned their backs on the Temple and their faces toward the sun and worshipped the sun toward the east: but we, our eyes to Jah." [58] Thackeray is surely right in seeing this as a ritualistic correction of an earlier orientation of the rite in sun worship, something which is still felt even in its disavowal. He proceeds to analyze the scriptural passages quoted as a basis for the celebration. In Zech. xiv the festival is connected with the Jewish triumph in the Messianic Age, after the final victory over all nations, a triumph which will register in continuous daylight and a never ceasing flow of water from Jerusalem. Into the details of Thackeray's analysis of the Psalms for the festival we need not go: but besides noting their references to literal hope for water, to the sun, and to the messianic triumph, he points out in them such spiritualizations of these figures as the Old Testament rarely gives us:

> As the hart panteth after the *water brooks*, so panteth my soul after *thee, O God*. My soul *thirsteth* for God, for the *living* God. . . . I *pour out* my soul within me. . . . All thy *waves* and thy *billows* are gone over me. . . . *In the night* his song shall be with me. . . . I will say unto God my *rock*. . . . Oh send out *thy light* and thy truth; let them lead me: let them bring me unto thy *holy hill*, and to thy *tabernacles*.[59]

This seems to me to go far beyond the language of a Canaanite fertility rite, though, like most development in religion, it expresses a deeper meaning given to the old rite itself, whose original meaning has been supplemented, not lost, in the advance. It is this sort of mysticism which, as Thackeray notices,[60] Jesus is made to claim for himself in the Fourth Gospel. For it is at the Feast of Tabernacles that he says: "If any man thirst, let him come unto me, and drink. He that believeth on me, as the scripture hath said, out of

56. H. St. John Thackeray, *The Septuagint and Jewish Worship* (Schweich Lectures, 1920), London, 1921, 62.

57. *BT, Rosh Hashanah,* 16a (ET, 60).

58. Mishnah, *Sukkah,* v, 4; *BT, Sukkah,* 51b (ET, 243). See Ezek. viii, 16. The formula was spoken when the procession of priests reached the western gate of the Temple. It is perhaps worth suggesting in passing that this is another indication of the Judaizing of a pagan observance, and that the verse was found a convenient (and perhaps not inappropriate) formula for rejecting the pagan source of the ritual, while the ritual itself was taken into Judaism.

59. Pss. xlii, xliii.

60. Op. cit., 66 f.

his belly shall flow rivers of living water." On which the evangelist comments: "But this spake he of the Spirit." [61] Jesus soon is quoted again: "I am the light of the world: he that followeth me shall not walk in darkness, but shall have the light of life." [62] Mere coincidence? We seem to have in these verses the Christianizing of a mysticism recognized in the festival by Jews, certainly by hellenized Jews: for the pith of the matter is found still in water and light.

2. Hellenistic Influences

IT IS NOT surprising that people who have studied this festival and the festivals of the pagans should see them to have many points in common, on all levels of meaning.[63]

A specific word for the lulab was of course lacking in Greek, but in II Mac. x, 7, it is called "a thyrsus and seasonable branches," while Josephus [64] calls it "a thyrsus of palm branches as described elsewhere," by which he refers to a passage [65] in which he calls the lulab an εἰρεσιώνη, and names palm, myrtle, and willow as included in it. The εἰρεσιώνη was a branch of olive or laurel wound round with wool and hung with fruits; it was dedicated to Apollo and borne about by singing boys at the festivals of Pyanepsia and Thargelia, while offerings were made to Helios and the Seasons; it was afterwards hung up over the doors of the temple and of houses.[66] Pyanepsia was a harvest and vintage festival in which Dionysus early took a place; it was probably the parallel to Tabernacles which Josephus had in mind, since Thargelia, a fertility festival honoring Apollo, was held in May. *Thyrsus* and *eiresione* make a significant pair of terms for the lulab, especially since the Greek word *thyrsus* appears in two such different Jewish writings as II Maccabees and the *Antiquities*. That is, they suggest again the conclusion that the ancient Jews themselves commonly compared their Feast of Tabernacles to the harvest festivals of the Greeks. Casanowicz [67] says that such an assumption "ignores the spirit and tendency of the Judaism of the Maccabean period," to which we can say only that it is precisely that ancient Jewish document, II Maccabees, which first makes the comparison, and that our ideas of the Judaism of the period must follow, not prejudge, the sources. That the members of the family of the Maccabees, like the strict rabbis, would have opposed such a comparison is very clear, but it is equally clear that the parallel was a commonplace among Jews of the day.

The comparison of Tabernacles to rites of Dionysus comes out also in two pagan

61. John VII, 37 f. Thackeray, ibid., seems right in following Abrahams and seeing in "belly" a reference to the navel, i.e., the omphalos or center, which for Jews was Jerusalem. That is, as in Zech. XIV, 8, "living water" was to flow from Jerusalem, and the believer would be so identified with the spiritual source of life that living water would flow from his omphalos also. It is notable that an omphalos appears on a Jewish grave (see above, III, fig. 781).

62. John VIII, 12.

63. The bibliography on this subject is very extensive. See esp. Heidel, op. cit., 236–247; Pedersen, op. cit., 740–745; Riesenfeld, op. cit., 154.

64. *Antt.*, XIII, 372: νόμου ὄντος παρὰ τοῖς Ἰουδαίοις ἐν τῇ σκηνοπηγίᾳ ἔχειν ἕκαστον θύρσους ἐκ φοινίκων καὶ κιτρίων.

65. *Antt.*, III, 245. Sverre Aalen, *Die Begriffe "Licht" und "Finsternis" im Alten Testament, im Spätjudentum und im Rabbinismus*, 1951, 145 f., dismisses these passages too lightly.

66. See LS, s.v. εἰρεσιώνη; Heidel, op. cit., 245 f.

67. In *JE*, VIII, 206.

writings. The less important of these is a passage in Tacitus [68] which recalls that there was a golden vine in the Temple, and this fact, coupled with a report that the Jewish priests wore garlands of ivy, and chanted to the accompaniment of pipes and cymbals, had led people, Tacitus said, to suppose that the Jews were worshiping Father Liber. Tacitus himself rejects the suggestion, because the rites of the Jews seemed to him so much lower in tone than the Dionysiac ceremonies. But his details are probably correct, and if he thought Judaism too degraded to recognize Liber pater, his informants certainly did not. There actually was a great golden vine in the Temple, for Josephus describes it.[69] As to the statement that the priests wore crowns, a Jewish document (Jub. xvi, 30) orders that crowns be worn by all those celebrating Tabernacles, from which it would appear that Tacitus was referring specifically to that feast.[70] It is reasonable to suppose that these two widely divergent sources, Tacitus and Jubilees, establish the fact, ignored by the rabbis in the Talmud, that the hellenistic custom of wearing wreaths had indeed become a feature of the Jewish festival. It may be this custom which lies behind the fact that the lulab and the crown are often presented together in our art.[71] The procession with music and singing may in the same way echo the beginnings of the great dance already described as the high point in the observance of Tabernacles.

A passage even more important for our immediate purpose is the description of Tabernacles in Plutarch:

> In the first place, the time and manner of celebrating their greatest and most perfect feast is quite appropriate to Dionysus. For in celebrating the so-called fast in the vintage season they set out tables with all sorts of autumn fruits under tents and huts woven out of sprigs of vine and ivy. And they call the first day of the feast "Tabernacles." But a few days later they celebrate another feast which they call, not by symbols [72] merely, but explicitly, the feast of Bacchus. And they have also a festival which is a sort of carrying of the twigs ($\kappa\rho\alpha\delta\eta\phi\rho\rho\iota\alpha$[73]) and of the thyrsus, during which they carry thyrsi into the temple. What they do when they have gone in we do not know, but they probably perform the rites of Bacchus. For they use little trumpets, as the Argives do at the Dionysiac festivals, to call upon God. Others go before them playing on lyres, people whom they call Levites, an appellation deriving from Lysius [i.e., "the saving God," applied to Dionysus] or rather Evius [likewise Dionysus].[74]

Plutarch goes on to cite other customs of the Jews which indicate that their God is actually Dionysus, but this is all he has to say of Tabernacles. Büchler [75] has elaborately

68. *Hist.*, v, 5.

69. *Antt.*, xv, 395 (xi, 3); *BJ*, v, 210 (v, 4).

70. A. Büchler, "La Fête des cabanes chez Plutarque et Tacite," *REJ*, XXXVII (1898), 181–202, admits that the crowns would be specifically Greek (p. 196). See above, p. 149.

71. See above, III, fig. 471.

72. Büchler, op. cit., 183, explains that the vine and ivy and fruits had earlier been symbols of Bacchus.

73. $K\rho\alpha\delta\eta\phi\rho\rho\iota\alpha$ is listed in LS only with reference to this passage, with the meaning "bearing of fig-tree branches at a festival." $K\rho\alpha\delta\eta$ means a bunch of twigs on a branch of any kind, and though it is especially used for fig branches, it does not necessarily have this meaning specifically. The myrtle and willow twigs of the lulab would answer to the meaning of the word perfectly well. See Büchler, op. cit., 187.

74. *Quaestiones convivales*, iv, vi, 2 (671d–f).

75. Loc. cit.

analyzed the evidence of both Tacitus and Plutarch, and concludes that they had written sources which were somewhat contradictory, but composed by pagans who were eye-witnesses of events in Jerusalem. This conclusion follows from the fact that a Jewish writer would have described what went on inside the Temple, and these writers stop outside. It is especially noteworthy, he thinks, that no information about the torch dance, the most bacchanalian feature of the festival, had reached either Tacitus or Plutarch, for they would certainly have mentioned it had they known of it. Büchler says that the thesis of both Plutarch and Tacitus, that in this festival the Jews were worshiping Dionysus, is not worth discussion, and he is of course right.[76] Actually, however, the argument of these pagans works both ways: if they saw similarity between the Jewish and the Dionysiac rites, in that devotees of both religions carried what they called thyrsi, it must have been conscious comparison of the same sort in the minds of the Jews which made them too speak of their lulabs as thyrsi. If Jews were thus comparing and appropriating, we cannot a priori say where that process may have stopped, though we are sure that it stopped short of identifying Dionysus with the Jewish God—at least among the majority of Jews, since otherwise the Jewish cult as such would quickly have disappeared.

But we have seen that the Jews took more than the term thyrsus from the Greeks. They wore crowns; they offered a libation of water and wine which was most appropriate in relation to Dionysus as savior of the dead; they performed a dance truly bacchanalian in character, in which the lights had wicks made from the drawers of the priests; and at the dance the women had to be especially protected from the men. The only hypothesis which will make room for all these peculiar features of the feast is that at some time, probably in the days before the Maccabees and their reforms, Tabernacles had been elaborated to draw in the most desired features of the pagan autumn festival of Dionysus (or Dionysus-Zeus-Helios-Apollo, for probably local Syrian amplifications were represented). There is no reference to the drinking of wine at Tabernacles, but otherwise the parallel is amazingly complete. What the Maccabean reaction and the rise of the Pharisees and rabbis did was to hold the celebration in check, and see that the women were decently segregated from the men; but otherwise the innovations stood. The festival was probably too popular for the rabbis to do more, and indeed they seem to have enjoyed it thoroughly themselves.

To what extent did the ideology of the pagans come in with the pagan rites, and how much of it, if any, remained in the general celebration of Tabernacles in regions not under rabbinic influence? Three sources survive for answering that question—the references to Tabernacles in Philo, the testimony of the Midrash, and the evidence of the late cabbalistic writings.

3. In Philo

PHILO mentions Tabernacles in two passages, of which the first is concerned with the sacrifices prescribed for the festival.[77] The second and more important discussion [78] is a

76. Ibid.
77. *Spec.* I, 189.

78. *Spec.* II, 204–213.

part of his allegory of the festivals in general, which I have treated elsewhere.[79] In this it appears that Philo regards each festival in turn as a rite in the true Jewish Mystery by which man is led into immaterial reality. Most of these rites Philo calls "eucharists," whereby it appears that the meaning of the word was changing from that of "thank offering" to the sense of "rite of participation in the flow of God's power and nature to man."

Tabernacles also becomes a "eucharist." Philo presents the meaning of the festival under six heads.

First, he says,[80] the feast occurs at the time of the autumn equinox, which symbolizes equality (of night and day). It is this cosmic equality which we are called upon to honor in the feast, for equality is the "source and fountain of justice (δικαιοσύνη)," it is "light without a shadow," while inequality is injustice and darkness. The first meaning, then, is a cosmic and metaphysical one: namely, in honoring equality, one honors the cosmic and metaphysical source of justice or of light. With this we are at once plunged into the depths, or lifted to the heights, of Philonic allegory. The festival is made into a seasonal one in the sense of a celebration of the time when light is at that special stage of balance which makes it a stream of justice, so that by implication the festival is dedicated to the stream of Light-Justice flowing from God to man. Philo makes no further explanation of the "source and fountain," apparently because in this series of his writings he is giving a greatly abbreviated account of Jewish rites for the gentile reader, and accordingly he suggests but does not elucidate the deeper mystical elements in Judaism. That justice is a beneficent flow from God to man, the supreme gift of God to man, and that all flow from God is to be described in the figure of the Light-Stream (a variant of the conception more generally known as "Philo's Logos")—these are ideas that I have elaborated in *By Light, Light:* they are so important a part of Philo's thinking that here I can only refer to the larger study. If that background of thinking is implicit in so brief a reference, Philo means that Tabernacles is in the first instance a celebration of the fact that justice, a quality of inner harmony and mastery within man which is at once the vehicle and end of his salvation, is, as with Paul, a gift of the streaming goodness and nature of God.

The second purpose of Tabernacles is, says Philo, to teach us that we should offer a thanksgiving to God, a eucharist to "the One who brings to perfection . . . the One who is the Cause of all good things." [81] That is, the fruits of the season are but a token of God's more general function as the Cause by which all things are brought to their perfection. It is naturally to be supposed that Philo is referring to the perfection of the cosmos, and to the individual who seeks perfection in it.

Philo's third and fourth explanations of Tabernacles are based upon the symbolism he sees in the tents or booths. The third is apparently only whimsical; for he says that tents are used in the festival because as long as the fruit is growing one must expose oneself to the weather to cultivate it, but once it is gathered in one may have rest and protection.[82] This

---

79. "Literal Mystery in Hellenistic Judaism," *Quantulacumque, Studies Presented to Kirsopp Lake,* 1937, 227–241.

80. *Spec.* II, 204.

81. Ibid.: τῷ τελεσφόρῳ θεῷ καὶ πάντων τῶν ἀγαθῶν αἰτίῳ.

82. *Spec.* II, 206 f.

seems to be mere fancy, although it may be quite mystical in intent, and may signify that divine shelter from the effort of life to which the mystic aspires. Of this we cannot be sure. The idea strangely recalls the tents of the harvesters earlier mentioned.[83] The fourth explanation definitely takes us back to the mystical.[84] The tents, Philo says, with the explanation of Leviticus in mind, are a symbol of the life of the fathers in the wilderness, that is—in accordance with his elaborate allegory of the migration—a symbol of escape from sin to righteousness. Those who have had this experience, he says, necessarily become "eucharistic," thankful, while they pray that God will never let them return to the evils they have transcended. Thus Tabernacles is the eucharist of the mystic journey, the migration from the world of matter and sin to that of spirit.

This is reinforced by Philo's two last explanations. For the fifth interpretation [85] returns us to the cosmic light, now typified in the fact that the feast is held not merely at the time of the equinox, but at a time of the month when the moon shines all night, so that there is at no time complete darkness. Philo still has in mind the "light without a shadow" of his first explanation. The sixth interpretation [86] applies especially to the closing day, the eighth, which gives Philo opportunity, by allegorizing the number eight, to bring in the world of Forms or Ideas, τὰ νοητά, the Conceptuals, the immaterial world in contrast to the material:

> The eight is the first cubic number: in the transition away from the immaterials it is the beginning of that which is potentially a solid substance, while it is the limit of the Conceptuals. The Conceptuals [change] into solid (material) nature as the numbers rise to higher powers.[87]

This is a peculiar conception, quite Neoplatonic, designed to explain the descent from the One to the material world. Philo is saying that this descent is like the complications which develop in the system of numbers as the numbers expand to their successive powers, go from simplicity to multiplicity. In this progression, or degeneration, as the Neoplatonic mind would consider it, the number eight seems to Philo to mark the point of transition between the immaterial and the material world. Since it was links, bridges, to the immaterial world which all this type of thought was seeking, the number eight would thus have been of great religious importance. This is the sixth meaning of the Feast of Tabernacles: celebrated for eight days, it is a mystic means of transition to the immaterial world. The eighth day, Philo says, is the *exodion*,[88] the "closing," but he is certainly punning on the term Exodus, his symbol of the migration from the material to the immaterial.

In this exposition it is hard to see exactly what Philo's model was. He follows the prescriptions of Leviticus more than those of Exodus or Deuteronomy, but there are anomalies in his treatment. For while, in what I call his first mention of Tabernacles,[89] he tells of the sacrifices in the Temple prescribed in Num. XXIX, 12–34, there is a second

83. See above, p. 148.

84. *Spec.* II, 207–209.

85. Ibid., 210.

86. Ibid., 211–213.

87. Ibid., 212; I am accepting Cohn's suggestion of μεταβαίνει for completing the sentence. See

Colson's and Heinemann's notes ad loc.

88. *Spec.* II, 211. The word *exodion* is used in LXX for the last day of the festival: Levit. XXIII, 36; Num. XXIX, 35.

89. *Spec.* I, 189. See above, p. 158.

discussion [90] which does not bring in the Temple at all, and the command in Deut. xvi, 16,[91] to go to the Temple for celebration of the feast is ignored. Likewise, the lulab and ethrog fail to appear. The festival is at once agricultural, seasonal, and, in its feature of tents, commemorative of the migration from Egypt. All that the celebrants do, Philo says, is to dwell in tents for seven days, and "honor God with songs and speeches, and importune God, propitiate him with supplications, so that he will not try them any more with evils." [92] It is hard to believe that the festival was not celebrated in some such way as this in Alexandria by the mass of people who could not go to Jerusalem. If the lulab and ethrog were used in Alexandria at all, as I suspect they were, Philo does not mention these articles, perhaps because they were too peculiarly Jewish to attract the gentile readers he was addressing in this series of writings. Of one thing we may be sure. To Philo the festival has become a celebration of delivery from the evils of material life; it is a seasonal revelation of the saving radiation of God to man which culminates in justice, and indeed it exemplifies, implements, the transition from the material to the immaterial world. He says nothing of the feast as representing a way to immortality, but the hope of immortality is a popularized form of mysticism, and everywhere the symbols of union with the god or God which the few understand in terms of mystic rapture are taken by the many to refer to glorification in a life after death.

Tabernacles has proved a festival most elastic in meaning. Beginning as an early Canaanitic celebration, it was Judaized by being given a place in the law of Moses under various codes: its original meaning, agricultural and, it is probable, primitively mystical ("magical" for those who prefer that term), was covered up as the festival was made into a celebration of the migration from Egypt. But its agricultural nature could not be concealed, and its gaiety, which made it an occasion for dancing according to Judg. xxi, 16–24, persisted—has persisted, indeed, to the present, for nowadays dances are often given by Jewish congregations during the feast. This feature made it easy to reinterpret the festival in the days of syncretism with hellenistic ways, and it was apparently then that it took on new aspects. The dance in the Temple became a bacchanalian celebration, with even the lights taking on new (or was it a very old?) meaning, namely, that Life is Light. There was a libation rite which was exactly the sort of ceremony used by the pagans in rituals to assure immortality, and the whole was so Dionysiac, with its "thyrsi" and citrons, and the crowns probably worn by the chief celebrants, that pagans took it for granted that the festival was dedicated to Dionysus. At the same time, for Philo, and, if he is in any sense typical, for thoughtful Jews influenced by Greek thinking, the ceremony was a mystic one, a eucharist celebrating escape from evil and passage into the justice given by the immaterial Light of God, which is Life.

4. In the Midrash

WITH ALL of this in mind one reads with fresh awareness the *Midrash Rabbah* on Leviticus,[93] a work roughly contemporary with the later elements (Gemara) of the Talmud

90. *Spec.* ii, 204–213.

91. And by implication in Exod. xxiii, 16 f.; xxxiv, 22 f.; Levit. xxiii, 33–36.

92. *Spec.* ii, 209.

93. *MR, Leviticus*, xxx, 1–16 (ET, 380–395). A review of the *recht nette Deutungen* of this section will

itself, but by no means so carefully censored. Here, in contrast to the approach in the Talmud, it is not the law of observance but interpretation of the cult which interests the commentators, and when we come to the discussion of Tabernacles we are embarrassed by the variety of interpretations, for they are so numerous and diverse that they at first seem like fancies rather than established and recognized symbolic interpretations of the feast. Thus we are told that if Israel fulfills the command to take up the lulab she will be assured of conquering the nations of the world.[94] We find an elaborate list of instances in which God "created them afresh," in the sense of redemption of the penitent from sin, of revival of messianic hope, of salvation from enemies, and of promise of new life after death. The passage goes on: "What then have we to do? To take the lulab and the ethrog and praise the Holy One, blessed be he," [95] with the assumption that doing these things will continue to bring the same rewards.

It is further taught that at Tabernacles, when all Israel stands before God with the palm branches and citrons, God gives them the full pardon of Rosh Hashanah and Yom Kippur; at Tabernacles, as at these other festivals, God says: "Let bygones be bygones; from now on we shall begin a new account." [96] The ceremony brings rain,[97] but mystically the lulab, myrtle, willow, and ethrog represent man's spine, eye, mouth, and heart,[98] so that they would appear to symbolize some sort of offering of the entire person. Indeed, there is a whole series of suggestions as to what the lulab and ethrog mean, in the form of interpretations of these four objects. In one group [99] the citron is the "fruit of the *hadar*": here it is pointed out that Aquila translated "*hadar* as that which lives (*hu dar*) by the water" (the rabbi obviously had in mind the Greek ὕδωρ).[100] In the next group each of the four articles in turn "symbolizes the Holy One, blessed be he." [101] In the next, *hadar*, the ethrog, is Abraham, who lived to a great age; the palm is Isaac bound to the altar; the myrtle is Jacob, who had many children; the willow is Joseph, who died before his brethren.[102] The four objects could by similar reasoning be made to represent Sarah, Rebekah, Leah, and Rachel.[103]

It is perhaps my great interest in a Judaism that especially emphasized Abraham and Sarah, Isaac and Rebekah, and Jacob and Leah, while it gave a fading and minor place to both Joseph and his mother Rachel, which makes me feel that, far from representing idle fancy, these lists of names used as symbols have come from Jews who, like Philo, found the highest, the true Judaism not in the written law but in the mystic salvation which the Jewish Patriarchs had brought to man.[104] The Midrash does not pause, but goes on to

be found in Hamburger, *RE*, II, 669 f. The *Sifra*, on Leviticus, adds little of interest (see transl. of J. Winter, 596–604); it is very close in tone and content to the talmudic *Sukkah*.

94. *MR, Leviticus*, xxx, 2.

95. Ibid., §3.

96. Ibid., §7.

97. Ibid., §13.

98. Ibid., §14.

99. Ibid., §8.

100. Explanations of the three other objects, the

palm, myrtle, and willow, are common places which need not be repeated.

101. Ibid., §9.

102. Ibid., §10.

103. Ibid.

104. The conception is discussed at length in my *By Light, Light, passim*, and more briefly in the last chapter of my *Introduction*. The salvation brought by the Patriarchs will be discussed at length in connection with the shofar, below, pp. 172–194.

make the four objects represent together another group, the Great Sanhedrin, the rabbis, the disciples, and the scribes.[105] Israel, the Midrash continues, is made up of learned men who possess good deeds, of learned men lacking in good deeds, of men who possess good deeds but no learning, and of men lacking in both, but when these are bound together like the lulab, they, as Israel, save one another: the lulab then represents the hope of united Israel.[106] At the end of the section it appears that the performance of the rites of the feast promises punishment of the wicked, the rebuilding of the Temple, and the coming of the "King Messiah." [107]

The Midrash has thus given us a really powerful group of interpretations, and I see no reason why it should not be taken to reflect at least in part what Jews actually felt at the feast as they celebrated it at the time of these writings. The rites were to induce rain, obviously, but much more is here. Tabernacles no longer commemorates the pilgrimage in the desert (the booths are not mentioned), and the harvest celebration has likewise disappeared. In place of both is a festival which centers in objects—the ethrog and lulab —which represent God's greatness, his forgiveness, his life-giving power, the saving Patriarchs, rabbinic legalism, the union of Israel, punishment of the wicked, the restoration of the Temple, and messianic hope. Almost every aspect of the life and aspiration of Israel is here. To assure all this to himself, the faithful Israelite takes up the lulab and the ethrog: in these all the symbolic meanings of the festival have come to express themselves.

Another midrash, on the Psalms, reads:

> What is the meaning of the verse: "In thy right hand bliss for ever more!" [Ps. xvii (xvi), 11]. This refers to him who takes the lulab in his right hand; just as the victorious athletes take the palm tree as a sign of their victory, so the victorious [Jew] carries the lulab. [108]

Here the palm tree in its pagan association with immortality is explicitly made parallel to the Jewish lulab, itself a symbol of "bliss for ever more." Marmorstein quotes this as an explanation of the appearance of the lulab on Jewish tombstones, and he is undoubtedly right.[109]

5. In Jewish Mysticism

ALL OF this, I say, is Tabernacles. But I do not believe that even this exhausts the meaning of the festival at the time of which we are speaking. For while the rabbis have hinted at the mystical Patriarchs of whom Philo tells, and to whom the Psalms used in the ritual make cryptic references, the talmudic comments in general conspicuously lack

---

105. *MR, Leviticus,* xxx, 11.

106. Ibid., §12. By a slightly different approach the same conclusion is reached in *BT, Menahoth,* 27a (ET, 174).

107. *MR, Leviticus,* xxx, 16.

108. Quoted by Marmorstein in *PEF,QS,* 1921, 187.

109. The widespread association of the palm branch (or branch of any kind) with immortality in mystic paganism has recently been recalled once more by H. Seyrig, "Le Rameau mystique," *AJA,* XLVIII (1944), 20–25. The eschatological significance of Tabernacles is the special theme of the essay "Tabernacles" in Israel Abrahams, *Studies in Pharisaism and the Gospel,* II, 1924, 50–55. See also Aalen, op. cit., 256 f.

Philo's mysticism. Yet as mystical Judaism survived rabbinic censorship, so the mystical notion of Tabernacles survived. To trace this phenomenon through the mystical literature of Judaism is beyond my power. The early cabbalistic book *Bahir* contains some highly obscure remarks about the lulab and ethrog. The first passage seems to connect Israel with a cosmic Tree by whose twelve roots the world is held together.[110] The second reference [111] includes a parable of a king who planted nine male palm trees, and with them one ethrog tree to be the female for the nine males. A still more cryptic passage follows in which the ethrog is linked with erotic verses from Canticles, and it is explained that the female body has more openings than the male. Scholem confesses that he does not follow the argument here, but he sees in it a reference to the ten *sephiroth*, the highest principles in the sublime world of Cabbala. That is, to the cabbalistic author of this book the ethrog and lulab had deep mystical significance, though that significance cannot be accurately recovered.

The *Zohar*, the great cabbalistic text of thirteenth-century Spain,[112] has some even more interesting passages. The booth, we are told,[113] recalls the "kindness" of God in the wilderness, where the cloud of Aaron was the "kindness," and Israel was adorned as a bride for God. Thus when a man sits in his booth he is still under the Shekinah, and Abraham and five other righteous ones and David make their abode with him, to round out the number seven. That is, we are by the feast taken into a Mystery of seven Patriarchs which recalls Philo's allegories; and Rab Hamnuna the Elder tells how he stood at the door of his booth to welcome these visitors, a passage reminiscent of Abraham's welcome of the holy visitors, which meant so much to Philo. The peculiar allusions make sense when we know that in the *Zohar* the Shekinah, or the cloud, was a sexual coming of God to Israel, and that Moses had intercourse with it.[114] Here it is Israel which is the bride, but by implication (it was probably too bold to say outright) the individual Israelite who went into his booth, the Shekinah, at Tabernacles shared also in this ineffable experience.

In the *Zohar* the obligation of observing the feast is also communal, but the next section,[115] which treats of the four emblems of Tabernacles, throws the writer back into discussion of the sacred marriage. This passage is obscure in its application to Tabernacles, but is illumined in a quite different passage,[116] where the sacred marriage, clearly the old ἱερὸς γάμος, is explained as the linking of Israel with the supernal world. [The union begins at Passover,[117] but is not consummated in the higher grades until Tabernacles, when

110. *Bahir*, ed. G. Scholem, 1923, §67, pp. 70 f.

111. Ibid., §§117 f., pp. 125–127.

112. See Scholem, *Jewish Mysticism*, 153–239, and above, p. 92, n. 137.

113. *Zohar*, v, *Emor* (Levit.), 103b (ET, V, 135 f.).

114. According to Scholem, *Jewish Mysticism*, 223, but his reference, *Zohar*, I, 21b–22a, shows no such statement in the English translation. Pre-

sumably this is the passage which, the editor tells us, was omitted in the rendition for English readers.

115. *Zohar*, v, *Emor* (Levit.), 104a,b (ET, 137).

116. Ibid., 95b (ET, 120 f.).

117. "On this night (the first night of the Passover) when there is the divine wedlock and universal joy in which Israel participate": ibid., 95b (ET, 121).

all is complete. Sexual figures are not unusual in Cabbalism.[118] But it is interesting that the Feast of Tabernacles should in both the *Bahir* and the *Zohar* supply a pretext for the image, and I suspect—though the surmise cannot be proved—that a mystical interpretation, in terms of Patriarchs and mystic marriage, was a strong element in the celebration of Tabernacles in the period of the Roman empire, as it may have been from hellenistic, or even, in a more primitive way, from ancient Canaanitic times. Indeed, Lowenthal [119] recalls that, however little the allusion may be recognized, the meditation suggested in modern prayer books to accompany the waving of the boughs of the lulab is, "While I wave them, may streams of blessing flow in upon me," while in the booth one prays, "Bid the stream of life flow in on thy servant," a formula which, he says, is taken directly from the Cabbalists.

C. CONCLUSIONS

PERHAPS WE are at last ready to understand why it is that the lulab and ethrog appear so prominently with other Jewish emblems in the Jewish funerary art of the Greco-Roman period.

In the designs found on tombs, forms identified as the lulab and ethrog normally are presented together with other Jewish cult objects, especially the menorah, though the two often occur by themselves. When used with the other emblems, there can be no doubt that they represent specifically the Jewish ritual objects. Berliner [120] many years ago observed that the lulab so often becomes the palm branch (exactly like the palm branch which appears on heathen and Christian graves as a symbol of the hope of immortality, if not as the magic bough which itself gave immortality) that he doubted whether any symbol found on Jewish graves was ever intended to represent a lulab. Many of the forms seem to me certainly to be lulabs. But the resemblance Berliner noted still remains. The lulab as used in ritual, and as sometimes pictured, was the traditional bundle of twigs. But one suspects that it could often be represented as only a palm branch because the Jewish object, which was basically a palm branch, actually meant to the Jew, in itself and in its association with Tabernacles, just about what the palm branch meant to pagans, and to Christians later—the hope and achievement of immortality or of mystic consummation.

No more appropriate symbol could be put upon a tombstone. But the lulab had this meaning in an assertively Jewish sense, which encompassed also the Jewish God, the Law, the Patriarchs, and messianic hope. If Tabernacles had borrowed so much from paganism that, as regards idea and representation alike, it was in some respects hard to tell the difference between the Jewish festival and the rites of Dionysus, the Jew knew the difference exactly, intransigently. The lulab and ethrog represented his Jewish hope, here and in the hereafter. That it was for the individual much like the hope of the pagan mystic, the hope that death is only the beginning of the greater eucharist wherein man takes to him-

---

118. See Scholem, *Jewish Mysticism*, 222–225.

119. Marvin Lowenthal, *A World Passed By*,

1933, 20 f.

120. Berliner, *Juden in Rom*, I, 58.

self the divine attributes of immortality, cannot obscure the fact that the Jew wanted this
hope realized in the Jewish way represented by the lulab and ethrog.[121]

121. I have the feeling throughout my exposition in these volumes that I am skirting, rather than exploring, many of the problems involved. For instance, the palm branch may have quite other associations. David Katz, *Gestalt Psychology*, 1950, 158 f., talks of an experiment of Volkelt, reported in a work not accessible to me, in which children were shown the form ✳ and then asked to draw it from memory. They drew the form 𖢃 , a sort of drawing, Katz remarks, which "is produced by an attitude in which emotion plays a definite part." When presented with this palm-branch form and with the form ✕, children thought the former resembled the original star more closely, adults thought that the latter did so. This opens up a world of possible associations for all such forms which I am not attempting to investigate.

CHAPTER SEVEN

The Shofar

THE SHOFAR, or trumpet of ram's horn, has often been mentioned among the symbols appearing in the Jewish remains we are studying.[1] In Jewish ritual the straight horn of the wild goat was at one time used interchangeably with the curved horn of the ram, but by Greco-Roman times the goat's horn was generally superseded by the ram's horn, which is the shofar of the monuments. In the Temple the shofar and a pair of trumpets were used together, and it is this pair of trumpets, apparently, that is represented on coins of the Second Revolt,[2] though it appears nowhere else. Outside the Temple probably only the shofar of ram's horn was used, as it is today. Eisenstein [3] lists a number of occasions on which the shofar was blown: "every day during the month of Elul except on the day preceding Rosh ha-Shanah . . . a later innovation," or only on the New Moon of Elul; to arouse the people to repentance on fast days; to proclaim an excommunication;

1. The best accounts of the shofar which I have seen are found in J. D. Eisenstein and F. L. Cohen in *JE*, XI, 301–306; Cyrus Adler, "The Shofar, Its Use and Origin," *Proceedings of the U. S. National Museum*, XVI (1893), 287–301, with plates XLVI–XLIX; Berthold Kohlbach, "Das Widderhorn (Shôfar)," *Zeitschrift des Vereins für Volkskunde*, XXVI (1916), 113–128. The material in Kohlbach is carefully reproduced and considerably amplified in the first part of the famous study of Theodor Reik, "The Shofar (the Ram's Horn)," in his *Ritual: Psycho-analytic Studies*, London, 1931 (New York, 1946), 221–361. Reik's study, like so much Freudian investigation of the history of religion, presents a great deal of acute observation, in spite of what seems to me its general neurotic compulsion to account for everything in man, past and present, in terms of the few categories of human motivation the Freudian system allows. He makes the shofar represent the craving of the son to kill the father and take his place, the guilt which follows this desire, and the castration fear attending the guilt, all within the frame of the universal totemism which seemed to Freud the basis of all religion. For this I cannot see that Reik presents any evidence at all, yet he ecstatically exclaims (p. 291) over his results: "Ethnology has proposed the hypothesis of 'elementary thought' (Bastian), but it was reserved for psycho-analysis to find the fundamental affective basis of this concept and to endow it with living content. Only psycho-analysis could show that everywhere in primitive society similar institutions result from the play of mental forces which are eternally the same. Only psycho-analysis has been able to hear amidst the manifold and confusing richness of sounds the hidden dynamic melody which solemnly and eternally rises from the deep and dominates chaos." That I do not share what seems to me the auditory hallucination of Reik's last sentence by no means keeps me from recognizing that much valuable interpretation is in his study.

2. See above, III, fig. 696; cf. Reifenberg, *Coins*, plate XIII, nos. 174, 182. For this use of trumpets, see Eisenstein in *JE*, XI, 301.

3. Op. cit., 304.

to announce a new rabbinic decision; at funerals; to announce a New Moon; and to call to rest for the Sabbath.

It is thus perhaps a mistake to discuss the shofar simply as a cult instrument associated with the New Year, for it seems generally to have been used to mark a distinctive occasion.[4] But in the popular mind all other uses of it have always been quite secondary to that connected with the New Year and the Day of Atonement. The blowing of the shofar to proclaim a New Moon or Sabbath, or to herald a new halachic decision, must have had little importance except immediately in rabbinical circles, and its use at funerals seems to have been quite sporadic and rare,[5] though it is most appropriate to be recalled in view of the representations of the shofar found on tombstones. Before discussing the meaning of the shofar, it will be well to review the occurrences of the motif in the art.

A. THE SHOFAR ON THE MONUMENTS

In Palestine, in contrast to what is commonly found in the diaspora, I have seen only one tombstone bearing a shofar; on this stone it stands with a lulab, flanking a menorah.[6] Tombstones in the usual sense are rare in Palestine, however, and funerary symbolism is more apt to appear on the walls or on the small objects in the tombs. Thus on one lamp [7] the shofar is likewise with a menorah and a lulab; on four very similar lamps,[8] a menorah and incense shovel are with the shofar, while on another [9] a group of the chief cult symbols, the shovel, the lulab, the ethrog, and the shofar, is on one side of a menorah, and an amphora with a vine growing from it is on the other. On one glass [10] a shofar is with a menorah and lulab; on two glasses a menorah is flanked by objects that I have guessed to be a shofar and an ethrog.[11] A fine little piece of carved bone has a menorah flanked by a shovel on one side and by a shofar and an ethrog on the other.[12]

In synagogues the same kind of grouping occurs. What is perhaps the earliest appearance of the shofar is on a capital at Capernaum,[13] where, balanced by a shovel, it flanks a menorah. It is to be found thereafter in nineteen synagogues so similarly presented that individual description is unnecessary. In one case, the shofar is alone beside a menorah.[14] In eight instances, a shofar and lulab flank a menorah,[15] and in two others [16] a shovel is added to these. A shofar and shovel balance an ethrog and what is probably a lulab in one synagogue mosaic, and these presumably are also the objects represented in a second.[17] The same group appears in one synagogue relief,[18] and perhaps it is a shofar

4. Kohlbach, op. cit., 115–118, lists a large number of occasions for noncultic use of the shofar.

5. Kohlbach, op. cit., 128, recalls that on the death of a rabbi in Sassin in 1814, the body was brought into the synagogue, a procession of the Torah was held around it, and the shofar was blown.

6. See above, III, fig. 99; I, 88.

7. See III, fig. 346.

8. See III, figs. 334–337.

9. See III, fig. 340.

10. See III, fig. 443.

11. See III, figs. 396, 411.

12. See III, fig. 444.

13. See III, fig. 478.

14. See III, fig. 566.

15. See III, figs. 571, 574–576, 583, 592, 624, 666.

16. See III, figs. 618, 656.

17. See III, figs. 651 f.

18. See III, fig. 572.

balancing a lulab and ethrog which is depicted in another.[19] In two others some unidentified object balances a shofar.[20] The effect of all of these together is to lead us to suppose that what is presented here is the vocabulary of cult objects which appears in full at Beth Alpha,[21] though at Beth Alpha the Torah shrine is central, and the menorah and all the other objects are presented in pairs, one symbol on each side of the shrine. We shall conclude at the end of this volume that, as in the elaborate symbolism of a Christian rose window, the symbols all together had a combined impact which was important in itself. But just as in the case of the rose window we should be in danger if we assessed the totality without analysis of the parts, so in the Jewish symbolism we must continue to study each symbol by itself.

In similar groupings—groupings which as such seem to me to have no significance— the shofar appears on ten tombstones in the Catacomb Monteverde in Rome,[22] and on two tombstones and a sarcophagus in the Catacomb Vigna Randanini.[23] One tombstone there, which I have not reproduced,[24] bears simply the words "Salpingius, infant," with a shofar on each side and two leaves (perhaps intended for ethrogs) below. There is here certainly a connection between the name and the shofar, but whether the name became a Jewish name [25] because of the importance of the shofar, or the object was put beside the epitaph because of the name, it is impossible to say with confidence, though I suspect strongly that Jews gave their children this name because of the feeling of sanctity and the Jewish association which the shofar in itself conveyed. The shofar appears three times with other cult objects in the murals of the Catacomb Torlonia,[26] and on ten tombstones from various parts of Italy.[27] It is similarly on an inscribed gravestone from Alexandria,[28] on one from Nicomedia in Asia Minor,[29] and on two from Gammarth.[30] It is displayed with the menorah, and an object that is perhaps an ethrog, in the mosaic of the synagogue of Hammam Lif.[31] On lamps it is not so common in the diaspora as in Palestine, but it appears on one lamp from Ephesus,[32] on one from Syria,[33] and on one from Malta.[34] It is with a menorah, lulab, and ethrog on a unique glass bottle from Ephesus,[35] and occurs with other Jewish objects on nine gold glasses.[36] Finally, it is found on a number of rings and amulets.[37]

Several facts seem to me to come out of these appearances of the shofar. Its use on amulets would indicate that it was thought to have active symbolic power. Its constant recurrence on graves, or on objects to be buried with a corpse, suggests that it had some

19. See III, fig. 584.

20. See III, figs. 577, 580.

21. See III, fig. 639.

22. See III, figs. 710, 715, 717, 720–722, 724 f., 727 f.

23. See III, figs. 768 f., 787.

24. Frey, *CIJ*, no. 162.

25. For other instances of the use of the name among Jews, see Frey's note ad loc.

26. See above, III, figs. 806, 808, 817.

27. See III, figs. 837, 846 f., 849, 851, 893. See also Frey, *CIJ*, 484, and nos. 523, 600, 652.

28. See above, III, fig. 896.

29. See III, fig. 977.

30. See III, figs. 872 f.

31. See III, fig. 891.

32. See III, fig. 928.

33. See III, fig. 941.

34. See III, fig. 958.

35. See III, fig. 961.

36. See III, figs. 962, 965–968, 970, 973 f., 976.

37. See III, figs. 1010 f., 1013 f., 1016 f., 1023, 1026, 1034.

sort of eschatological significance, so that it could supposedly help the deceased in the next world; its association with the ethrog, lulab, or shovel in such a great majority of the designs in which it appears suggests that the shofar as used in the festivals had this significance also. It is not a shofar as such, but the shofar of the High Holydays which we are encountering, as well as, perhaps, the shofar of funerals.

In shape the shofar resembles the Dionysiac drinking horn, but among the Jewish representations collected, I have seen only one form that suggests a drinking horn,[38] and since the horn in Dionysiac representations is always a drinking horn [39] (though sometimes hard to distinguish from a cornucopia), I see no reason to think that Jews felt any parallelism between the Dionysiac drinking horn and their shofar.[40] The horn is universally one of the commonest primitive musical instruments: thus it is surprising that its introduction into Jewish ritual seems to have occurred relatively late,[41] and I have been able to find no Canaanitic or Syrian counterpart to the shofar.

A Dionysiac parallel comes at once out of the liturgy, however, for in the ceremonies in honor of Dionysus apparently one of the earliest elements was the blowing of "trumpets" to mark or herald the vernal resurrection of the god. Dionysus was supposed to die and go into the depths of the lower world in the winter; then, in a rite of spring which we may suppose was not practised exclusively at the one place we know of, Lake Alkyonia near Lerna, a lamb was thrown into the lake and a horn sounded over it. The lamb was intended to placate the warder of the gates of Hades, and the blast of the trumpet was to awaken Dionysus and call him forth.[42] Plutarch tells of this custom,[43] and it is to this same rite that he compares the Jews' use of the shofar: "They [the Jews] use little trumpets as the Argives do at the Dionysiac festivals to call upon God." [44] That is, the Jewish horns much resembled the Dionysiac trumpets,[45] and it may be supposed that basically the two

---

38. Cf. the three little objects in the third opening from the bottom of the vine, at the left, in III, fig. 632; see I, 242.

39. The drinking horn was pictured by Greeks more commonly in the earlier period than later: see Roscher, *Lex. Myth.*, I, 1095, line 25; 1099, line 41. It would amount to a large study in itself to collect the representations of drinking horns in Greek and Roman art. A few examples that I happened to note, probably because in these cases the horn especially recalled the shofar in form, may be listed as follows: the horns in an Attic relief of Dionysus, *JDAI*, XI (1896), 104; those pictured on later Greek vases, on a table before banqueters, ibid., II (1887), 125; the forms reproduced in *Mon. Ant.*, XXII, ii (1914), plate XCIII; drinking horns painted as hanging on a wall in Pompeii, *NSA*, 1934, plate XII. See also above, III, fig. 637.

40. On the superficial level of symbolism to which I am keeping myself, this statement stands. But the object was the same in both religions, and

it may be that when the devotee of Dionysus drank his immortalizing wine from the horn of a ram (or bull), the association of the wine with the sacrificial animal, which in Christianity still survives in the image of the "blood of the Lamb," was definitely felt. That which, as we shall see, constituted the saving power of the ram's horn in Judaism comes very close, then, to the value of the Dionysiac horn. If the horn in Judaism had phallic association, as we may suppose it had in Dionysiac usage, that association was probably completely unconscious.

41. Adler, op. cit., 293–297; F. Brown, S. R. Driver, and C. A. Briggs, *Hebrew and English Lexicon*, s.v. שׁפר; Cohen in *JE*, XI, 301.

42. Farnell, *Cults*, V, 183–185; see p. 305, n. 89, for the classical references.

43. *On Isis*, 35 (364 F).

44. *Quaestiones convivales* IV, vi, 2 (671 E).

45. The juxtaposition of the shofar and the name Salpingius in a Jewish epitaph has already been noted above, p. 169.

practices were indeed similar, and that the Jewish ritual usage in the same way went back to a blast to awaken God to assure the growth of the crops. Or, since the blowing of the shofar was prescribed in observance of the New Moons in general (Num. x, 10; Ps. LXXXI, 3 f.), it may originally have summoned or awakened the moon-god. At least it is interesting that while it was to be blown over the sacrifices on all the solemn feast days,[46] the shofar was from early times uniquely associated with Rosh Hashanah, the New Moon par excellence, the New Moon of the New Year. There may be some importance in the fact that the new moon is shaped like a horn, and that the use of the horn as a symbol of the new moon in cult (e.g., the horns of altars, and of Minoan-Mycenaean art) is probably much older than the discovery that an animal horn would make a sound if blown. Such speculation cannot be pursued farther, however, for it has already taken us quite beyond all evidence.[47]

If such meanings were originally associated with the horn, it is clear that by the beginning of the Christian era, if not long before, they had been forgotten in Jewish liturgy, even in the liturgy of the Temple, because Jews were now actively setting forth other explanations of the shofar.

B. *THE SHOFAR IN THE TRACTATE ROSH HASHANAH*

FOR THE EXPLANATIONS current at the time when the art of our study arose, one turns naturally first to the relevant tractate in the Babylonian Talmud, the *Rosh Hashanah;* but we are disappointed to find that this document, except for a few passages, is concerned largely with problems of how the days of the festivals were to be determined each year, and how Jews in the diaspora could be informed about the proper dates, especially that of the New Year. With this goes a considerable discussion about the making and blowing of the shofar.[48] But in one passage it is said: "From the beginning of the year sentence is passed as to what shall be up to the end of it." [49] This conception is elaborated in another passage,[50] where the Mishnah explains that there are four seasons of judgment each year: at Passover the "produce," probably the crop of winter grain, is judged; at Pentecost, fruit; at Tabernacles, rain; and at the New Year "all creatures pass before God like children of Maron," i.e., one by one, or, as it is restated in the Gemara, "man is judged on New Year, and his doom is sealed on the Day of Atonement." That is, the special significance of the New Year and Yom Kippur is personal—a significance still vividly felt in Jewish ritual. And so two statements are reported in this connection, bearing most

---

46. Num. x, 10.

47. My colleague Harald Ingholt recalls in a note to me that "the Hebrew *halal,* 'to shout with joy,' comes from the noun of the same root, or with the same radicals, meaning 'new moon,' Arabic *hilâl.* . . . As far as I can see the Hebrew verb originally denoted the joyous shouting at the sight of the new moon." Mention should be made of a recent study of the origin of Yom Kippur, though

it contains no discussion of the shofar: Julian Morgenstern, "Two Prophecies of the Fourth Century B.C. and the Evolution of Yom Kippur," *HUCA,* XXIV (1952/3), 1–74.

48. Maurice Simon has an excellent brief outline of the tractate in the introduction to his translation of it (publ. 1938).

49. *BT, Rosh Hashanah,* 8a (ET, 30).

50. Ibid., 16a,b (ET, 57–64).

importantly on the meaning of the New Year rites. To the question, "Why do we blow on a ram's horn?" one rabbi answers that it is to remind God of the "binding" of Isaac, and make him ascribe the merit of that deed to the worshipers as though they all had done it. Another explains that because God has commanded it, we blow the horn with the elaborations traditional for the day in order to confuse Satan, for if at the beginning of the New Year Satan be not confused, it is clear that he will put catastrophe into what is being ordained for that year.[51]

The ordaining for the year is shortly explained: three books are opened on the New Year, one for the thoroughly wicked, one for the thoroughly righteous, and one for the intermediate category of men. The fate of the first two is determined at once, but that of the intermediate group (into which most worshipers would put themselves) is suspended till the Day of Atonement, when it is finally decided whether to write them in the book of the bad or the book of the good. This statement suggests that each writing is final, but since the whole process is repeated every year, it is not surprising to learn that there will be still the same three groups on the Day of Judgment, when the intermediate ones will go to Gehenna, "squeal" for a time, and then be taken up, apparently to join the righteous in everlasting life.[52] This sounds extremely grim, and is meant to sound so, but all can be mitigated by repentance, since "great is the power of repentance that it rescinds a man's final sentence." [53] It can also be mitigated by certain rituals, for "whenever Israel sin, let them carry out this service before me, and I will forgive them." [54] This last refers to the reading of the passage of the Torah which sets forth the thirteen attributes of God, but "this service" must often have been thought to refer to the ritual of the New Year and the Day of Atonement as a whole, since reconciliation with God was precisely the purpose of that ritual. For it is especially "in the ten days between New Year and the Day of Atonement that the individual can find God." [55]

For all the frequent mention of the shofar in the talmudic *Rosh Hashanah*, then, little space is given to its significance. Important interpretations are, to be sure, suggested: the shofar is blown to recall the sacrifice of Isaac, to confuse Satan, and because God commanded it. But these interpretations are almost lost sight of in the far greater concern of the rabbis with the laws for correct observance of Rosh Hashanah.

C. THE AKEDAH

To one of these three interpretations we must pay considerable attention—that which connects the blowing of the shofar with the sacrifice or "binding" of Isaac, the Akedah.[56]

51. Ibid., ET, 60 f. Simon quotes Rashi as saying that the devotion of the Jews to the Law is what confuses Satan, but Eisenstein (in *JE*, XI, 304) has a more elaborate explanation, namely, that at the first great series of blasts Satan thinks the Jews are just complying with the Law; at the second, that the Messiah is coming; at the third, that the resurrection is at hand, when his power will end. Where Eisenstein got this I do not know. The difficulty

encountered by God himself in adapting the decrees of New Year to later circumstances is discussed in *BT, Rosh Hashanah*, 17b (ET, 69).

52. Ibid., 16b–17a (ET, 64).

53. Ibid., 17b (ET, 68).

54. Ibid.

55. Ibid., 18a (ET, 72).

56. The term Akedah literally means "binding," but refers to all the incidents of the story of

This tradition is discussed at considerable length in the midrashic writings of the rabbinic period, but references to it in the Talmud show that it was completely accepted by the early legalists.

1. In the Talmud

THE LONGEST talmudic section of this tradition is in the Palestinian Talmud.[57] The passage begins with a statement that the salvation of Isaac is equivalent to that of Israel itself. This is explained by showing how Abraham did not protest against the command to sacrifice Isaac, though it seemed to annul God's previous promise that Isaac was to have a mighty posterity. Thus Abraham is said to have prayed that if the children of Israel should get into trouble, and have no advocate, God would himself be their advocate as he recalled Isaac bound on the faggots for the sacrifice. Such deliverance will come when God himself blows the shofar.[58] Indeed, R. Hanina adds, as Abraham saw the ram getting free from one bush only to be caught in another, so the children of Israel will be subjected to the rule of Babylonia, Media, Greece, and Rome, but will in the end be delivered through this blast of God himself on the shofar. With this conception the sounding of the shofar becomes clearly the original of the Christian "last trump," at least as heralding the Messianic Age.[59] But in the Jewish tradition the trumpet is no other, still, than the shofar of the Akedah.

These are the important allusions to the shofar and the Akedah in the Talmud. On the second day of the celebration of the New Year the story of the sacrifice of Isaac is still read from Genesis, and then by orthodox tradition there is recited a prayer ascribed to Rab, the great rabbi of the third century:

> Remember in our favor, O Lord our God, the oath which thou hast sworn to our father Abraham on Mount Moriah; consider the binding of his son Isaac upon the altar when he suppressed his love [of his son] in order to do thy will with a whole heart! Thus may thy love suppress thy wrath against us, and through thy great goodness may the heat of thine anger be turned away from thy people, thy city, and thy heritage! . . . Remember today in mercy in favor of his seed the binding of Isaac.[60]

The prayer remains in the liturgy, though it is often omitted, since the halachic rabbis do not like its implications. It is a part of their general antipathy to the principle of the "merit of the Fathers," the doctrine that later Israelites would be forgiven their sins because God had been so pleased with the virtues of the Old Testament heroes. The rabbinic antipathy to the idea of the atoning force of this vicarious merit is well expressed in the

---

the call to Abraham to sacrifice his son, and of the events on Mount Moriah.

57. *JT, Taanith*, II, 4, 65d (FT, VI, 157); partly transl. into German in Strack-Bill., III, 242. See also *BT, Sanhedrin*, 89b (ET, II, 595 f.), to be discussed shortly. The relation of the shofar to the Akedah is discussed by Shalom Spiegel, "The Legend of Isaac's Slaying and Resurrection," in

Alexander Marx Jubilee Volume, II, 1950 (in Hebrew), 471–547, esp. 504 f., 514, 518.

58. Zech. IX, 14.

59. Matt. XXIV, 31. In I Cor. XV, 52, the trumpet is introduced as signal for the resurrection; we shall see that this idea is also involved in the meaning of the Akedah.

60. As quoted by Max Landsberg in *JE*, I, 303*a*

saying put into God's mouth as at the time of Elisha: "Hitherto did you have the merit of the Fathers; but from now on will each man depend upon his own works." [61] Landsberg represented such a point of view when he wrote:

> This turn given to the attempted sacrifice of Isaac is certainly in conflict with the prophetic spirit [i.e., the rabbinic spirit]. The occurrence is never again mentioned in the Bible; and even in the Talmud voices are raised in condemnation of its conception as a claim to atonement.

But if we are to understand the shofar in the graphic presentations we are discussing, we must quickly come to see that Landsberg has definitely (certainly not in ignorance) misrepresented a powerful tradition in rabbinic writings. To him the very idea of atonement is distasteful; yet Yom Kippur is the Day of Atonement, and the desire for atonement was and still is the very heart of the religious feeling of the day. Landsberg is strictly correct: references to the elements of atonement, specifically to the Akedah, are rare in the Talmud, though the rabbis quoted express the doctrine unmistakably. But the Midrash elaborately attests that there was much more to rabbinic Judaism than the halachic emphasis of the Talmud, and it is to the former that we return for the story of Isaac, and the meaning of the Akedah. [62]

2. *In the Midrash*

FIRST AS to the shofar itself. In the Midrash the shofar is connected with the New Year and the Day of Atonement on the ground that they are days of determining, repentance, and judgment. For here it is first explained that the New Year is the anniversary of the creation of the world, and so on that day "sentence is pronounced upon countries, which of them is destined to the sword and which to peace, which to famine and which to plenty." [63] The passage goes on to show how on that day God created, judged, and then pardoned Adam, and this happens to Adam's descendants each year on the same day. The story is then told of how Jacob watched the angels, that is the princes, of Babylon, Media, and Greece in turn ascend the ladder toward heaven, but all had to turn back. Edom (Rome) then tried it and was, at the time of writing, still going up; but God had promised to send him down, however high he might climb. God then invited Jacob to climb, but Jacob was afraid. He learned after it was too late that God had planned to keep him aloft forever, had he tried it, and the penalty of his timidity was that his descendants

61. A. Jellinek, *Bet ha-Midrash*, IV (1857), 16; quoted by Gustaf H. Dalman, *Jesaja 53*, 1914, 42.

62. The most important study of the Akedah is found in Spiegel, op. cit. Still of value are: Israel Lévi, "Le Sacrifice d'Isaac et la mort de Jésus," *REJ*, LXIV (1912), 161–184; Dalman, op. cit., 37–41; Ginzberg, *Legends*, I, 271–285, with notes in Vol. V; H. J. Schoeps, "The Sacrifice of Isaac in Paul's Theology," *JBL*, LXV (1946), 385–392; Riesenfeld, *Jésus transfiguré*, 86–96; David Lerch, *Isaaks Opferung christlich gedeutet*, 1950 (Beiträge zur historischen Theologie, ed. by G. Eberling, XII).

Moore, *Judaism*, I, 535–552, discusses the problem of atonement and expiatory suffering—like Landsberg, to belittle it, though he admits (p. 541) that in the later liturgy, as well as in the Palestinian Targum, and in the younger midrashim, the Akedah has a much larger place.

63. *MR*, *Leviticus*, XXIX, 1 (ET, 369). This, J. J. Slotki remarks ad loc. in his translation, is the old "shofar benediction," now called *Zikronoth*, or "Remembrance," in the Additional Service for Rosh Hashanah.

had to serve those four princes. But the end is to be a happy one: after all the others have been humiliated,[64] Israel, we gather, will some day make the ascent never to come down again.

All of this, it seems, is a sample of the deterministic judgment that marks the New Year. What has it to do with the shofar? The passage goes on to explain that God sits on the throne of judgment on this day, presumably to set the fate of nations and individuals; but when he hears that trumpeting he rises from the throne of judgment and sits upon the throne of mercy.[65] The blowing of the shofar is not enough in itself, it is stated: it must be accompanied by a genuine change of conduct, and we recall from the *Rosh Hashanah* [66] that the one who blows as well as the one who hears must "put his mind to it," or the religious duty is not performed. In this statement, then, the blowing of the shofar has become a summons to man to repent and to God to be merciful. Then follow the ten days of penitence, closing with the Day of Atonement, the exercises of which culminate in a single long blast on the shofar, which means to the worshipers that the rites are accomplished, and that thereby atonement is consummated. Incidentally, we have seen this judgment represented in a Jewish prayer book of the thirteenth century, fig. 94. Under an arch, that is, in heaven, stands a figure holding a balance. Jewish sensitivities would require that this be called the "divine judgment" rather than "God judging," but the values are the same.

Such associations might well have been recalled by putting the shofar on a tombstone: but the very fact that the horn so often was thus employed in the Roman period, and never, or practically never, appears in such use today, strikingly suggests that at that time all this symbolism had a fresh vividness which even the solemn rites now practised hardly convey. For this deeper meaning we turn to the midrashic tradition on the Akedah.

The *Midrash Rabbah* on Genesis contains the most elaborate discussion of the sacrifice of Isaac.[67] The test which God put upon Abraham, the account begins, was designed to show forth Abraham's righteousness "like a ship's ensign . . . in order that the equity of God's justice may be verified in the world," [68] for God knew very well that Abraham could stand such a test.[69] In Jub. xvii, 16–xviii, 12, God is challenged by the devil—here called "Prince Mastema"—to put Abraham to this trial, and the tradition reappears in the Talmud.[70] It is probably with reference to this episode that, as we have seen, the devil is discomfited by the shofar. The talmudic passage has Satan accusing Abraham of failing to make sacrificial offerings on the occasion of the banquet celebrating Isaac's birth. In the midrash we are discussing, the incident arises from the fact that Abraham has not been offering rams and bullocks; according to one tradition Abraham reproaches himself, according to another the heavenly court criticizes him for the omission.[71] We stop to recall that this was the situation of Jews living away from the Temple before its destruction, and

64. Ibid., §2 (ET, 370 f.).
65. Ibid., §§3 f., 6, 9 f. (ET, 372 f., 376 f.).
66. *BT, Rosh Hashanah,* 28b–29a (ET, 130–133).
67. *MR, Genesis,* LV (ET, 482–503).

68. Ibid., LV, 1 (ET, 482), and 6 (ET, 485).
69. Ibid., §2 (ET, 482 f.).
70. *BT, Sanhedrin,* 89b (ET, II, 595 f.). Cf. Strack-Bill., I, 141; Lerch, op. cit., 9–12.
71. *MR, Genesis,* LV, 4 (ET, 484).

of all Jews afterwards. If the atoning sacrifices of the Temple were really necessary for removal of guilt, there was little hope for anyone who could not come to the Temple. As we continue it will appear that this interpretation of the Akedah, which makes it a substitute for Temple sacrifice, antedates the destruction of the Temple, and this circumstance is the first among many which will suggest to us that the idea of the Akedah as a permanent atonement probably had its origin in the diaspora, and, never popular with the halachic rabbis, was accepted by rabbinic Judaism afterwards when, like Abraham, no Jews could offer sacrifice in the Temple.

God, the same midrash explains, knew better than Abraham or the heavenly court: he knew that if it were asked of him, Abraham would sacrifice even his own son,[72] from which we understand that the sacrifice was made to exhibit Abraham's (and Isaac's) righteousness to others, not to convince God of Abraham's complete fidelity. At once Jews in the diaspora might take comfort, for it was not any sacrifice in itself, whether of bulls or of a son, that God needed. The attitude of Isaac was similarly assured in advance. For an argument between Isaac and Ishmael, of which two accounts are given, ends in the one version in God's recognition that Isaac is willing to sacrifice himself, in the other with Isaac's declaration of his willingness. And when Isaac had thus spoken, "said the Holy One, blessed be he, 'This is the moment!' "[73] We are reminded of the Greek sacrifice, which could use only willing victims, and of Christ, who "gave himself." The conception of vicarious sacrifice, the innocent willingly giving himself for the guilty, is already beginning to appear in one of its most important aspects. Of course Isaac's willingness to be sacrificed was also a model and inspiration for Jewish martyrs,[74] as Christ's sacrificing of himself has inspired Christian martyrs.[75]

The next section, more cryptic, seems to say that by thus offering himself Isaac "came before the Lord."[76] Abraham, however, was the one especially "lifted like an ensign,"[77] for when God called him, and he answered "Here am I," it meant that God was exalting him to priesthood and kingship.[78] Priesthood is obviously appropriate for one who is about to make a sacrifice, but it is conspicuous that, as is said of Christ in the Letter to the Hebrews, it was to the "priesthood of Melchizedek" that God exalted Abraham—a priesthood, the passage reveals, whose unique characteristic, in the famous language of Ps. cx, 4, is that of being a "priesthood for ever." Abraham's sacrifice and priestly mediation, in having the value of "for ever," is made available for the faithful of every generation. Here is a sacrifice again like Christ's in that it need not be repeated, for it is timeless and eternal.

---

72. Ibid.

73. Ibid.

74. This interpretation is very old: see IV Mac. VII, 14; cf. XIII, 12, XVI, 20, XVIII, 11. It persists in modern times: see Morris Silverman, *High Holiday Prayer Book*, 1951, 108; Spiegel, op. cit., 473, 517.

75. We need recall only the line in the beloved song of the American Civil War, "As He died to make men holy, let us die to make men free."

76. The sacrifice of Isaac was acceptable, whereas the sacrifice of a son by Mesha, King of Moab, was not: *MR, Genesis*, LV, 5 (ET, 485).

77. Ginzberg, *Legends*, V, 249, n. 229, has an interesting comment on the dispute in the tradition as to whether Isaac or Abraham was more glorified in the Akedah.

78. *MR, Genesis*, LV, 6 (ET, 486).

The passage adds, as we have seen, that Abraham was also made a king by this sacrifice, but in what sense he became a king is not explained, except that his kingship is compared to that of Moses. The writer in the *Midrash Rabbah* understands, and takes it for granted that his reader does: he need not explain what kingship really implies, and I can only suppose that he assumes the reader to comprehend the generally current meaning of the term, which Philo also reads so richly into his explanations of the function and power of the Patriarchs. In this idea of kingship, the king's essential function, besides that of exercising the priestly office, was to be a mediator between man and God, a guide to lead man into the true right, which the king was uniquely empowered to see in the nature of God; indeed, true right was a part of the king's own nature, insofar as he was a true king. To express this theory of royal power, the king was called *lex animata*, the Law of Nature or of God become incarnate and vocal for men. Even more, the true king was the savior of his people: "in the case of ordinary men, if they sin, their most holy purification is to make themselves like the rulers, whether it be law or king who orders affairs where they are." [79] A king "will put in order those who look upon him. . . . For to look upon the good king ought to affect the souls of those who see him no less than a flute or harmony" [80]—the flute or harmony which was a means of purification in mystic rites. This sort of thinking Philo especially applied to Moses, in expositions that consistently made him the savior of his people as well as the priest par excellence. Indeed, each of the great Patriarchs was for him the *lex animata*.[81] In the *Midrash Rabbah* the parallel with Moses is at once felt, but typically, in a passage praising Abraham, Moses is represented as having been less fully king and priest. We recall that Christ is also the King in Christian explanations of his office.

Thus Abraham was commanded to take his beloved son (the element of love is beautifully stressed) and go with him to the land of Moriah.[82] The place, Moriah, is then given a number of allegorical meanings. Moriah was traditionally "the spot where in later times the Chamber of Hewn Stones in the Temple stood and the Great Sanhedrin sat and sent forth religious teaching to all Israel." [83] In the Midrash it is accordingly the place whence instruction went forth to the world, or the source of religious reverence. It is compared to the holy Ark of the Covenant, from which go forth light and religious reverence, and to the inner sanctuary of the Temple, whence issue speech (*dibbur*) and retribution. So Moriah is also the place of final judgment from which God will hurl the nations into Gehenna, the place corresponding to the heavenly Temple, the "place that God will show thee," the seat of world domination, "the place where incense would be offered." [84] All of these associations seem to me important. Moriah is clearly identical with the site of the Temple, Mount Zion—an identification that is soon considerably expanded.[85] Even

79. Ecphantus, as quoted in my study, "The Political Philosophy of Hellenistic Kingship," *Yale Classical Studies*, I (1928), 77.

80. Diotogenes, as quoted ibid., 72.

81. See my *By Light, Light*, 181–198.

82. *MR, Genesis*, LV, 7 (ET, 487).

83. Freedman (in a note ad loc., ibid., ET, 487),

states this not as a tradition but as a fact.

84. *MR, Genesis*, LV, 7 (ET, 488).

85. Ibid., LVI, 10 (ET 500 f.). Riesenfeld, op. cit., 90 f., points out that this identification is as old as II Chron. III, 1, i.e., goes back to c. 400 B.C., and is recalled in Jub. XVIII, 13 and Josephus, *Antt.*, I, 226 (xiii, 2). Some idea that the sacrifice of

more importantly, the identification continues the process of generalizing the action of Abraham and Isaac, making it into an act of universal validity, and incidentally bringing into the episode more and more of the meaning of the New Year and its judgment.

Abraham saddled his ass in the early morning, the allegory continues,[86] but this too is generalized. Abraham's act was one of love, and as such it counteracts the deeds of hate of others. Abraham was like Joseph in this: Abraham's deed of love counteracted Baalam's saddling of his ass in hate, just as Joseph's preparing of his chariot in love counteracted Pharaoh's hateful preparation of a chariot. Hence from this point of view too the act of Abraham was one of vicarious rectification of evil.

Abraham went forth, and on the "third day" he saw the place to which he was being led.[87] The Midrash then interprets the "third day" in a way that again recalls Christian speculation; the parallel immediately quoted is: "After two days he will revive us, on the third day he will raise us up, that we may live in his presence," [88] and soon the parallel is with Jonah's three days in the fish's belly. The third day is a day of resurrection and revelation—all of which seems written with the judgment of the New Year in mind.

The place to which Abraham and Isaac were led was a mountain which they saw covered by a cloud (the Shekinah),[89] but the servants could not see it, and so they had to stop with the asses.[90] The mountain (which is still Jerusalem in the allegory) will some day be alienated from God, the rabbis interject, but will be restored by the Messiah, who will come riding upon an ass—a statement which seems cryptically to make the Messiah a second Isaac. The Midrash is so much later than the Gospels that it is extremely dangerous even to suggest that possibly this conception is older than the Gospels, and prompted the story of the Triumphal Entry. But one must admit the possibility.[91] Abraham promised the servants that he and Isaac would return when they had worshiped, and this suggests to the writer of the passage a list of rewards for worship, a list which we need not reproduce. So Abraham and Isaac set off together.

First Abraham "laid the wood on Isaac his son"; on this verse it is most surprisingly commented that he was "like one who carries his cross on his shoulder." [92] This detail so strikingly brings to mind the crucifixion of Jesus that it seems impossible that there was no relationship. To conclude finally that the detail in the Midrash must have come from

---

Isaac was the prototype of the sacrifice in the Temple seems indicated by the passage in Chronicles, but the fact that there the site of the Temple is called Moriah by no means justifies putting back into so early a period the whole tradition of the Akedah as it is developing before us. See also Schoeps, op. cit., 388, n. 12.

86. *MR, Genesis*, LV, 8 (ET, 488).

87. *Ibid.*, LVI, 1 (ET, 491).

88. Hos. VI, 2.

89. G. Friedlander, in *Pirke Eliezer*, 225, n. 9, says that this detail is Philonic. It is so in a general way, but not specifically, for there is no exact parallel to be adduced.

90. *MR, Genesis*, LVI, 2; cf. *MR, Ecclesiastes*, XI, 7, 1 (ET, 231 f.).

91. In *Pirke Eliezer*, XXXI, it is said that the same ass was ridden by Moses when he came to Egypt, and that it will again be ridden by the Messiah (with quotation of the classic prophecy in Zech. IX, 9).

92. *MR, Genesis*, LVI, 3 (ET, 493): in ET, the word is softened to "stake," but A. Wünsche, GT (1885), reads *Kreuz*, and Levy, *Wörterbuch*, s.v. צלוב, makes the meaning unequivocal, and adds that the same thing is said in *Pesiqta Rabbathi*, §31, 57b. See also Strack-Bill., I, 587, and III, 324; Schoeps, op. cit., 387; Spiegel, op. cit., 509.

the Christian story, however, seems rash, even though the Christian story is so much earlier than the composition of the Midrash. The detail of Jesus carrying his cross may have come from some tradition about Isaac, but this seems also unlikely. Yet the resemblance remains, and one begins to see why the halachic rabbis did not like the theme of the Akedah. As expanded, it made a striking Jewish parallel to the idea of the atonement of Christ's death.[93] The parallel actually appears in Christian literature earlier than we can find it in Jewish writings. Important in Origen, who probably considerably antedates the Midrash,[94] it was mentioned by Melito nearly a century before Origen. In one fragment Melito says of Christ:

> He bore the wood upon his shoulders as he was led up for sacrifice like Isaac by his father. However, Christ suffered, but Isaac did not suffer, for he was a type of the Christ who was to suffer in the future.[95]

The parallel is much elaborated in this and other fragments,[96] and is mentioned in another newly found sermon of Melito.[97] It seems to me quite possible that the Christian comparison of the death of Christ with the sacrifice of Isaac had behind it some sort of Jewish tradition in which the wood that Isaac carried was likened to the cross carried by a criminal, rather than that later Jews took the idea from Christians.[98]

As the two walked this last part of their journey, Abraham went through his supreme trial. Samael, the wicked one, offered many arguments to induce Abraham to stop, and tried also to disturb Isaac.[99] But, as told in one of the most moving passages in the Midrash, both resisted; they went on, father and son together, to slaughter and be slaughtered.[100]

When they reached the mount, Abraham prepared the altar, while Isaac hid himself lest Samael strike him with a stone, maim him, and so make him unfit for sacrifice.[101] Then Abraham bound him, bound him indeed at his own request, lest he tremble and so invalidate the sacrifice.[102] Abraham put his son on the altar, and reached for the knife, but as he did so his tears fell into the eyes of his son,[103] and the angels likewise wept,[104] so that their tears fell upon the knife and dissolved it.[105] Thereupon Abraham proposed to

93. Lerch, op. cit., 19 f., is likewise perplexed by the passage, but does not think that the idea was taken by the rabbis from Christian tradition, nor that it is the Jewish source of Christian interpretation of Isaac.

94. Lerch, op. cit., 52, in a digest of Origen, *Homilies*, VIII, vi, 6–8.

95. J. von Otto, *Corpus apologetarum Christianorum saeculi secundi*, 1872, IX, 416 f., fr. IX.

96. See also ibid., frr. X–XII, and the discussion in Lerch, op. cit., 27–38.

97. Campbell Bonner, *The Homily on the Passion by Melito*, 1940, §§59, 69 (Studies and Documents, ed. by Kirsopp and Silva Lake, XII).

98. Lerch, op. cit., 277, n. 2, opposes Schoep's thesis that a Jewish tradition of Isaac lies behind Christian allegories. Proof is impossible, but that the Jewish tradition is the older still seems to me the more likely of the two possibilities.

99. Later legends greatly elaborated this: see B. Beer, *Leben Abrahams*, 1859, 61–63.

100. *MR, Genesis*, LVI, 4 (ET, 493).

101. Ibid., §5 (ET, 494).

102. Ibid., §8 (ET, 497).

103. Ibid. This was taken as the cause of Isaac's later blindness, but the blindness was also explained as the result of Isaac's having looked at the Shekinah as he lay bound on the altar: *MR, Deuteronomy*, XI, 3 (ET, 174).

104. *MR, Genesis*, LVI, 5 (ET, 495).

105. Ibid., §7 (ET, 497).

strangle Isaac, and it was at this point that God declared that he knew that Abraham loved him; indeed God is represented as saying to Abraham: "I ascribe merit to thee as though I had bidden thee sacrifice thyself and thou hadst not refused." [106] God ordered Abraham to spare Isaac, and Abraham discovered the ram caught by its horn in the bush, took the ram, and prayed: "Sovereign of the Universe! Look upon the blood of this ram as though it were the blood of my son Isaac, its *emurim* (sacrificial parts) as though they were my son's *emurim*." [107] According to another rabbi the prayer was: "Sovereign of the Universe! Regard it as though I had sacrificed my son Isaac first and then this ram instead of him." This prayer, the passage assures us, was answered. It was the ram that was killed, but the substitution was so complete that the effect was as though Isaac himself had been the victim.[108] The meaning of the whole incident then appears, when Abraham says:

> I suppressed my feelings of compassion in order to do thy will. Even so may it be thy will, O Lord our God, that when Isaac's children are in trouble, thou wilt remember that binding (*akedah*) in their favor and be filled with compassion for them.[109]

The conception of substitution is indeed elaborate here. The ram is substituted for Isaac, and Abraham's compassion will become God's compassion. The symbol of all this for later generations, and in liturgy, is to be the shofar, the passage assures us. For Israel, in spite of all that has been done for them, will still sin: "Yet they will be ultimately redeemed by the ram's horn, as it says, 'And the Lord God will blow the horn.' " [110] This is specifically the shofar of the New Year, as R. Hanina, son of R. Isaac, said:

> Throughout the year Israel are in sin's clutches and led astray by their troubles, but on New Year they take the shofar and blow on it, and eventually they will be redeemed by the ram's horn, as it says, "And the Lord God will blow the horn." [111]

This passage is approximately repeated in Leviticus *Rabbah*,[112] immediately after the following statement:

> When the children of Isaac give way to transgressions and evil deeds, do thou recollect for them the binding of their father Isaac and rise from the Throne of Judgment and betake thee to the Throne of Mercy, and being filled with compassion for them have mercy upon them and change for them the Attribute of Justice into the Attribute of Mercy! [113]

The shofar is also given a messianic or eschatological significance. Israel will continue to sin, and will become subject to the four great empires: yet each time they will be saved

---

106. Ibid.
107. Ibid., §9 (ET, 499).
108. This identification is elaborated in *MR, Numbers*, XVII, 2 (ET, 700 f.), where Abraham is made to say: "Sovereign of the worlds! Regard the act as though the blood of Isaac were being sprinkled before thee! . . . O consider the act as though I had flayed the skin of Isaac before thee."

And God answers: "By your life! I regard it as though your son had been offered first! This ram represents him!"
109. *MR, Genesis*, LVI, 10 (ET, 500).
110. Ibid., §9 (ET, 498); Zech. IX, 14.
111. *MR, Genesis*, LVI, §9 (ET, 499).
112. *MR, Leviticus*, XXIX, 10 (ET, 377).
113. Ibid., §9 (ET, 376).

by the ram's horn.[114] The brief talmudic statement paraphrased above has taken on a wide significance:

> Why do we blow the ram's horn? The Holy One, blessed be he, said: Sound before me a ram's horn so that I may remember on your behalf the binding of Isaac the son of Abraham, and account it to you as if you had bound yourselves before me.[115]

The remarkable explanation of the value of the Akedah given in Genesis *Rabbah*, and the allusions to it in Leviticus *Rabbah* and in the passages of the Talmud we have quoted, are by no means unique in the rabbinic writings. Actually the use of the Akedah, the appeal to the merit of Isaac, is only a special development of a larger conception—that the individual is saved not only by his own virtue but also by applying to himself, or by God's applying to him, the merit of the Patriarchs. Rabbi Levi, in the name of R. Hama, son of R. Hanina, tells a parable:

> A king's son was to be tried before his father. His father said to him: "If you wish to be acquitted by me in judgment this day, appoint such-and-such a man as advocate and you will be acquitted by me in the judgment." So the Holy One, blessed be he, said to Israel: "My children! If you wish to be acquitted by me in judgment on this day, you should recall the merit of the Patriarchs and you will be acquitted by me in judgment." [116]

The passage goes on to name the Patriarchs as Abraham, Isaac (identified with the blast of horns), and Jacob, and the judgment is said to be that of the seventh month, that is, of Rosh Hashanah. Hama, son of Hanina, was a Palestinian rabbi of the third century. It may be that in him we are nearer than we usually are in rabbinic tradition to the Judaism of the decorated synagogues, for he came of wealthy ancestors who built many synagogues. "On one occasion," writes S. Mendelsohn, "while with his colleague Hoshaiah II he was visiting the synagogues at Lydda, he proudly exclaimed, 'What vast treasures have my ancestors sunk in these walls!' " [117] Hoshaiah, who admired the synagogues less and had apparently a more halachic mind, answered that it was not so much treasure as lives which had been sunk into the walls, lives which could have been devoted to the study of the Law if the money had been given for the support of scholars. Apparently Hama's ancestors valued the highly expensive (probably also elaborately carved) walls of the synagogues more than they did legalistic study. His father, Hanina, as we shall see, had the same interests.[118]

The parable just quoted reproduces with amazing identity the idea, "If any man sin he hath an Advocate with God the Father." So Isaac "goes and sits at the entrance of Gehinnom to deliver his descendants from the punishment of Gehinnom." [119] Not only does he save from punishment, but individual resurrection is promised through his merit: "Through the merits of Isaac, who offered himself on the altar, the Holy One,

---

114. Ibid., §10 (ET, 377).

115. *BT, Rosh Hashanah,* 16a (ET, 60 f.). See above, p. 172.

116. *MR, Leviticus,* xxix, 7 (ET, 374).

117. *JE,* VI, 187; W. Bacher, *Die Agada der palästinensischen Amoräer,* 1892, I, 447. Neither of these scholars gives a reference for the story.

118. For the tradition of Hanina, see Bacher, op. cit., I, 1–34; for that of Hama, ibid., 447–449.

119. *MR, Song of Songs,* VIII, ix, 3 (ET, 317).

praised be his name, will eventually raise the dead." [120] Indeed, the Jewish tradition of imputed merit presents the same peculiar combination as that found in Christianity, where the Savior is one who saves by self-sacrifice, by personal advocacy, and also through a more abstract treasury of merit stored up by his deeds of supererogation and those of the saints, which can be imputed to others to compensate for their sins.[121] The idea of a treasury of merit is presented most succinctly and vividly in a parable told by R. Aha. He is commenting upon the incident in which Moses reminded God of Abraham, Isaac, and Jacob, to persuade him to soften his wrath against the Israelites for having worshiped the golden calf:

> A king's friend deposited with him ten precious pearls. After a time, this friend died, leaving one only daughter behind, whom the king subsequently married and made the chief lady of the land, also giving her a necklace of ten pearls which she placed round her neck. In course of time, she lost that necklace and the king sought to divorce her, saying: "I will drive her out of my house, I will banish her from my presence." Her best friend then appeared before the king and tried to appease him, but the king would not hearken to him, repeating: "I will banish her from me." The friend then said: "Why, your majesty?" "Because I gave her ten pearls and she lost them," he replied. "Well, in spite of this," he urged, "by thy life thou must become reconciled to her and forgive her." But the king still would not hearken to him. When the friend saw the king's intention and that he refused to be appeased, but vehemently declared, "I will drive her out," he then said to him: "Thou dost seek to drive her out because of the ten pearls she lost? Dost thou not know that I am aware that her father had deposited ten pearls with thee? Well, let these ten pearls [she lost] be in exchange for those [her father had deposited with thee]." So, when Israel perpetrated that act, God was angry with them and said: "Now therefore let me alone, that my wrath may wax hot against them, and that I may consume them" (Exod. xxxii, 10); but Moses pleaded: "Lord of the Universe! Why art thou angry with Israel?" "Because they have broken the Decalogue," [God] replied. "Well, they possess a source from which they can make repayment," urged he. "What is that source?" [God] asked. Moses replied: "Remember that thou didst prove Abraham with ten trials, and so let those ten [trials serve as a compensation] for these ten [broken commandments]." This is why he said: "Remember Abraham, Isaac, and Israel." [122]

Thus R. Hama, whose interest in atonement has already been mentioned, represents God as saying to Abraham:

> From thee I will raise up protectors and righteous men. . . . If thy children fall into transgression and evil deeds, I will see what great man there is among them who can say to the Attribute of Justice, "Enough!" And I will take him as a pledge for them.[123]

120. *Pesiqta de Rab Kahana*, XXXII, 200a, as quoted by Schoeps, 390. See GT of A. Wünsche, 299.

121. In *MR, Lamentations*, Proem (ET, 46), Abraham, Isaac, Jacob, and Moses present themselves as advocates before God, each pleading his special act of merit: Abraham's merit is that he offered his son, Isaac's that he willingly assented to being sacrificed.

122. *MR, Exodus*, XLIV, 4 (ET, 509 f.). There were a great many rabbis named Aha. Any of the three called Aha I, Aha II, and Aha III in *JE*, I, 276, could have been the source of this parable, since to all of them somewhat kindred sayings are ascribed.

123. *MR, Song of Songs*, I, 14, 3 (ET, 84); cf. the remark of Bacher, op. cit., I, 470, n. 2.

The treasury of merit, we are told, was enriched by the succession of righteous ones, including all the heroes of the Old Testament—"New and old have I laid up for thee, O beloved" [124]—right down to Hillel, R. Johanan b. Zakkai, and R. Meir.

Was Isaac sacrificed? Clearly the story in Genesis, and the discussions of it in the *Midrash Rabbah*, say that in his person he was not; the passages hitherto adduced show that the ram stood for Isaac by substitution only. But there is a tradition—probably quite old, since it appears in the *Sifra* [125]—that alludes to Isaac's ashes. The Jerusalem Talmud and the Babylonian Talmud both make the same allusion in commenting on the mishnaic command to sprinkle ashes upon the Torah shrine and upon the worshipers when they celebrate the special rites for rain. The Babylonian Talmud says only that these ashes are to recall the "ashes of Isaac," [126] a statement ascribed to R. Hanina, father of that R. Hama whose ancestors sank so much money into the walls of the synagogues at Lydda; both father and son seem to have been especially interested in the Akedah. The Jerusalem Talmud adds the detail that Isaac's ashes "are as a pile on top of the altar." [127] Again we must supplement cryptic remarks in the Talmud with statements in the midrashim. In one midrashic passage "our Rabbis" are quoted as saying that God did not need to be reminded of Isaac, "because he saw Isaac's ashes, as it were, heaped up upon the altar." [128] Three passages in the *Midrash Rabbah* on the Song of Songs say that Isaac was "brought as an offering like a handful of frankincense on the altar," [129] was actually "offered on the altar like a handful of frankincense," [130] and "was bound on the altar like a cluster of henna because he atones for the iniquities of Israel." [131] Here Isaac seems definitely to offer his merit in the form of incense.

Even the blood of Isaac is brought in. Most accounts insist that Isaac came out of the ordeal completely unscathed, but to the great R. Joshua b. Hanania, who flourished in the second century, is attributed the saying that Isaac shed on the altar a quarter of a log

124. *MR, Leviticus*, II, 11 (ET, 31); Song of Songs VII, 14. Indeed, in *BT, Sotah*, 14a (ET, 73 f.), the substitutionary implication of Is. LIII, 12, is ascribed to Moses, in a way so strongly suggestive of Christianity that the passage has been thought to be an answer to Christianity. Cf. Moore, *Judaism*, III, 166, n. 254. In *MR, Genesis*, XLVII, 6 and LXXXII, 6 (ET, I, 403; II, 757), Simeon b. Lakish is quoted as saying: "The Patriarchs are [God's] chariot, for it says, 'And God went up from Abraham.'" Scholem, *Jewish Mysticism*, 77 f., takes this to mean that the Patriarchs are the basis of God's throne or *merkabah*, or that man's soul is the throne of glory. S. Fisch, *Ezekiel*, 1950, p. xii (Soncino Books of the Bible) prefers to interpret it as meaning that "the patriarchs were the Divine Chariot on earth, in that they brought the Glory of God down to the mundane sphere." But in *MR, Genesis*, LXVIII, 12 (ET, II, 625), the same rabbi is quoted as saying, "[God] showed [Jacob]

a throne of three legs," to which R. Levi is quoted as adding, "[God said to him]: 'Thou [Jacob] art the third leg,'" a passage to which Solomon alludes, but which Fisch did not consider. It seems to confirm Scholem's interpretation of these passages. Merkabah mysticism seems to have gone far in glorifying the Patriarchs, for Abraham and Isaac must have been the other two legs.

125. *Bechukkotai*, VIII (GT, 660).

126. *BT, Taanith*, 16a (ET, 74).

127. *JT, Taanith*, II, 1, as translated for me by Nemoy (in FT, 152, the passage seems to have been misunderstood).

128. *MR, Leviticus*, XXXVI, 5 (ET, 462). Schoeps, op. cit., 389 f., has a considerable collection of midrashic passages containing this idea.

129. *MR, Song of Songs*, IV, 6, 2 (ET, 202).

130. Ibid., III, 6, 2 (ET, 152).

131. Ibid., I, 14, 1 (ET, 81). See below, p. 189, n. 159.

of blood.[132] So important was this conception that in the approximately contemporary *Mekilta* it is said: "When I [God] see the blood [of the Passover on the houses of Jews in Egypt] I see the blood of the sacrifice of Isaac." [133] Later midrashim [134] make it appear that Isaac's soul actually departed from his body just as Abraham was about to strike with the knife, and did not return until the heavenly voice told Abraham to substitute the ram; thus when Abraham unbound him from the altar, Isaac said: "Blessed art thou, O Lord, who quickenest the dead!" [135] Later legends also recount that the ram was the bellwether of Abraham's flock; as a pet it had been named Isaac, and after it was sacrificed and burned to ashes it came to life again.[136] We feel that the identification of Isaac and the ram has become almost dreamlike substitution. What the "dream" is saying is that in sacrificing the ram Abraham sacrificed Isaac—that Isaac truly died on the altar, and came to life again, as did the ram. In this is the hope of atonement for Israel: it is the eternally valid sacrifice made by the "priest for ever," [137] and it is this merit par excellence which the shofar invokes on the New Year and the Day of Atonement.

How old the conception is that Isaac died in the sacrifice, and then returned to life, cannot be said. It seems to lie behind Heb. XI, 17–19, where it is said that Abraham was ready to sacrifice Isaac, in spite of his hope of having descendants through his son, because he believed that God could "raise up even from the dead; from whence he did in a figure receive him back." We cannot know whether at the time when the Letter to the Hebrews was written the idea had developed only so far as to be a figurative presentation, or whether the author of Hebrews has blunted the story in order to reserve the value of resurrection for the Christian Savior.[138]

We are unable to trace this conception of substitutionary sacrifice and atonement to its source. The Akedah is not the only element in the observance of the New Year and Yom Kippur in which the conception emerges, in view of the apparently very old rite of the scapegoat which, laden with the sins of Israel, was thrown from a cliff on the Day of Atonement. Similarly, the idea of substitutionary atonement was probably never completely absent from the sacrifices offered on the altar in the Temple. Reik may be correct in thinking that the shofar blowing was originally a bringing of God, who was the ram, into the power of man; that the shofar was the divine phallus, and that it was also endowed with power to utter the voice of the Ram-God. God spoke from Sinai, Reik properly recalls, and Israel was commanded in Exodus to approach the mount "when the ram soundeth long." [139] This sound was apparently identical with "the voice of the Lord our

132. *Mekilta of R. Simeon b. Yohai*, on Exod. XVI, 2; Schoeps, op. cit., 389.

133. *Mekilta of R. Ishmael, Pischa*, VII (ed. Lauterbach, I, 57; see editor's note ad loc.).

134. Ginzberg, *Legends*, I, 281 f.; V, 251, n. 242 f.

135. The sentence is from a Jewish prayer of blessing, the Amidah.

136. Ginzberg, *Legends*, V, 252, nn. 245 f. Ginzberg, esp. in his notes, greatly enriches the

Akedah interpretation from later midrashim, but I have pointed out that the basic ideas appear in the older sources. See also Spiegel, op. cit., 473.

137. Abraham is the "priest for ever after the order of Melchizedek" in *BT, Nedarim*, 32b (ET, 99); *MR. Genesis*, LV, 6, 7 (ET, 486, 488). See above p. 176.

138. Lerch, op. cit., 39–46.

139. Exod. XIX, 13. Reik's translation here seems to me correct.

God" which, it is said in Deuteronomy, the people could not long endure,[140] and with the voice in which "the Lord will roar from Zion" according to Amos.[141] So at the moment of greatest tension toward the end of the traditional liturgy of the Day of Atonement, the experience of atonement would appear to culminate in the feeling that when the shofar is blown it becomes the direct voice of God, which seems to say to the penitents, *Vos absolvo*.

Parenthetically I would say that I see no reason to follow Reik [142] in asserting that all meaning in the shofar goes back to a totemistic God who is killed, and arouses the oedipal guilt and castration fear, although I have no more ingenious theory of its origin. Search for original meanings in symbolism seems to me, valuable as such meanings are when they can be found, usually to introduce a tendency to oversimplification. The origin of man's religious rites is hopelessly and forever lost. Our earliest prehistoric relics belong to a period when the race was perhaps already hundreds of thousands of years old, and there is every reason to suppose that religious symbolism had even then become so complicated that no analysis of any kind can recover what Reik calls the original "hidden dynamic melody," if there ever was one. Reik [143] tells us that he did not get his "first clear enlightenment respecting the shofar from the rich material available, but from the peculiar biblical passages occurring in Exodus XIX" which we have just quoted. That is, like all other allegorists who put strange interpretations upon old texts, he uses a few phrases which fit his purpose as the crux of his interpretation, and largely ignores the rest of the evidence. The "rich material" which suggested nothing to Reik seems to me to include the evidence that the shofar was the voice of God: it also seems to include even clearer evidence that whatever its original meaning, a new idea has become associated with the shofar when we reach the Greco-Roman period, an idea which dominates the minds of the haggadic writers—namely, that the shofar represents not the oedipal killing of the father by the son, but the killing of the son by the father, a theme whose corollary is the concept of an eternal priesthood, a permanent atonement. If, then, we are to understand the shofar as a symbol in the period we are considering, we must not run from the complexity of the "rich material" to the simplicity of some proof text, or of some quite hypothetical "dynamic melody." That is, we must, in spite of both the halachists and the psychoanalysts, take the Akedah and its symbolism of atonement seriously in all its implications and complications.

3. In the Cabbala

FOR UNDERSTANDING the meaning of the Akedah and the shofar as symbolic equivalents, and of both as carrying the idea of a substitutionary atonement in which the merit of Abraham and Isaac turns God from justice to mercy, it is important to see that while the story of the Akedah fell into steady neglect in halachic tradition, it continued to be highly important in the mystic Judaism of cabbalistic tradition. In a late midrashic teaching Moses asks God, "Will not the time come when Israel shall have neither Tabernacles nor

---

140. Deut. v, 25; cf. IV, 12.

141. Amos I, 2.

142. See above, p. 169, n. 1.

143. Op. cit., 246.

Temple? What will happen with them then?" To which God answers, "I will then take one of their righteous men and retain him as a pledge on their behalf, in order that I may pardon all their sins." [144] This is part of the medieval development of the general doctrine of vicarious merit.[145]

In the *Zohar* [146] the story of the Akedah is told much as in the *Midrash Rabbah*, though it is not connected with the Day of Atonement. But the sacrifice of Isaac is the sacrifice of incense: Mount Moriah means "the mountain of myrrh," [147] and

> Isaac purified himself and in intention offered himself up to God, was at that moment etherealised, and, as it were, he ascended to the throne of God like the odour of the incense of spices which the priests offered before him twice a day; and so the sacrifice was complete.[148]

That is, the sacrifice of Isaac himself was indeed complete. A little before this it is explained that the perfect priesthood of Melchizedek effected the union of the letter hē, the earth, with the letter waw, the heavens, "and so [the letter] hē ascended and was joined in a perfect bond." [149] This, the passage assures us, is what happens on the Day of Atonement.

On the other hand, in discussing the blowing of the shofar on that day, the *Zohar*, while it keeps all the values of the Akedah, nowhere directly alludes to it. Isaac is, however, the hero in that discussion. First the Patriarchs are given a position as high as in Philo's allegory:

> Great kindness did God show Israel in choosing the patriarchs and making them a supernal holy chariot for his glory and bringing them forth from the supernal precious holy River, the lamp of all lamps, that he might be crowned with them.[150]

In the exposition which follows it appears that the great judge of the Day of Atonement is Isaac himself, and the business of the Day of Atonement is to soften the wrath of Isaac, and to turn him from justice to mercy. This is done by blowing the shofar. There seems to be allusion to a supernal shofar, which is the "illumination of all"; in the passage just

144. *MR, Exodus*, xxxv, 4 (ET, 432). The teaching is attributed to a rabbi named Hoshaiah, but it is quite uncertain whether this is the R. Hoshaiah of the fourth century (*JE*, VI, 475; Bacher, op. cit., III, 565). This midrash is dated by Strack (*Intro.*, 215) in the eleventh or twelfth century.

145. A rich collection of passages on this doctrine from all periods of Judaism is presented in Dalman, *Jesaja 53*, 19–35, where (p. 23) the quotation will be found. One of the strangest details is the statement, *Zohar, Emor*, 101a (ET, V, 128), that while a sinner is himself lost if his sins outweigh his good deeds, these good deeds are not lost, but are accounted to the credit of some righteous man who needs additional merit to complete his garment of good works.

146. *Zohar, Vayera*, 119a–120b (ET, I, 371–376).

147. Ibid., 120a (ET, I, 373).

148. Ibid., 120b (ET, I, 375). On Isaac's offering himself as incense, see below, n. 159.

149. *Zohar, Lech Lecha*, 87a (ET, I, 290). The hē which ascends to join with the waw is obviously the lower hē. See note, ibid., ET, 383.

150. *Zohar, Emor*, 99a (ET, V, 124). My exposition from here on is based upon §§99a–101a (ET, V, 127). For the blowing of the shofar on the New Year, when Isaac becomes the head of the Patriarchs, see *Zohar, Vayikra*, 18a,b (ET, IV, 357 f.). A "perpetual Fire, the Fire of Isaac," is mentioned in *Zohar, Zav*, 30b (ET, IV, 381).

quoted it is the "lamp of all lamps." This lamp ceases to shine (in mercy) when Isaac prepares himself for judgment, "takes hold of his sons." The supernal shofar then shines out, makes men repent; they blow the shofar below, which "awakens another supernal *Shofar*, and so mercy is awakened and judgment is removed." The various sounds of the shofar that men blow correspond to the voices in the supernal shofar. A first series of three blasts is directed, one blast each, to the three Patriarchs. The first blast sets Abraham on his throne; the second, "of broken notes," breaks down the wrath of Isaac; the third summons Jacob, who takes a position on the other side of Isaac, and he and Abraham restrain Isaac from violence. Two other series of blasts (we need not repeat all the details) have a similar effect, which is summarized as follows:

> This is the purpose which these blasts should serve, being accompanied by repentance before God. Thus when Israel produce the blasts of the *shofar* with proper devotion, the supernal *Shofar* returns and crowns Jacob so that all is properly arranged. . . . Joy is universally diffused.

In all of this there is a lacuna in the development, but it is clear that Isaac has come to take on another of the prerogatives ascribed to Christ in Christian theology: by virtue of his being the victim sacrificed for man, Isaac has become the great heavenly judge. And just as the cross is the primary symbol of the mercy of the heavenly Judge of the Christians, the shofar has become the symbol of the hope of mercy before Isaac. That it is the symbol of mercy to be obtained before Isaac as the final judge in the next world is an interpretation I have not seen in any early documents of Jewish mysticism, and the idea, I strongly suspect, is an appropriation of a Christian value—the value that the individual sacrificed for man by the Father has become the final judge of man, a judge incredibly severe, but one whose severity can be mitigated by appeal to symbols which recall his sacrifice of himself.

A later Cabbalist, Isaac Luria, prepared a "Meditation on Blowing the Shofar on New Year's Day" which reads as follows:

> May it be thy will, O God of heaven and earth, God of Abraham, Isaac, and Jacob, great and awe-inspiring God, that thou mayest send all the pure angels, the faithful messengers, who are eager to favor Israel: *Patzpatzya* who is charged to bring to light the merits of Israel when they blow the shofar, *Toshbash* whose duty it is to confuse Satan, and the great angels *Hadarniel* and *Tusniel* whose task it is to bring the shofar-blasts before thy throne of glory. Let thy mercy over thy people prevail, and look down upon the ashes of our father Isaac which are accumulated upon the altar.[151]

The sacrifice of Isaac was, for Luria, still really being performed, and his ashes were upon the altar for God to regard when the shofar of the New Year was blown. The tradition of the vicarious value of the Akedah persisted long indeed in Judaism and has never entirely died out. A reflection of this prayer, or one of similar content, seems to appear in Morris Silverman's recent modern formulation of the liturgy:

151. Quoted by A. Z. Idelsohn, *Jewish Liturgy* [1932], 50.

O may the remembrance of his [Isaac's] virtue be before thee now as the ashes of offering in thy Temple court. Remember the binding of Isaac and be gracious unto his posterity.[152]

But I do not find anywhere in modern ritual the direct idea that it is the shofar which has the power to revive the merit of Isaac's virtue in God's mind.

It is worth passing note that the Falasha Jews still celebrate a festival, corresponding to the festival of the New Year, called "Light Has Appeared," or the "Commemoration of Abraham," in which the Akedah is the theme of central interest, though the older custom of blowing the shofar on the day is now given up.[153] It is the horn of the ram of the Akedah, however, which Elijah will blow on Mount Zion on the Last Day.[154]

It may seem that in this interpretation of the redemption sought at the New Year (which essentially includes Yom Kippur, when the horn is also blown), I have presented Judaism too much as a religion of redemption. Far as medieval and modern rabbinic Judaism have gone in obscuring this element, it has never ceased to occupy a prominent place in the Jewish attitude toward the great festivals of the New Year. T. H. Gaster,[155] an authoritative spokesman for modern as well as traditional Judaism, has recently published an epitome of the meaning of these festivals. He describes them as having several aspects. First, "individuals purge their sins by the threefold process of introspection, confession, and *regeneration.*" Secondly, the house of Israel restores itself "to that state of holiness" required to fulfill its work for God among men. Thirdly, this "process of purgation" is effected by a combination of human supplication and divine forgiveness, worked out under the covenant, in which, as Israel is obligated to holiness, God is obligated to mercy: "the Blessing of God can therefore be *compelled* by righteousness as well as entreated by prayer; and one purpose of Yom Kippur is so to *compel* it." Fourthly, it is not only the righteousness of the living generation that may be applied to this end; the merit of Israel's ancestors—from the biblical Patriarchs down—has, so to speak, accumulated a substantial credit with God upon which it is possible and permissible for their descendants to draw. The italics in the quoted statements are mine: in describing Judaism I should not myself have dared use so "Christian" a term as regeneration, or so magical a word as "compel." Gaster does not mention the shofar here, but it is clear that at least in ancient times, the shofar was regarded as a direct means of transferring merit, and of "compelling" God. Certainly Israel has never lost its belief in the vicarious merit of the Fathers.

D. SYMBOLISM OF THE SHOFAR

HOW THE AKEDAH came to be a part of the symbolism of the shofar of the New Year, if not the most important part, cannot, I repeat, be traced. But two things have come from the material we have been examining—the place of the Akedah as an element in Jewish tradition,[156] and the rich significance of the shofar. One question remains, however: How

152. Silverman, *High Holiday Prayer Book,* 426.

153. Wolf Leslau, *Falasha Anthology,* 1951, p. xxxii (Yale Judaica Series, VI).

154. Ibid., 28.

155. In *Commentary,* XVI (1953), 258.

156. I do not profess to have done more than open the subject. E.g., Scholem, *Jewish Mysticism,* 151, quotes an anonymous Cabbalist as saying that

much of all this meaning of atonement and final judgment are we to associate with the shofar as it appears on the Jewish monuments we are studying? To suppose that all of this significance, or much of it, was consciously behind each representation of a shofar on a tombstone is as absurd as to suppose that the full scope of the mystical meaning of the cross is in the mind of every Catholic who buries his father under a cross. But the cross on the grave refers to that range of symbolic values to some extent in every case. The elaborate explanations of the more deeply pious are not extraneous ideas superimposed upon the simple, direct sense of the protection inhering in the symbol itself: rather, the person who uses the symbol is at a greater or lesser remove from understanding of its full range of meaning as developed in the minds of the mystics.

Since the shofar was so persistently and elaborately connected with the Akedah in Jewish tradition, it is hard to believe that the Jews who used these symbols did not have the Akedah in mind when they represented the shofar on their tombs. Proof of this is of course not forthcoming, since we have no documents deriving from the Jews who made the monuments. But there is at least some evidence of such an association.

It was when I had learned of the meaning of the Akedah to Jews that I first began to see point in the little design over the niche for the Torah scrolls in the Dura synagogue.[157] Here is a very early painting, done by quite other hands than those which decorated the synagogue so profusely later. On the left is a menorah, and beside it an ethrog and a lulab; in the center is the façade of a sanctuary, and then, fitted in as best the space permitted, a representation of the Akedah. What long perplexed me was why this scene should have been thus crowded into that space, which might have been given to other cult objects, such as a shofar, a wine jar, a drinking cup—the emblems commonly found with those used at the opposite side. It now appears that the Akedah is here for the simple reason that it too had great importance in Jewish cult, and simply takes the place of the shofar.

That this Akedah scene refers to the New Year, usually symbolized by the shofar, seems more likely in the light of two details of the design. In general the elements of the painting are a quite necessary part of the scene—the ram caught in the bush, Abraham with raised knife, and Isaac bound on the altar, while God's hand appears above, in the critical moment of interference. But in the upper corner there is a figure standing at the door of a tent, and this recalls to us that Sarah played a definite part in the story as told in connection with the New Year: for when Abraham and Isaac returned to her in the tent, and she heard how nearly Isaac had been killed, she cried out six times—"corresponding to the six blasts" of the shofar—and died.[158] The figure before the tent seems to me then most probably that of Sarah,[159] and her presence as one of the elements of the scene ap-

---

the second stage of mystic ascent, that of being purified of earthly or bodily ties, is represented in the test put upon Abraham, when he had to give up his "only beloved son."

157. See above, III, fig. 602.

158. *MR, Leviticus,* xx, 2 (ET, 253 f.).

159. That this figure is Sarah seems assured by the parallel found in a scene of the Akedah painted in a Coptic chapel in Egypt. See A. Fakhry, *The Necropolis of el-Bagawāt in Kharga Oasis,* 1951, 73 (Service des Antiquités de l'Egypte: The Egyptian Deserts). Here Sarah (her name inscribed above her head), stands beside the altar with a box in one hand and a small object in the fingers of the other. She is apparently putting incense on the sacrifice, an act very important in view of the

pears to me to emphasize the fact that the Akedah accompanies the other cult implements in lieu of the shofar. That is, the associations of the designs at Dura in themselves suggest that it is the Akedah as associated with the New Year which is represented, and that Akedah and shofar were interchangeable symbols. In any case, the representation of the Akedah here and in the Beth Alpha floor [160] appears to underline an importance in the incident which the interpretations we have found make it most easy to understand.

Indeed, we have seen four amulets engraved with the Akedah scene which seemed Jewish,[161] and we concluded inevitably that this was a motif regarded as having such power that wearing it on one's person would bring protection in this world, and probably in the next also. If the device was held to have such potency in individual use, we can hardly suppose that any less power could have been attributed to it when painted, or represented in mosaic, in a synagogue. The power could, we have seen, be indicated more succinctly by the shofar itself, and this, as easier to draw, and easier to present along with other Jewish tokens of potency, was the more common way of representing and thereby invoking that power.

We cannot leave the subject without returning to the problem suggested by the fact that conceptions of vicarious atonement are associated with the Akedah. We have seen the Akedah take on many interpretations which may have been borrowed from Christians, such as the idea that Isaac in carrying the wood carried his cross, that he died and came to life again, that he shed his blood for the People, and that he is to be the judge in the Last Judgment (anticipated in the yearly judgment of the Day of Atonement). We must again ask: At what point did the borrowing begin, and what part of the story may have lain behind, and itself created, the similar Christian thinking about Jesus? [162] It is obvious that the blowing of the shofar was a very old element in the celebration of the New Year, as the primitive instrument itself would clearly indicate; and the identification of Mount Moriah with Mount Zion was also old.[163] Yet it is highly probable that such elaborate explanations of the shofar and of the Akedah as we have found in the Jewish literature came into Jewish thinking at a much later time than did the blowing of the shofar, or even the transfer of the scene of the sacrifice to Mount Zion. Abraham's act in freely offering his willing son came to be given such stress that it was made a synonym for the eternal priesthood functioning through all later generations, for the never failing atonement. The original story suggests a legend artificially formed to rebuke and put an end to the practice of

---

passages in *MR, Song of Songs* (quoted above, p. 183) saying that Isaac offered his merit in the form of incense. Incidentally, the Coptic painting shows two knives in the air between Abraham's back and the hand of God (Abraham holds a third knife in his hand). Fakhry and everyone he has consulted are quite at a loss to explain the two extra knives.

160. See above, I, 246–253.

161. Above, III, figs. 1038–1041; cf. II, 224.

162. In Strack-Bill., II, 110 f., the horn of the Akedah and the shofar are treated as underlying the allusion to the "horn of salvation" and to "the oath which he swore unto Abraham our father" in the Benedictus, Luke I, 69, 73. The authors present their usual collection of uncritically assembled quotations to illustrate this, but nothing shows by any means decisively that either verse implies an intention to identify the little Jesus with the Isaac of the Akedah.

163. See above, p. 177.

sacrificing the first-born son. But in the material we have reviewed, sacrifice is made once
for all, with universal validity—a basic idea so powerful that it became the dominant explanation of the death of Jesus. Whence came this idea and when was it adopted into
Judaism?

Unfortunately neither Josephus nor Philo gives us here the help we should expect.
When Josephus tells the story of the Akedah he adds no significant details to the biblical
narrative.[164] Philo's treatment of the life of Isaac has so largely vanished that I long ago
suspected it to have been for some purpose suppressed by Christians for the reason that it
said so much about the sacrifice and atoning value of Isaac which Christians wanted to
say of Christ alone. Not only have we lost Philo's *On Isaac*, which he wrote to follow his
On Abraham, but those sections of *Questions and Answers on Genesis* which treat of the birth of
Isaac and the Akedah are also missing. The Akedah is mentioned in *On Abraham*, but there
it is made only a part of the allegory of the two Patriarchs, especially of the interpretation
of Abraham. In Philo's total allegory Isaac was really a higher type than Abraham, a being equaled only by Moses. Isaac and Moses were "self-taught"—"perfect from the beginning," men who did not, like Abraham and Jacob, reach the heights by labor and
climbing, but were from boyhood the full representation of God's power to men. As such,
the special attribute of Isaac was that of his Hebrew name, "Laughter," and this Philo
makes to mean the supreme happiness of God, which man shares in mystic rapture. The
sacrifice of Isaac represents, then, Abraham's willingness to subordinate his desire for
personal happiness in his desire for God himself; it taught Abraham, and teaches us after
him, that the goal of striving is the supreme desirability and virtue of God himself, not the
happiness which union with God brings. The only way in which we can keep the joy of
God is to be constantly ready to give it back to God who gives it. We must fix our attention
upon God, not upon his gifts, if we wish to keep the gifts.[165] That is, in the few Philonic
references to Isaac that we have, he is one who leads the Jew into the consummation of
mystic achievement in the hellenistic sense.

As to the Akedah, Philo calls it a "thank offering"—here *charisterion* instead of his
usual *eucharisterion*.[166] The difference seems to me of no importance. We have seen that the
Jewish festivals all become "eucharists" to Philo, in that they become, through the giving
of thanks, mystic rites of passage from the material to the immaterial. The two words occur
so often in this sense in Philo's writings that when he applies *charisterion* to the Akedah it is
clear that the Akedah too has this mystic meaning for him. Indeed, Philo goes on at once
to explain that the transition from changing matter to the changeless Existent One is
symbolized by the binding of Isaac, by which Isaac lost his power of movement or
change.

Philo also comments on the shofar of Rosh Hashanah, but does not connect this horn
with the horn of the ram in the Akedah; it is the horn of war turned into what another

164. *Antt.*, I, 222–236 (xiii, 1–4); Lerch, op. cit.,
25–27.

165. *Abr.* 201–205; *LA* III, 209. Other interesting

allegories (here irrelevant) on details of the narrative are to be found in *Som.* I, 64 f., 193–195; *Post.*
17–20; *Migr.* 140; *Fug.* 132–136.

166. *Immut.* 4.

hellenistic Jewish document calls the "trumpet of peace." [167] The explanation recalls the eighth of the Homeric Hymns, in which Ares is transformed into a god who gives man peace by making him victorious in the conflict within his own soul. The shofar is also to Philo the shofar of Sinai, whose voice was the true Law—the unwritten Logos in contrast to the written law—which was sent out by the blowing to all men.[168] That is, Philo has a profoundly mystical and spiritual interpretation of both the Akedah and the shofar, but in his passing allusions to the one or the other he nowhere relates the two, and where the connection arose cannot be said: but one cannot help speculating on the problem.

The central point about the Akedah story as later interpreted is that it teaches not only that the Jews are heirs of the promise made to Abraham and of the Law given to Moses, but also that these heroes in their very persons are intercessors for and saviors of their descendants. The idea of the value accrued through the merit of the Fathers appears frequently in Jewish writings, especially in the haggadic midrashim, but was never quite congenial to the halachic spirit. In contrast, the conception is enormously expanded in Philo's treatment of the Patriarchs: in his thinking they are, as incarnate representations of the unwritten law of God and nature, much more important than the Code in any halachic sense. His view of them is that they actually were the Wise Men, the *Sophoi*, of pagan dreams, and that "the Wise Man [in this case he is speaking of Abraham] is the savior of the race, the intercessor before God, the one who seeks pardon for the sins of those akin to him." That is, the Wise Man is a "savior" in the sense of the mystery religions, though the term *Sophos* has come from Stoic philosophy. What I have described as Philo's "mystery religion" is the old Jewish cultus shot through with new meaning, such meaning as that in the sentence just quoted—the meaning that as we appropriate to ourselves the mystic achievements of the Fathers, we can become sharers in their virtues, in the sense of being initiates. Philo said that he himself was "initiated into Moses." In short, the concept of the Patriarchs as saviors has an inherent compatibility with Philonic thinking which it has never had with halachic thinking, since the whole idea of a savior whose merits we assume to ourselves is the idea which most differentiates Hellenism (and Christianity) from "normative" Jewish thought.

At the moment there is the deepest disagreement on the question as to whether Philo's ideas are an expansion of such "native" or rabbinic thinking as the concept of the Akedah presented, or whether the teachings about the Akedah and the merit of the Fathers conveyed in the haggada are reflections of the Philonic, or, better, hellenized Jewish adaptation of Old Testament texts and rites to Greek mystery. The interpretation of the Akedah, even in rabbinic tradition, has revealed to us the old hellenistic idea of the dying and rising redeemer. But as a whole it offers a conception I do not know in Greek thinking. For it expresses not only the familiar hellenistic idea that the savior who died broke the iron curtain of death so that we can hope to live like him after death as we identify ourselves with his death and resurrection; it goes on to indicate that his blood was shed willingly for

---

167. The so-called pseudo-Justinian *Oratio ad Graecos:* see *By Light, Light,* 303. Cf. Philo, *Spec.* II, 190–192.

168. *Spec.* II, 188–189. Cf. *Migr.* 47–52; *Decal.* 47–49.

our redemption, and he has become not only the mystic figure with whom we may be identified, but also, though at times our final judge, more often our intercessor and advocate with the Father. The whole seems a peculiar blending of the spirit of Isaiah and Deutero-Isaiah with hellenistic conceptions, and is precisely the blending which we know as the basic interpretation of Jesus in Christian theology. If in later versions of the Akedah we have suspected the presence of Christian innovations, the theme impresses me for the most part as a pre-Christian formulation which, I believe, was formative in Christian thinking. It appears to me, however, even in its rabbinical form, strongly hellenized. For the fact that atonement is centered in the Patriarchs, and associated with the Law and the Messiah, is as deeply Jewish as the figure of a dying and rising personal savior whose ashes are before God seems to me hellenistic.

In Philo we see the idea in its more fully hellenistic setting, but not in an essentially different form. The great difference between the rabbinic Jewish and the hellenistic conception, as the two appear to me here, consists in the transition from the explanation of the Akedah as a story of Isaac spared from the sacrifice by divine intervention, to an interpretation which represents Isaac as actually the eternal sacrifice atoning by his merit for all men who blow the shofar. The either-or of Judaism versus Hellenism as the source of the conception disappears when we see that the later idea would have been as impossible without both contributions as would be the idea of green without both blue and yellow. To argue whether Philo, later Christianity, and the doctrines of the merit of the Fathers and of the saving power of the Akedah are basically Greek, or "Jewish with a hellenistic veneer," is as pointless as to argue whether green is blue with a yellow veneer or vice versa. It is another instance of senseless debate of the sort that William James compared to an argument as to whether the left leg or the right leg is more important in walking, or whether a child is more closely related to its father or to its mother. The conception into which we have come seems to me to be so completely a composite that while in rabbinic writings the color is more blue, and in Philo's writings more yellow, the conception in both cases is green; the Isaac of the Akedah and the Christ of theology are brothers, sons of the same two parents, Hellenism and Judaism, though one may resemble the father more, the other the mother. Or, may I say explicitly, in the doctrines of vicarious merit and of the Akedah, even as propounded by the rabbis, I see influence of hellenistic thinking, influence which I suspect was felt in the first instance not in the circle of the rabbis themselves, but in such centers and among such people as "Philo the Jew" represents.

With this we have come, I believe, to the meaning of the shofar on the tombstones. Probably in the minds of those who used the symbol, there was no uniform shade of green. We may assume that the shofar meant for all Jews of the time hope of a life to come, or it would not have been put on tombstones. Insofar as this is true, the thinking was green, if I may keep the figure. But where for some the symbol may have had all the implications of the Greek conception of the *Sophos* and the *lex animata*, for others it must have carried, much more simply, what the rabbis came to tolerate, however grudgingly, as the tradition of the merit of the Fathers. Even where hellenistic admixture was greatest, however, the Jewish feeling must still have been very strong, as it was with Philo. The people buried with the shofar on their graves were Jews who had blown the shofar and hoped for life in the other world through the shofar: "Eventually they will be redeemed by the ram's horn."

Nevertheless, much as has been found in the Akedah story to illumine the symbolism of the shofar, the shofar cannot be taken ever to have represented only the personal quest for mercy. Like every good religious symbol, it gathered into itself, in one way or another, all the aspirations and promises of the religion which used it. Thus we may well close our exploration with the often quoted ten reasons for blowing the shofar given by Saadya b. Joseph, called Saadya Gaon, in the tenth century. As abbreviated by Idelsohn,[169] they are:

1) To proclaim the sovereignty of God on the anniversary of creation.

2) To stir the people to repentance.

3) To remind the people of the revelation on Mount Sinai.

4) To remind us of the messages of the Prophets.

5) To remind us of the destruction of the Temple.

6) To remind us of Isaac's sacrifice.

7) To cause the human heart to tremble.

8) To remind us of the Day of Judgment.

9) To remind us of the blasts of the Shofar of redemption which Messiah will sound.

10) To remind us of the resurrection [when again the trumpet will sound].

Such a symbol, a sign of repentance bringing hope of mercy and restoration for the nation and the individual alike, might well be carved upon the graves of Jews. Jewish ritual still associates the Akedah and the shofar.[170] But the custom of putting the shofar on graves seems to have disappeared as the vivid symbolism of all the cult objects has faded, or as Jews have largely come to ignore those meanings which, in the period we are trying to reconstruct, had such deep importance for their ancestors. Yet Jews are still Jews because, among other things they do, they blow the shofar.

169. Op. cit., 210 f. They are given in full by Adler, op. cit., 290 f. A modern version, with interesting alterations, is published by Silverman, op. cit., 167 f.; cf. S. M. Lehrman, *The Jewish Festivals*, 1948, 123–125.

170. Silverman, op. cit., 165–170. But Silverman, 107 f., uses the interpretation of modern critics earlier referred to, according to which one of the chief motives of the narrative was to put an end to human sacrifice. He undoubtedly is correct as regards the original meaning of the biblical story, but his explanations omit the idea that Isaac was actually sacrificed, as it appears in the thinking of the rabbis. M. Friedmann, "The New Year and Its Liturgy," *JQR*, I (1888/9), 62–75, does not mention the Akedah at all.

CHAPTER EIGHT

The Incense Shovel

AMONG THE implements of Jewish cult we have been discussing is a quite surprising object which we have seen represented a number of times. It was at first variously identified, but scholars now generally agree that it is an incense shovel or fire pan.

A. THE INCENSE SHOVEL ON THE MONUMENTS

A CORINTHIAN capital in the synagogue at Capernaum presents the object clearly as most commonly encountered.[1] It is balanced by a shofar at the other side of a menorah. This, the earliest known appearance of the incense shovel, can be dated at the end of the second century. It is a sort of rectangular box, open at the top, with a short handle. A carved plaque—probably part of a screen—from the synagogue at Nawa shows the form even more clearly.[2] The synagogue has not been excavated,[3] and its date is undetermined, but I should guess that it was built not more than a century later than the synagogue at Capernaum. The plaque shows a large central menorah, with the incense shovel and a lulab on the right, and something that is perhaps a shofar on the left. The open-top box with handle is here very clear. We find what is probably the same object represented on a carved plaque from the synagogue at Pekiin.[4] Here a central menorah is flanked at the left by a lulab and an ethrog, and at the right by a shofar and something that seems to be the form we are considering. The photograph shows no handle, but the open-top box is so clear that I can see no reason to doubt such an identification. Indeed, Ben Zevi and Klein said that they could see traces of a handle on the stone.[5] The plaque is perhaps to be dated as contemporaneous with the synagogue at Nawa.

In three other synagogues the object is pictured in mosaic. We find it also on two companion plaques which flanked an inscription in the synagogue at Isfiya.[6] Both are damaged, but on each the shovel appears quite clearly beside a shofar at one side of a central menorah. An ethrog and what was presumably a lulab balance these. Here for the first time we meet with a spotted effect in the center of the shovel, markings which may repre-

1. See above, III, fig. 478.
2. See III, fig. 618.
3. Cf. I, 236.
4. See III, fig. 572.
5. Cf. I, 219, n. 308.
6. See III, figs. 651 f.

sent draught holes in the bottom, or "round objects" in some way essential to the symbolism. They may also have been intended to stand for the coals on the censer. The same combination of forms has appeared in the synagogue of Jerash in the middle of a donor's inscription,[7] that is, a menorah with shovel and shofar at the left, a lulab and ethrog at the right. In one panel of the great mosaic of the synagogue at Beth Alpha is collected the whole vocabulary of cult utensils.[8] A central Torah shrine is flanked by pairs of birds, lions, and trees, and also by cult objects, each in turn presented at either side—menorah, ethrog, lulab, shofar, and shovel. The shovels pictured in mosaic would not be recognizable if we had not first seen the ones in carving; but their square or rectangular bodies with the short handles are by this time unmistakable. The shovel at the right in the panel at Beth Alpha likewise shows the mottled center we have seen on the Isfiya stone.

The device appears also on six lamps from Palestine or its vicinity. On one,[9] besides a shrine and a menorah, and two strange objects, one perhaps an *ascia*, there is also a very clear shovel at the right, flanked in turn by a pair of "round objects." Here are six of the marks like holes in the bottom, clearly indicated. On the lamps, however, the design is usually that of a central menorah with a shofar on one side, a shovel on the other. For example, of four such lamps,[10] one has two shovels, empty,[11] but on the other three there is in each shovel a small mound, which I take to stand for coals with incense sprinkled on them. Another lamp [12] has a design which Reifenberg believes to have originated in Alexandria, in which a vase with a vine growing from it is on one side of the central menorah, and a lulab, an ethrog, a shofar, and a shovel on the other. One of the clearest representations is on a little bone carving [13] from Beth Shan; here the object seems to me indisputably a shovel. Again the bottom is apparently pierced with holes. It was reported that a "snuff shovel" was found carved or painted on one of the tombs in Sheikh Ibreiq.

All of these examples are from Palestine or near by. On Jewish monuments of western origin, the shovel appears only twice so far as I know. A stone from Carthage [14] shows a menorah flanked by a shofar and a shovel of the Palestinian type. But a tombstone from the Catacomb Monteverde in Rome presents an indubitable shovel standing alone.[15] It is the only Jewish instance in which the shovel appears as a symbol by itself, and since it has a long handle it may have some reference different from that of the others. It recalls a similar object occurring in Egyptian burial ornament of the Roman period. In the funerary painting shown in fig. 114,[16] a shovel is placed in one hand of the deceased, and a spray of leaves is in the other; the figure is surrounded by symbolic representations in the marginal panels. In such a setting the device clearly has symbolic value, though in what terms I cannot say. Incidentally, the shovel appears, in exactly the Palestinian form, on Punic stelae, as in fig. 117,[17] where, between a pair of caducei, we find even the holes, indicated here as

7. See III, fig. 656.

8. See III, fig. 639.

9. See III, fig. 293.

10. See III, figs. 334–337.

11. See III, fig. 334.

12. See III, fig. 340.

13. See III, fig. 444.

14. See III, fig. 873.

15. See III, fig. 703.

16. From R. Pagenstecher, *Nekropolis*, 1919, 92, fig. 62.

17. From A. Delattre, *Musée Lavigerie de Saint-Louis de Carthage*, I, 1900, plate IV, 3 (Description de l'Afrique du Nord: Musées et collections archéo-

"round objects." Delattre, not knowing what the object was, covered his perplexity by saying: "One must see in it without doubt a libation table." But the handle makes it in all probability a shovel. It is in any case a Punic instance of the form we are discussing. Presumably, like much Punic symbolism, it came to Carthage from the East. Aside from the single Carthaginian instance, the shovel in the form of a censer has appeared on Jewish monuments only in Palestine, so that both as a symbol and as a cult object it probably came into Judaism under eastern influence.

By what right may we regard these objects, or all of them but the long-handled example at Rome, as incense shovels? It is clear that if we are to do so we must, first, establish that the form is that of an incense shovel, and, secondly, demonstrate the relevance of such an object to Jewish cult.

As to the form, the similarity between these representations and actual incense shovels or fire pans known from the Near East has been pointed out in the first volume. Several specimens of censers found in Palestine are shown in our illustrations,[18] as well as one found at Dura, and now in the Yale University Art Gallery.[19] Similar objects are to be seen in many of the museums of Europe. Not one of the examples displayed, or known, is demonstrably of Jewish origin, but they definitely identify the device found in Jewish iconography as representing objects of this kind. They are called *batillae* or *vatillae*, and pagans, Jews, and Christians would seem to have used them in Palestine. None of them have what I have been suggesting might be draught holes, but such perforations would have made them more useful, and Jews may have been clever enough to construct them in this way.

There is always the possibility that our shovel is in reality a *mḥtyt*, or snuff dish, an object which Kennedy and Holmes [20] think might have had the form we have been considering, and which was used to carry away the burnt ends of the wicks of the menorah in the Temple. There was also a sort of shovel which was used as a musical instrument, and another for removing ashes from the altar.[21] None of these identifications appears to offer as much likelihood, however, as the presumption that the objects represented are censers, since they seem to have equal importance with the shofar and menorah, and to such a dignity the other utensils just named could hardly aspire.

The form, then, has established itself as being apparently that of a portable censer, and it would appear that it was considered by Jews in this period to be a symbol of great significance. Our next task is to establish the relevance of such an object in Judaism.

B. JEWISH USE OF INCENSE

INCENSE FUMES as a concomitant of religious worship have had a great variety of uses and interpretations.[22] Certainly one of the basic reasons for burning incense has always

---

logiques de l'Algérie et de la Tunisie, VIII, i). Delattre says (p. 26) that the symbol *paraît à plusieurs reprises sur les stèles puniques.*

18. Above, III, figs. 433, 436–438; cf. I, 173 f.
19. See III, fig. 439.
20. In *HDB*, I, 365 f. The same suggestion is

made by the anonymous author of the *Gallery Book* of the Palestine Archeological Museum. See above, I, 174, n. 83.

21. Mishnah, *Tamid*, III, 8, and v, 5 f.; see Danby, *Mishnah*, notes ad loc.

22. The only general study of the subject I know

been that people liked the odors, and offered them to God on the assumption that he would like them also. Benzinger [23] thought that this covered everything, and that any other explanation was "far-fetched," but we cannot thus dismiss the direct testimony of those who have been actual users of incense in all ages.

Incense was used widely in the ancient world in casting spells, in worshipful approach to kings, or, according to G. F. Moore, as a demonifuge,[24] and also as a fumigant of direct medicinal value. Among the Egyptians and Romans it was used as an accompaniment of sacrifices and libations. All ancient peoples used it at funerals and graves, where it was thought to have had much greater power than merely that of counteracting the odor of decay. For among the ancients the appearance of a god was marked by a beautiful aroma,[25] and Blackman has shown that in Egypt, when a corpse was censed, "the body was re-vivified not by restoration of its own exudations, but by receiving those of Osiris," [26] since incense, as smoke or odor, indicated divine presence, was itself divine presence. In Jewish tradition, the coming of death as a heavenly being was announced to Abraham by "a smell of sweet savour . . . and a flashing of light." [27] Thus incense becomes a form of sacrifice, *ture et vino sacrificium facere*, or of prayer, *ture et vino supplicare*,[28] that is, the libation and the incense are direct acts of prayer or of sacrifice. To the modern Catholic, incense is likewise a form of prayer.[29]

It has often been pointed out that incense came into the Hebraic cult relatively late. Presumably the actual use of incense long antedated its acceptance in the Temple, but it is striking that while priests in the earlier times had each his own incense burner (probably an object much like the shovels we have before us),[30] the incense altar itself was apparently not in the Temple of Solomon, and is thought, though with some doubt, to have been in the Temple built immediately after the Exile. By Greco-Roman times, however, the offering of incense on the incense altar was completely accepted as one of the forms of sacrifice in the Temple. The older ambulatory use of incense, by which objects or persons could be fumigated or protected, seems to have survived in later Temple cultus only in the incense

---

is that of E. G. C. F. Atchley, *A History of the Use of Incense in Divine Worship*, 1909 (Alcuin Club Collections, XIII). See also J. A. MacCulloch, "Incense," *HERE*, VII, 201–205. Special studies are: on Greek and Roman usage, A. Pfister, "Rauchopfer," PW, Ser. II, Vol. I, 267–286; on Egyptian, A. M. Blackman, "The Significance of Incense and Libations in Funerary and Temple Ritual," *ZaeS*, L (1912), 69–75; on Israelite and Jewish, J. D. Eisenstein and I. Benzinger, "Incense," *JE*, VI, 568–571; on Christian, E. Fehrenbach, "Encens," CL, V, 2–21.

23. Op. cit., 571. Many others have similarly thought that Jews burned incense with the sacrifices only to counteract the stench of the burning animals.

24. "Incense," *EB*, II, 2165–2169.

25. See, e.g., the Homeric Hymn to Dionysus.

26. Op. cit., 75. Blackman (p. 73) quotes from a mortuary text about incense: "The god's dew [approaches] toward thy flesh," where the "god's dew" is the incense.

27. Ὀσμὴ εὐωδίας . . . καὶ φωτὸς ἀπαύγασμα : Montague R. James, *The Testament of Abraham*, Cambridge, 1892, 97, lines 16 f. (Texts and Studies, II, ii); G. H. Box, *The Testament of Abraham*, 1927, 28.

28. For many references regarding these phrases, see Besnier in DS, V, 552 f.

29. See *Catholic Encyclopedia*, s.v. "Incense."

30. In the Old Testament it was called *maḥtâh:* see Atchley, op. cit., 33. Kennedy and Holmes, in op. cit., 365, reason from this Hebrew root and the prescribed usages that the censer was a "bowl-shaped implement furnished with a short handle—in other words, a species of ladle." This is very close to the form we are discussing.

burner which the high priest carried on Yom Kippur into the Holy of Holies "lest he die." [31] According to the biblical provision, the priest, as he entered the inner sanctuary, was to carry in one hand the pan of coals and in the other a spoon of incense, which he was to empty on the coals after going in. This was the literal interpretation later defended by the Pharisees and rabbis against the Sadducees who, as the priestly class, felt uneasy about venturing even a first look at the inner room with its Shekinah "lest they die," and developed the practice of having the high priest put the incense on the coals before going behind the curtains, so that he would have the protection of the smoke screen from the beginning.[32]

In ancient translations, however, the cloud of incense became confused with the "cloud" of the earlier verse—"I will appear in the cloud upon the mercy seat" [33]—so that the incense smoke itself became the manifest Shekinah. Hence the incense smoke would be, first, a protecting agent in its own right; secondly, as we shall see, it would represent, or carry to God, the prayers and aspirations of the worshipers; and thirdly, it was the very presence of Deity. Such a confusion of symbolism appeared in the pagan conceptions of incense and also in the Jewish conceptions of the shofar, according to which the sound of the shofar was the highest form of prayer from men to God: it reminded God of the sacrifice of Isaac, and at the same time was the voice of God to men. This association of God himself, or his power or presence, with the incense smoke is clearly what lies behind the expression used by Eastern Jews: "To hate a thing as the devil hates incense." [34]

A talmudic passage [35] comments on the biblical account of how Aaron stopped a plague by carrying incense among the people. In the narrative it is said, "He put on the incense and made atonement for the people," [36] but in the comment the power ascribed to the incense is limited to the offsetting of the sin of slander. According to the Old Testament passage, however, Korah protested Aaron's exclusive right to burn incense, was killed, and then Aaron vindicated his right. For when the people rebelled over the execution of Korah, God became very angry and smote them with plague; and this plague ceased when Aaron burned incense for them and so made atonement for their sin. This

---

31. Levit. XVI, 12 f.

32. J. Z. Lauterbach, "A Significant Controversy between the Sadducees and the Pharisees," *HUCA*, IV (1927), 173–205, has expounded this controversy at length, and come through to the suggestion that the view of the Sadducees in the matter looked to magic, while the Pharisees were trying to replace this attitude with a more spiritual conception. It seems to me just as likely that the Pharisees here had caught the Sadducees out on a matter of law, and turned literalist just to make a point against their traditional opponents. Philo, who, we shall see, is far from "magical" in his approach to such matters, as usual takes the Sadducean practice for granted: *Spec.* I, 72 (see below, p. 207).

33. Levit. XVI, 2; cf. Lauterbach, op. cit., 200 f.

34. For the Jewish use of the expression, see Lauterbach, op. cit., 196, n. 21. R. Marcus, in *Journal of Religion*, XXXII (1952), 158, has suggested that in holding to the literal command that the incense be lighted only within the Holy of Holies, the rabbis were trying "to deprive the high priest of some of his glory by forcing him to send up the cloud of incense behind the veil of the Holy of Holies, where the spectators could not see him." This explanation seems to me inadequate, though it does still imply that the incense had great significance.

35. *BT, Zebahim*, 88b (ET, 420).

36. Num. XVI, 46–48; cf. Wisd. XVIII, 21; Atchley, op. cit., 39.

incident must have affected all later uses of incense, so that incense, especially that burned on the Day of Atonement, became indeed a companion to the shofar as a means of atonement. We now recall that in the Akedah story, Mount Moriah is identified with Jerusalem as "the place where incense would be offered," [37] and that Isaac is "brought as an offering like a handful of frankincense on the altar," indeed is offered "like a cluster of henna because he atones for the iniquities of Israel." [38] The Akedah, incense, and atonement are here being deliberately combined, and I see no reason to doubt that people believed that there was atoning power in the incense of Yom Kippur quite as in the shofar, and that the rabbis, when they made Isaac himself into an offering of incense, were showing that the two were really one. The comment which limited the power of incense to apply only to the sin of slander was apparently not typical of all rabbinic thought.

Older Jewish tradition, as just said, regarded incense as a form of prayer: "Let my prayer be set forth as incense before thee; the lifting up of my hands as the evening sacrifice." [39] This becomes very explicit in the Apocalypse, where "the four living creatures and the four and twenty elders" have "each one . . . golden bowls full of incense, which are the prayers of the saints." [40] But early Christians, in spite of these sayings, held incense in such horror because of its association with emperor and idol worship that they apparently did not employ it in their own cult for several centuries, though they could not resist using it at graves, especially at the graves of martyrs. [41]

Incense is of course often mentioned in Talmud and Midrash, but in the great majority of instances with reference only to the incense which had been burned much earlier in the Temple. Only a few passages that I know can even be imagined to allude to contemporary use of incense, but the shovels depicted in synagogues and on graves force us to scrutinize these passages closely. One says:

> Formerly God used to receive sacrifices from on high, as it is written, "And the Lord smelled the sweet savour" [Gen. VIII, 21]. Now he receives below, and so it is written, "I am come into my garden, my sister, my bride. I have gathered my myrrh with my spice": this refers to the incense of spices and the handful of frankincense. [42]

It would be rash to assert that the contrast intended in this passage is to set the animal sacrifice of the Temple over against incense offered in the synagogues. That is at least a possible interpretation, but does not at all assure us that incense was burned in synagogue ritual.

Fancy might also play with the frequently repeated legend of the family of Abtinas, who had the monopoly of making incense for the Temple, since they held, as a special family secret, the formula for an incense which when it was burned produced a straight column of smoke that went like a shaft to the roof. To try to break this monopoly the Sages imported incense makers from Alexandria; the smoke of their incense, however, produced no such column, but simply spread out at once, and so the Sages recalled the house of

37. See above, p. 163.
38. See above, p. 183.
39. Ps. CXLI, 2.
40. Rev. V, 8; VIII, 3 f.

41. Pfister, op. cit., 285 f.; Fehrenbach, op. cit., 8–10.
42. *MR, Song of Songs,* V, i, 1 (ET, 230).

Abtinas, even though these men would not return until their fees had been doubled.[43] To ingratiate themselves with the Sages, they said that they kept the secret in their family because if this incense ever became widely known it might be offered to idols. In the early second century, the story concludes, R. Johanan b. Nuri met an old man of this house carrying a scroll on which was the formula that had been kept so strictly in the family "when the members of my father's house were virtuous. . . . But now," he said, "here it is," and gave the rabbi the scroll. When R. Akiba heard of the incident he burst into tears, so much had he admired the integrity of the family.[44] The formula seems to have been preserved. In it fifteen ingredients and their proportions are named,[45] though the traditional number is often given as eleven.[46] It is possible that the story in which the last of the family of Abtinas gave the formula to the rabbis, causing Akiba to burst into tears, indicates the spread of the use of incense from the Temple (now destroyed) to the synagogue. This is also a guess which establishes nothing.

In another treatise, "our Rabbis"—a formula which usually introduces early material—are quoted as saying, "When one compounds incense for experimenting [alchemy?] or in order to hand it over to the community, he is culpable; if in order to smell of it, he is guilty," [47] which may refer to a current use of incense in synagogues, or may be simply an academic expansion of Exod. xxx, 37–38. The comments of later rabbis which follow this statement take its reference back to the incense burned in the Temple. It may be that the rabbis first quoted were protesting against making incense available for general use (in synagogues or houses, or for magical rites), a protest which, like that against the making of seven-branched menorahs, was perhaps ineffectual.

Another possible indication of the use of incense by Jews at this time is found in a blessing prescribed in the Mishnah:

> If wine is brought to them . . . after the meal, one should say the Benediction for all, and he, too, should say the Benediction over the burning spices even though they are brought in only after the meal is over.[48]

In the Gemara this is expanded:

> When do they say the blessing over the incense? As soon as the smoke column ascends. . . . Whence do we learn that a blessing should be said over sweet odours? Be-

43. A special chamber in the Temple, in which Abtinas prepared the incense, is mentioned in *BT, Tamid,* 25b, 26b, 27a.

44. The story is told, in almost identical form, in *BT, Yoma,* 38a (ET, 176–178); *JT, Yoma,* III, 9 (FT, V, 199 f.); *MR, Song of Songs,* III, vi, 4 (ET, 155–157).

45. *BT, Kerithoth,* 6a (ET, 40); balm, onycha, galbanum, frankincense, myrrh, cassia, spikenard, saffron, costus, aromatic rind, cinnamon, lye from leeks, Cyprus wine, salt of Sodom, and one ingredient the name of which the translator leaves in Hebrew, *ma'aleh 'ashan.* Rabbi Nathan wanted to add to this a bit of Jordan resin, and apparently

others wished to add honey, but this, the passage says, would make the incense unfit. Omission of any of the ingredients named in this list entailed the death penalty. Urine could be used in place of the Cyprus wine, though urine could not be brought into the Temple. For this latter, white wine is substituted in *JT, Yoma,* IV, 5 (FT, V, 209).

46. *MR, Song of Songs,* I, xiv, 3 (ET, 82 f.); III, vi, 4 (ET, 155). Benzinger, op. cit., 570, recalls that Josephus speaks of thirteen ingredients (*BJ,* v, v, 5; VI, viii, 3).

47. *BT, Kerithoth,* 6a (ET, 38).

48. Mishnah, *Berakoth,* VI, 6, as transl. in Danby, *Mishnah,* 7; cf. *BT, Berakoth,* 42a (ET, 259).

cause it says, *Let every soul praise the Lord.* What is that which gives enjoyment to the soul and not to the body?—You must say that it is fragrant smell.[49]

Here is direct evidence that incense was blessed and burned in homes. It is most interesting that the odor of the burning incense is associated with the soul as contrasted to the body.

Another allusion to early use of incense appears in a passage in the *Zohar* discussing the incense burned in the Temple: "In accordance with the Chaldaic rendering it is forbidden to burn incense anywhere save on coals of fire taken with the censer from the altar." On the common assumption of talmudic scholars that a prohibition indicates a practice, this would seem to suggest that people were actually burning incense, especially since the *Zohar* says just before this that incense "is able to banish sorcery and all evil influences from the house." According to the *Zohar* the burning of incense is replaced by reciting the "section of the Incense" not only daily, but twice a day, and even before "all other services of hymn and prayer." [50] The actual burning of incense as an accompaniment of all prayer, or at least once a day, seems only just out of sight behind this passage.

We are reminded sharply of the spices used in the Habdalah, the ceremony of closing the Sabbath and going over into the days of work. These spices also are thought to have direct effect upon the soul. They are said to cheer the soul saddened by the departure of the Sabbath,[51] or to be a substitute for the special Sabbath angel who comes to each man at the Sabbath and at the separation leaves him in a fainting condition, from which he is revived by smelling the spices.[52] Indeed, there are traces of connection between the Habdalah ceremony and the Day of Atonement, and the use of spices on both occasions possibly presents one such trace.[53] The smelling of spices, however, like the ceremony of incense at the meal, has often been interpreted simply as indulging in a sensory pleasure.

There is also a direct reference to the burning of spices on festival days:

> [Rabban Gamaliel I] declared three decisions of a lenient character: one may sweep between the [banqueting] couches on a festival, and put spices [on the coals] on a festival, and roast a kid whole on the night of the Passover. But these things the Sages forbid.[54]

The translators in general explain this, like the preceding passage, as referring to the burning of spices by the wealthy for perfume—an interpretation that seems quite doubtful to me. The point about sweeping between the couches I do not understand, but the reference

49. *BT, Berakoth,* 43a,b (ET, 263 f.).

50. *Zohar, Vayaqhel,* 218b–219b (ET, IV 243–247).

51. Segal, *The Sabbath Book,* 136.

52. A. Kingsley Glover, *Jewish Laws and Customs,* 1900, 44; cf. *JE,* VI, 119, 121. See Freedman on *BT, Pesahim,* in ET, 540, n. 8. In Cabbalism this conception of the direct working of the odor of the spices is much elaborated: "The sweet smell provides sustenance for the soul, it brings a substance which enters the soul but is too tenuous for absorption by the body." See *Zohar, Vayaqhel,* 208b (ET, IV, 208 f.).

53. Suggested by M. Zobel in *EJ,* VI, 755–763, with reference to material beyond my competence. Zobel does not consider the spices.

54. This is stated in identical terms in Mishnah, *Betzah,* II, 7, and Mishnah, *Eduyyoth,* III, 11. The passage as I present it here combines elements from the translation in Danby, *Mishnah,* 184 and 428, and from the two *BT* tractates as rendered resp. in ET, 116 and 121.

to the roasting of a kid is clearly one of the rare allusions we find to what must have been a great matter—the question whether, once the Temple was destroyed, or even before that, when one lived in the diaspora and could not get to Jerusalem for the Passover observance, one might not still have a whole roast lamb or kid for the Passover meal.[55] We recall the trouble incurred over the matter by one Theodosius in Rome. That is, the passage deals with a problem highly important for Jews. The Sages won out, and even today it is customary to have almost any meat for the Seder meal except lamb, which is ordinarily represented by only a symbolic piece of roasted lamb bone.[56] The reference to spices, in view of our shovels, seems to me quite probably a reference to a similar controversy: was it permissible to burn incense on a festival—especially on the holiday with which incense was particularly associated, the Day of Atonement? Rabbi Gamaliel said yes, but the other Sages again triumphed, and, like the roasting of a lamb for the Seder evening, the custom was generally repressed, but not, as it appears, before it had left its trace in the use of the shovels we are considering.

There are suggestions also that in the period we are studying Jews burned incense for the dead, as was done in paganism and in Christianity. One passage seems to refer to a custom of sprinkling spiced wine before a coffin, but the text is such that I cannot use it as direct evidence.[57] Another passage,[58] however, reads:

> The Rabbis taught: . . . Do not bring incense [59] to be burned or spices into a house of mourning. But this is not [correct]. For Bar Kappara taught: One should not say a benediction for incense or spices in a house of mourning, which implies that while we do not say a benediction, they may yet be taken into the house. That presents no difficulty: the former ruling is for the house of mourning, while the latter ruling is for the house of comforters.

The last sentence is quite differently interpreted by the German and the English translator. Yet, again on the principle that a prohibition indicates a practice, one thing is clear, namely, that incense and spices were often taken into houses of mourning, either while the corpse was still in the house or later, and that a blessing was pronounced over the incense and spices, however they were used. The rabbis, who like the Sages of the preceding quotation finally won their point, did not like the practice, and forbade it. But it was so popular that one rabbi, at least, went on record as approving it, provided only that the blessing

55. That a lamb or a kid could be used interchangeably for the Passover offering appears clearly in Mishnah, *Pesahim*, VIII, 2 (Danby, *Mishnah*, 147).

56. Actually the *Shulchan Aruch* (*Orach Chayim*, §476, 1) legislates for modern practice following the distinctions made in *BT*, *Pesahim*, 74a (ET, 383), which rules out a whole roast lamb under any conditions for the Passover eve. In some places, it is clear, roast meat was used, even roast lamb. The law is that one should follow local custom, but not

to the point of having a whole lamb roasted. The safest course is that now taken by the great majority of Jews, namely, not to serve lamb at all. On the incident of Theodosius, see above, I, 14 f.

57. *BT*, Sanhedrin, 48a; ET, I, 321 (see Shachter's note ad loc.).

58. *BT*, *Moed Katan*, 27a (ET, 176; GT, IV, 224).

59. Lazarus translates the Hebrew word of the text as "perfumes," but explains in a note that it means "spices to be burned on 'coals' in fumigation pans," i.e., incense.

was omitted. It has been suggested that the incense was used to cover the odor of putrefac-
tion or to fumigate for protection against disease. But since Jewish burials took place always, if possible, not more than twenty-four hours after death, the first would have been
quite unnecessary, while fumigation—which to us means sterilization—to the minds of the
ancients had to do with evil spirits, and so at once became a sort of religious rite.

We are now ready to see what no one till now has seen—the implications of the fact
that four graves of the period we are studying, where the lamps and other artifacts found
led to the presumption that these were Jewish burials, contained actual incense burners.
In commenting upon these earlier,[60] I said that they imply an association of incense with
burials, whether literally or only in that the dead were provided with symbolic censers.
These censers are not shaped like those we are considering, but rather like little incense
altars; they are open-top square boxes with four legs, or taller objects that look like
dovecotes. In spite of the differences in form, there seems to me to be a definite connection
between these burners and the frequent representations of the incense shovel on funerary
objects. I should still incline to believe that the portable shovel was a ritualistic object
appropriate for a ceremony, and so I feel that the actual shovel predicates association with
some such rites as those of the Day of Atonement. But the importance of incense in relation to the dead seems doubly attested by the two sorts of censers connected with Jewish
burials.

All such use of incense has entirely disappeared from orthodox Judaism, but the
customs of the Yemenite Jews are here most illuminating. This community, who now have
almost all migrated to Israel, lived since perhaps 400 A.D. in the Arabian kingdom of Yemen,
and preserved their ancient traditions as they had known them throughout the centuries.
Hence it is interesting that the Yemenite Jews often use incense, and in the following
circumstances. First, incense is highly important in marriage rites. Before marriage the
bride is bathed, anointed, and then taken home by a group of women, one of whom carries
a burning censer.[61] They burn incense for the groom as part of the ceremony of con-
gratulating him before the wedding.[62] A burning censer is carried in the procession in
which the bride is led to the groom.[63] Secondly, incense is of great importance in child-
birth. When the birth is difficult, the woman is censed "until the incense pierces into her
body, and she gives birth." [64] After the child is born an egg is broken and incense is burned
to protect the child from the evil spirit Lilith.[65] The house is censed, the new mother and
child are censed, as well as all women who come to call, and the smoke must go up the
clothes of the women.[66] A feast is held to celebrate the birth, on which occasion the mother
is also censed,[67] while for some time the child is censed every day.[68] Thirdly, incense has
a role in connection with death: the corpse is censed while in the house [69] (clearly a survival of the use of incense in the house of mourning as we have just found it mentioned

60. Above, I, 165, n. 13.

61. Erich Brauer, *Ethnologie der jemenitischen
Juden*, 1934, 136.

62. Ibid., 144.

63. Ibid., 156.

64. Ibid., 182–184.

65. Ibid., 186.

66. Ibid., 187.

67. Ibid., 188–190.

68. Ibid., 192.

69. Ibid., 222.

in the Talmud), and throughout the procession to the grave the corpse is censed.[70] Fourthly, incense is burned in magical healing rites [71] and in black magic.[72] These usages described by Brauer comprise just about all the functions of incense we have found, except for the specific censing of the Shekinah by the high priest on the Day of Atonement.

It will be recalled that there was a dispute in talmudic circles as to whether incense might be burned at festivals. It is, then, extremely interesting that Professor Goitein of the Hebrew University in Jerusalem could tell me that before a festival the Yemenite women go to the synagogue, open the curtains or doors of the Torah shrine, and cense the scrolls. It is clear that the rabbis won out, even to some extent, among the Yemenites. For although the high priest, in carrying the burning coals to the Holy of Holies and putting incense on them, had from time immemorial broken the law prohibiting manipulation of fire on a Holyday, for the ordinary Jew to do so was too much.[73] So the festival incense is used by Yemenites to sanctify the scrolls on the day before a festival. Jews in the Greco-Roman synagogues may well have resorted to the same compromise. But that the Yemenite usage is a direct descendant of the practice of offering incense to the Shekinah in the Temple seems by all means the most likely hypothesis, since upon the Torah shrine and its scrolls, itself called an ark, was centered, by transference from the Temple, much of the feeling that worship must be directed toward the Shekinah. If one could no longer worship facing the Ark in the Holy of Holies (though one still worshiped toward Jerusalem), one worshiped facing the ark which contained the Torah. It is no mere chance that curtains still hang before the ark in the synagogue, as they hung before the Holy of Holies.

No direct literary evidence has been produced to show that Jews burned incense in their synagogues during the Greco-Roman period. But in the light of the material we have been recalling, one turns back with a new sense of possibilities to the large number of incense shovels portrayed on the monuments in association with symbols of the High Holydays, symbols which it seemed worth while to put on graves for their potency and their expression of eschatological hope. Among the Yemenites, it is clear, incense is a thing of potency, something attractive to God and abhorrent to demons, as it is in Christianity. That it is so much used at funerals suggests again that it was credited with power as a demonifuge, and also that it probably carried eschatological value, which is the value likewise felt in censing the corpse at a Christian funeral. It appears to me highly probable that the representations of the incense shovel in the Jewish remains attest a wide use of in-

70. Ibid., 224.

71. Ibid., 361.

72. Ibid., 367.

73. According to one of the laws of the Sabbath set forth in the Falasha treatise *Te'ezaza Sanbat*, the only labor allowed on the Sabbath is "the bringing of sacrifices, incense, offerings, and gifts before God," and the law goes on apparently to include the festivals: Leslau, *Falasha Anthology*, 20. This may be only an antiquarian reference to incense, as the allusion to sacrifices seems at first glance to be; yet the Falasha Jews do offer sacrifices, especially a lamb on the eve of Passover, though not if that day is a Sabbath: ibid., xxvi f., xxxi; D. Lifchitz, "Un Sacrifice chez les Falacha, juifs abyssins," *La Terre et la vie*, IX (1939), 116–123. The reference to incense may, then, similarly be realistic. Instances of incense burning among Jews could certainly be found elsewhere. Jonas Greenfield has told me of a synagogue of Syrian Jews in Brooklyn, N.Y., where incense is regularly burned.

cense in connection with the High Holydays, especially in the eastern countries, where the device chiefly appears, and that like the other symbols, it had come to have an eschatological association, so that Jews wanted to have it in their graves as well as in the synagogues. It seems also likely to me that as the proscription of incense burning became effective and the practice ceased, the aromatic spices of the Habdalah, which did not need to be burned, took the place of incense as something "good for the soul." The odor of the spices may well have also carried on the idea that incense was a prophylaxis against demons as one went out to secular life after the Sabbath.

Philo also gives suggestions, but does not settle our problem at all. He too knows incense as simply a means of sensory titillation employed by the rich,[74] and says nothing which suggests a ritualistic use of incense in the synagogues he describes, though this is not especially significant, since he tells us almost nothing about any cultic practices in the synagogues.[75] He mentions ritual incense only as he comments on the Pentateuch, and here his interpretations are as inconsistent as usual. He contrasts the incense altar with the menorah on the ground that as the menorah symbolizes the heavens, so the incense altar is the earth, and the incense is the *eucharistia* of the earth.[76] In another passage he says [77] that the four ingredients for incense specified in the scriptural formula represent the four elements of nature, and that since the universe is made up of four elements, the incense is the *eucharistia* of the universe: "it is the entire universe, formed by the divine Sophia, which is offered as a whole burnt offering morning and evening." In both of these concepts we have *eucharistia* as much more than a "giving of thanks." The term "giving of thanks" came into Christianity as the name of the chief sacrament of Christians—the Eucharist— from a Judaism which still blesses a great variety of things by giving thanks over them. "When he had given thanks" reflects what is still the Jewish formula of *berakoth*. But in calling the incense offering a *eucharistia*, Philo shows that he considers that one who offers incense partakes sacramentally in the cosmic worship offered by all nature, a thoroughly mystical point of view.

A step beyond this appears when Philo thinks in terms of the contrast between the material and the immaterial. The cosmic worship is a highly mystical approach to God, Philo tells us,[78] but throughout he considers this Persian or generally Oriental approach to God through astralism and the material universe as being inferior to a Platonic approach, where the escape is from matter in any sense to the immaterial. In terms of this immaterial approach, incense is given an entirely new interpretation: sacrifice in the form of a bloody burnt offering is on behalf of man's material aspect (and, we understand, of everything material) while the incense offering is the worship offered by the "leading part" within man, the λογικὸν πνεῦμα, the higher mind or spirit, which is shaped in the divine image, that is, made like the Logos.[79] This is an awkward attempt to paraphrase in biblical language the idea that man's highest mind is a presence of the divine Logos within him, and

74. *Sacr.* 43.

75. Usually Philo speaks of synagogue worship as "philosophizing": *Som.* ii, 123–127; *Mos.* ii, 216; *Legat.* 156; cf. *Cont.* 28.

76. *Mos.* ii, 101, 105.

77. *Heres* 196–200; cf. §226.

78. See my *By Light, Light*, 95–120: "The Mystery of Aaron."

79. *Spec.* i, 171; cf. Colson's note ad loc.

that the worship of God by this part of man is on an entirely different footing as compared with the worship offered by his material aspect. For this inner presence is in the image of the great Logos, in the sense that both are immaterial. Incense, then, represents the approach of man's immaterial nature to the immaterial Logos of God. Such an immaterial approach distinguishes the higher formulation of Jewish Mystery from the lower: this distinction is to Philo especially symbolized in the contrast between the ordinary holy places of the Temple and the Holy of Holies, into which only the high priest goes, and only on the Day of Atonement. This inner room, and especially the Ark of the Covenant within it, as described in the Bible, constitute the basic symbol for all of Philo's metaphysics. He calls the Holy of Holies directly the "intelligible world," that is, the world of immaterial reality approached only by reason.[80]

> For what is inside is unseen by anyone except only the high priest, as he enters according to his duty once a year; and even to him everything is invisible. For he takes with him a brazier full of coals and incense, and the great quantity of vapor which this naturally gives forth covers everything round about, beclouds the eyesight, and creates a barrier through which sight cannot penetrate.[81]

This is a description according to the usage which the Talmud, as we have found, regards as Sadducean rather than Pharisaic,[82] for it indicates that the priest got no initial look at the room as he would have had if he had put the incense on the coals after entering, but was so blinded by the fumes as he went in that he saw nothing inside the room. Philo must have thought that the high priest put the incense on the coals outside the room. This is unquestionably the way in which the high priest of Philo's day, a Sadducee, did enter the Holy of Holies, and Philo is for once letting the literal text stand as factually correct about current Temple usage. It is interesting that whenever Philo discusses a point that is in dispute between Pharisees and Sadducees, he can usually be trusted to represent the Sadducean view.[83]

Of course the high priest carried in also blood of the bullock which had been offered as a sin offering just before he entered, and he removed his ornate high-priestly robe and put on one of plain white linen. The ornate robe to Philo's thinking is proper for administration of material matters; it symbolizes to him the honor and glory which are values in the material realm. In this robe, he says, the high priest represents "true opinion," the highest type of understanding Plato thought possible in relation to the material world.[84] But when the high priest put this robe off for the one of plain white linen, he seemed to Philo to go into something quite different. The white robe for entering the Holy of Holies symbolized to him radiant light (the divine Light-Stream).[85] Such a contrast

80. *QE* II, 94, as translated by Marcus: "I have said that the simple holy (parts of the tabernacle) are classified with the sense-perceptible heaven, whereas the inner (parts), which are called the Holy of Holies, (are classified) with the intelligible world. The incorporeal world is set off and separated from the visible one by the mediating Logos as by a veil."

81. *Spec.* I, 72.

82. See above, p. 199.

83. For other instances, see my *By Light, Light,* 78–80, 192 (n. 65), 345.

84. *QE* II, 107.

85. *Som.* I, 216–218.

presented itself to him also in the two different robes put upon persons being inducted into the mystery of Isis and Osiris: at the lower stage the initiate donned the variegated robe of Isis, while the culmination of the rite was marked by his putting on the pure white "light-form" (φωτοειδές) of the robe of Osiris.[86] Now, it is conspicuous that while the ordinary robes of the Aaronic high priest were never worn after the destruction of Jerusalem and the Temple, the plain white robe did continue in use in the home and synagogue for the leader of the prayers at Passover and on the High Holydays. To take off the ornate robe, Philo says, is "to lay aside opinions and impressions of the soul," so that the high priest shall enter the inner sanctuary naked (γυμνός), with no display of colored borders or sound of bells, to pour as a libation the blood which is the soul (τὸ ψυχικὸν αἷμα), and to offer as incense the whole mind to God our Savior and Benefactor.[87]

Philo's incorporation of the incense offering into the deepest part of his mystic symbolism goes along with the significance he gives to the white robe of the high priest—which came out of the Temple for celebrating the festivals. Certainly Philo in Alexandria was offering his whole mind to God, his Savior and Benefactor, and probably, like later Jews, was wearing the white robe in his home or in the synagogue while he did so. It becomes increasingly likely that he had an incense shovel also, and that at some time in the course of the ceremonies of the High Holydays, along with blowing the shofar, he burned incense in his shovel.

That all Jews in Alexandria or Capernaum could have burned incense, or worn the white robe, or blown the shofar, with Philo's depth of mystic appreciation, it would be absurd to say. But I suspect that just as they blew the shofar, so also they wore the white robe, and that as Yemenite Jews still burn incense, they also at some point burned incense in an incense shovel.

86. Plutarch, *On Isis*, 77 (382 C). See my *By Light, Light,* 113–120.
87. *LA* II, 56.

Conclusions

THE CULT OBJECTS which the Jews of the Greco-Roman period depicted on their synagogues and tombs have gone far to confirm the surmise that they were Jewish substitutes for pagan symbols similarly used.

The pagan tombs and sarcophagi of the hellenistic and Roman centuries display a great number of devices which indicate hope for a life after death, and which probably were thought, by their very presence on the tomb, to be of some direct help in achieving immortality for the deceased. We have seen in the earlier volumes that Jews used a great number of these pagan emblems along with their own symbols, and what they may have had in mind when they did so will be the concern of the volumes which follow. But for Jews the simplest way of securing for themselves the values implied in hellenistic burial practice was to adapt pagan usage by putting Jewish symbols on their graves, symbols which, from the way in which they were used, presumably would assure immortality to the Jew just as the pagan ones promised future life to the pagan, but would assure it in Jewish terms.

Such an adaptation would necessarily imply that the Jewish cult symbols had taken on an eschatological reference by no means implicit in the original purpose of the object represented, and quite beyond their connotations in that Judaism of later centuries which was oriented by the legalism of the rabbis. For the followers of legalistic Judaism have not put these symbols on their graves and have read little of eschatological hope into either their forms or their uses. Yet our examination of the place of the cult objects themselves in the rituals, and of the comments of Jewish mystical writers upon their meaning, has made it seem likely that such a wider, if not deeper, feeling about the values they carried was general in the period we are studying. To reach this conclusion, we have had to take only one unsupported step—the step which brought us to the assumption that the eschatological and mystical association was much more common among Jews in the Greco-Roman period than it has ever been in Judaism at any time since, and that those who made the monuments of that time found in this association the true meaning of Jewish cult and of its symbols.

The tombs have kept their silence, and the ornament of the synagogues is unexplained in any contemporaneous literary documents. What their builders were thinking must always be ultimately a matter of inference. Those who hold to the theory that the graphic designs were meaningless decoration, or to the notion that they must be explained, if at all, from halachic and rabbinic postulates, are taking an inferential step quite as undocumented as the one which I have suggested. The final inference as to the ideas that lay behind the Jewish monuments can be made, I believe, only after we have studied the complete picture—the symbolic forms themselves, their history, their cultic associations, the explanations given them in various Jewish traditions, and finally the places and circumstances in which they are represented. I simply want to stress that I am as aware as anyone can be that the final step—namely, my conclusion that the symbols have mystical and eschatological reference—is unsupported by direct evidence, and is offered only as presenting the greater probability. I do not see how any conclusions other than those I have reached can seem more probably correct to one who takes into view all the considerations I have discussed. That I have brought out everything that may be relevant I cannot hope, and anyone who can add evidence that I have overlooked will do me a great service. But any additional evidence will still be additional, and will have to be discussed as such.

The Jewish cult symbols on the monuments have at least all proved to have been given mystic and eschatological interpretation in Jewish literary documents—with the exception of the façade, which is not mentioned in such writings. But the way in which the façade was used indicates, more clearly than does the use of any of the other forms, that it had, and still has, at least subconsciously, definite association with immortality. Here is the clearest example we have yet seen of the stubborn persistence of a value along with a form, even though little explanation of the form seems to have been offered in any of the various religions that utilized it. As Jews built it into a tomb portal or the front of a synagogue, as it became the mizrach, or pre-eminently as it came to represent the Torah shrine, the façade indicated that God had come to man, and that through its doorways man could go to God in mystical union, or into immortal life.

The other Jewish cult emblems have no such connections with pagan forms as the façade has, with the exception of the incense shovel; here identification is less certain, and the probability that its meaning has been correctly explained is by no means so high as in the case of the other objects. But the menorah, the lulab and ethrog, and the shofar are idiomatically Jewish, and all appear as emblems on graves in such a way that their eschatological implication seems to me inescapable. At the same time, the references to them in Jewish writings, and their use and associations in Jewish cult, appear to justify the conclusion not only that they were at the time symbols of mystical achievement and immortality, but also that Jews put them on the tombs with such meanings consciously in mind. Specifically, the menorah seems to have become a symbol of God, of his streaming Light and Law; it was the Tree of Life, the astral path to God, and the mediating female principle, the Mother. The lulab and ethrog carried on the association with Tabernacles as a festival of rain and light, but took on mystical overtones, to become a eucharist of escape from evil and of the passing into justice as the immaterial Light comes to men. They came even to signify the mystic marriage. But all of these mystical interpretations looked to immortality. The shofar was the great symbol of God's mercy and forgiveness, of imputed merit available to every man from the treasury of merit stored up through the virtuous acts of the Fathers, especially of Isaac, so that it too became an eschatological symbol.

The manner in which Jews used these symbols in ornamenting their synagogues recalls what has long been recognized about the Jewish borrowings from pagan symbolism, namely, that the symbolic vocabulary taken from the pagans and adapted in synagogue decoration is almost if not entirely a funerary vocabulary. The implication seems obvious that synagogue worship, at the time when these borrowings occurred, was oriented in mysticism and the hope of life after death. To the impression made by these borrowed symbols we can now add the impressions gained from our studies of the uses made of Jewish cult objects. These were, indeed, represented in the synagogue decorations in ways in which halachic Jews have never thought of representing them, but their primary symbolic use seems to have been in connection with graves. The cluster of such symbols found in the synagogue of Beth Alpha [1] corresponds closely to the cluster that appears in the Catacomb Torlonia in Rome,[2] but has a relevance in the catacomb which it does not immediately manifest in the synagogue—the relevance of its essentially eschatological implications. Transferred from the tombs to the synagogues, the symbols must indicate that synagogue worship was concerned with life after death in a sense far beyond anything that appears in synagogue worship under rabbinic guidance.

We have already come a long way, I believe, in our search for light on the question which is the central interest of our entire study, namely, the question as to what sort of Judaism produced all this art. The feeling is that it was an intensely loyal Judaism, loyal in its belief that the Jewish faith offered man the true knowledge of the nature and will of God, and that the institutions of Judaism defined the duty of man in this life and were his promise of security after death. But the Jews who lived under hellenistic and Roman influence had come to ask questions of their Jewish tradition, as they looked to it for consolations—questions which had much more importance for them than for the rabbinic scholars, who, especially in Babylonia, were more segregated from pagan impact than the mass of Jews in the Greco-Roman world. Many of these questions had crept into the thinking of the rabbis, and are sporadically reflected in their writings; but the questions did not have the same immediacy for the rabbis that they had for the Jews who built and worshiped in the synagogues, and who were interred in the graves most commonly found.

The new questions were, first, the one with which Philo was most concerned: How could Judaism take men from the material to the immaterial? The second was a question which Philo's mysticism made largely irrelevant for him, but which was crucial for the mass of pagans and Christians, as well as for Jews: How could religion take man into a blissful immortality? Philo's answer, and apparently that of many of his associates in Alexandria, was to turn Judaism into the true Mystery, by which he had in mind the sort of conception in which educated and thoughtful pagans saw the true meaning of the mystery cults—salvation from bondage to the flesh and its desires, and release to share in

1. See above, III, fig. 639 (cf. fig. 632).   2. See III, fig. 817.

the freedom of immaterial reality. At the same time the great majority of pagans were seeing in their mysteries a means of escaping from material bondage to a redemption which would help them to face the great judgment after death, and make them ready for acceptance in the future life. We saw such a pagan hope expressed in the Sabazian paintings of a tomb in Rome.[3] Correspondingly, the great majority of Jews in the period appear to have been regarding their Judaism as the true Mystery in this more popular sense. As in paganism, there was no feeling of a discrepancy between the two levels, the eschatological and the mystical; hence Jews probably as a matter of course conceived Judaism as a Mystery in both senses. And as ordinary pagans put the symbols of their mysteries on their sarcophagi, ordinary Jews put the cult symbols of their Mystery in the same places and, presumably, with the same basic intent. Christians have ever since used Christian symbols in the same way.

That modern Jews find in their religious traditions the answers to modern social problems makes them no less Jews. Similarly, the fact that the Jews of the Greco-Roman world were finding in their religion the answers to the problems which concerned all men in their day detracted by no means, I believe, from their loyalty to Judaism, and does not compromise their right to a place in Jewish history, even though all that the Talmud can say of many of their practices is that one or another rabbi did not stop them.

Such is the impression that we derive from the Jewish cult symbols as we find them in the synagogues and on the graves of the period. We are ready to see not only that it was possible for the Jews of the period to interpret and use the symbols of their own cult in this way, but also that they were so close to the thinking of their neighbors (just as modern Jewish idealists are close to the idealism of gentiles) that they could take a host of pagan symbols which appeared to them to have in paganism the values they wanted from their Judaism, and blend them with Jewish symbols as freely as Philo blended the language of Greek metaphysics with the language of the Bible. We must constantly assume that to their minds the borrowed symbols only enriched their Judaism, just as for Philo the terminology of Greek metaphysics seemed only to express more accurately what he felt to be the real meaning of Scripture, and as modern Jews avail themselves of the terminology of current social and philosophical thought only to bring out more clearly the intent of their Jewish forefathers.

Whether this reasoning about the symbols which Jews borrowed from the pagans is true, we can establish only by elaborate analysis of those symbols—analysis of their meaning in paganism, and of the ways in which Jews used them. To this analysis the following volumes will be devoted. Volume V, as it deals with fish, bread, and wine, will in a sense be transitional: for in these three symbols we shall see elements long present in Jewish life, yet represented in pagan forms on the Jewish monuments. The more purely pagan symbols will be discussed in Volume VI. It becomes possible properly to treat these only now that we have seen how much the Jewish emblems in themselves suggest that the Jews who made the monuments were faced with new problems in the Greco-Roman world, and were solving them in Jewish terms and with Jewish loyalty.

3. See III, figs. 839–843; cf. II, 45–50.

INDEXES

Avi-Yonah, M., 4 f., 28, 71, n., 74, n., 112, n.
Ayazin, tomb at, 117, n.

Baal, 59
Baal-berith, 148
Baalam, 178
Baby, *see* Child
Babylon, 22, 54
Babylonia, 15, 102, 134 f., 173, 211
Bacchus, 47, 157. *See also* Dionysus
Bacchism, 52, n., 59
Bacher, W., 88, n., 152, n., 181, n., 182, n., 186, n.
Bachofen, J. J., 28, n.
Bacon, Francis, 28, n.
Baentsch, B., 73, n.
Bagdad, mihrab from, 139
Bainton, R. H., 111, n.
Banqueting bolster, 144, n.
Bar Kappara, 203
Bar Kokba, 114
Barca, 104
Baron, S. W., 21, 78, n.
Baumeister, A., 107, n.
Becker, C. H., 139, n.
Beer, B., 179, n.
Bees, N., 79
Bekker, E., 79
Belial, 23 f.
Bellak, L., 30, n.
Beni Hasan, 104, 142
Benjamites, 148
Benoit, F., 104, n., 105, n., 109, n., 117, n.
Benouville, P., 107, n.
Ben Zevi, *or* Ben-Zevil, I., 74, n., 195
Benzinger, I., 132, n., 147, n., 198, n., 201, n.
Berliner, A., 165
Besnier, M., 198, n.
Beth Alpha synagogue, Akedah in, 190; cluster of cult utensils in, 74 f., 89, 121, 127–29, 130, n., 135, 169, 196, 211; three-door façade on, 113, n.
Beth Shan, 196
Betyl, 112, 118 f.
Beyer, W. H., 74, n., 77 f., 81, 87, 146, n.
Bezaleel, 91
Billerbeck, P., 145, n., 147, n., 173, n., 175, n., 178, n., 190, n.
Bird, *on* breastplate, 127; *on* Coptic cloth, 138; eating grapes, 4, 37, 44, 46, 69 f., 76, 81; *with* menorah, 72, 74–76; *on* mizrach, 125; prohibited on images, 16; *with* shrines, 121–24, 134, 137; *on* synagogues and graves, 26, 44

Birt, Th., 143 f.
Blackman, A. M., 198
Blau, L., 8–10, 127, 128, n.
Blaufuss, H., 15, n., 16, 17, n., 19, n.
Blinkenberg, C., 16, n.
Boat, 102 f.
Boaz, column of, 122, n.
Bonner, Campbell, 26, 80, 179, n.
Book, 42, 68, 142, 144. *See also* Scroll
Book of the Dead (Egyptian), 143
Booth, 148–50, 153, 159, 164 f.
Bordeaux, ring from, 81
Bourguet, P. du, 138, n.
Box, G. H., 198, n.
Brauer, E., 204, n., 205
Bread, 26, 79, 113, 137
Breastplate of the Law, 127
Briggs, C. A., 170, n.
Brooks, Cleanth, 31, n., 41
Brown, Donald F., 112, n.
Brown, F., 170, n.
Brunner, A. W., 123
Büchler, A., 157 f.
Bull, 11, 14, 42, 60, 68, 76, 100, 132, 144, n.
Burney, C. F., 132, n.
Burning bush, 74, 82
Butler, H. C., 104, n., 112, n.
Buxtorf, Johannes, 123, n.

Cabbala, 61, 92, 129
Cabbalism, 62, 133, 165, 202, n.
Caesarea, coin from, 114
Canaanites, 53 f., 148 f., 155, 161
Capernaum synagogue, bacchic scene in, 9; menorah in, 75; screen in, 116 f.; shofar in, 168; shovel in, 195; three-door façade on, 113, n.; Torah shrine in, 115 f.
Capricorn, 13, n., 72
Carrousel, Arc du, 108
Carthage, 94, n., 196 f.
Casanowicz, J. M., 116, 130, n., 145, n., 156
Casey, Robert P., 49, n., 59, n.
Cassirer, E., 31, n.
Catacombs—
  Christian, 5
  Jewish, 3 f., 44, 67; Catacomb Monteverde, 69, 81, 142, 169, 196; Torlonia, 7, 128, 130, 133, 140–42, 169, 211; Vigna Randanini, 7, 70, 76, 142, 169
Cathedral, *see* Church
Censer, 196 f., 204

2. CITATIONS

Italic numerals refer to pages in this volume.

LIST OF ILLUSTRATIONS

ILLUSTRATIONS

Discussion of the objects or designs listed below will be found in the text as indicated by the page numbers in parentheses. Acknowledgments for the figures individually likewise appear there. Names of museums, collections, etc., accompanying the captions give the present location of the item designated. The abbreviation PM means that the object so marked is in the Pierpont Morgan Library, New York.

1. For the dating of these periods, which is much in dispute among specialists, I am arbitrarily following Miss Porada's scheme; see above, p. 100, n. 1.

ILLUSTRATIONS

1

2

3

4

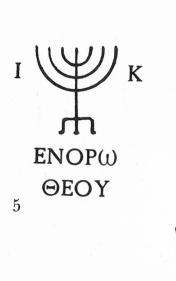

I K

ENOPω
ΘEOY

5

שלא של

7

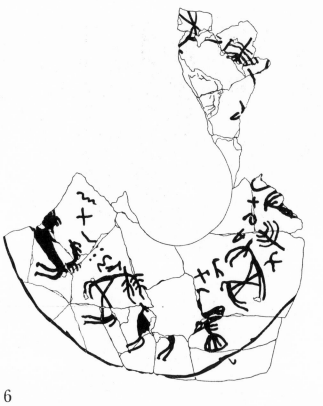

6

8

9

10

11

13

14

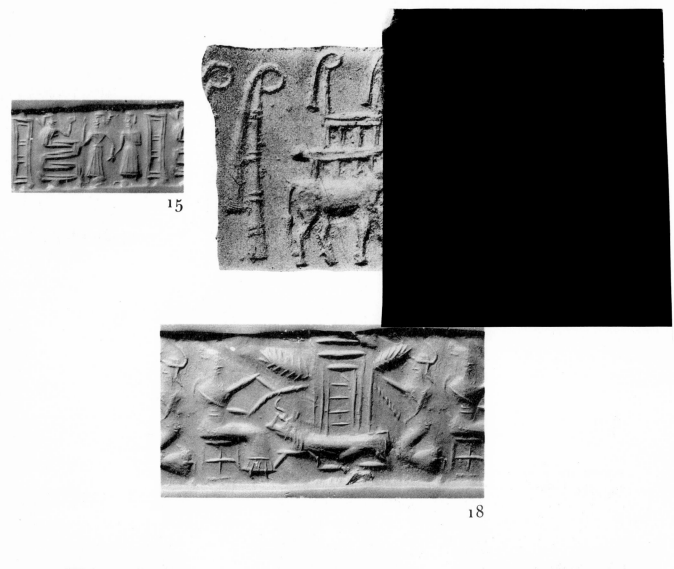

15

18

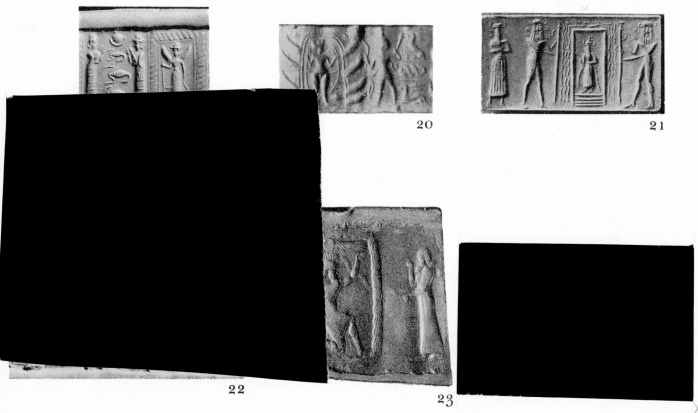

20

21

22

23

X

26

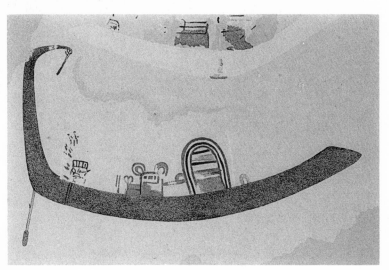

27

30

31

32

33

34

35

37

38

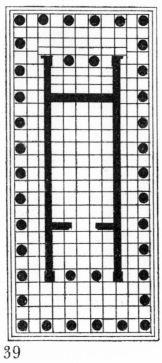

39

4¹

4²

44

43

45

46

48

59

60

61

62

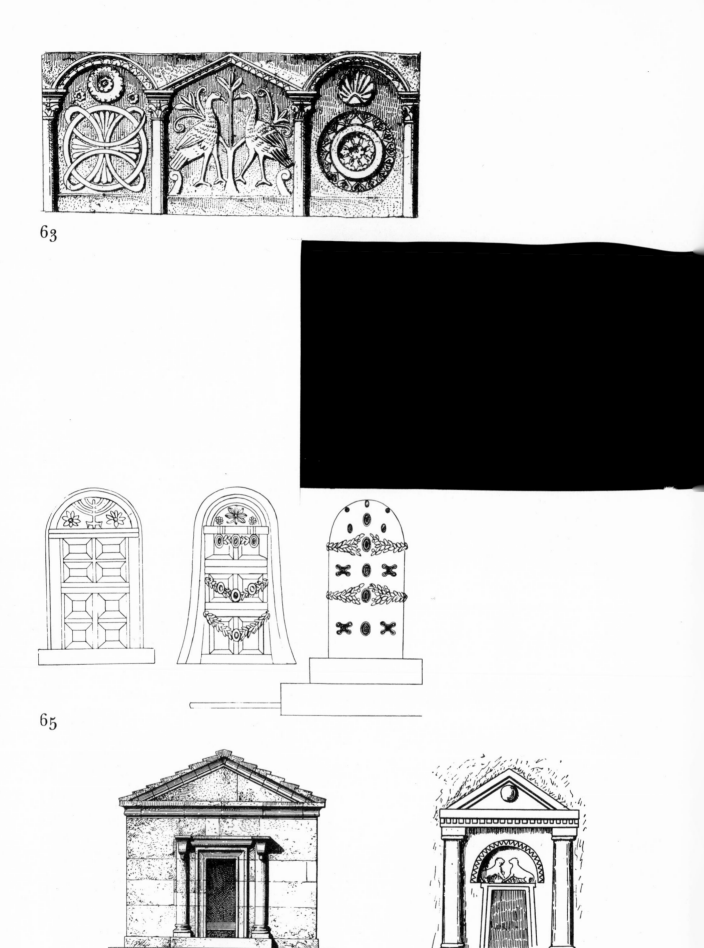

63

65

66   67

68

69

70

71

72

73

74

75

76

77

78

79

80

81

82

84

83

87

88

89

90

91

93

92

94

95

97

98

99

100

102

103

104

105

106

107

108

109

110

111

112

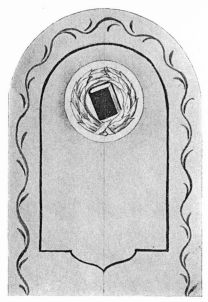

113

114

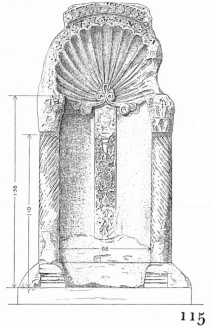

115

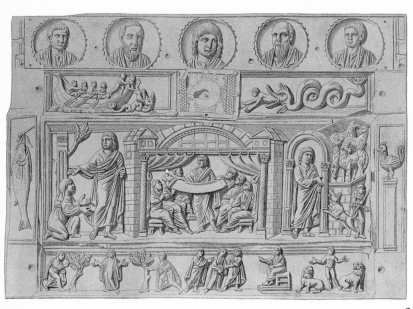

116

117